NATIONAL GEOGRAPHIC
KIDS™

ALMANAC 2011

NATIONAL GEOGRAPHIC

Two bottlenose dolphins frolic in the waters of the Caribbean.

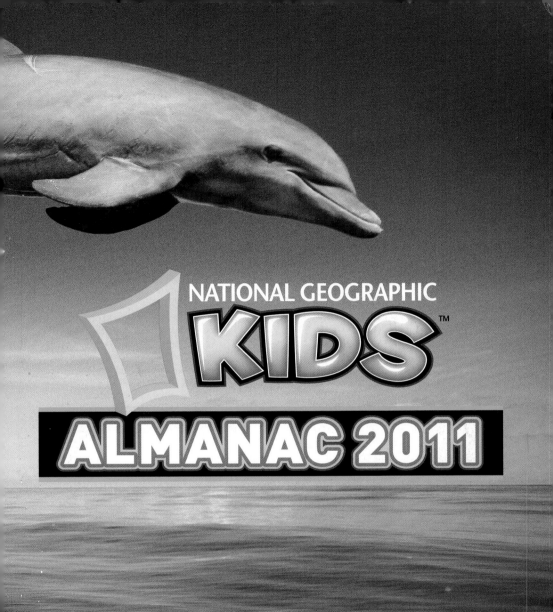

NATIONAL GEOGRAPHIC
KIDS™
ALMANAC 2011

NATIONAL GEOGRAPHIC

WASHINGTON, D.C.

National Geographic Children's Books gratefully acknowledges the following people for their help with the *National Geographic Kids Almanac 2011*.

Curtis Malarkey, Julie Segal, and Cheryl Zook of the National Geographic Explorers program; Truly Herbert, National Geographic Communications; and Chuck Errig of Random House

Your World 2011

Jenny Mehlow, Public Relations, San Diego Zoo

Tia B. Viering, Head of Communications, New7Wonders

Amazing Animals

Dr. Thomas R. Holtz, Jr., Senior Lecturer, Vertebrate Paleontology, Dept. of Geology, University of Maryland

Dr. Luke Hunter, Executive Director, Panthera

"Dino" Don Lessem, President, Exhibits Rex

Kathy B. Maher, Research Editor, NATIONAL GEOGRAPHIC magazine

Kathleen Martin, Canadian Sea Turtle Network

Barbara Nielsen, Polar Bears International

Andy Prince, Austin Zoo

Julia Thorson, translator, Paris, France

Chris Sloan, NATIONAL GEOGRAPHIC magazine

Dr. Sylvia Earle, National Geographic Explorer-in-Residence

Dennis vanEngelsdorp, Senior Extension Associate, Pennsylvania Department of Agriculture

Going Green

Eric J. Bohn, Math Teacher, Santa Rosa High School

Stephen David Harris, Professional Engineer, Industry Consulting

Cid Simões and Paola Segura, National Geographic Emerging Explorers

Super Science

Tim Appenzeller, Chief Magazine Editor, NATURE

Dr. José de Ondarza, Associate Professor, Department of Biological Sciences, State University of New York, College at Plattsburgh

Lesley B. Rogers, Managing Editor, NATIONAL GEOGRAPHIC magazine

Abigail A. Tipton, Director of Research, NATIONAL GEOGRAPHIC magazine

Erin Vintinner, Biodiversity Specialist, Center for Biodiversity and Conservation at the American Museum of Natural History

Barbara L. Wyckoff, Research Editor, NATIONAL GEOGRAPHIC magazine

Dr. Enric Sala, National Geographic Visiting Fellow

Geography Rocks

Dr. Mary Kent, Demographer, Population Reference Bureau

Dr. Walt Meier, National Snow and Ice Data Center

Dr. Richard W. Reynolds, NOAA's National Climatic Data Center

United States Census Bureau, Public Help Desk

Dr. Spencer Wells, National Geographic Explorer-in-Residence

Carl Haub, Senior Demographer, Conrad Taeuber Chair of Public Information, Population Reference Bureau

Glynnis Breen, National Geographic Special Projects

History Happens

Dr. Gregory Geddes, Lecturer, Department of History, State University of New York, College at Plattsburgh

Dr. Robert D. Johnston, Associate Professor and Director of the Teaching of History Program, University of Illinois at Chicago

Dr. Fredrik Hiebert, National Geographic Visiting Fellow

Sylvie Beaudreau, Associate Professor, Department of History, State University of New York

Karyn Pugliese, Acting Director, Communications, Assembly of First Nations

Parliamentary Information and Research Service, Library of Parliament, Ottawa, Canada

Micheline Joanisse, Media Relations Officer, Natural Resources Canada

Culture Connection

Dr. Wade Davis, National Geographic Explorer-in-Residence

Deirdre Mullervy, Managing Editor, Gallaudet University Press

Awesome Adventure

Jen Bloomer, Media Relations Manager, The National Aquarium in Baltimore

Dereck and Beverly Joubert, National Geographic Explorers-in-Residence

Wonders of Nature

Anatta, NOAA Public Affairs Officer

Douglas H. Chadwick, wildlife biologist and contributor to NATIONAL GEOGRAPHIC magazine

Drew Hardesty, Forecaster, Utah Avalanche Center

Dr. Robert Ballard, National Geographic Explorer-in-Residence

Paperback ISBN: 978-1-4263-0630-3
Hardcover ISBN: 978-1-4263-0631-0

Contents

Your World 2011 — 8

Amazing Animals — 18

Going Green — 92

COOL CLICK

Throughout this almanac, our virtual pet, Zipper the dog, alerts you to cool clicks—Web links that will help you find out more!

Your World
2011

A high-tech light show celebrates the opening of the tallest building on Earth. Located in Dubai, in the United Arab Emirates, the 2,717-foot (828-m) -tall Burj Khalifa skyscraper has more than 160 stories, 57 elevators, and the world's highest swimming pool!

NEW
World's
Tallest
Skyscraper!

LIFE ON MARS?

Martians aren't really little green men with bulging eyes and alien superpowers. But it is possible that life exists (or existed) on Mars. In 2011, the Mars Science Laboratory, or rover, will head to the red planet to test soil and rocks for signs of life, past and present. Luckily, only tiny, microscopic life-forms could have lived there, so earthlings have nothing to fear.

Go online to add your name to a microchip that will travel on the Mars rover.
marsparticipate.jpl.nasa.gov/msl/participate

COMEBACK CAT

It seems an impossible mission: to pinpoint a hidden den of newborn Canada lynx kittens. But researchers from the Colorado Division of Wildlife know they are close.

In a small plane above the snowy wilderness, the team tracks a mother cat to a remote spot. Watching warily, she growls as the researchers gently weigh her two kittens and tag them with microchips before returning them to their den.

These kittens and others are a sign of hope. Humans wiped out the Canada lynx from this part of its range in the 1970s. But a decade ago, wildlife experts captured more than 200 lynx in Canada and Alaska, in the northern U.S., and set them loose farther south in Colorado.

These newborns are the grandkittens of the relocated cats. By tracking their movement, scientists can ensure that the wild cats continue to bounce back.

Blue Whale Secrets
REVEALED!

An almost 200-ton (181 t) blue whale breaks through the ocean's surface, its blowhole blasting water 20 feet (6 m) into the air. Sitting in a boat just ten feet (3 m) away, research biologist John Calambokidis springs into action. He uses a pole to attach a high-tech video camera called a Crittercam to the whale's back.

Created by National Geographic, Crittercams have been used on more than 50 species of land and marine animals. "The cameras allow us to look at the world from an animal's point of view," says Crittercam inventor Greg Marshall. When the cameras fall off, they send out radio signals so the scientists can find them.

The technology is helping solve mysteries about endangered blue whales, the largest animals ever to have lived on Earth. "We can see what happens deep underwater," says Calambokidis, cofounder of Cascadia Research. Among other discoveries, the cameras have revealed that blue whales dive as deep as 1,000 feet (305 m) and that their calls—one of the loudest sounds on Earth—are sometimes used to attract mates.

What's next for Crittercam? Soon the cameras will be able to record whale calls and other sounds more clearly. Experts hope to find out if loud underwater noises, often created by ships, are dangerous to blue whales. This knowledge could help scientists protect these giants of the sea.

A CRITTERCAM IS ATTACHED TO A BLUE WHALE WITH A GIANT SUCTION CUP.

Researchers in the inflatable boat at left had a special permit that allowed them to get this close to endangered blue whales.

AVERAGE LENGTHS OF ADULT AND BABY BLUE WHALES

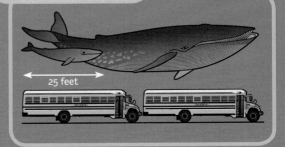

25 feet

11

Meet the Dalai Lama

What if you became the leader of your people when you were just 15 years old? That's what happened to Lhamo Thondup, known as the Dalai Lama. In 1950 he became the political leader of Tibet, now a part of China. But the Dalai Lama is more than just the head of his government. Promoting peace, compassion, and tolerance, he is also the spiritual leader of millions of people. Here's what this hero for peace wants to tell you.

NATIONAL GEOGRAPHIC KIDS: How can kids really help solve problems such as poverty and terrorism through peace?

THE DALAI LAMA: You need patience and determination. Study and become an expert in something, because education can bring compassion, peace, and harmony. That will bring self-confidence and stability. When you have all that, then you can influence others as an example. That's the way to create more peaceful communities.

NGK: Can one kid really make a difference in the world?

THE DALAI LAMA: Yes. Because if everyone works hard, we can all make a difference.

NGK: How can kids promote peace everyday?

THE DALAI LAMA: Look at situations from all angles, and you will become more open. We all have to live together, so we might as well live together happily. Realizing this helps you feel as if this whole world is one home.

NGK: You have been recognized for your concern about the environment. Why is it so important to protect the planet?

THE DALAI LAMA: We need to care for every part of the Earth and the life upon it, because this affects future generations.

NEW 7 WONDERS OF NATURE

Vote Now!

new7wonders.com

The Grand Canyon in the United States, the Great Barrier Reef in Australia, and the Bay of Fundy in Canada are just a few of the finalists competing to be one of the new 7 Wonders of Nature. Hundreds of millions of votes will be cast worldwide. The winners will be announced in 2011, so vote soon!

AUSTRALIA'S AYERS ROCK (ALSO CALLED ULURU) IS ONE OF THE NOMINEES.

> In the wild, orangutans are the largest animals that spend most of their lives in trees.

TIGERS CUDDLE WITH APES

Bogor, West Java, in Indonesia

Tigers don't normally snuggle with orangutans. The big cats are meat-eaters, after all. But when Demis and Manis, the tiger cubs, were rejected by their mother, zookeepers at Taman Safari Zoo thought they might like the company of two other orphan siblings: Nia and Irma the orangutans. "The first time I put them together, they just played," says zookeeper Sri Suwarni. The four shared toys, wrestled, and took naps together. Then one morning, Nia and Irma, began hugging Demis the tiger, and he lick-kissed them back! "That's when I knew they were true friends," Suwarni says. As the tigers grew, their natural instincts started showing, so Suwarni moved them into a separate exhibit. Now two other apes Suwarni is raising also have made a new friend—a leopard cub.

ELEPHANTS LIVING LARGE

Basking in the sunshine and soaking up attention from adoring fans, Ranchipur the Asian elephant is getting rock star treatment. The 12,000-pound (5,443 kg) pachyderm and three elephant friends have moved into fancy new digs at the San Diego Zoo, in California, U.S.A. Their new 2.5-acre (1-ha) pad comes complete with "utilitrees," fake trees that have built-in misters, heaters, and plenty of places to hang toys. Ranchipur lives in one of many zoos that are giving their elephant exhibits a luxury makeover. But these changes aren't just for show. "To keep elephants mentally and physically healthy, the new exhibit designs imitate the animals' environment in the wild," says elephant expert Mike Keele.

In nature the pachyderms travel in herds and can walk more than five miles (8 km) a day on grass and dirt. So to thrive in zoos, elephants need buddies to hang out with and room to roam. Plus, soft floors are a must to protect the animals' feet from arthritis and disease. Some will even have swimming pools, which encourage natural bathing behavior. "The trend for zoos is better and better care," says Keele.

Breeding programs at many of these zoos are also helping elephant species survive. That's good news for the lovable pachyderms, which are at risk of becoming extinct in the wild.

ROSE-TU THE ASIAN ELEPHANT PLAYS IN A POOL AT THE OREGON ZOO, IN THE U.S.A.

ERUPTION
as seen from space

FLYING OVER THIS SPEWING VOLCANO WAS TOO DANGEROUS FOR AIRPLANES, but this aerial photo was taken from a safe distance—more than 200 miles (322 km) above the Earth! An astronaut on the International Space Station (ISS) snapped this amazing picture of the Sarychev volcano in Russia during a powerful eruption. Using a digital camera, astronauts have taken pictures of hurricanes, meteor craters, Mount Everest, and other amazing sights down here on Earth.

First-Class RECYCLING

Flying to your next vacation spot? How about spending your next holiday *living* on an airplane instead? Well, on a recycled airplane, that is.

Some clever architects are turning retired airplanes into recycled homes and hotels, such as this resort in Quepos, Costa Rica.

Planes are designed to withstand extreme temperatures, so they make for well-insulated and sturdy structures.

And you won't be short on legroom in these luxury aircraft, which often come equipped with Jacuzzis, master bedrooms, hardwood floors, and outside "wing" decks. These jets can't fly anymore, but some rotate to show your favorite view from the window seat. This is one lofty idea that's really taking off!

See-Through Fish

Everyone wants to look inside this freaky fish's head. This Pacific barreleye is the first to be photographed with its see-through dome intact. But looks can be deceiving. What appears to be eyes are really nostrils (or nares). Barrel-shaped eyes, topped with big green lenses, are actually protected inside its head. This deep-sea creature lives mostly in the dark, so its lenses may filter traces of light, while its eyes rotate to look for prey.

EYES

NARES (NOSTRILS)

MOUTH

15

2011: What's Ahead

JANUARY
17th

Happy birthday to *The Lord of the Rings* author, J.R.R. Tolkien, born in 1892.

FEBRUARY
6th

TOUCHDOWN! It's **Superbowl XLV** for the **National Football League** in the U.S.A.

MARCH
18th

The Messenger spacecraft will begin its year-long orbit of the planet Mercury.

APRIL
22nd

Celebrate **Earth Day!** Plant a tree, pick up trash, just be good to the Earth.

MAY
2nd–**8**th

Stock up on apples, it's **Teacher APPRECIATION WEEK.**

JUNE
26th–July **17**th

The **6th FIFA Women's World Cup** kicks off in Germany. Go girl power!

JULY
June **25**th–July **4**th

Head to Athens, Greece, to see the **Special Olympics World Summer Games.**

AUGUST
1st–**7**th

Break out your big red nose and your floppy shoes—it's time to celebrate **National Clown Week** in the United States!

SEPTEMBER

Don't be afraid to get dirty at Great Britain's **NATIONAL MUD FESTIVAL of Wales.**

OCTOBER

Bask in the glow of 29,000 jack-o'-lanterns at the **KEENE PUMPKIN FESTIVAL** in New Hampshire, U.S.A.

NOVEMBER
20th

Universal CHILDREN'S Day

DECEMBER

This month marks the **100th anniversary** of the first expedition to reach the **SOUTH POLE!**

PLUG IN THIS CAR!

People are really charged up about electric cars. **Some of these eco-friendly autos are already for sale, and more will hit the road in 2011.**

Instead of running on polluting gasoline, these green machines "fuel" up on electricity by plugging into high-powered chargers. So what's stopping this great idea from getting rolling? There aren't very many places to recharge.

Hot Movies in 2011*

PUSS IN BOOTS

HARRY POTTER

Cars 2: World Grand Prix

Harry Potter and the Deathly Hallows: Part II

Kung Fu Panda: The Kaboom of Doom

Puss in Boots

*release dates and titles subject to change

*B*OWWOW-ABUNGA!

There's a new breed of dog in town: the extreme dog! While most pooches act as if sneaking food from the table is living dangerously, some aren't happy unless they're catching awesome waves or a fast ride.

Take Bandit the Boston terrier. He digs adventure so much that he surfs whenever he can. Bandit craves the waves, but his first love is riding motorcycles. "That's where he learned to balance," says owner Mark Shaffer.

"Dogs like Bandit are unique individuals," veterinary behaviorist Jacqui Neilson says. "Like people, dogs that enjoy daring activities have a special personality, talent, or athletic ability."

BANDIT (RIGHT) AND HIS BUD R.J.

17

Amazing Animals

Face to face with a green sea turtle
in Bora-Bora, part of French Polynesia.

WHAT IS Taxonomy?

Since there are billions and billions of living things, called organisms, on the planet, people need a way of classifying them. Scientists created a system called **taxonomy**, which helps to classify all living things into ordered groups. By putting organisms into categories we are able to better understand how they are the same and how they are different. There are seven levels of taxonomic classification, beginning with the broadest group, called a domain, down to the most specific group, called a species.

Biologists divide life based on evolutionary history and place organisms in three domains depending on their genetic structure: Archaea, Bacteria, and Eukarya. (See p. 118 for "The Three Domains of Life.")

Where do animals come in?

Animals are a part of the Eukarya domain, which means they are organisms made of cells with nuclei. There are more than one million species named, including humans. Like all living things, animals can be divided into smaller groups, called phyla. Generally, there are thought to be more than 30 phyla into which animals are grouped based on certain scientific criteria, such as body type or whether or not the animal has a backbone.

It can all be pretty confusing, so there is another less complicated system that groups animals into two categories: vertebrates and invertebrates. About 95 percent of all animals are invertebrates.

Chinese stripe-necked turtle

SAMPLE CLASSIFICATION
GIRAFFE

Domain:	Eukarya
Phylum:	Chordata
Class:	Mammalia
Order:	Artiodactyla
Family:	Giraffidae
Genus:	*Giraffa*
Species:	*G. camelopardalis*

TIP
Here's a sentence to help you remember the classification order:
Dear Philip Came Over For Good Soup.

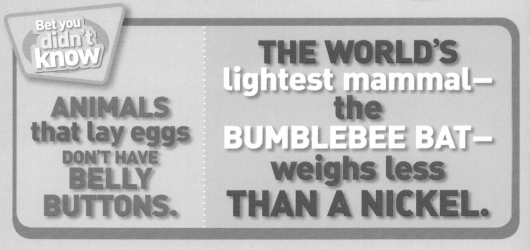

Bet you didn't know

ANIMALS that lay eggs DON'T HAVE BELLY BUTTONS.

THE WORLD'S lightest mammal— the BUMBLEBEE BAT— weighs less THAN A NICKEL.

Vertebrates Animals WITH Backbones

Fish are cold-blooded and live in water. They breathe with gills, lay eggs, and usually have scales.

Amphibians are cold-blooded. Their young live in water and breathe with gills. Adults live on land and breathe with lungs.

Reptiles are cold-blooded and breathe with lungs. They live on both land and water.

Birds are warm-blooded and have feathers and wings. They lay eggs, breathe with lungs, and usually are able to fly. Some birds live on land, some in water, and some on both.

Mammals are warm-blooded and feed on their mothers' milk. They also have skin that is usually covered with hair. Mammals live on both land and water.

Bird:
White-faced owl

Fish:
Gray reef shark

Invertebrates Animals WITHOUT Backbones

Sponges are a very basic form of animal life. They live in water and do not move on their own.

Echinoderms have external skeletons and live in seawater.

Mollusks have soft bodies and can live either in or out of shells, on land or in water.

Arthropods are the largest group of animals. They have external skeletons, called exoskeletons, and segmented bodies with appendages. Arthropods live in water and on land.

Worms are soft-bodied animals with no true legs. Worms live in soil.

Cnidaria live in water and have mouths surrounded by tentacles.

Brown tube sponges

Earthworms

Arthropod:
Red-kneed tarantula

Cold-blooded versus Warm-blooded

Cold-blooded animals, also called ectotherms, get their heat from outside their bodies.

Warm-blooded animals, also called endotherms, keep their body temperature level regardless of the temperature of their environments.

21

Amazing Animal Friends

KIPPER AND MI LU

GETTING HER GOAT

Kromdraai, South Africa

Bok-Bok the goat passed the ultimate friendship test: She helped save the life of Clover the rhinoceros! Sure, they were close before the rescue. Bok-Bok would give the rhino first dibs on alfalfa meals and huddle with Clover during rainstorms to keep them both warm. But no one expected Bok-Bok to leap into a dam after her rhino pal fell in! "Bok-Bok was a much better swimmer and started bumping Clover to push her out—but it didn't work," says Rhino & Lion Nature Reserve manager Ed Hern. "So she started bleating until someone came to help." You goat, girl!

BOK-BOK AND CLOVER

A DEER FRIEND

Prescot, England, United Kingdom

Most dogs would have no problem accepting a new puppy in the house. But a baby deer? Kipper the golden retriever thought, "Why not?" Mi Lu the deer came to live with Kipper's owners shortly after the deer had been orphaned at Knowsley Safari Park. Curator Nick Ellerton took the scared fawn into his home, but it was Kipper who took charge. "Kipper came to Mi Lu's rescue," Ellerton says. "He would lie beside Mi Lu, licking and comforting him." Outside, the pals played every day in the woods. "They loved chasing each other," Ellerton says. Mi Lu has since rejoined the deer in the park, but he hasn't forgotten Kipper. The two still visit regularly for playful romps!

New deer antlers are covered in what feels like velvet. But it is actually soft skin that eventually comes off.

TOKOLOS AND BABOON PALS

DOG PADDLE

Namibia, in Africa

It's not surprising for a dog to dive into a pool after a ball. But when Tokolos the Jack Russell terrier is followed by four baboons, that's something to see! Tokolos and his monkey pals—Elvis, Kanna, Lonny, and Tennis Ball—race each other to see who can get to the ball first. Then they dunk each other just like kids! Out of the water, Tokolos runs after the baboons until they playfully scamper up trees. Later the monkeys will groom Tokolos—a sure sign of friendship in the animal world. "Tokolos loves it when they look for ticks in his fur," says owner Marlice Van Vuuren.

Tokolos has all different kinds of pals—baboons, cheetahs, and meerkats—that he plays with every day at Harnas Wildlife Sanctuary. "He watches me care for the animals, so he thinks he's supposed to do that, too," says Van Vuuren.

Do Animals Have FEELINGS?

A scientist sat observing wild chimpanzees in Tanzania, in Africa. The chimp she called Flint had always been unusually attached to his mother. Even as an adolescent, he shared her nest at night. When his mother died, Flint withdrew from other chimps. He hardly ate. He climbed a tree to the nest he and his mother had shared. For a long time he stood there, staring into space. "It was as though he were remembering," says Jane Goodall, the world-famous chimp expert who witnessed the scene.

Stories like this suggest that animals have emotional feelings. Add up all such stories (there are many), and they suggest something more: evidence. It is evidence that researchers like Goodall hope will convince skeptics of something most people with pets already believe: that animals do have feelings.

Not everyone agrees that there is proof of animal emotions. Why the doubt? "You can't do an experiment to find out," says Joseph LeDoux, professor of neuroscience. "An animal can't tell you, 'Yes, that's how I feel.' So there's no way you can prove it."

Scientists used that same argument with Goodall nearly 50 years ago. But she didn't buy it. "Look into a chimp's eyes," she says, "and you know you're looking into the mind of a thinking, feeling being."

Sometimes that feeling is grief. Flint was so distraught after his mother's death that he starved to death—an extreme reaction to grief. Elephants also seem to mourn their dead. They stare at and touch their relatives' bodies and sometimes even carry their bones around.

But LeDoux says this doesn't prove feelings. Complex emotions—such as jealousy, grief, or embarrassment—may require a neocortex, the wrinkled outer part of the brain. Only primates and a few other animals have this brain structure.

Though most scientists believe that many animals do have some feelings, they also suspect that animal feelings are different from human feelings. How different? We may never know for sure.

Goodall believes that as researchers continue to observe animals and compare their findings, they will eventually gather enough data to draw some conclusions. "Until then, let's give all creatures the benefit of doubt," suggests Goodall.

Jane Goodall sits quietly observing chimpanzees, animals she has studied for more than 40 years.

ANIMAL MYTHS BUSTED

NG KIDS PUTS THESE TALL TALES TO THE TEST.

Animals do some pretty strange things. Giraffes clean their eyes and ears with their tongues. Snakes see through their eyelids. Some snails can hibernate for three years. But other weird animal tales are hogwash. NG KIDS finds out how some of these myths started—and why they're not true.

MYTH Opossums hang by their tails.

HOW IT STARTED Opossums use their tails to grasp branches as they climb trees. So it's not surprising that people believe they also hang from branches.

WHY IT'S NOT TRUE A baby opossum can hang from its tail for a few seconds, but an adult is too heavy. "Besides, that wouldn't help them survive," says Paula Arms of the National Opossum Society. "Why would they just hang around? That skill isn't useful—there's no point."

MYTH Ostriches bury their heads in the sand when they're scared or threatened.

HOW IT STARTED It's an optical illusion! Ostriches are the largest living birds, but their heads are pretty small. "If you see them picking at the ground from a distance, it may look like their heads are buried in the ground," says Glinda Cunningham of the American Ostrich Association.

WHY IT'S NOT TRUE Ostriches don't bury their heads in the sand—they wouldn't be able to breathe! But they do dig holes in the dirt to use as nests for their eggs. Several times a day, a bird puts her head in the hole and turns the eggs. So it really *does* look like the birds are burying their heads in the sand!

MYTH Penguins fall backward when they look up at airplanes.

HOW IT STARTED Legend has it that British pilots buzzing around islands off South America saw penguins toppling over like dominoes when the birds looked skyward.

WHY IT'S NOT TRUE An experiment testing the story found that penguins are perfectly capable of maintaining their footing, even if they're watching airplanes. "But the reality isn't funny," says John Shears, who worked on the survey. "Low-flying aircraft can cause penguins to panic and leave their nests."

25

ANIMAL TOOLBOX

Crabs, bears, and primates—all are ingenious tool users that get what they want!

MOBILE HOME

Hermit crabs carry other species' shells for protection from predators. As a crab grows, it finds a bigger shell.

THROUGH THE ROOF

Seals often make dens in Arctic snow at the edge of the sea. Observers report that a hunting polar bear that smells a seal will often lift a chunk of ice and use it to smash a hole through the den's roof. Then the bear grabs a meal of seal.

DRIP-DRY

Not anxious to get soaked during a rain shower, this orangutan creates an umbrella from a giant leaf.

GROUPIES!

Fish swim in schools, and cattle hang out in herds, but check out these weird names for other animal groups.

- a cloud of grasshoppers
- a sloth of bears
- a business of ferrets
- a troop of monkeys
- a plague of locusts
- a bloat of hippos
- an army of caterpillars
- a crash of rhinos

- a stand of flamingos
- a murder of crows
- a gaggle of geese
- a string of ponies
- a skulk of foxes
- an ostentation of peacocks
- a knot of toads
- a trip of goats

- a rafter of turkeys
- a peep of chickens
- a husk of hares
- a paddling of ducks
- a bale of turtles
- a pod of whales
- a drift of hogs
- a smack of jellyfish

GAGGLE OF GEESE

National Geographic photographer Darlyne Murawski combines her background in art and biology to showcase the lives and ecology of lesser-known organisms. Here she lies on her back to photograph caterpillar larvae.

HOW TO GET GREAT ANIMAL PHOTOS

Tips from the pros at National Geographic

1. Learn as much as you can about the animal and observe it for a while before you take any pictures.

2. Get on the animal's schedule. This may mean getting out of bed early!

3. Get as close to the animal as possible without taking a risk. Crouch or lie down so that you're at the animal's eye level.

4. When photographing animals in zoos or aquariums, visit when the animals are most active—usually feeding time or early or late in the day.

5. Be patient. The best shots come when you photograph animals on their terms rather than your own.

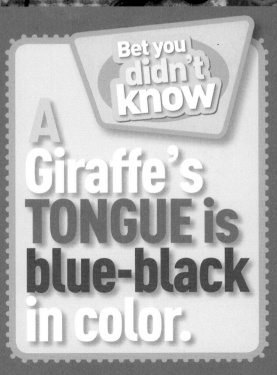

Bet you didn't know

A Giraffe's TONGUE is blue-black in color.

Wolf Speak

Understanding the secret language of a wolf pack

Calling all pack members! Meet us over here **to go hunt!**

To all who can hear: If you're not in our pack, **stay off our turf.**

It's all good. **C'mon, let's go.**

I f you want to understand wolf speak, you need to use your ears, eyes, and even your nose. Wolves talk to each other using their voices, body language, and, yes, body odor.

Wolves live in packs. Their survival depends on working as a team to find food, protect pack members, and raise pups. Being able to clearly read and express each wolf's rank is a matter of great importance.

Read My Lips and Ears and Shoulders

From head to tail, wolves express information through subtle and obvious body language. Facial expressions and how high a tail is held tell a wolf's confidence level or where it fits within the pack. The higher a wolf ranks, the higher it stands and holds its head, ears, and tail. The lower it ranks, the lower it drops everything, even flopping to the ground belly side up. Wolves also puff up their fur or flatten it to express themselves.

From Growl to Howl

Yips, yaps, barks, and squeaks are all wolf sounds. Wolves usually use vocals when interacting with each other. Scientists have trouble eavesdropping on these shy animals, so little is known about wolves' private conversations. But they're sure vocalizations are important. Even a three-week-old puppy can mimic almost all the adult sounds.

The howl is a wolf's long-distance call. In a forest, a howl might be heard six miles (10 km)

away. On the tundra it can be heard up to ten miles (16 km) away. A wolf may howl to locate its pack. Or it may be announcing its availability to join or form a new pack. Packs howl together in a chorus to strengthen the team, warn other wolves away from their territory, or coordinate movements of packs.

Talk to the Paw

With a sense of smell a hundred times better than a human's, it's no wonder scent is an important part of wolf communication. Wolves intentionally leave their

scent by marking trees and bushes with urine. They also secrete messages with scent glands in their feet and other body parts.

These odors aren't generally obvious to humans, but for wolves, sniffing tells all: the identity of an animal, its social status, whether it's an adult or a youth, how healthy it is, what it's been eating, if it's ready to breed, and much more.

As scientists keep learning how to understand wolf speak, they use their best tools—sniffing, spying, and eavesdropping.

GRAY WOLVES

You Are Here

CONTINENTS: EUROPE AND ASIA

COUNTRY: RUSSIA

SIZE: WORLD'S LARGEST COUNTRY, FOLLOWED BY CANADA, THE UNITED STATES, AND CHINA

LOCATION: NORTHWESTERN COUNTRYSIDE

Your plane lands in northern Russia. As you approach wolf territory, you hear them first. *Ow-oooo! Grrr!* Then you spot the pack of wolves. Wrestling and playing, they look like they're celebrating. They're actually psyching themselves up for a hunt. Wolves' preferred prey includes moose. One moose can weigh twice as much as the entire pack. Confidence and teamwork mean survival. Only about one in ten attacks on a moose is successful.

Packs are led by the dominant male and female,
sometimes called the alpha wolves. Your heart pounds when you see the alpha female lunge toward a younger wolf in the pack. It falls down, exposing its neck to show submission. Growling, the alpha holds the young wolf down by its throat. Even from a distance, you understand the conversation. She's reminding the juvenile that she's in charge. The pup's submissive response means, "Yes, ma'am!" Communication and leadership help the pack survive.

You notice that the alpha pair really seem to like
each other. The power couple nuzzles and cuddles; they're likely to remain lifelong partners. The two leaders rally the pack, and all but one adult trot off to hunt. Left behind: the pups and an adult babysitter. You watch as the wolves, working as a team, successfully bring down a moose. They eat their fill in about half an hour. Then they return home, and the pups nip at their snouts, begging for dinner. The adults immediately regurgitate undigested meat for the pups and babysitter to eat. Happy that a more appetizing meal is waiting for you on the plane, you slip away to begin your next adventure.

BY THE NUMBERS

1 litter of pups is born each year in a typical pack.

3 times bigger than a coyote, the gray wolf is the largest wild member of the dog family.

13 years is the average life span of a gray wolf in the wild.

22 pounds (10 kg) of meat may be wolfed down at one meal.

40 miles an hour (64 kph) is a wolf's top running speed.

100 times stronger sense of smell than a human's. A gray wolf can sense the presence of an animal up to three days after it's gone and smell prey more than a mile (1.6 km) away.

ARCTIC ANIMALS

Wind whips across the ice at 45 miles an hour (72 kph). Blizzards cut visibility to zero. Temperatures plunge to -50°F (-45°C). Not many creatures can survive the fierce Arctic winter.

One survivor is the cunning arctic fox. It doesn't even try to escape. Nor does it sleep through the coldest and darkest months of the year. Instead, the arctic fox depends on three special survival tricks.

TRICK 1: When hunger strikes, the arctic fox often steals a meal. It creeps across the sea ice in search of the leftovers of another Arctic winter resident—a polar bear.

TRICK 2: The arctic fox stores food, which is less risky than stealing from bears. In the spring foxes steal snow goose eggs from nests and bury them in secret spots. Months later the foxes come back, dig up the eggs, and have a feast.

Arctic foxes have been known to steal and store as many as 3,000 eggs during the nesting season. Burying the eggs in the cool ground keeps them fresh for months.

TRICK 3: The arctic fox dresses for success. Nature designed its whole body for heat conservation (see box below). The fox even changes coats with the seasons. In the summer the arctic fox's back, sides, and tail are a dusky brown. But by mid-November the fox sheds the last traces of its summer look for pure white winter fur that helps it blend with the snowy background. This coat is super-thick and mostly made of fleece. The long, coiled hairs are especially good for holding in body heat.

During the worst winter weather the arctic fox curls up into a ball to save heat and stay cozy, even as the brutally cold Arctic winds blow.

THE ANATOMY OF A
SURVIVOR

Small ears, a short muzzle, rounded body, and squat legs are all less likely to lose body heat than larger, lankier body parts. Extensive, complicated networks of veins and capillaries within each pad on a fox's foot keep warm blood flowing through, supplying feet with extra heat.

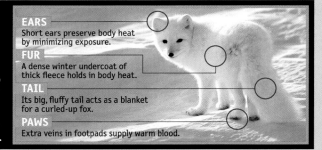

EARS
Short ears preserve body heat by minimizing exposure.

FUR
A dense winter undercoat of thick fleece holds in body heat.

TAIL
Its big, fluffy tail acts as a blanket for a curled-up fox.

PAWS
Extra veins in footpads supply warm blood.

Wild Hare

Fur and speed: These are the keys to an arctic hare's survival.

Winter weather is often bitterly cold in the tundra of North America and Greenland where arctic hares live. But a coat of thick, luxurious fur, along with pads of thick hair on the soles of its feet, keep a hare toasty warm. By curling into a tight ball with only its hind feet touching the ground, a hare stays snug. The tighter the curl, the warmer it remains.

An arctic hare's fur helps conceal it from predators. White fur camouflages it as snow in winter. In the southern part of their range, hares grow darker coats that help them blend into the rocky terrain.

Standing on its hind legs and using its excellent eyesight and sense of smell, a hare stays alert for enemies. If one gets too close, the hare hops away, leaping six to nine feet (2 to 3 m) in one hop. At speeds of up to 30 miles an hour (48 kph), an arctic hare could keep up with a city car—though off-road cruising is more its style.

BEAR NECESSITIES

How Polar Bears Survive the Deep Freeze

In a polar bear's Arctic home, winter temperatures get unbelievably cold. But imagine running around outside in a heavy down jacket. Even if it's cold out, you might start to feel too warm. Much like you in that jacket, a polar bear is so well insulated that it can easily become overheated. Sometimes it cools off with a mouthful of snow or by lying flat to expose its belly directly to the snow. To keep from overheating, a polar bear usually moves slowly and doesn't run much.

So what keeps the polar bear so toasty? The most visible protection is its thick fur coat. The coat has two layers: an outer layer of long, dense guard hairs and an undercoat of short woolly hairs. A polar bear may look white, but underneath its hair its skin is black, which absorbs heat.

Another way a polar bear copes with the cold is with built-in insulation: a layer of blubber under its skin that can be more than four inches (10 cm) thick.

Many polar bears spend the winter living on slippery sea ice. Luckily, their paws are perfect for getting around on a slick, cold surface. Rough pads give them a nonslip grip, and thick fur between the pads keeps their feet warm. Sharp, curved claws act like hooks to climb and dig in the ice.

So bring on the snow, wind, and icy water. Because when it comes to keeping warm, a polar bear's got it covered!

KEY: WHERE POLAR BEARS LIVE

The Bear Facts

ICY HOME Polar bears live in the far north, on sea ice and on land. Scientists estimate that some 20,000 to 25,000 polar bears roam the Arctic.

HANDY PAWS Partially webbed front paws help polar bears swim. The bears may use their back paws like rudders—to steer.

SEA BEAR Polar bears, seen swimming as far as 150 miles (241 km) offshore, are the only bears considered to be marine mammals.

BIG BOYS Polar bears usually bear twins. A newborn weighs about a pound; an adult male, about 1,400 pounds (635 kg).

SNACKING When a polar bear hunts, it looks for baby seals resting in dens under the snow near the water's edge.

SNOW BABIES

Baby polar bear cubs are born in mid- to late-December inside a snow den built by their mother. She usually has one or two cubs. The den is about the size of a refrigerator, and so is mom, so it's not roomy.

As newborns, cubs are about the same size as a loaf of bread and weigh about a pound (.5 kg). They have no teeth, their eyes are closed, and their fur is not thick. They need their mother's warmth and protection 24/7.

By early April, when cubs leave the den for the first time, they weigh 20 to 30 pounds (9 to 14 kg). By two years old the cubs have learned all the bear lessons they'll need for their 30-year life span. Then the young bears find their own territory and start preparing for having their own cubs.

PANDAMONIUM

Like a toddler at snack time, a giant panda sits with its legs stretched out in front of it and munches on bamboo. The tough bamboo is no match for the panda's powerful jaws and the crushing force of its huge molars. In one day, it'll polish off 20 to 40 pounds (9 to 18 kg) of bamboo! Bamboo—a grass that grows tall like a tree—sprouts so fast you can actually watch it grow. Even so, nearly 138 giant pandas starved to death in the mid-1970s. Today, there are between 1,000 to 3,000 pandas left in the wild. Another loss would devastate the endangered population.

BLOOMING BAMBOO

For pandas, bamboo is the perfect food and shelter. Ninety-nine percent of a panda's diet is bamboo. Stems, shoots, leaves—pandas devour it all. That is, until the bamboo begins to flower. Even the hungriest panda isn't likely to eat it at that stage, because bamboo is not nutritious or appetizing as it flowers.

One blooming plant wouldn't be a big deal, but bamboo is peculiar. Unlike most plants, when one bamboo flowers, all of the bamboo plants of the same species do, too. After flowering, bamboo drops its seeds to the forest floor. Then the plant dies. If a majority of a forest is the same species of bamboo, then pandas are suddenly out of food.

FINDING FOOD

You would think that a panda would be able to hunker down and wait out the flowering by surviving on other plants and small animals. But many species of bamboo sprouts aren't big enough to be edible for at least five to seven years. That means a small area—or an entire forest—goes from a bamboo buffet to starvation-central practically overnight—and stays that way.

Scientists know very little about the bamboo flowering process because it happens so infrequently. Some haven't flowered in 120 years—when your great-grandparents or maybe even great-great-grandparents were still in diapers. In the past, pandas would just search for other sources of bamboo. Today there's a short supply of dining digs because roads, farms, cities, logging, and mining isolate forests. The pandas can't get to a suitable new forest because their homes are surrounded by human activities.

LOOKING AHEAD

To halt habitat destruction, China has stopped most logging. The government also created some 50 nature reserves for pandas. And scientists are working with zoos worldwide to create an extensive panda breeding program with a goal of rebuilding the wild population. All this support gives giant pandas—and their bamboo habitat—a green future.

Where Bears Live

Bear Ranges

- American Black Bear
- Asiatic Black Bear
- Brown Bear
- Giant Panda
- Polar Bear
- Sloth Bear
- Spectacled Bear
- Sun Bear

Striped pattern indicates overlapping ranges.

0 — 3,000 miles
0 — 4,000 kilometers

BROWN BEARS

CLOSE-UP

Look, Ma. No Hands!

Open wide! Fish—it's what's for dinner. This salmon did not look before it leaped, so it's about to end up as brown bear food. Salmon by the thousands leave the ocean and head upstream to mate and lay eggs every fall. Attracted by the fish feast, brown bears by the dozen gather along the banks of Brooks Falls in Katmai National Park in Alaska to fatten up before their long winter hibernation. Timing, luck, and patience helped photographer Joel Sartore catch this fish—just before the bear did.

5 COOL THINGS ABOUT ELEPHANTS

1 ELEPHANTS HAVE LONG MEMORIES

Elephants never forget. "They keep coming to places they like, no matter what," says wildlife photographer Frans Lanting. One elephant herd has been visiting the same tree every November for at least 25 years!

2 ELEPHANTS CHAT WITH FRIENDS

Elephants are always "talking" in some way. This is fine in the wild. But it's a problem when elephants join sightseers on safari through the jungle. Noisy elephants spook wildlife away. "We depended on quiet," says John Roberts, who managed elephants at a lodge in the Royal Chitwan National Park in Nepal, in Asia.

When pachyderm pals Chan Chun Kali and Bhirikuti Kali worked together, they were too chatty, so Roberts moved the elephants to separate camps, six miles (10 km) apart.

This worked during the day. But every night the chatterboxes started up again. They didn't rumble softly like most elephants do when "talking" long distance. "They shouted!" says Roberts. He wore earplugs to get some sleep.

3 ELEPHANTS THINK FOR THEMSELVES

The wild and wacky sport of elephant polo is popular in Thailand. During one game, a player couldn't quite hit the ball—he just kept swinging and missing. Finally his quick-thinking elephant took matters into her own hands. She picked up the ball and handed it to the player!

4 ELEPHANTS ARE GENTLE

Tender touching is important among elephants. They hug, pet, and guide others with their trunks. American cowboy Bob Norris adopted a baby African elephant named Amy. "We bonded immediately," he says.

5 ELEPHANTS HELP EACH OTHER

A retired circus elephant named Peggy might have drowned if another elephant hadn't come to her rescue! Peggy, an elephant with a partially paralyzed trunk, and her friend Betty Boop were bathing in a pond, when Peggy lay down on her side. Swimming elephants use their trunks as snorkels, but Peggy's was completely underwater. The elephant couldn't breathe or stand! Luckily Betty Boop rushed over and used her head to push Peggy back up on her feet and save her.

ELEPHANTS TO THE RESCUE

Trained elephants lent a helping "trunk" after a tsunami destroyed many of southern Asia's coastal towns in December 2004. In Thailand the pachyderms used their trunks to lift motorcycles (right) and cars from the wreckage. Elephants also helped out in other countries hit by the tsunami. One elephant was walking with an eight-year-old girl on its back when the tsunami struck. In shoulder-high water, the elephant carried the girl to safety. Guess that makes these animals huge heroes!

CONVERSATIONS WITH
APES

SURPRISING WAYS BONOBOS "TALK" WITH HUMANS

HMM . . . WHICH RING TONE DO I WANT?

RARING TO GO!

Panbanisha, a female bonobo (buh-NO-bo), often hitches a ride—but she'd probably rather drive. One day, while out in the woods of Georgia, U.S.A., Panbanisha suddenly leaped into a parked golf cart. By pushing the accelerator with her foot, she started the engine. Gripping the steering wheel with both hands, she looked over her shoulder and backed up. Next, she shifted gears and zoomed ahead. The only reason she stopped was because she rammed the cart into a tree! (She wasn't hurt.)

"We never taught her to drive," says primatologist Sue Savage-Rumbaugh. But that didn't prevent this smart ape from teaching herself.

JUST LIKE US?

Of the great apes—bonobos, gorillas, orangutans, and chimpanzees—bonobos are the most like humans. Savage-Rumbaugh decided to study them to see whether they could pick up language on their own, as humans do. It turns out that they can. In fact, Savage-Rumbaugh discovered that bonobos can learn to do lots of things on their own.

Growing up in a language center lab at an American university, Panbanisha and her brother, Kanzi, had human caretakers, watched TV, and played with toys. Now both drink from a glass, brush their teeth, and use the toilet. They also communicate.

At first, the apes simply listened—picking up the meanings of words by hearing people talk. Later they learned to say things by pressing symbols on a portable computer.

FIREFIGHTER?

Savage-Rumbaugh frequently took the apes hiking in the forest. Kanzi learned to make fires by watching her make them. Kanzi collected sticks, which he snapped with his foot and piled in a heap. He borrowed a lighter to ignite the blaze. The apes used the fires for roasting marshmallows! When it was time to leave, Kanzi doused the flames with a bucket of water. (CAUTION: Never light a fire without adult supervision!)

Savage-Rumbaugh hopes that as people learn more about bonobos, they'll grow to respect them and feel as strongly as she does about protecting them in the wild.

Above and Beyond

NATIONAL ZOO, WASHINGTON, D.C., U.S.A.

Like a nervous tightrope walker, Bonnie the orangutan stood on a platform tower 40 feet (12 m) above the ground. At this zoo, towers and cables connect the Great Ape House with a primate language exhibition in another building. Called the O-line, it lets orangutans travel naturally and decide for themselves where to spend their days.

Bonnie was the first to use it. But before she did, she tested each cable. She shook it, stood on it, and bounced up and down. Finally, she ventured across, leaving her baby behind. But what happened next amazed everyone watching. At the halfway point, Bonnie stopped . . . and stared.

"I'll never forget the look on her face," says biologist Rob Shumaker.

"It was thrilling for her to sit up there looking out over the zoo. She saw things she didn't know existed."

As employees cheered, Bonnie returned for her baby. And together they retraced her steps—so she could expand his world, too.

THE Great Koala RESCUE

Frightened and helpless, a baby koala clings to a tree branch. Below, his mother screams. Searching for dinner, the mother has gotten her head stuck in a fence.

For Australians, spotting a koala isn't unusual, but finding one in distress is. Desperate to save the koala, a family who happened upon the scene calls the Queensland Parks and Wildlife Services. Koala rescuer Vicki Pender is sent to help.

Pender knows she must act quickly to save the terrified animal that is frantically struggling to free herself. After giving the koala a tranquilizer to calm her down, Pender carefully cuts away the fence with bolt cutters.

CAUGHT IN HER TRACKS

Just as she is about to rush to the animal hospital, a yipping sound stops Pender in her tracks. High in a nearby tree, the baby calls for its mother. The rescuer tries to coax him from the tree, but he scampers away. Knowing the baby will not survive alone, Pender needs to act fast.

Quick action, experience, and a little luck help the rescuer nab the confused baby before he gets far. At the hospital veterinarians check both koalas for injuries. Every day, rescuers, scientists, and citizens work to help save koalas. Not too long ago millions of koalas thrived in Australian forests. Then people moved in, cutting down trees to build roads, houses, factories, and malls.

A Koala-Friendly Development

New South Wales, Australia

Dogs and cats are not allowed in Koala Beach Estates, a housing development in New South Wales, but koalas are more than welcome. The number of koalas in Australia has declined dramatically because eucalyptus trees, which koalas depend on for food and shelter, have been cut down to make room for houses and shopping centers. The builders of Koala Beach Estates, however, worked with the Australian Koala Foundation to preserve the existing eucalyptus trees and also plant new ones. All fences are raised one foot off the ground so koalas can move around easily. And residents agree not to keep cats or dogs because the pets might harm the koalas. The result? There are probably 30 or more koalas living at Koala Beach Estates!

A DANGEROUS LIFE

Koalas stay in the trees as much as possible, preferring to spend little time on the ground. A koala's life consists mainly of sleeping during the day and devouring up to two pounds (907 g) of eucalyptus leaves at night. Now there are fewer trees, and koalas face more dangers as they walk greater distances to go from tree to tree. They must walk through yards, across streets, and often into danger to reach eucalyptus. On the ground koalas can be hit by cars or attacked by dogs.

Because koalas are also sensitive to stress and unable to adapt to the changing environment, koalas' numbers have dropped drastically.

What are people doing to help save koalas? They're keeping pets in at night and planting trees for koalas to feed on. Warning signs remind drivers to watch out for koalas crossing roads. Most important, citizens continue to work hard to pass laws that protect koalas' remaining forests.

Luckily, the rescued koala and mother survived. After a short hospital stay, the rescuers released the healthy animals back into the wild.

City Gone WILD!

Wild animals have moved into the big city, and they're fitting in a little too well. Find and circle ten wild animals hiding in this scene. Look carefully— you might see them in some funny places.

ANSWERS ON PAGE 339

The Weird World of FROGS

Frogs survived the catastrophic extinction of the dinosaurs. But strangely, the world's frogs and toads have suddenly begun to disappear. Some species that were common 25 years ago are now rare or extinct. And individual frogs are showing up with deformities such as too many legs. Scientists are not sure exactly what is going on.

But scientists do agree that because frogs drink and breathe through their thin skin, they are especially vulnerable to pesticides and pollution. A deformed frog often indicates that all is not well with the environment. And frogs live just about everywhere on Earth.

Frogs are amphibians, which means "double life." They generally hatch in water as tadpoles and end up living on land as fully formed frogs.

Frogs' skin must stay moist, so they're usually found in wet places.

Because frogs are so sensitive to environmental changes, they act as an early warning system. Their dwindling numbers may be a sign that our planet is not as clean and healthy as it once was. By studying how frogs are affected by the environment around them, scientists may be able to predict—and sound an alarm—that a neighborhood needs to cut back on lawn fertilizers or that a chemical-dumping factory should clean up its act. The hidden message in frogs' familiar peeps and croaks? "I'm jumpy for a reason!"

RANDOM Question

Q Has it ever rained frogs?

A Yes! Frogs fell from the sky twice in the United States: in Kansas City, Missouri, in 1873, and again in De Witt, Arkansas, in 1942. Tornadoes and powerful storms sometimes vacuum up the surface of ponds, including the frogs living in the water. When the storm breaks up, frogs really *can* drop from the clouds!

CALLING ALL FROGS

Frogs bark, croak, cluck, click, grunt, snore, squawk, chirp, whistle, trill, and yap. Some are named for the noise they make. A chorus of barking tree frogs sounds like a pack of hounds on a hunt. The carpenter frog sounds like two carpenters hammering nails, and the pig frog grunts like—you guessed it—Porky's cousin! Here a male Australian red-eyed tree frog (above) inflates his throat pouch, which helps make his female-attracting calls louder.

TOADS and FROGS—WHICH IS WHICH?

Toads are actually a subgroup of the frog family. So scientifically speaking, all toads are frogs—but not all frogs are toads. Generally, the differences include the following:

AMERICAN TOAD **versus** BRONZE FROG

TOADS
- have bumpy, dry skin
- have short hind legs and move by short hops
- usually live in damp places

FROGS
- have smooth, moist skin
- have long, strong hind legs, and move by long leaps
- live in or near water

Superfrogs!

LARGEST
The Goliath frog, from West Africa, grows to about a foot long (.3 m). As frogs grow, they shed their skin. After bending and twisting their bodies to loosen the skin, they pull it over their heads like a sweater—and eat it!

SMALLEST
One of the smallest frogs in the world, this leaf litter frog fits on a coin. The tiny frog is found in Cuba. There are more than 4,500 species of frogs worldwide.

MOST POISONOUS
The bright colors of the golden poison dart frog from Colombia, South America, warn predators to stay away. The skin of one golden poison dart frog, the deadliest of all frog species, contains so much toxin that it could kill 20,000 mice.

COOLEST
The North American wood frog spends two or three months frozen each winter. Its breathing and heartbeat stop, and most of the water in its body turns to ice. These frogs use a sugar called glucose in their blood as a kind of antifreeze to protect their organs from damage.

Frog Facts

Frogs are carnivorous—they eat almost anything that moves and can fit into their mouths, including insects, worms, slugs, snails, small mammals, and even other frogs.

The unusual gastric brooding frog of Australia is now probably extinct. But check this out: Mother frogs would swallow their eggs, and the young hatched in their stomachs. About six weeks later—burp!—up and out came fully formed froglets!

When frogs swallow their food, their eyeballs close and go into their heads. The eyeballs help with digestion by applying pressure and pushing food down the throat.

Frogs can be different colors—green, brown, red, yellow, orange, and even blue.

Whooo-o Are You?

5 Owls
you ought to know

There are almost 200 species of owls. They range in size from 5 to 30 inches (13 to 76 cm) tall and live on every continent but Antarctica. Here are five owls and the fun facts about whooo-o they are!

pygmy owl

1 SAW-WHET OWL

This tiny owl, just seven inches (18 cm) tall, gets its name from its call, which sounds like a saw being sharpened on a stone. Owls make many different and distinct sounds, including hoots, screeches, trills, and chimes. Like most birds, owls sing to attract mates and call to keep other owls from intruding into their territory.

2 AFRICAN SPOTTED EAGLE-OWL

Owls' big eyes are ten times more sensitive to light than humans' eyes. That helps the birds see at night, which is when most owls, including the eagle-owl, hunt rabbits and other prey. Eyes that face forward give owls depth perception, or the ability to tell how far away things are—another useful ability for these hunters.

Sometimes these hunters have to hide from pests such as crows and smaller birds. When startled, many owls flatten their feathers and lengthen their bodies to look like a tree branch. Some have "ear" tufts (which are just feathers, not really ears) that mimic broken twigs, helping the birds blend in even better.

3 BURROWING OWL

Most owls live in trees in nests abandoned by other birds. But a burrowing owl looks for an abandoned animal den in the ground. If it's in an area with very soft, loose soil, the owl digs its own burrow. To hunt, it stands on the dirt mound near its burrow or on a higher perch if available and watches the area for lizards, mice, or insects. Once the owl spots its prey, off it goes, sometimes on foot, to catch dinner. Most owls live alone, but a burrowing owl often lives in a group called a parliament.

4 GREAT GRAY OWL

A tasty fresh mole caught by a parent means dinnertime for many great gray owl chicks. To feed the babies, an adult uses its sharp beak to tear the food into pieces. In owl families both parents feed the young. A female lays an average of four to six eggs. She lays each egg on a different day, so the chicks hatch at different times. That means some are smaller than others. If food is scarce, the smallest owl chick often starves. Owlets quickly learn to hunt, and most are on their own by the first winter. Sometimes parents bring live insects and small rodents to the nest so the young can practice hunting.

5 BARN OWL

Silent flight lets owls surprise their victims. Owls with long wings, like barn owls, usually hunt from the air. After catching its prey, an owl carries it back to a perch where it swallows its meal, usually whole. It can't digest bones, feathers, or fur. A few hours after it eats, the owl closes its eyes, makes a pained face, and regurgitates a big, tightly wrapped pellet of leftovers.

Wonder what kind of owl Harry Potter has? Learn about this "snow white" wonder online. kids.nationalgeographic. com/Animals/Creature Feature/Snowy-owl

COOL CLICK

5 COOL REASONS TO LOVE BATS

1 FLIP, FLAP, AND FLY
Bats are the only mammals that can truly fly. A bat's wings are basically folds of skin stretched between extra-long finger and hand bones.

2 VALUABLE DROPPINGS
Bat droppings, called guano, are super-rich in nitrogen, a main ingredient in plant food. The ancient Inca of South America protected bats as a valuable source of fertilizer for their crops. Guano is still used in farming today.

3 MARVELOUS MOSQUITO MUNCHERS
Many bats are born bug eaters, filling their bellies with moths, mosquitoes, and other winged insects. The brown bat gulps down as many as a thousand mosquito-size insects in an hour. Each night the bats from one Texas cave consume about 200 tons (181 t) of bugs, many of them crop-eating pests. That's about the weight of six fully loaded cement trucks.

4 EXTREME FLIGHT
Hoary bats migrate up to 1,000 miles (1,609 km) south from Canada each fall. Mexican free-tailed bats often fly up to 3 miles (5 km) high, where tailwinds help speed them along at more than 60 miles an hour (97 kph).

5 SUPERMOM STRENGTH
A newborn bat may weigh as much as one-third of its mother's weight, yet the mom can hold her baby while clinging by her toes to a crack in a cave's ceiling.

Going Batty

LITTLE BROWN BAT
"Little" is right—a brown bat weighs about as much as two small coins!

SHORT-TAILED FRUIT BAT
After just one night of dining, this bat can scatter up to 60,000 undigested seeds—crucial to rain forest plant growth.

COMMON VAMPIRE BAT
Vampires' main diet is the blood of cows and horses. Rarely do they take a bite out of humans.

WHITE TENT BATS
These fruit-eaters often create "tents" to roost in. They make bites in a large leaf so it folds over itself. Then the bats snuggle under.

FLYING FOX
There are about 60 species of bats called flying foxes (above). This kind sometimes roosts in a "camp" of up to a million individuals.

VELVETY FREE-TAILED BAT
This bat fills its cheek pouches with insects in midair, then chews and swallows them later.

PALLID BAT
Using big ears to listen for rustlings, a pallid bat locates and grabs its prey from the ground.

DESERT LONG-EARED BAT
Sonar emitted by this kind of bat echoes off prey, signaling where its meal lies.

OLD WORLD LEAF-NOSED BAT
Complex nose structures for hunting gave this bat its name.

Bet you didn't know

Bat Spit May Save Lives
A substance in the saliva of vampire bats could help victims of strokes survive, according to researchers at the University of Monash in Melbourne, Australia. Strokes happen when a blood clot blocks blood flow to the brain. An anticlotting substance in bat spit makes blood flow freely, so a bat can continue to feed. The researchers think the same substance may be able to dissolve blood clots in stroke patients. Fortunately the substance would be contained in medicine, and bats would not be required to bite patients!

Albino Animals

THESE ANIMALS FACE DANGER IN THE WILD

From mottled gray-and-white koalas to brilliantly hued reef fish, an animal's color serves a purpose. Color helps some species blend with their surroundings so they can hide from predators or sneak up on prey. The bright colors of some animals warn predators that they're poisonous, while others help attract a mate.

An animal's color comes from a pigment called melanin. Pigment cells color eyes, skin, fur, feathers, and scales. The specific colors the cells produce are determined by genes. Genes are a body's instructions on how to build the animal from head to toe, inside and out, down to the last detail.

But what happens if an animal's pigment cells cannot produce melanin? Animals without pigment have inherited a condition called albinism. In albinos, altered genes prevent pigment cells from making color. Albino animals are all white with pink or blue eyes. Many animal species can have the rare genes that cause albinism.

Albino animals face challenges in the wild. They stand out, which makes them targets for predators. Albino animals also may have trouble finding mates. Some birds, for example, reject albino partners. The reason may be that albinos lack the colors and patterns the birds rely on to choose a mate.

Below are a couple of examples of rare albino animals. Many albino animals, like those shown below, live in captivity, where they are protected and live longer than they would in the wild.

Alligator

Wallaby

BEST PERFORMANCE BY AN ANIMAL . . .

If animals got Grammy Awards, male humpback whales would win trophies for their long and varied songs. Here are a few more animal acts that might take home Grammys for their sensational singing skills.

LOUDEST VOCALIST

The winner is the blue whale. Its low-frequency rumblings can reach 188 decibels. That's louder than a jet airplane. The howler monkey is a close runner-up. Its booming voice can carry a distance of three miles (5 km).

BEST SAMPLER

Let's hear it for the mockingbird, famous for copying the songs of other birds. Many talented mockingbirds can belt out the calls and songs of at least 30 other kinds of birds in just 10 minutes.

STRANGEST SINGER

Give it up for the male grasshopper mouse! When threatened, this five-inch (13-cm)-long rodent rears up on its hind legs, points its nose to the sky, and howls like a wolf. Each shrill cry can be heard across the length of a football field.

HORSE? ZEBRA? BOTH!

Schloss Holte-Stukenbrock, Germany

When Eclyse was about to be born, people figured the animal would be a zebra. After all, that's what the mother was. But the newborn's mix of stripe patterns and solid hair told a different story: Her father was a horse! Eclyse is a zorse: half horse, half zebra. How did this happen? In the wild, horses and zebras would never mate. But Eclyse's parents lived close together at a horse farm. The result was a rare, unintentional zorse.

Eclyse looks like two animals melded into one, but she behaves more like a horse. She eats hay, whinnies, and hangs out with Pedro the horse. "But she's a little wild like a zebra," says Susanna Stubbe of Zoo Safaripark Stukenbrock, where Eclyse now lives. "She's a bit jumpy, even if a fly lands on her back." Eclyse is definitely a horse of a different stripe!

> The name Eclyse (ee-KLEEZ) is a combination of her parents' names: mom Eclipse and dad Ulysses.

PIG ATHLETES?

Moscow, Russia

Now even pigs can have gold medal dreams! During the third annual Pig Games, Russian pigs faced a fierce team of international competitors in sports such as pigball, pig swimming, and pig racing.

Russia's sporting swine live in a special complex where vets and coaches keep them in fabulous form. Nariner Bagmanyan, whose company organizes the games, says the well-trained Russian pigs were calm and focused before their events. Or maybe they just had their eyes on the prize: a tub of cooked carrots with cream!

The home team left their challengers in the dust, winning all three events. Russia's pigball players defeated the international team by a whopping 16 to 3. But Bagmanyan cuts the visiting athletes some slack: "To play soccer in a foreign country is probably difficult for everybody—even pigs."

WILD CAT
Family Reunion

There Are 37 Species of Wild Cats

Scientists divided them into eight groups called lineages after studying their DNA. Here are representatives from each lineage. The domestic house cat comes from the lineage that includes the sand cat.

not

CHEETAH
(46 to 143 pounds: 21 to 65 kg)

- Often scans for prey from a high spot
- Can sprint up to 70 miles an hour (113 kph)
- From Puma lineage, which includes three species

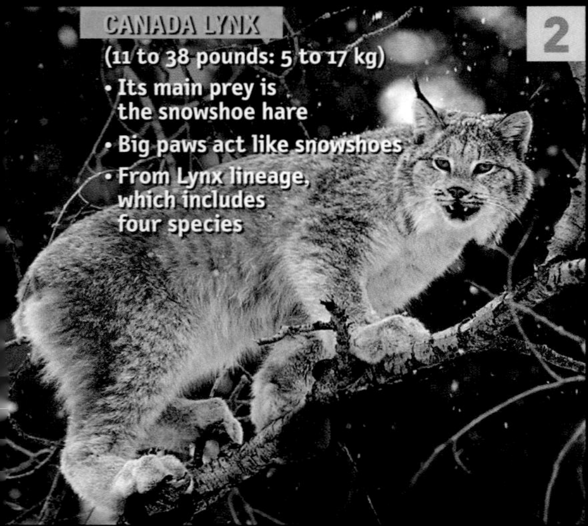

1

CANADA LYNX
(11 to 38 pounds: 5 to 17 kg)

- Its main prey is the snowshoe hare
- Big paws act like snowshoes
- From Lynx lineage, which includes four species

2

3

OCELOT
(15 to 34 pounds: 7 to 15 kg)

- Most of an ocelot's prey is small
- Found from Texas to Argentina
- From Ocelot lineage, which includes seven species

TIGER
(165 to 716 pounds: 75 to 325 kg)

- Tigers are the only striped wild cats
- These big cats will hunt almost any mammal in their territory
- From Panthera lineage, which includes seven species, such as the lion and jaguar

4

44

5

ND CAT (3 to 7.5 pounds: 1 to 3 kg)
he sand cat lives in dry deserts of northern
frica and the Middle East
arely drinks; gets water from food
rom Domestic Cat lineage, which includes
x species of cat

MARBLED CAT
(4 to 11 pounds: 2 to 5 kg)
- Its long, bushy tail is sometimes longer than its body
- Very little is known about this rare, nocturnal, and shy wild cat
- From Bay Cat lineage, which includes three species

6

SERVAL
7
(15 to 30 pounds: 7 to 14 kg)
- Longest legs, relative to its body, of any cat species
- Big ears used to listen for prey
- From Caracal lineage, which includes three species

FISHING CAT
8
(11 to 35 pounds: 5 to 16 kg)
- A strong swimmer, it has slightly webbed feet
- Eats mainly fish
- From Leopard Cat lineage, which includes five species

How to tell a cat by its
SPOTS

JAGUAR: little dots in the middle of larger rings
Home: mainly Mexico, Central and South America
Average Size: 80 to 350 pounds (36 to 159 kg)
Cat Fact: Third largest in the cat family after tigers and lions, the jaguar is the largest feline in the Western Hemisphere.

LEOPARD: rings without the jaguar's smaller dots inside
Home: much of Asia and Africa
Average Size: 62 to 200 pounds (28 to 91 kg)
Cat Fact: Some leopards are dark and look spotless. They're called black panthers.

CHEETAH: evenly spaced, solid black splotches the size of a human thumbprint
Home: parts of Africa
Average Size: 46 to 143 pounds (21 to 65 kg)
Cat Fact: On the fastest land animal, dark lines mark a cheetah's face from the inner corner of each eye to the outer corners of its mouth.

SERVAL: usually a series of single black dots that can vary from the size of a freckle to one inch (2.54 cm) wide
Home: many parts of Africa
Average Size: 15 to 30 pounds (7 to 14 kg)
Cat Fact: A serval uses its huge ears to hunt by sound, surprising prey with a pounce.

OCELOT: solid or open-centered dark spots that sometimes merge to look like links in a chain; fur in the center of open spots is often darker than background coat color.
Home: South, Central, and North America
Average Size: 15 to 34 pounds (7 to 15 kg)
Cat Fact: An ocelot's main prey is rodents.

MEET THE LIGER

Sporting stripes and sometimes a shaggy mane, ligers roar like lions and chuff like tigers. That's because ligers are a rare mix of a male lion and a female tiger.

Giants among the big cats, ligers can weigh almost as much as a lion and tiger combined. They can devour up to 30 pounds (14 kg) of raw meat a day, and their heads are as big around as a kid's bicycle tire!

There may be fewer than 30 ligers living today. But they aren't endangered. Zoologists and other scientists don't even recognize ligers as a species. Ligers would not exist in the wild, because lions and tigers wouldn't mate. The solitary tiger and the group-minded lion wouldn't be good partners.

WHERE DO LIGERS COME FROM?

In captivity, some caretakers have allowed the two species to share space. Kept together, a lion and a tiger *can* mate, resulting in an "accidental" liger cub.

Most ligers are intentionally bred by humans—often for personal gain by being sold to private zoos. People like them because they are odd.

AN ACTIVE DEBATE

Is it wrong to allow this to happen? Almost all scientists say yes. "It's just not natural," says Ron Tilson, director of conservation at the Minnesota Zoo.

Besides that, ligers are often unhealthy because of their mismatched lion and tiger genes. They're prone to blindness, weak hearts, deafness, and short life spans. No matter how playful and happy some ligers may seem, this genetic mix isn't right.

JAGUARS

You Are Here

CONTINENT:
SOUTH AMERICA

COUNTRY: BRAZIL

LOCATION: AMAZON
RIVER RAIN FOREST

LENGTH OF RIVER:
4,000 MILES
(6,437 KM);
SECOND LONGEST
RIVER ON EARTH

As your plane lands, the sun rises in Brazil's rain forest along the Amazon River. You make your way into the lush growth of the hot, dense forest. You're eager to spot a jaguar hunting. You and your guide search for a cat using a tracking device. The jaguar's spots camouflage it so well that the cat is hard to find. Finally, it appears, leaping suddenly from the underbrush into a small clearing.

You notice the jaguar's short, compact body and big head. A jaguar easily drags prey two or three times its weight great distances. To match that strength, you'd have to be able to drag three of your friends at once—with your mouth!

You watch as the jaguar settles into a hidden spot, waiting to ambush a deer. As the unsuspecting animal wanders by, the cat pounces, killing the deer by piercing its skull with its powerful bite. The jaguar is the only big cat that uses this method to kill prey. It can even bite through a tortoise's shell.

Like the lion, this cat likes to swim—and fish. Your guide tells you about the time he watched a jaguar wait patiently at the edge of a stream until a fish swam by. Then *swoosh!* The cat scooped the fish out with its paw for a snack.

COOL CLICK

To learn more about lots of other amazing animals, go online.
kids.nationalgeographic.com/Animals

LIONS
OF THE
KALAHARI
DESERT

How these specialized hunters adapted to their environment

E yes half-closed against the wind-blasted sand, a sleek, black-and-gold-maned lion strides along a dry riverbed in the Kalahari Desert. He is one of the lions that roam the desolate sand dunes of southern Africa's Kalahari and Namib deserts. These lions thrive in an intensely hot landscape. They have learned to go without water for weeks.

Life for a desert lion is very different from life as a lion in the grassy plains of Africa, such as in the Serengeti of Kenya and Tanzania. There, large prides of up to 20 lions spend most of their time together. A pride is very much like a human family.

Fritz Eloff, a scientist who spent 40 years studying the desert lions of the Kalahari, found that desert lions live, on average, in smaller groups of fewer than six. Family ties are just as strong, but relationships are long-distance. They often break up into smaller groups.

BUSY NIGHTS

Life for Kalahari lions is a constant battle against thirst and high temperatures. In summer during the day, the surface temperature of the sand can be 150°F (66°C). That's hot enough to cook an egg.

Not surprisingly, Kalahari lions hunt mostly after the sun has gone down. The big cats usually rest until the middle of the night, waiting for a cool desert wind.

Then they spend the rest of the night walking—looking for food.

In the Serengeti, food is very plentiful. Lions rarely have to walk more than a couple of miles before they find a meal. But life in the desert is not so easy. With only a few scattered animals such as porcupines and gemsboks—horse-size antelopes—for prey, desert lions have to walk farther and work harder to catch dinner.

FAST FACTS

TYPE: Mammal

DIET: Carnivore

SIZE: Head and body, 4.5 to 6.5 feet (1.4 to 2 m);

TAIL: 26.25 to 39.5 inches (67 to 100 cm)

WEIGHT: 265 to 420 pounds (120 to 191 kg)

GROUP NAME: Pride

PROTECTION STATUS: Threatened

BY THE NUMBERS

3 is the number of cubs in a typical litter of lions.

5 miles (8 km) is the distance the sound of a lion's roar can carry.

15 pounds (7 kg) of meat is a typical meal for an adult male lion.

36 miles an hour (58 kph) is a lion's top running speed.

2,200 pounds (998 kg) is the top weight of prey a pride can kill.

ROARRR!
On a still night, the sound of lions roaring can carry for five miles (8 km). Roaring often is used to tell other lions, "This is my piece of land."

DANGEROUS DINNER

When Kalahari lions do find something to eat, it is usually spiky or dangerous. One out of every three animals they catch is a porcupine. The desert lion's main prey is the gemsbok, which can provide ten times as much meat as a porcupine. But gemsboks are difficult to bring down; they've been known to kill lions by skewering them on their three-foot-long (1 m), saber-like horns.

Water is scarce in the Kalahari, so the desert lions have to be as resourceful at finding a drink as they are at finding a meal. One hot day, just as a light rain began to fall, Eloff watched two lionesses. Side by side, they licked the raindrops off each other.

Amazingly, these lean, strong lions have learned to survive, and by cooperating they manage to thrive in an inhospitable, almost waterless world.

Lions are the world's most social cats.

THE PRIDE

Lions are the only cats that live in groups, which are called prides. Prides are family units that may include up to three males, a dozen or so females, and their young. All of a pride's lionesses are related, and female cubs typically stay with the group as they age. Young males eventually leave and establish their own prides by taking over a group headed by another male.

THE MANE STORY

Only male lions boast manes, the impressive fringe of long hair that encircles their heads. Males defend the pride's territory, which may include some 100 square miles (259 sq km) of grasslands, scrub, or open woodlands. These intimidating animals mark the area with urine, roar menacingly to warn intruders, and chase off animals that encroach on their turf.

LADY LIONS

Female lions are the pride's primary hunters. They often work together to prey upon antelopes, zebras, wildebeest, and other large animals of the open grasslands. Many of these animals are faster than lions, so teamwork pays off.

HIDDEN HUNTER

How stripes help the tiger make a sneak attack

Crouching in the tall grass, a tiger waits patiently. Black stripes against a golden coat blend perfectly with brown and yellow stalks reflecting the sunlight. Perfectly still, the big cat is almost invisible as a large Indian bison approaches. The bison is unaware of the hidden danger. Suddenly the tiger springs from its hideout, pounces on its prey with a powerful leap, and pulls the bison to the ground. The bison didn't see its predator coming—until it was too late.

In their natural habitat, tigers live in a world of dappled sunlight and shadows. Patches of bright sunlight alternate with deep shadows in the dense, tangled forests and grasslands of Asia. A tiger's bold stripes break up the outline of its body and let it blend into the shadows.

SOLO STRIPES

Tigers are the only striped wild cat. Other wild cats are marked with spots or blotches, like cheetahs, or have coats with no pattern, like lions. Some scientists think that tigers' stripes may have evolved from a blotched coat pattern similar to that of the clouded leopard. Over time, the large spots may have disappeared, leaving the dark lines on the back edges of the blotches—the cloud patterns—to evolve into stripes.

No two tigers have exactly the same stripe pattern. Just as each human's fingerprints differ, so do each tiger's stripes.

Tigers' individual striping comes in very handy for scientists who study tigers in the wild—a difficult pursuit because the animals are hard to spot and are most active at night.

TIGER PHOTOGRAPHERS

Biologists used to rely on finding tracks and signs of kills to get a tiger population count in an area under research. Now they just get tigers to take their own pictures! Choosing trails that the big cats are likely to use, researchers set out special motion-detecting cameras throughout a study area. As a tiger walks by, it trips the camera's shutter. Because each tiger's stripes are different, researchers can recognize individuals in the photographs by the unique markings on each animal's head and body.

Unlike most other cats, tigers actually enjoy water. On hot days they spend hours playing in ponds or rivers, or just lounging in the water to beat the heat. Tigers are strong swimmers and are known to swim to islands as far as five miles (8 km) offshore.

THE MYSTERY OF THE
BLACK PANTHER

**Are you superstitious?
Do you think it's bad luck if
a black cat crosses your path?**

Many people once believed that black cats part-nered with the devil. They show up regularly in comic books, posters, and movies. But in real life they are as rare as parents who allow kids to eat dessert before dinner. What are these mysterious black cats and where do they live?

"Black panthers are simply leopards with dark coats," says scientist John Seidensticker. "If you look closely, you can see the faint outline of spots in the dark fur," he adds.

Biologists used to think that black panthers were a separate species of leopard. The fierce black cats had a reputation of being more aggressive than spotted leopards, the way dark-maned lions are more aggressive than those with lighter manes. But zookeepers noticed that normal spotted leopards and black leopards can sometimes be born in the same litter (see below)—just as kids in the same family can have blue eyes or brown eyes.

BLENDING IN

Overall, black leopards are extremely rare in the wild. They are almost never seen in the leopard's range in Africa, and only occasionally in India. But surprisingly, these black cats are the only leopards known in the forests of Malaysia, in Southeast Asia. Black leopards are so much more common there that the local forest people don't even have a word in their vocabulary for *spotted* leopards.

Scientists don't really know why black leopards are the norm in Malaysia. One theory is that animals living in dark, humid forests like those in Malaysia, tend to have darker fur for camou-flage. African leopards spend most of their lives in grasslands and forests where spots are prob-ably the best disguise.

The black cats are not evil creatures of witches and devils. They are cats at their best—evolving to blend with their habitat.

51

DOLPHINS IN DISGUISE

If you think *you* have a few odd relatives...

imagine having a second cousin who's six times your size or an uncle covered in scars from a lifetime of fighting. Welcome to the dolphin family, made up of more than 30 species that inhabit every ocean—and even some rivers. You probably know the common bottlenose dolphin, seen frolicking in aquariums. Now meet its surprisingly diverse relatives.

HOURGLASS DOLPHIN

Dolphin data Sailors once called these small mammals "skunk dolphins," but not because they smelled bad. The dolphin's white markings are similar to a skunk's stripe.

Spinning in air Leaping out of the water, hourglass dolphins make spectacular midair spins. "No one knows for sure why they spin," says Mark Simmonds, a dolphin biologist. "Theories include that they do it for fun, as a form of communicating to others, or to help get rid of parasites."

Where they live Frigid waters in the Antarctic

Dolphin data With its stubby dorsal fin and permanent grin on its beakless head, the Irrawaddy dolphin looks like a bottlenose dolphin reflected in a fun house mirror—recognizable but oddly misshapen. These dolphins, found in both coastal waters and some freshwater rivers, are experts at catching dinner. They spit streams of water to confuse fish, making them a cinch to snatch.

Perfect catch Fishermen in Myanmar, in Asia, appreciate the Irrawaddy dolphin's fishing skills, too. In a tradition carried down for generations, the fishermen signal the dolphins to drive schools of fish into nets. These special dolphins don't do it for free—they snap up fish that get away.

Where they live Along coasts of India and Southeast Asia, and in some Southeast Asian rivers

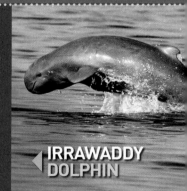

IRRAWADDY DOLPHIN

ORCA

Dolphin data Don't let its titanic size or "killer whale" nickname fool you. A male orca may grow to the length of a school bus, but it is actually a dolphin. It's also the sea's top predator, using team-work to hunt seals, sea lions, and other large prey—hence the killer alias. Researchers have even seen orcas gobbling up great white sharks!

Mother knows best Orcas love their moms. Elder females typically lead each family, or pod. Male orcas who wander off to mate in other pods return to their mothers' sides and never see their young. "It's unusual among mammals," says Val Veirs, who studies orcas. "This top predator gets all its marching orders from Mom."

Where they live Frigid coastal waters across the globe

BOTTLENOSE DOLPHINS

Dolphin data In the wild, these sleek swimmers can reach speeds of over 18 miles an hour (29 kph). They surface often to breathe, doing so two or three times a minute.

Superstars They are well known as the intelligent and playful stars of many aquarium shows. Their curved mouths give the appearance of a friendly smile, and they can be trained to perform complex tricks.

Where they live In tropical oceans and other warm waters around the globe

Dolphin data Small and curious, the Commerson's dolphin is known for its playful nature and striking black-and-white coloring. These sleek swimmers look like they're wearing white capes!

Boat buds Many dolphin species enjoy playing with boats, but Commerson's seem especially excited to surf on a ship's wake and twirl in propeller turbulence. "One time two dolphins spent more than an hour playing with our research boat," says Vanesa Tossenberger, who studies Commerson's dolphins. "It certainly makes our work easier."

Where they live Off the southern tip of South America

HOW TO ID A DOLPHIN

Dolphins are part of a group of marine mammals called cetaceans, which also includes whales and porpoises. As you can see, dolphins come in many shapes, sizes, and colors. So what makes a dolphin ... a dolphin?

DENTAL CHECKUP

Dolphins are considered toothed whales. They have conical teeth, unlike porpoises, which have spade-shaped teeth.

NOSE JOB

Most dolphins have a beak, called a rostrum, on their melon-shaped heads, although some family members, such as the orca, do not.

TEAM PLAYERS

"Of the toothed whales, the dolphin family is probably the most social and most diverse," says biologist Denise Herzing.

FINNED KIN

Many dolphins have a dorsal fin. The fin helps stabilize a dolphin as it swims and also helps regulate its body temperature.

COMMERSON'S DOLPHIN

UNDER the ICE

Jellyfish (right) with 30-foot (9-m) -long tentacles... sponges the size of bears... these are just a few of the surprises beneath the surface of Antarctica's frozen seas.

One such surprise is **sea spiders.** Found in oceans worldwide, they are less than an inch (2.54 cm) long. But in Antarctica they often reach the size of a human's hand. Luckily, people aren't their chosen snack food. They prefer to chow down on coral, anemones, and sponges.

SEABIRDS OF THE NORTH

Colorful Atlantic puffins perch on a grass-covered cliff in Iceland, Europe's westernmost country. These unusual birds are skilled fishers but have difficulty becoming airborne and often crash (unharmed) upon landing.

IN SEARCH OF THE GIANT SQUID

Do huge sea monsters with eyes the size of human heads and multiple arms that could wrap around a large ship exist? For centuries sailors have reported seeing such sea monsters. In fact, they sound a lot like a real deep-sea creature called the giant squid.

The giant squid may grow 60 feet (18 m) long and can weigh, literally, a ton (.9 t). It has a razor-sharp beak plus eight arms and two tentacles outfitted with hundreds of suckers. Its eyes are the largest of any animal. But until recently scientists only knew about this from examining dead or dying squid that were trapped in fishing nets or washed up on beaches. In 2004 Japanese scientists took the first photographs of a giant squid in its natural habitat, 2,950 feet (899 m) below the ocean's surface, and they have now also filmed and captured a live giant squid.

BIG AND SCARY

There may be something even bigger and scarier than the giant squid lurking in the ocean depths: the colossal squid. According to some marine biologists, the colossal squid has a heavier body than the more common giant squid. Scarier still, the suckers that line the colossal squid's arms and tentacle ends boast hooks that can bend while they grip. Ouch!

SQUID VERSUS SQUID

In a watery wrestling match between the two enormous squids, which would come out alive? "It probably comes down to weight," says Mark Norman, a senior curator of mollusks at Museum Victoria in Melbourne, Australia. "So I'd be putting my money on the colossal squid."

GREAT WHITE SHARKS

"We've located a great white shark," the captain tells you on the deck of the research vessel. You're off the coast of South Australia, near Spencer Gulf. The captain points to the shark cage tied to the boat's stern. "Hop in!" he tells you. "This is an opportunity you won't want to miss."

You check your snorkeling gear and then slip down feet-first into the cage. (A shark cage is built to keep great white sharks out. The cage's metal bars protect divers like you.) Slowly you're lowered, inside the cage, to just below the ocean surface. Soon you spot what you came to see. Your heart races as a six-foot (2-m) great white shark glides past the cage, turns, and swims by again. You are safe.

Steering Clear of SHARK BITES

Shark attacks on people are extremely rare. In the U.S., seven times as many people are bitten by squirrels as sharks every year. Here are tips to help you stay safe:

1 Stay out of the ocean at dawn, dusk, and night—when some sharks swim into shallow water to feed.

2 Don't swim in the ocean if you're bleeding.

3 Swim and surf at beaches with lifeguards on duty. They can warn you about shark sightings.

Great white sharks are the world's largest meat-eating fish. Their sharp teeth and powerful jaws are built to cut and tear their prey. The longest confirmed great white was longer than 20 feet (6 m)—about the length of 4 bathtubs! Your six-footer is a young shark.

Suddenly you see the shark's impressive teeth. The predator you're watching speeds by again—this time following a school of large fish. The shark grabs one that lags a bit behind the rest. In two gulps, the fish is gone. The scientist on board told you that great white sharks also scavenge, or eat dead animals they come across. They particularly like whales. Whale blubber, or fat, gives these large sharks an excellent source of calories. Now the captain hoists you out of the water because the time has come to head for dry land.

COOL CLICK

Want to color a picture of a great white shark? nationalgeographic.com/coloringbook/sharks.html

6 COOL THINGS YOU DIDN'T KNOW ABOUT SHARKS

1 TEETH TO SPARE

If great white sharks had tooth fairies, they'd be rich! A great white loses and replaces thousands of teeth during its lifetime. Its upper jaw is lined with 26 front-row teeth; its lower jaw has 24. Behind these razor-sharp points are many rows of replacement teeth. The "spares" move to the front whenever the shark loses a tooth.

2 BOX OFFICE BULLY

Great white sharks are superstars. Before the *Star Wars* series, the 1975 movie *Jaws* was Hollywood's biggest moneymaker. *Jaws*, about a great white on the prowl, cost $12 million to film but made $260 million in the U.S. Not bad for a fish story!

3 SPEEDY SWIMMERS

Great white sharks can sprint through the water at speeds of 35 miles an hour (56 kph)—seven times faster than the best Olympic swimmer! Scientists on the California coast tracked one shark as it swam all the way to Hawaii—2,400 miles (3,862 km)—in only 40 days.

4 CHOW DOWN, TUNA BREATH!

Picky eaters they're not. While great white sharks prefer to eat seals, sea lions, and the occasional dolphin, they've been known to swallow lots of other things. Bottles, tin cans, a straw hat, lobster traps, and a cuckoo clock are among the items found inside the bellies of great white sharks.

5 EAR THAT?

Great white sharks have ears. You can't see them, because they don't open to the outside. The sharks use two small sensors in the skull to hear and, perhaps, to zero in on the splashing sounds of a wounded fish or a struggling seal!

6 HOT ON THE TRAIL

Unlike most fish, great white sharks' bodies are warmer than their surroundings. The sharks' bodies can be as much as 27°F (-3°C) warmer than the water the fish swim in. A higher temperature helps the great white shark swim faster and digest its food more efficiently—very useful for an animal that's always on the go!

Sensitive Sharks

What's the secret weapon a great white shark or a black-tip reef shark uses to track its prey? Gel in the snout! The clear gel acts like a highly sensitive thermometer, registering changes in water temperature as slight as a thousandth of a degree, according to one scientist. Tiny changes in the ocean's temperature tend to occur in places where cold and warm water mix, feeding areas for smaller fish—a shark's next meal. Once the gel registers a change, it produces an electrical charge that causes nerves in the snout to send a message to the shark's brain that says, "Let's do lunch!"

BY THE NUMBERS

ABOUT **12** species of sharks are considered dangerous.

YOU ARE **250** times more likely to be killed by lightning than by a shark.

THERE ARE **375** different species of sharks found in the world's oceans.

THERE WERE **43,674** more injuries associated with toilets than with sharks.

MEET THE NAT GEO EXPLORER

SYLVIA EARLE

Sometimes termed "Her Deepness," Earle is an oceanographer, explorer, author, and lecturer whose knowledge of the sea is immense. Earle has led more than 60 expeditions and logged more than 6,000 hours underwater, including leading the first team of women aquanauts during the Tektite Project in 1970 and setting a record for solo diving to a depth of 3,300 feet (1,006 m).

How did you become an explorer?
It was really easy. I started out as a kid asking questions—Who? How? What? Where? When? And especially, Why? And I never stopped. Explorers and scientists never lose their sense of wonder, never stop asking questions, and always keep looking for answers.

What was your closest call in the field?
I have been surrounded by hundreds of sharks, dived in submersibles more than two miles (3 km) under the sea, and had my air supply run out when I was more than a thousand feet (305 m) away from my home base underwater.

How did you get involved with National Geographic?
I loved reading the NATIONAL GEOGRAPHIC magazine as a child, and I still do. Then, as a scientist, I lived underwater for two weeks in 1970, and I was asked to write about the experience for NATIONAL GEOGRAPHIC! Since then I have written more stories for the magazine and worked on a lot of films and books.

Would you suggest that kids follow in your footsteps?
I followed my heart—and it led into the sea. I hope every child will have a chance to realize his or her dreams. Every person has a special, unique pathway that unfolds as opportunities arise and choices are made. There is an urgent need for everyone who cares about exploring and protecting natural systems, above and below the sea, to get busy and go for it!

EMPEROR PENGUINS

1 Emperors are the largest of the 17 penguin species.

2 One colony can number as many as 60,000 penguins.

3 These penguins can live 20 years or more in the wild.

4 Emperors eat fish, squid, and shrimplike krill.

5 Parents feed chicks every three to four days.

Penguin Party

The loudmouthed penguins at this party have a lot to say. Use the clues in the word balloons to match each penguin to its species name. Fill in the correct letters below.

ANSWERS ON PAGE 339

1. Rockhopper
2. African
3. Chinstrap
4. Emperor
5. Erect-crested
6. Little
7. King
8. Macaroni
9. Magellanic
10. Yellow-eyed

A

GO PICK ON SOMEONE YOUR OWN SIZE.

B

DUDE, WHICH ROCK STAR DO I LOOK LIKE?

C

MY HAIR ALWAYS STANDS UP STRAIGHT, NO MATTER HOW MUCH GEL I USE.

I LOVE GOING ON SAFARI.

D

LOOK ME IN THE EYE WHEN I'M TALKING TO YOU.

E

YOU ARE ALL MY SUBJECTS.

IT'S A GOOD THING MY HEAD IS STRAPPED ON, OR I'D PROBABLY LOSE IT.

WHEN I GROW UP, I'M GOING TO BE KING.

G

I'M NAMED AFTER A FAMOUS EXPLORER.

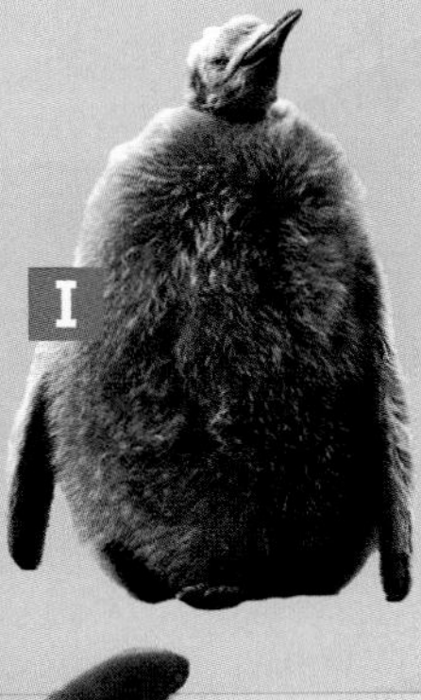

F

H

I'M ALWAYS USING MY NOODLE.

I

J

59

Human activity poses the greatest threat to Earth's biodiversity—its rich variety of species. Loss of habitat puts many species, including those in this section, at great risk. Experts estimate that species are becoming extinct at a rate 100 to 1,000 times faster than would occur naturally.

THREATENED!

SAVING THE Sea Turtle

How people are saving these threatened creatures

Green sea turtles were important to the fishermen on Mafia Island off Tanzania's coast, in Africa—because they could sell the turtle meat!

That attitude began to change when fishermen hauled in a 50-year-old green sea turtle with a shell as wide as a car tire. There was nothing special about the turtle. Mafia Island fishing boats had netted thousands just like her before. But what happened next was special: Instead of killing her, the fishermen spared the turtle's life.

Sea Life Needs Sea Turtles

Sea turtles play a key role in Mafia Island's chain of life. Green turtles act as natural undersea lawn mowers. Fish and other sea creatures use the huge sea grass beds near Mafia as a safe place with plenty of food for raising their young. Sea grass beds need sea turtles to graze on them in order to stay healthy.

Four of the world's seven sea turtle species swim in the waters off Mafia. Green turtles are the most common. Even though it's illegal to harm these threatened animals, Mafia Islanders had traditionally eaten turtle meat. They also ate turtle eggs found in nests. Other sea turtle species in the world include: hawksbill, leatherback, loggerhead, Kemp's ridley, flatback, and olive ridley turtles. Populations of all these sea turtles are in distress.

Success Saving Sea Turtles

Thanks to a program funded by the World Wildlife Fund, fishermen have learned about the value of sea turtles. Fishermen who guard a nest or turn over a live sea turtle to scientists—for data collection and release—can earn money. For fishermen, sea turtles have become the gift that keeps on giving.

The program seems to have worked. Killing turtles and taking their eggs has almost completely stopped.

All this success started when that first green sea turtle was saved. Unfortunately, sea turtles throughout the oceans still face many dangers, such as pollution and deep-sea fishing nets. But at least they're not being eaten as much anymore!

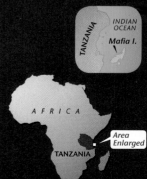

INDIAN OCEAN
TANZANIA
Mafia I.

AFRICA

TANZANIA

Area Enlarged

Will the RED PANDA survive?

A mask marks one of the cutest faces in the forest. The red panda looks a little like a raccoon, a bit like a fox, and somewhat like a puppy. Soft, cuddly reddish fur blankets its body, which is a tad larger than a big house cat's. These harmless creatures live in the high mountain forests of the Himalaya in southeastern Asia. But their numbers in the wild are dwindling.

As loggers and firewood collectors chop down trees, and ranchers allow overgrazing by domestic livestock, the fragile mountain habitat of the red panda erodes.

SPECIALIZED DIET

The diet of the red panda also makes it vulnerable, because it is one of just a few mammal species in the world that eat mainly bamboo. It's not the most nutritious stuff. This giant grass has tough stems and leaves that make it difficult to chew and digest. A bamboo diet doesn't give red pandas much energy, so they have to conserve as much as possible.

SLOW-MOVING SLEEPYHEADS

Red pandas save energy simply by keeping activity to a minimum. They spend six to eight hours a day moving around and eating. The rest of their time is spent resting and sleeping. Their bodies are built to conserve energy. When the weather is cold, the pandas curl into a tight ball on a tree branch and go into a very deep sleep. This reduces their metabolism, or the amount of energy they use. When red pandas wake up, their metabolism returns to normal. But as soon as they go back to sleep their metabolism drops again, saving energy.

SAVING THE BLUE IGUANA

F ound only on the Caribbean island of Grand Cayman, in the Cayman Islands, the blue iguana is one of the most endangered species of lizards in the world. They can't protect themselves against threats such as the houses and roads being built, or predators such as snakes, cats, and dogs. When the number of these wild, dragonlike creatures dropped to fewer than 25 several years ago, experts took action. They began breeding them in captivity. The program has been so successful that over 250 blue iguanas now live wild on the island. Luckily, it may be blue skies ahead for these living "dragons."

BY THE NUMBERS

There are 8,782 vulnerable or endangered animal species in the world. The list includes:

- **1,142 mammals**, such as the snow leopard, the polar bear, and the fishing cat.
- **1,223 birds**, including the Steller's sea eagle and the Madagascar plover.
- **1,414 fish**, such as the Thailand giant catfish.
- **469 reptiles**, including the American crocodile.
- **711 insects**, including the Corsican swallowtail butterfly.
- **1,895 amphibians**, such as the Round Island day gecko.
- **And more**, including 18 arachnids, 606 crustaceans, 235 corals, 97 bivalves, and 939 snails and slugs.

COOL CLICK

To find endangered species by state, country, and other groupings, check out the U.S. Fish and Wildlife Service. ecos.fws.gov/tess_public

PANDA BABY BOOM!

Today, Su Lin is a confident, maturing, female giant panda, but just a few years ago she was barely the weight of a stick of butter! (See her grow below.)

Born in 2005, Su Lin lives at the San Diego Zoo in California. She was one of 19 captive pandas born that year. Since the giant panda is an endangered species, it is great when cubs are born in captivity.

PANDAS AT RISK

The exact number of giant pandas in the wild is hard to estimate, but scientists think that fewer than 2,500 of these animals live in the mountains of central China. About another 300 giant pandas live in zoos and breeding stations, mostly in China. Giant pandas are among the rarest of the world's living mammals.

DAY 1
08-02-2005
22:37:35

The panda gently holds her newborn, Su Lin, in her mouth moments after giving birth.

DAY 3

A newborn panda doesn't have its parents' black-and-white markings.

WEEK 2

She's almost 10 inches (25 cm) long and weighs 13 ounces (369 g). Black markings begin to show.

WEEK 6

Cubs grow fast. She already weighs more than four pounds (2 kg).

WEEK 13

WEEK 11

The cub gets her first tooth. "Stay tuned," say zoo doctors. "More teeth to come!"

In keeping with Chinese tradition, the cub is named 100 days after her birth. Her name is Su Lin, which means "A Little Bit of Something Very Cute."

Polar Bears
Listed as Threatened

Polar bears were recently added to the list of threatened species and received special protection under United States law. In his statement, former U.S. Secretary of the Interior Dirk Kempthorne noted that the decline of Arctic sea ice is the greatest threat to the bears.

Polar bears live in the Arctic and hunt seals and other fatty marine mammals from sea ice. They also travel, mate, and sometimes give birth on the ice. But sea ice is melting as the planet warms, and it is predicted to continue to do so for several more decades. "Because polar bears are vulnerable to this loss of habitat, they are—in my judgment—likely to become endangered in the foreseeable future," Kempthorne said.

Although many scientists say that human activity is directly responsible for the melting sea ice, the polar bear protections will not by themselves change U.S. climate policy.

The listing of the bear adds protection for the animals and provides a means to limit the impacts from activities such as oil and gas production. Hunting of polar bears as a food source by certain native people and trade in native handicrafts made from polar bears will continue. However, importing polar bear products from Canada (where trophy hunting is legal) is banned in the United States.

A study found that two-thirds of the world's polar bears could go extinct by 2050. Saving the polar bear will depend on international cooperation. Permanent sea-ice habitat is likely to remain in areas outside of the U.S., particularly in Canada and Greenland, until the end of the century (see range map on p.31).

Scientists view these areas as refuges that could allow some polar bear populations to survive over the long term and repopulate the Arctic if temperatures decrease and sea ice returns. Scientists believe that there is still time to save polar bears and their Arctic habitat if we take action on climate change soon.

When you're a Canada lynx's lunch, it's *always* a bad hare day.

An endangered Canada lynx perches on a stump. A snowshoe hare, ever alert, crouches on the snow. White on white, the hare is betrayed only by its black, marblelike eyes. Suddenly the lynx bounds, pounces ... and just misses as the hare flees. The cat sniffs briefly and then sits on its haunches in deep, melting snow. It's late spring in the far north.

Animal

Elephant Seal

After being swept out to sea alone, an elephant seal pup that hadn't yet learned how to swim washed up on a beach. The confused and exhausted baby began crying for his mother.

The owner of a nearby house called the rescue hotline at the Marine Mammal Center, a wild animal hospital in Sausalito, California. Volunteer Kat Rudd left immediately to find the pup and bring him back.

The week-old pup desperately needed food. Elephant seal pups with curly black fur like his are in the earliest stage of development and are totally dependent on their mothers for milk.

After rushing him to the animal hospital, staff assessed the pup's physical condition as well as his emotional state. After a few hours of human-free relaxation, medical treatment began.

After about a month of training, the seal, now named Chamomile, had gained a taste for the seafood he would have to find for himself and had learned to swallow a fish in one gulp: He was a Fish School graduate.

Three months after he was rescued, Chamomile was ready to return to the wild. He was taken to a protected beach with a group of other rehabilitated seal pups and set free.

The baby leopard knew his mother wanted him to stay in the den until she returned. But when his mom didn't come back, the starving cub crawled out into the African wilderness of Kenya's Tsavo East National Park hoping to find food. After being found by men patrolling the park, he was delivered to the home of Nana Grosse-Woodley and her husband, the park warden, who named the cub Mtito after a nearby river.

Mtito was wounded and sick. The cub had probably been attacked by a hawk or an eagle. After it was treated by a vet, Grosse-Woodley had to decide the leopard's future. Mtito's mother had almost certainly been killed by poachers, and there wasn't a facility that could prepare him for survival in the wild. Grosse-Woodley had reared some animal orphans in the past, so she adopted him and moved him into her home. Winning Mtito's trust was essential. To raise Mtito for return to the wild, Grosse-Woodley needed the leopard to form a strong family bond with her. But she also formed a bond with Mtito.

The cub would wander off to practice stalking prey, but he'd always return when called. When Mtito was about nine months old, Grosse-Woodley and her husband built an enclosure for him three miles (5 km) away and visited him every day for walks. Then, when he was 18 months old, they moved him to a perfect hunting ground beside a river. This meant plenty of prey for Mtito, who was not yet fully grown.

Mtito would disappear for days, then weeks or months. Everything had gone according to plan. Last year Mtito was spotted in the park looking healthy and very big—and perfectly at home in the wild.

Rescues Badger

During a torrential rainstorm in England, a farmer stumbled across a tiny, almost furless, badger cub in serious trouble. He scooped up the cub and took her to an animal rescue center.

By the time the cub arrived at the center, Secret World, it was wriggling and making a badger's distinctive chirping.

Less than 48 hours old, the baby badger's mother would not have willingly abandoned her cub. The staff believed the cub's home flooded and the mother lost the newborn while moving other cubs out.

The biggest concern for the cub, now named Gale, was her low body temperature. The staff put the orphan in a warm incubator and gave her a hot water bottle and a stuffed animal to snuggle up to.

When Gale was six weeks old she opened her eyes for the first time. At ten weeks she began to crawl. During four months of preparation for release, Gale lived with other rescued badgers. They learned survival skills and got their first taste of wild badger food: earthworms.

When Gale was nine months old, she and five other badgers were ready for the real world. They were taken to the countryside and set free.

Leopard

AYE-AYES OF MADAGASCAR

The aye-aye's odd-looking fingers, pointy teeth, big eyes, and huge ears give some people the creeps.

Seeing an aye-aye is considered very bad luck to many superstitious residents of Madagascar, the African island country where these animals live in the wild. In parts of the country, people kill aye-ayes on sight, hoping to prevent anything "evil" from happening. The aye-aye's bad reputation isn't helped by the fact that it's active only at night, when things can seem a lot scarier to people.

The truth about this five-pound (2-kg) animal, a type of lemur, is that it's harmless. In the wild, aye-ayes live mostly in trees. When they leave their nests, where they spend daylight hours sleeping, their forest home is dark. Big eyes help them see and look for food. Aye-ayes' favorite food is insect larvae.

The main threat to aye-ayes is loss of habitat due to farming and logging in Madagascar. Added to that danger are the people who kill them because of lingering beliefs that aye-ayes bring bad luck. We can only hope that fears about the animals will disappear at the same time aye-ayes' numbers grow.

AFRICA

MADAGASCAR

MADAGASCAR

AREAS WHERE AYE-AYES MAY LIVE

ANIMAL KILLERS
BUSTED!

GUNNING FOR TROUBLE

The bald eagle bodies arrived at the lab by the dozens, shot, with their tails and wings missing. No gun had been heard, and no hunter was sighted where police had discovered the corpses.

But the killer left key evidence. The casings, or outer shells, of his bullets littered the ground beneath the telephone wires where he'd shot the U.S.-protected, national birds.

A gun leaves telltale nicks and scratches on the bullets it fires. "We can match both the bullets and the casings to a particular weapon by the marks left on them after they've been fired from the gun," says deputy lab director Ed Espinoza.

Back in the lab the forensic scientists recovered the bullets that killed several eagles. Then they fired a test round of bullets from a gun seized from a suspect.

Using a high-powered microscope, investigators compared scratches from the test round to scratches on bullets found in the eagles. They matched perfectly. Thanks to the scientists' eagle eyes, the suspect was charged. Bald eagles are now safe from this bad guy.

CRIME SCENE EVIDENCE

BULLET

CRIME SCENE EVIDENCE

FEATHER SAMPLE

YOU CAN HELP SAVE THIS LEMUR'S HABITAT!

Anything you do to preserve the planet helps all living things, including the ring-tailed lemurs that live in the African island nation of Madagascar. And yes—just one kid, like you, can make a difference. Here are ideas for five small, easy things you can do.

1 CUT TRASH, NOT TREES. In your kitchen, reach for a cloth towel instead of paper towels to dry your hands. In public bathrooms, use the air dryer or limit yourself to one paper towel. Changing daily habits can reduce the number of trees that are cut down each year and can help save important habitats for animals such as lemurs.

2 USE FISHY WATER. When you clean out your fish tank, dump the water into your garden instead of down the drain. You'll cut water waste and the nutrients from the fishy water will fertilize your plants.

3 KEEP OUT THE HEAT. On hot, sunny days close your blinds or curtains to block out the heat from the sun. If each home in the United States cut the use of air-conditioning by 10 percent annually, the energy savings could power 1.6 million homes for a year.

4 COLLECT CANS. The next time you're at a friend's party or barbecue, ask if you can collect the aluminum soda cans to recycle. Just one recycled can saves enough energy to run a small radio for more than ten hours.

5 USE FEWER CUPS. Instead of using several glasses a day, pick your favorite and use it all day. If you use fewer dishes, you will reduce the number of times your family runs the dishwasher. You'll save energy and about 100 glasses of water for each load of dishes you and your family eliminate.

COOL CLICK

For more about helping Earth, go online. preserveourplanet.com

Bugs, Bugs, and More Bugs!

Those creepy crawlers are the most diverse group of the animal kingdom. From the phylum Arthropoda, insects are considered to be the most successful life-form on the planet! There are so many millions of insect species that scientists can't even agree on the number. They live everywhere—in every habitat—from the frozen tundra to the arid desert. They even live on you!

The most common thing among arthropods is that they have a hard outer shell, called an exoskeleton. They also have segmented bodies, which include three parts: **head**, **thorax**, and **abdomen**. There are two classes in the arthropod phylum: Hexapoda (insects) and Arachnida (spiders, ticks, mites, scorpions, and their relatives).

> The study of insects is called entomology.

abdomen

head

thorax

INSECTS Helping Out

Insects aren't just about bugging you. There are lots of ways they are beneficial to humans. Here are some of the most common ways insects help us.

FOOD: Bees make honey, and some insects are eaten by people.

PRODUCTS: Beeswax, dyes, and silk

POLLINATION: They pollinate plants so that humans can grow fruit and vegetable crops, making insects responsible for billions of dollars worth of the food we eat.

AND THEY'RE PRETTY TO LOOK AT, TOO!

Bet you didn't know

Some HONEYBEE queen bees QUACK!

A FLEA can JUMP a HUNDRED times its body length—that's like YOU JUMPING to the TOP of a 34-story BUILDING.

Bee Mystery

Millions of honeybees are vanishing, and their disappearing act has experts stumped.

Honeybees are more important than many people realize. A lot of what we eat is directly or indirectly pollinated by the bees, including apples and almonds. Ice-cream manufacturers are even worried that one day they'll have to stop making fruit and nut flavors, such as strawberry, banana, raspberry, and rocky road.

So what is the cause of this bizarre *bee*-havior? No one knows for sure. In one year beekeepers nationwide lost 36 percent of their colonies, with some beekeepers losing more than 70 percent to a new problem called colony collapse disorder.

According to bee expert Dennis vanEngelsdorp, he used to see up to 40,000 of the insects inside every hive. "Now many hives have no bees—dead or alive," he says. The insects just fly away and die.

But what is the culprit? The experts know the bees' immune systems are having trouble fighting disease. "We are now fairly sure that the collapse of colonies is caused by a bee flu, but we don't know why the bees are suddenly getting the flu," says vanEngelsdorp. Investigators are working hard to solve the puzzle and put these busy bees back in business.

WHAT'S ALL THE BUZZ ABOUT?

The ancient Egyptians were the first known beekeepers.

Honeybees dance to communicate with each other.

BY THE NUMBERS

- Honeybees fly **50,000** miles (8,047 km) to collect enough nectar for one pound (454 kg) of honey.
- A honeybee's wings beat about **11,400** times a minute.

CLOSE-UP

Stupid antennae.
I can't wait to get cable!

Some kinds of short-horned grasshoppers are called locusts. Locusts that migrate in swarms eat all the grasses, crops, and trees in their path.

Grasshoppers can't tune in to the Plant Channel with the antennae on top of their heads, but they *can* use them to find food. Antennae are like hands that can smell. Most grass-hoppers are plant-eaters, so antennae come in, well, handy! Scientists separate the more than **11,000 kinds of grasshoppers** into two groups. Based on the length of their antennae, grass-hoppers are either short-horned or long-horned. This one's a "shortie." Maybe *that's* why it can't get good TV reception!

One giant swarm of migrating locusts during the 1870s stretched 300 miles (483 km) long and 100 miles (161 km) wide.

5 COOL THINGS ABOUT Butterflies

VICEROY

1 Butterflies ARE COPYCATS.

The orange-and-black viceroy, like many species of butterflies, has evolved to outsmart its hungry predators by mimicking the appearance of the poisonous monarch. Animals won't eat the viceroy for fear of a nasty stomachache.

SOME butterflies shimmer.

2

BLUE MORPHO

Like all butterflies, the blue morpho butterfly has microscopic scales on its wings. Its scales make this brilliant blue insect iridescent. When you look at it from different angles, it appears to change color from light blue to purple—or even neon blue.

3 Butterflies LIVE ALMOST EVERYWHERE.

Butterflies live on all continents except Antarctica. Lepidopterists, or scientists who specialize in butterfly biology, estimate that there are about 20,000 species of butterflies worldwide.

4 SOME butterflies ARE world TRAVELERS.

RED ADMIRAL

The red admiral is found on several continents. It makes a remarkable round-trip journey between Africa and Europe. Monarch butterflies migrate from Canada to Mexico.

5 SOME butterflies ARE tiny.

The grass blue holds the Guinness World Record as the smallest butterfly. It's about the size of a penny.

71

Who's SMARTER ... Cats or Dogs?

CATS FLUSH

Russ and Sandy Asbury were alone in their Whitewater, Wisconsin, home when they suddenly heard the toilet flush. "My husband's eyes got huge," says Sandy. "Did we have ghosts?"

Nope. Their cats just like to play with toilets. Boots, a Maine coon cat, taught himself to push on the handle that flushes. Then his copycat brother, Bandit, followed. "It's kind of eerie," Sandy admits. "Bandit follows me into the bathroom and flushes for me—sometimes even before I'm finished!"

Now the cats use the stunt to get attention. They go into a flushing frenzy if supper's late!

These cats just play in the bathroom, but some cats can be trained to use the toilet instead of a litter box. For their lucky owners, cleanup is just a flush (instead of a scoop) away. Meanwhile, Fido's just *drinking* from the toilet.

DOGS "GO" ON CUE

To housebreak a pup, take him outside and watch closely. When he starts to urinate, say the same phrase, such as "right there," each time. Within weeks, he'll associate the phrase with the action.

Buffy, a keeshond belonging to Wade Newman of Turin, New York, has never had an "accident" in the house. In fact, the smart dog sometimes plans ahead. Once, called in for the night, she came running. "But suddenly she stopped, cocked her head, and took off in the other direction," Newman says. "I was kind of annoyed." But it turned out Buffy was simply getting ready for bed—by "going" first, after which she obediently ran back to Newman. Now, *that's* thinking ahead!

DOGS SNIFF

Sometimes dogs can drive you crazy! That reportedly happened to one woman whose sheepdog started to sniff at her back every time she sat down. Exasperated, she asked her husband to take a look. All he saw was a dark mole. Nothing to worry about, thought the woman. Then one day she was sunbathing when her dog tried to nip off the mole with its teeth.

That did it. The woman went to the doctor and found out the mole was a deadly form of skin cancer. Her dog probably saved her life.

Dogs' noses have about 4 times as many scent cells as cats' noses and 14 times more than humans.' It makes some breeds terrific at sniffing out mold, termites, illegal drugs, missing persons, and, apparently, even cancer. Now, if only those noses didn't feel so cold!

CATS PREDICT EARTHQUAKES

Early one evening in 1976 people in northeastern Italy were all asking the same question: What is wrong with my cat? Many pets were running around, scratching on doors, and yowling to go out. Once out, they didn't come back (except for mother cats, who returned to get their kittens). Then, later that day, a major earthquake hit!

Cats may feel very early vibrations or sense the increase in static electricity that occurs before a quake. Whatever they're sensing, it's one more reason to pay attention to your cat.

So, which *is* smarter . . . a cat or a dog?

Actually, this is a trick question, and there's no simple answer.

Dogs and cats have different abilities. Each species knows what it needs to know in order to survive. "For that reason, we can't design a test that is equal for both animals," says Bonnie Beaver, a veterinarian at Texas A&M University. "When people ask me which is smarter, I say it's whichever one you own!"

DOGS PLAY THE PIANO

Forget "sit" and "shake." Chanda-Leah, a toy poodle who died in 2006 at the age of 12, settled down at a computerized keyboard and plunked out "Twinkle, Twinkle, Little Star." Flashing red lights under the white keys told her which notes to hit.

"She loved to show off," says owner Sharon Robinson of Ontario, Canada, who says the secret to training is practice and patience. That must be true, because Chanda knew a record-breaking number of tricks! She's the trickiest canine ever listed in *The Guinness Book of World Records*.

CATS WALK TIGHTROPES

Animal trainers of cats that appear in movies and TV commercials train the feline actors to walk on tightropes, wave at crowds, and open doors.

"Cats can do a lot, like jump through hoops, retrieve toys, and give high fives," says Beaver. But unlike dogs, they won't work for praise. "Cats are motivated by food," she says, "and it's got to be yummy."

NAUGHTY PETS

NAME	Midnight
FAVORITE ACTIVITY	Washing his face in his owner's glass
FAVORITE TOY	Straw
PET PEEVE	Drinking out of a cat bowl

MMM.... REFRESHING!

TOP TEN MOST POPULAR DOG BREEDS	TOP TEN MOST POPULAR CAT BREEDS
1. LABRADOR RETRIEVER	1. PERSIAN
2. GERMAN SHEPHERD	2. EXOTIC
3. YORKSHIRE TERRIER	3. MAINE COON
4. GOLDEN RETRIEVER	4. SIAMESE
5. BEAGLE	5. ABYSSINIAN
6. BOXER	6. RAGDOLL
7. BULLDOG	7. SPYHNX
8. DACHSHUND	8. AMERICAN SHORTHAIR
9. POODLE	9. BIRMAN
10. SHIH TZU	10. ORIENTAL
(According to the American Kennel Club, 2010)	(According to the Cat Fanciers' Association)

Why should cats and dogs get all the attention? Here's what makes other pets so special. See if one of them is right for you.

HORSE

If you have the time and money, pick one for its behavior, not its breed. Horses can take you for a ride!

Q Do FROGS REALLY EAT their OWN SKIN?

A Yes. In a process called molting, most frogs twist and wriggle out of their skin as often as once a month or more. By chowing down on the used skin, the frog takes in nutrients and water without having to hunt for food. A new skin has already formed underneath, so losing the skin is, well, no skin off the frog's back.

GOLDFISH

Too busy? Goldfish won't chew up your shoes if you come home late.

NauGHty PETS

OH-BOY-OH-BOY-OH-BOY! THIS IS THE BEST CHEW TOY EVER!

NAME Casper

FAVORITE ACTIVITY
Counter surfing

FAVORITE TOY
Oven mitt

PET PEEVE
Leftovers

PARAKEET

Parakeets can be trained to talk and will perch on your finger.

Pampered PET

Pampering your pet could cost you an arm and a paw! Here are some ways to give your pet the royal treatment.

LUXURY SUITE AT PET SPA	**$75** A NIGHT
PROFESSIONAL MASSAGE	**$30**
CUSTOM-BUILT DOGHOUSE	**$6,000**
CUSTOM-MADE PET SOFA	**$400**
HAND-KNITTED SWEATER	**$250**
GOURMET DOG TREATS	**$5**

PRICES ARE ESTIMATED IN U.S. DOLLARS

In the 1800s Hai Lung, a long-haired Pekingese, had his own servant and snoozed in a basket lined with red silk. The royal pup couldn't even chow down on his chopped liver until the food had been inspected by his owner—the ruler of China!

Try This! Happy Birthday Cake

YOU WILL NEED
- **SEVERAL CANS OF WET DOG OR CAT FOOD**
- **ASSORTED DOG OR CAT TREATS**

WHAT TO DO
Shape the wet food into cake layers. You can use plastic containers as molds.

Decorate the cake with kitty or doggie treats.

Sing "Happy Birthday" and watch your pet dig in.

Remember to monitor your pet to make sure it does not overeat.

Prehistoric TIME LINE

HUMANS HAVE WALKED on Earth for some 200,000 years, a mere blip in Earth's 4.5-billion-year history. A lot has happened in that time. Earth formed, and oxygen levels rose in the millions of years of the Precambrian time. The productive Paleozoic era gave rise to hard-shelled organisms, vertebrates, amphibians, and reptiles. Dinosaurs ruled the Earth in the mighty Mesozoic. And 64 million years after dinosaurs became extinct, modern humans emerged in the Cenozoic era. From the first tiny mollusks to the dinosaur giants of the Jurassic and beyond, Earth has seen a lot of transformation.

THE PRECAMBRIAN TIME

4.5 billion to 542 million years ago

- Earth forms from exploding stars when a new star gathered a swirling disk of dust and gases around it.
- Low levels of oxygen made Earth a suffocating place.

THE PALEOZOIC ERA

542 million to 251 million years ago

- The first insects and other animals appeared on the land.
- 450 million years ago (m.y.a.), the ancestors of sharks began to swim in the oceans.
- 430 m.y.a. plants began to take root on land.
- More than 360 m.y.a., amphibians emerged from the water.
- Slowly the major landmasses began to come together, creating Pangaea, a single supercontinent.
- By 300 m.y.a., reptiles had begun to dominate the land.

What Is a Dinosaur?

Strong, huge, fierce—these are some words people generally associate with dinosaurs. But not all dinosaurs were big or mean; in fact, they had lots of different characteristics. One quality stands out about dinosaurs, though—they endured. Dinosaurs were some of the most successful animals that have ever lived. After all, they managed to stay on Earth for more than 150 million years! They lived all over the world and dominated all other land creatures. Dinosaurs were reptiles, animals with many common features including a backbone, and scaly, waterproof skin. To date, there are at least 1,000 known reptile species, and more fossils are discovered all the time.

DINO TIMES

THE MESOZOIC ERA

251 million to 65 million years ago

The Mesozoic era, or the age of the reptiles, consisted of three consecutive time periods (shown below). This is when the first dinosaurs began to appear. They would reign supreme for more than 150 million years.

TRIASSIC PERIOD

251 million to 199 million years ago

- Appearance of the first mammals. They were rodent-size.
- Appearance of the first dinosaur
- Ferns were the dominant plants on land.
- The giant supercontinent of Pangaea began breaking up toward the end of the Triassic.

JURASSIC PERIOD

199 million to 145 million years ago

- Giant dinosaurs dominated the land.
- Pangaea continued its breakup, and oceans formed in the spaces between the drifting landmasses, allowing for sea life, including sharks and marine crocodiles, to thrive.
- Conifer trees spread across the land.

CRETACEOUS PERIOD

145 million to 65 million years ago

- The modern continents developed.
- The largest dinosaurs developed.
- Flowering plants spread across the landscape.
- Mammals flourished and giant pterosaurs ruled the skies over the small birds.
- Temperatures grew more extreme. Dinosaurs lived in deserts, swamps, and forests from the Antarctic to the Arctic.

THE CENOZOIC ERA—TERTIARY PERIOD

65 million to 2.6 million years ago

- Following the dinosaur extinction, mammals rose as the dominant species.
- Birds continued to flourish.
- Widespread volcanic activity
- Temperatures began to cool, eventually ending in an ice age.
- The period ends with land bridges forming, which allowed plants and animals to spread to new areas.

Who Ate What?

Herbivores
- Primarily plant-eaters
- Grew up to 100 tons (91 t)—the largest animals ever to walk on Earth
- Up to 1,000 blunt or flat teeth to grind vegetation
- Many had cheek pouches to store food.
- Examples: *Styracosaurus, Parasaurolophus*

Carnivores
- Meat-eaters
- Long, strong legs to run faster than plant-eaters; ran up to 30 miles an hour (48 kph)
- Most had good eyesight, strong jaws, and sharp teeth.
- Scavengers and hunters; often hunted in packs
- Grew to 45 feet (14 m) long
- Examples: *Velociraptor, Gigantoraptor, Tyrannosaurus rex*

TYRANNOSAURUS REX

Dino Poo

You may wonder how we could possibly know what dinosaurs actually ate. Well, paleontologists search for coprolites, or fossilized waste. Yep, that's right, the poo of the prehistoric world has told us much of what we know about what plants dinosaurs ate. Coprolites contain digested plant material, which can help us learn about a dinosaur's diet. Coprolites aren't the only things that can help scientists learn about the dinosaur diet—teeth, habitat, and plant fossils also provide insight.

GIGANTORAPTOR

DID YOU KNOW?
Different species of dinosaurs lived at different times. Some dinosaurs would have never met, being separated by up to 164 million years!

VELOCIRAPTOR

SINOSAUROPTERYX

MAMENCHISAURUS

PARASAUROLOPHUS

ERKETU

Paleontologists learn about dinosaurs by studying fossils—plant and animal remains that have been preserved in rock.

Bet you **didn't know**

Some think that **dinosaurs may have LIVED** to be **50 to 150 YEARS OLD!**

TUOJIANGOSAURUS

STYRACOSAURUS

MONONYKUS

DINO Classification

Classifying dinosaurs and all other living things can be a complicated matter, so scientists have devised a system to help with the process. Dinosaurs are put into groups based on a very large range of characteristics.

Scientists put dinosaurs into two major groups: the bird-hipped ornithischians and the reptile-hipped saurischians.

Dinosaur Superlatives

Smallest
Hesperonychus was a tiny dinosaur, reaching about 19 inches (50 cm) in length.

Scariest looking
Tyrannosaurus rex was a huge, meat-eating dinosaur.

One of the heaviest
Argentinosaurus is thought to have weighed up to 100 tons (91 t)! Only the blue whale is larger.

Smartest
If a large brain compared to body size indicates intelligence, then the **Troodon** may have been the smartest. This fast little meat-eater with excellent eyesight lived during the Cretaceous period.

Dumbest
Stegosaurus was among the dumbest—it had a brain the size of a walnut!

Longest name
Micropachycephalosaurus (23 letters)

First dinosaur to be named
Megalosaurus, named in 1822 by the Reverend William Buckland.

Ornithischian

"Bird-hipped"
(pubis bone in hips points backward)

Ornithischians have the same shaped pubis as birds of today, but today's birds are actually more closely related to the saurischians.

Example: *Styracosaurus*

Saurischian

"Reptile-hipped"
(pubis bone in hips points forward)

Saurischians are further divided into two groups, the meat-eating Theropoda and the plant-eating Sauropodomorpha.

Example: *Tyrannosaurus rex*

Within these two main divisions, dinosaurs are then separated into orders and then families, such as Stegosauria. Like other members of the Stegosauria, *Stegosaurus* had spines and plates along the back, neck, and tail.

COOL CLICK

What's the largest, most complete, best preserved *T. rex?* Learn about a fossil named Sue at the Field Museum.
fieldmuseum.org/sue

21 DINOS YOU SHOULD KNOW

Dinosaur (Group) *Example*
What the name means
Length: XX ft (XX m)
Time Range: When they lived
Where: Where they are found

1 *Aucasaurus* (Saurischian)
Lizard from Auca
Length: 13 ft (4 m)
Time Range: Late Cretaceous
Where: Argentina

2 *Brachiosaurus* (Saurischian)
Arm lizard
Length: 98 ft (30 m)
Time Range: Late Jurassic
Where: U.S. (Colorado); Tanzania

3 *Camptosaurus* (Ornithischian)
Bent lizard
Length: 23 ft (7 m)
Time Range: Late Jurassic
Where: U.S. (Colorado, South Dakota, Utah, Wyoming); England, U.K.

4 *Carcharodontosaurus* (Saurischian)
Shark-toothed lizard
Length: 40 ft (12 m)
Time Range: Late Cretaceous
Where: Algeria; Egypt; Morocco

5 *Carnotaurus* (Saurischian)
Meat-eating bull
Length: 25 ft (8 m)
Time Range: Late Cretaceous
Where: Argentina (Patagonia)

6 *Herrerasaurus* (Saurischian)
Herrera's lizard
Length: 17 ft (5 m)
Time Range: Late Triassic
Where: Argentina

9 *Lambeosaurus* (Ornithischian)
Lambe's lizard
Length: Up to 54 ft (16 m)
Time Range: Late Cretaceous
Where: U.S. (Montana); Canada (Alberta)

7 *Hypsilophodon* (Ornithischian)
High-ridged tooth
Length: 8 ft (2 m)
Time Range: Early Cretaceous
Where: England; Spain; Portugal

10 *Lesothosaurus* (Ornithischian)
Lesotho lizard
Length: 3 ft (1 m)
Time Range: Early Jurassic
Where: Lesotho

8 *Iguanodon* (Ornithischian)
Iguana tooth
Length: 33 ft (10 m)
Time Range: Early Cretaceous
Where: Europe

11 *Maiasaura* (Ornithischian)
Good-mother lizard
Length: 30 ft (9 m)
Time Range: Late Cretaceous
Where: U.S. (Montana)

12 *Microraptor* **(Saurischian)**
Small thief
Length: 22 inches (56 cm)
Time Range: Early Cretaceous
Where: China (Liaoning Province)

13 *Oviraptor* **(Saurischian)**
Egg thief
Length: 8 ft (2 m)
Time Range: Late Cretaceous
Where: Mongolia

14 *Protoceratops* **(Ornithischian)**
First horned face
Length: 8 ft (2 m)
Time Range: Late Cretaceous
Where: Mongolia; China

15 *Stegosaurus* **(Ornithischian)**
Roofed reptile
Length: 30 ft (9 m)
Time Range: Late Jurassic
Where: U.S. (Colorado, Utah, Wyoming)

Bet you didn't know

THE LARGEST DINOSAURS WERE VEGETARIANS.

16 *Tarchia* **(Ornithischian)**
Brainy one
Length: 18 ft (6 m)
Time Range: Late Cretaceous
Where: Mongolia

18 *Troodon* **(Saurischian)**
Wounding tooth
Length: 12 ft (4 m)
Time Range: Late Cretaceous
Where: U.S. (Alaska, Montana, Wyoming); Canada (Alberta)

17 *Therizinosaurus* **(Saurischian)**
Scythe lizard
Length: 36 ft (11 m)
Time Range: Late Cretaceous
Where: Mongolia

19 *Tyrannosaurus rex* **(Saurischian)**
Tyrant lizard
Length: 41 ft (12 m)
Time Range: Late Cretaceous
Where: U.S. (Western); Canada (Western)

20 *Utahraptor* (Saurischian)
Utah plunderer
Length: 20 ft (6 m)
Time Range: Early Cretaceous
Where: U.S. (Utah)

21 *Velociraptor* (Saurischian)
Swift robber
Length: 7 ft (2 m)
Time Range: Late Cretaceous
Where: Mongolia; China

BONUS—3 PREHISTORIC BIRDS

2 *Baptornis*
Diving bird
Length: 4 ft (1 m)
Time Range: Late Cretaceous
Where: U.S. (Kansas)

1 *Archaeopteryx*
Ancient wing
Length: 12–20 in (30–50 cm)
Time Range: Late Jurassic
Where: Germany; Portugal

3 *Iberomesornis*
Intermediate Spanish bird
Length: 8 in (20 cm) wingspan
Time Range: Early Cretaceous
Where: Spain

SuperCroc ROCKED!

What's 40 feet (12 m) long, tips the scale at 10 tons (9 t), and eats dinosaurs for lunch? It's SuperCroc! National Geographic Explorer-in-Residence Paul Sereno dug up this bus-length, dino-era crocodilian's giant bones and teeth in Africa. We now know that about 110 million years ago, SuperCroc (aka *Sarcosuchus imperator*) was the toughest bully on the block. As if its six-foot (2-m) -long jaws weren't enough, this scaly, muscle-bound monster hid most of its bulk underwater while scoping out its next banquet-size dinosaur meal. Then, a sudden splash, the scramble of heavy footsteps, and...gulp! What's for dessert?

Q Did PEOPLE and DINOSAURS ever live at the same time?

A Absolutely not! Dinosaurs died out 65 million years ago, long before people lived on Earth.

What Does a Paleontologist Do?

Ask a Scientific Question
Example: Did reptile-hipped dinosaurs hunt? If so, what did they eat?

Find a Fossil
Example: Map the area, search, and record finds.

Get It Out of the Ground
Example: Dig up the remains.

Conserve
Example: Clean it up; repair it as needed.

Reconstruct
Example: Compare the fossil with others and with living things to learn about what it was.

Tell People
Example: Write about or exhibit the discovery.

For more detailed information on the paleontology process, check out the Project Exploration website.
projectexploration.org

What Killed the Dinosaurs?

Sixty-five million years ago the last of the nonbird dinosaurs went extinct. So did the giant mosasaurs and plesiosaurs in the seas and the pterosaurs in the sky. Many kinds of plants died, too. Perhaps half of the world's species died in this mass extinction that marks the end of the Cretaceous and the beginning of the Paleocene period.

Why did so many animals die out while most mammals, turtles, crocodiles, salamanders, and frogs survived? Birds escaped extinction. So did many plants and insects. Scientists are searching for answers.

Asteroid or Volcano?

Scientists have a couple of theories: a huge impact, such as an asteroid or comet, or a massive bout of volcanic activity. Either of these might have choked the sky with debris that starved Earth of the sun's energy. Once the dust settled, greenhouse gases locked in the atmosphere may have caused the temperature to soar.

Regardless of what caused the extinction, it marked the end of *Tyrannosaurus rex*'s reign of terror and opened the door for mammals to take over.

Bet you didn't know

Modern-day **BIRDS** are descendants of **THEROPOD DINOSAURS;** that means **THEROPODS NEVER WENT EXTINCT!**

SEA MONSTERS
A PREHISTORIC ADVENTURE

Prehistoric animals didn't just live on the land—they swam through the sea, too. These wondrous sea monsters ruled the deep with supersize eyes, fearsome teeth, and extremely long necks.

The National Geographic giant-screen film *Sea Monsters: A Prehistoric Adventure* (available on DVD) features many of these prehistoric marine creatures.

TYLOSAUR

Tylosaurus proriger

The 29-foot (9-m) -long tylosaur is the unchallenged ruler of the Cretaceous ocean. It ambushed its prey, crushing victims with its sharp, cone-shaped teeth.

OTHER COOL STUFF

Tylosaur had a nose for nastiness. Some scientists think its long, bony snout had dozens of nerve endings that sensed prey in murky waters. As soon as the meal was detected, the nerves triggered a bite response to quickly seize the prey.

Filmed in the Bahamas, *Sea Monsters* features computer-generated sea monsters and real water backgrounds. The digital sea monsters were added later.

To find out even more, check out the film and its website. nationalgeographic.com/sea monsters/index.html

WHEN MARINE REPTILES AND DINOSAURS LIVED

About 250 million years ago

The first marine reptiles appeared.

About 230 million years ago

Dinosaurs first walked on the Earth.

About 65 million years ago

Most marine reptiles and dinosaurs became extinct.

XIPHACTINUS

Xiphactinus audax

This 17-foot (5-m) -long fish had fangs that seized prey so it could swallow its victims whole. But this fierce predator sometimes got choked up. Many *Xiphactinus* fossils have been found with undigested fish in their rib cages—a sign that the prey may have choked the killer fish.

OTHER COOL STUFF
Shaped like a torpedo, *Xiphactinus* was a fast swimmer.

DOLLY

Dolichorhynchops osborni

Living 82 million years ago, these dolphin-size air breathers hunted fish and squid in shallow waters. But they had to brave dangerous, unknown seas when their prey migrated into deeper water.

OTHER COOL STUFF
Dollies used large, winglike flat paddles to "fly" through the water. But they had to be careful. Dollies that dived too deep and surfaced too quickly could suffer a deadly condition called "the bends," according to expert Kenneth Carpenter.

CRETOXYRHINA

Cretoxyrhina mantelli

Like today's great white shark, the 20-foot (6-m) -long *Cretoxyrhina* had razor-sharp teeth that cut victims into chunks.

OTHER COOL STUFF
Cretoxyrhina never ran out of teeth! Worn-out teeth were replaced by new ones. Good thing, because *Cretoxyrhina* would even eat bones. Anything it couldn't digest, it would just throw up.

WILDLY GOOD ANIMAL REPORTS

Your teacher wants a written report on the velvety free-tailed bat. By Monday! Not to worry. Use the tools of good writing to organize your thoughts and research, and you'll create an animal report a bat would flap about.

Velvety free-tailed bats in flight

STEPS TO SUCCESS Your report will follow the format of a descriptive or expository essay (see p. 300 for "How To Write a Perfect Essay") and should consist of a main idea, followed by supporting details, and a conclusion. Use this basic structure for each paragraph as well as the whole report, and you'll be on the right track.

1. Introduction
State your main idea.
The velvety free-tailed bat is a common and important species of bat.

2. Body
Provide **details, supporting points,** for your main idea.
The velvety free-tailed bat eats insects and can have a large impact on insect populations.
Ranges from Mexico to Florida and South America.
Like other bats, its wings are built for fast, efficient flight.

Then **expand** on those points with further description, explanation, or discussion.
The velvety free-tailed bat eats insects and can have a large impact on insect populations.
  Their diet consists primarily of mosquitoes and other airborne insects.
Ranges from Mexico to Florida and South America.
  They are sometimes encountered in attics.
Like other bats, its wings are built for fast, efficient flight.
  They have trouble, however, taking off from low or flat surfaces and must drop from a place high enough to gain speed to start flying.

3. Conclusion
Wrap it up with a summary of your whole paper.
Because of its large numbers, the velvety free-tailed bat holds an important position in the food chain.

KEY INFORMATION

Here are some things you should consider including in your report:

What does your animal look like?
To what other species is it related?
How does it move?
Where does it live?
What does it eat?
What are its predators?
How long does it live?
Is it endangered?
Why do you find it interesting?

FACT FROM FICTION: Your animal may have been featured in a movie or in myths and legends. Compare and contrast how the animal has been portrayed with how it behaves in reality. For example, penguins can't dance the way they do in *Happy Feet.*

PROOFREAD AND REVISE: As with any awesome essay, when you're finished, check for misspellings, grammatical mistakes, and punctuation errors. It often helps to have someone else proofread your work, too, as they may catch things you have missed. Also, look for ways to make your sentences and paragraphs even better. Add more descriptive language, choosing just the right verbs, adverbs, and adjectives to make your writing come alive.

BE CREATIVE: Use visual aids to make your report come to life. Include an animal photo file with interesting images found in magazines or printed from websites. Or draw your own! You can also build a miniature animal habitat diorama. Use creativity to help communicate your passion for the subject.

THE FINAL RESULT: Put it all together in one final, polished draft. Make it neat and clean, and remember to cite your references (see p. 253 for "Reveal Your Sources").

WATCH OUT!
How to Conduct an Animal Observation

BOOKS, ARTICLES, and other secondhand sources are great for learning about animals, but there's another way to find out even more. Direct observation means watching, listening to, and smelling an animal yourself. To truly understand animals you need to observe them.

VISIT

YOU CAN FIND ANIMALS in their natural habitats almost anywhere, even your own backyard. Or take a drive to a nearby mountain area, river, forest, wetland, or other ecosystem. There are animals to be seen in every natural setting you can visit. To observe more exotic varieties, plan a trip to a national park, aquarium, zoo, wildlife park, or aviary.

OBSERVE

GET NEAR ENOUGH to an animal to watch and study it, but do not disturb it. Be patient, as it may take a while to spot something interesting. And be safe. Don't take any risks; wild animals can be dangerous. Take notes, and write down every detail. Use all of your senses. How does it look? How does it act? What more can you learn?

RESEARCH

COMPARE YOUR own observations with those found in textbooks, encyclopedias, nonfiction books, Internet sources, and nature documentaries. Even classic stories from literature can provide great information and context as you do your research. And check out exciting animal encounters in National Geographic's book series *Face to Face with Animals*.

TIP:
Binoculars are a good way to get up close and personal with wild animals while still keeping a safe distance.

COOL CLICK

Love to watch animals having fun in their own habitats? See amazing wildlife videos captured by National Geographic's Crittercam. nationalgeographic.com/crittercam

Going Green

A splendid leaf frog—a rarely seen species—hangs onto a tree in Costa Rica.

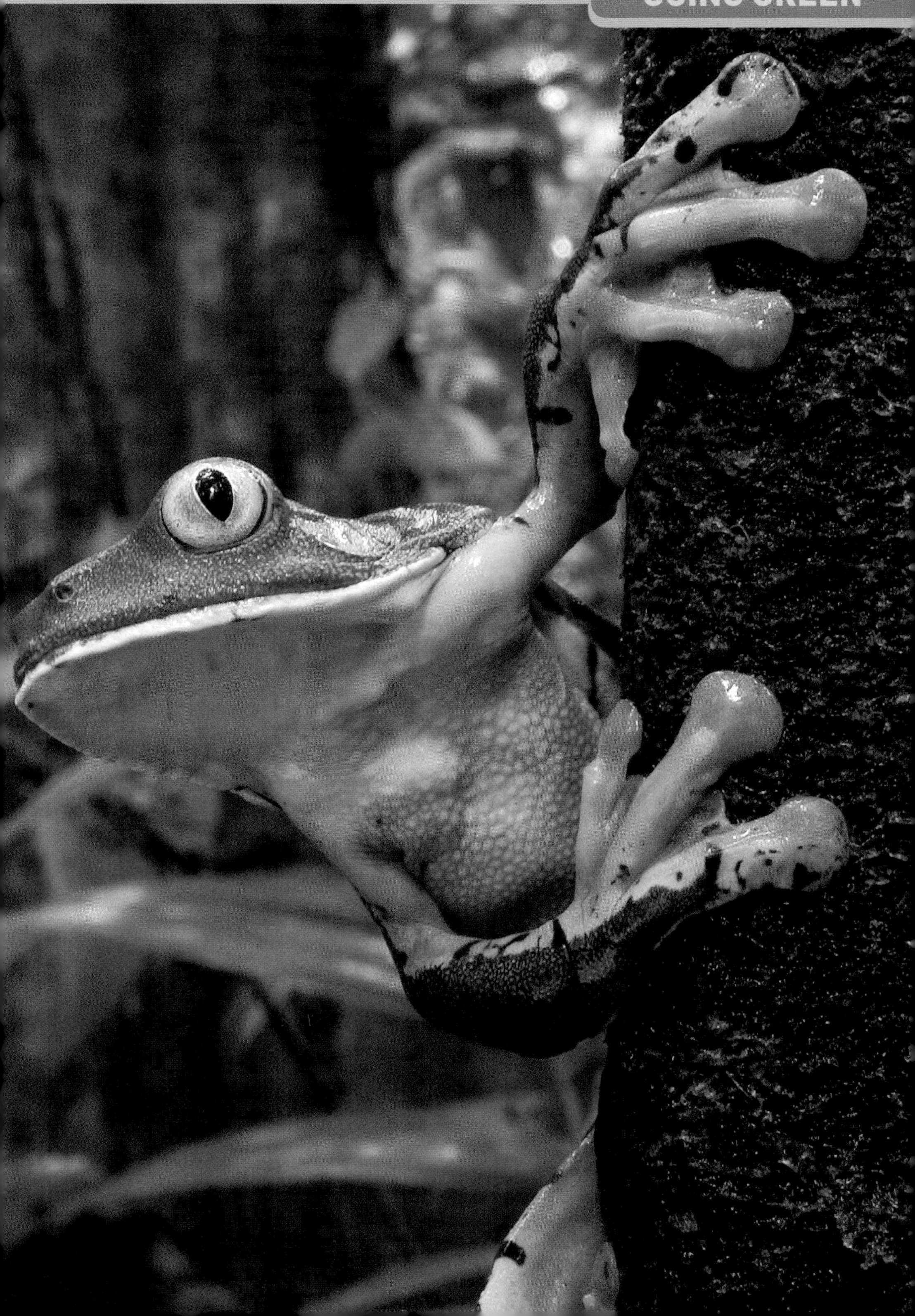

9 Tips to Save EARTH

1 Recycle newsprint, cardboard, plastic, and other household waste. This can reduce emissions of carbon dioxide (CO_2), a greenhouse gas that many scientists believe contributes to global warming.

2 Walk, ride your bike, or carpool. Driving 15 minutes less a week can save 900 pounds (408 kg) of CO_2 a year.

3 Buy snacks in bulk. By doing away with individual wrappers, you'll throw away less of the 5 pounds (2 kg) of trash each person pitches every day.

4 Put on a sweater. Don't turn up the heat when you're chilly. Wear more clothes and turn down the temperature! Doing so can keep 300 pounds (136 kg) of CO_2 out of the air each year.

5 Always turn off the lights when you leave a room.

6 Change incandescent lightbulbs to compact fluorescent lights. Just one could save 500 pounds (227 kg) of coal a year.

7 Plant a tree to put more oxygen into the atmosphere.

8 Drive better. Ask your parents to drive a more fuel-efficient car. An electric or hybrid car can save 5,600 pounds (2,540 kg) of CO_2 a year.

9 Stop water waste. In many homes, toilets use more water than anything else. An older toilet may use more than 5 gallons (19 L) of water each time it's flushed! Try this only with an older toilet and with a parent's permission. Clean out a one-gallon plastic jug (a milk or juice container will work), and make sure you take off any labels. Fill the jug with stones to make it heavy. Place the jug into the toilet tank, being very careful that it doesn't touch any of the toilet's inner workings. Now every time that toilet is flushed, it's using a gallon of water less than it used to!

Try This!

Did you know that the average U.S. household receives one-and-a-half trees' worth of unwanted mail each year? Much of it is trashed, unopened.

SAVE TREES!
KEEP JUNK OUT OF YOUR MAILBOX.

Millions of trees are cut down each year to produce junk mailings. Challenge your family to limit unsolicited incoming mail. With your parents' help, go online to register with the Direct Marketing Association at dmachoice.org. It will help reduce the number of trees that are cut down and the energy used to make and transport the 62 billion pieces of junk mail delivered annually. Use any unwanted mail you still receive as scrap paper and recycle it.

ECO-LINGO

climate change

A long-term and worldwide change in temperature, rainfall, snowfall, fog, frost, hail, wind, and storms. Gradual warming and cooling of Earth's climate has been a natural process throughout its history.

fossil fuel

Coal, petroleum, and natural gas that is burned to generate heat or power. The less we use, the better.

carbon dioxide (CO_2)

Every time you breathe out, you release CO_2 gas. Burning forests to clear land and using fossil fuels for energy emit carbon into the atmosphere, where it combines with oxygen to form CO_2. A little CO_2 in the atmosphere is a good thing; a lot is bad. Trees and other plants filter out CO_2, but their destruction reduces this natural filtering process.

global warming

An increase in Earth's average surface temperature. The increase in CO_2 and other gases—such as methane—is the major cause of this warming. By 2100 Earth's temperature may rise by several degrees, melting glaciers, drying up wetlands, and raising sea levels.

Environmental Hot Spots

Around the world people are putting more and more pressure on the environment. They are dumping pollutants into the air and water and removing natural vegetation to extract mineral resources or turn the land into cropland for farming. In more developed countries industries create waste and pollution; farmers use fertilizers and pesticides that run off into water supplies; and motor vehicles release exhaust fumes into the air. In less developed countries forests are cut down for fuel or to clear land for farming; grasslands are turned into deserts as farmers and herders overuse the land; and expanding urban areas face problems of water quality and sanitation.

OCEAN ALERT!

It may seem as if the world's oceans are so vast that nothing could hurt them. Unfortunately, that's not true. The oceans suffer from people dumping stuff that they don't want (pollution) and taking too much from the ocean that they do want (overfishing). You can help turn this problem around.

You probably already know how to help fight pollution: Participate in stream, river, and beach cleanups; don't litter; and don't dump things into storm drains. But you may not realize that too many fish—including the bluefin tuna above—are taken from the sea. Some overfished species are disappearing, such as sharks and bluefin tuna.

People kill tens of millions of sharks every year. The desire for shark fin soup is one big reason so many sharks die. These fish are caught, their fins cut off to be sold, and the rest of their bodies are thrown back into the sea.

Many fish are slow growing and live decades or even centuries. Chilean sea bass live up to 40 years. Orange roughies can live to be more than 100 years old. And, rockfish can live to be 200! When there aren't enough of these slow-growing fish, the species is threatened because the fish often are taken from the sea before they are old enough to reproduce. These species could disappear.

95

Pollution
Cleaning Up Our Act

So what's the big deal about a little dirt on the planet? Pollution can affect animals, plants, and people. In fact, some studies show that more people die every year from diseases linked to air pollution than from car accidents. And right now more than one billion of the world's people don't have access to clean drinking water.

A LITTLE POLLUTION = BIG PROBLEMS

You can probably clean your room in a couple of hours. (At least we hope you can!) But you can't shove air and water pollution under your bed or cram them into the closet. Once released into the environment, pollution—whether it's oil leaking from a boat or chemicals spewing from a factory's smokestack—can have a lasting environmental impact.

KEEP IT CLEAN

It's easy to blame things like big factories for pollution problems. But some of the mess comes from everyday activities. Exhaust fumes from cars and garbage in landfills can seriously trash the Earth's health. We all need to pitch in and do some house cleaning. It may mean bicycling more and riding in cars less. Or not dumping water-polluting oil or household cleaners down the drain. Look at it this way: Just like your room, it's always better not to let Earth get messed up in the first place.

Too Much Light!

Seattle, Washington, U.S., at night

Bright lights threaten more than stargazing.
For some wildlife it's a matter of "light" and death. Light pollution, which is excessive or obtrusive artificial light, can affect ecosystems in many ways. For example, it blocks bugs from navigating their way, disorients birds, and misdirects turtles and frogs.

Declining Biodiversity
Saving All Creatures Great and Small

Earth is home to such a huge mix of plants and animals—perhaps 100 million species—and scientists have officially identified and named only about 1.9 million so far! Scientists call this healthy mix biodiversity.

THE BALANCING ACT

The bad news is that half of the planet's plant and animal species may be on the path to extinction, mainly because of human activity. People cut down trees, build roads and houses, pollute rivers, overfish, and overhunt. The good news is that people care. Many scientists and volunteers race against the clock every day, working to save wildlife before time runs out. By building birdhouses, planting trees, and following the rules for hunting and fishing, you can be a positive force for preserving biodiversity, too. Every time you do something to help a species survive, you help keep Earth rich.

WILDLIFE BIODIVERSITY

Insects, Centipedes, and Millipedes

Other Animals

Mammals

A whitetip reef shark swims along a coral reef.

Habitat Destruction
Living on the Edge

Even though tropical rain forests cover only about 7 percent of the planet's total land surface, they are home to half of all known species of plants and animals. Because people cut down so many trees for lumber and firewood and clear so much land for farms, hundreds of thousands of acres disappear every year.

SHARING THE LAND

Wetlands are also important feeding and breeding grounds. People have drained many wetlands, turning them into farm fields or sites for industries. Over half the world's wetlands have disappeared within the past century, squeezing wildlife out. Finding a balance between the needs humans and animals have for land is the key to lessening habitat destruction.

A jaguar in the rain forest

97

Overpopulation

It's Getting Crowded in Here

Every 60 seconds more than 250 people are born. Based on expected birth and death rates, experts predict that our planet could be home to more than nine billion people by the early 2040s. That's a big increase from the nearly seven billion who populate Earth now. The world's two most populous countries are China and India. They have more than a billion people each.

TOO LITTLE FOR TOO MANY

The United States and other wealthy countries have fewer people but use up much more of the world's resources. Countries that use a lot of resources and countries that have a lot of people put pressure on the planet. To feed everyone, we must either grow more food on existing farms or carve new farmland out of wilderness areas, which is not as simple as it seems. Disposing of massive amounts of waste, producing enough heat and electricity, and curbing rising pollution are some of the other challenges that must be met before everyone on Earth can live comfortably. In an effort to slow population growth in China, most couples there must ask permission from the government to have more than one child. Some countries have found that providing citizens with more education and better job opportunities has helped slow population growth. Still the world population continues to increase.

Farmers working in a rice paddy

World Food

Earth produces enough food for all its inhabitants—the nearly seven billion and growing—but not everyone gets enough to eat. It's a matter of distribution. Food-producing regions are unevenly spread around the world, and it is sometimes difficult to move food supplies from areas of surplus to areas of great need.

STILL NOT ENOUGH

In recent decades, food production has increased, especially production of meat and cereal grains (corn, wheat, and rice). But increased yields of grain require intensive use of fertilizers and irrigation, which are not only expensive but also can be a threat to the environment.

MORE PEOPLE, FEWER RESOURCES

"Developing countries with so many people can't afford to waste food, water, and energy," says Karen Kasmauski, who photographed a story on population growth for NATIONAL GEOGRAPHIC. "In the U.S. we think we can afford to waste resources, but we can't. We're stealing from future generations. Rich societies like ours often think that overpopulation is only a problem in countries where the birth rate is very high. But a family with a gas-gulping SUV and a huge house they must heat and cool is a bigger environmental threat."

Do your part to help conserve resources.

1. Learn to recognize the difference between *wanting* things and *needing* them. Advertising aimed at kids often targets "wants."
2. Don't waste food. Think about what went into growing, packaging, and transporting the things you eat.
3. Recycle glass, paper, and plastic.

CHANGING THE LAND

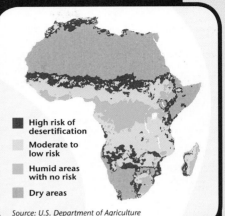

- ■ High risk of desertification
- ■ Moderate to low risk
- ■ Humid areas with no risk
- ■ Dry areas

Source: U.S. Department of Agriculture

Overgrazing, removal of vegetation by farmers, and unreliable rainfall are turning some land in Africa into deserts—a process called desertification.

ENVIRONMENTAL TRAGEDY

This grappler truck works at a logging operation. Harvesting trees provides income for workers and products for consumers but poses a serious long-term threat to the environment.

Global Warming

Feeling the Heat?

In the past century average temperatures rose 1°F (.56°C). That may not seem like a lot, but evidence shows that it is enough to change weather patterns and shift the directions of ocean currents. All of this is an effect of global warming. The heat is melting glaciers and polar ice sheets, causing sea levels to rise and habitats to shrink. This makes survival for many animals a big challenge. Warming also means flooding along the coasts and drought for inland areas.

The world's climate changes naturally, but now people are speeding up the process. Everyday activities, such as driving cars that use gasoline and burning fossil fuels, contribute to global warming. These kinds of activities produce greenhouse gases, which seep into the atmosphere and trap heat. Scientists predict that temperatures may continue to rise by as much as 10°F (-12°C) over the next hundred years.

METHANE is the second **BIGGEST CAUSE** of GREENHOUSE **WARMING.**

Gas from COWS is a big contributor to **GLOBAL WARMING.**

A World at RISK

Glacier National Park
London
Rotterdam
Alps
Caucasus
Tian Shan
Himalaya
Tokyo
New York
Shanghai
New Orleans
Alexandria
Dhaka
Hong Kong
Miami
Mumbai
Dakar
Bangkok
Lagos
Mt. Kenya
Kilimanjaro ice cap
Jakarta
Quelccaya ice cap
Rio de Janeiro
Buenos Aires

Global Warming

Habitat loss due to global warming
(risk over next 100 years)

- ■ Critical
- ■ High
- □ Low

- • City vulnerable to sea-level rise
- △ Melting glaciers

CLOSE-UP

Phew! That STINKS!

The biggest flower in the world is this very stinky Sumatran corpse flower. This rare and ancient lily from the tropical rain forests of Sumatra, Indonesia, is best known for its sickening smell (like rotting dead animals). Luckily it doesn't bloom very often!

MEET THE NAT GEO EXPLORERS

CID SIMÕES AND PAOLA SEGURA

As sustainable agriculturists and development experts, this husband-wife team is protecting the planet—and Brazil's small farmers—one fruit tree at a time.

What was your closest call in the field?

Fortunately we have not had any close calls—only fun troubles, like fighting angry ants and bees, getting stuck in mud, getting covered with dust, and having to walk a lot when the car is broken or without gas.

How would you suggest kids follow in your footsteps?

Many people believe that agriculture is boring and hard work, but you can have a lot of fun. Like genetics, agriculture is one of a few sciences in the world where you can create a new "creature," like when we breed two flowers together to make a new one. A new creature can help hungry people, cure diseases, or even help bring peace and harmony. You just need to play with soil, plants, and water!

What is one place or thing you'd still like to explore?

We would love to keep exploring the world of microorganisms. There are millions and billions of them working for and against us. To learn how to control them and use their power in our favor is very important for the balance of the planet.

Bet you didn't know

6 incredible facts about rain forests

1 One-quarter of all **BUTTERFLY** species on Earth live in South American **rain forests.**

2 **Tropical rain forests** are a habitat for **80 percent** of the WORLD'S **INSECT** species.

3 **Antarctica** is the ONLY CONTINENT that has **NO** rain forests.

4 **The Amazon** rain forest is home to **giant rodents** called **capybaras—** that are about as tall as **German shepherds.**

5 **Rainbow-colored grasshoppers** live in the rain forests of **Peru.**

6 **The world's BIGGEST** flower—found in the Indonesian rain forest— can grow **wider than a car tire.**

What in the World?

SAVE THE RAIN FOREST!
The rain forest is home to these animals—and many others. To identify the animals, unscramble the letters below the pictures.
ANSWERS ON PAGE 339

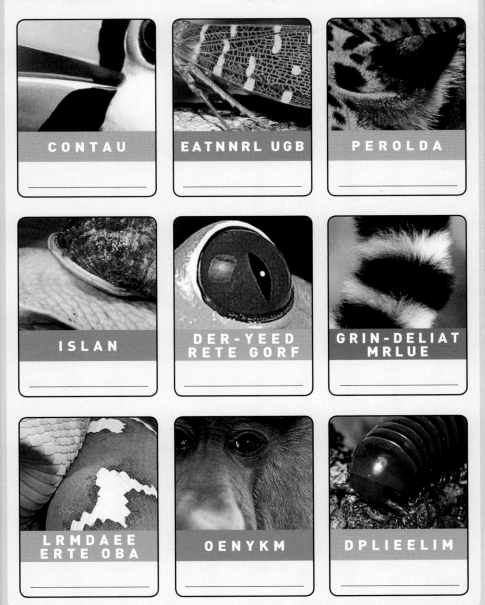

CONTAU

EATNNRL UGB

PEROLDA

ISLAN

DER-YEED RETE GORF

GRIN-DELIAT MRLUE

LRMDAEE ERTE OBA

OENYKM

DPLIEELIM

World Energy & Minerals

Almost everything people do—from cooking to powering the International Space Station—requires energy. But energy comes in different forms. Traditional energy sources, still used by many people in the developing world, include burning dried animal dung and wood. Industrialized countries and urban centers around the world rely on coal, oil, and natural gas—called fossil fuels because they formed from decayed plant and animal material accumulated from long ago. Fossil fuel deposits, either in the ground or under the ocean floor, are unevenly distributed on Earth, and only some countries can afford to buy them. Fossil fuels are also not renewable, meaning they will run out one day. And unless we find other ways to create energy, we'll be stuck. Without energy we won't be able to drive cars, use lights, or send emails to friends.

TAKING A TOLL

Environmentally speaking, burning fossil fuels isn't necessarily the best choice either—carbon dioxide from the burning of fossil fuels, as well as other emissions, are contributing to global warming. Concerned scientists are looking at new ways to harness renewable, alternative sources of energy, such as water, wind, and sun.

COOL CLICK To learn more about global trends, go online. nationalgeographic.com/earthpulse

OIL, GAS, AND COAL

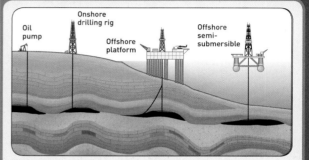

This illustration shows some of the different kinds of onshore and offshore drilling equipment. The type of drilling equipment depends on whether oil or natural gas is in the ground or under the ocean.

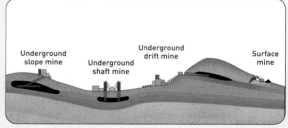

The mining of coal made the industrial revolution possible, and coal still provides a major energy source. Work that was once done by people using picks and shovels now relies heavily on mechanized equipment. This diagram shows some of the various kinds currently in use.

WORLD PRIMARY ENERGY SUPPLY

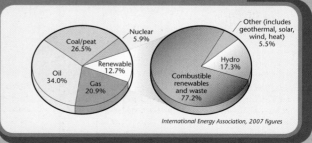

International Energy Association, 2007 figures

Alternative Power

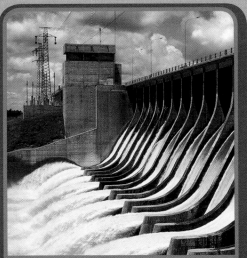

HYDROELECTRIC POWER

Hydroelectric plants, such as Santiago del Estero in Argentina, use dams to harness running water to generate clean, renewable energy.

SOLAR POWER

Solar panels on Samso Island in Denmark capture and store energy from the sun, an environmentally friendly alternative to fossil fuels.

GEOTHERMAL POWER

Geothermal power, from groundwater heated by molten rock, provides energy for this power plant in Iceland. Swimmers enjoy the warm, mineral-rich waters of a lake created by the power plant.

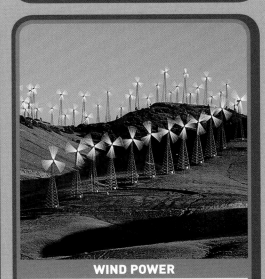

WIND POWER

Strong winds blowing through California's mountains spin windmill blades on an energy farm, powering giant turbines that generate electricity for the state.

HELP CLEAN UP
A LOCAL BEACH OR RIVERBED.

A few hands can make a real difference when it comes to cleaning up local beaches and riverbeds. These waterways can get really polluted with litter and debris. Help restore these habitats to their original beauty by picking up trash with your friends. You may even save a few animals along the way.

THE LARGEST **WIND TURBINE** in the world, located in Emden, Germany, stands **50 STORIES TALL** and can power **4,500 HOMES.**

GREEN ENERGY

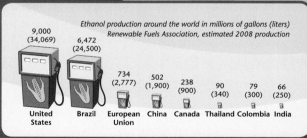

Ethanol production around the world in millions of gallons (liters)
Renewable Fuels Association, estimated 2008 production

9,000 (34,069) — United States
6,472 (24,500) — Brazil
734 (2,777) — European Union
502 (1,900) — China
238 (900) — Canada
90 (340) — Thailand
79 (300) — Colombia
66 (250) — India

In the United States, Iowa is the leading producer of ethanol, a clean-burning, renewable, nonfossil fuel energy source made from corn.

ENERGY FROM WATER

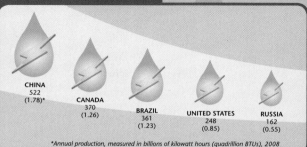

CHINA 522 (1.78)*
CANADA 370 (1.26)
BRAZIL 361 (1.23)
UNITED STATES 248 (0.85)
RUSSIA 162 (0.55)

Annual production, measured in billions of kilowatt hours (quadrillion BTUs), 2008

Hydroelectric dams harness the power of rivers to produce clean, renewable energy for industrial and home use. China leads the world in hydropower production.

Turning GREEN

Every day the media is filled with stories about global warming, pollution, and dwindling resources. Headlines warn of environmental risks that may threaten our way of life. The United States is the source of a quarter of the world's greenhouse gas emissions, and Americans generate more than 254 million tons (227 million metric tons) of trash each year and only recycle about 33 percent of their waste. The average American also uses 32 times more resources than a person in the African country of Kenya. But there's a bright side to these grim statistics. Everyone can help the environment by making simple lifestyle changes, such as using cars that run on alternative fuels. It is up to each of us to make changes that take advantage of these environmentally friendly developments.

SHARE THE ROAD

Biking to work or school reduces the use of gasoline, a source of greenhouse gases, and it is healthy, too.

COOL CLICK Zipper the Web dog has green tips for you. Check them out online.
kids.nationalgeographic.com/Stories/SpaceScience/Green-tips

A GREEN RIDE

Can a motorcycle be both superfast and eco-friendly?

The Die Moto bike clocks in at more than 130 miles an hour (209 kph) and holds a world land speed record for diesel motorcycles. Even better, the speedster does so on biodiesel. Unlike diesel or regular fuel, which are produced from oil from the earth, biodiesel is made mainly from vegetable oil—the same stuff that's used for cooking! Biodiesel is cleaner and emits fewer pollutants into the air.

GREEN HOUSE
THE LATEST ECO-TECHNOLOGY FOR YOUR HOME

You just moved into the coolest house on the block. From top to bottom, inside and out, your green house cuts natural resource use and decreases CO_2 emissions by using smart design and construction that emphasize renewable resources. Your house is all about recycling, which significantly decreases waste that would otherwise go to landfills. Check out some of the sustainable and biodegradable items in your unique eco-friendly home.

1 A ROOFTOP GARDEN provides insulation for the house, makes oxygen, and absorbs CO2.

2 SOLAR PANELS, facing south, use sunlight to generate electricity for the whole house.

3 DOUBLE-PANED WINDOWS reduce the need for heating and air-conditioning systems, keeping your house comfortable year-round.

4 The TALL DESIGN OF THE HOUSE uses less land.

5 BRICKS for the exterior walls are made from recycled materials.

6 You have CHAIRS made from recycled seat belts and LAMPS made of RECYCLED CHOPSTICKS.

7 STRATEGICALLY PLACED TREES provide indoor climate control by shading out summer heat and letting in light and warmth when the leaves fall in autumn.

8 The DECK is made from recycled plastic.

9 A PASSIVE SOLAR SYSTEM uses concrete, brick, stone, and tile to absorb and maintain heat from the sun.

10 WOOD for the stairways and furniture comes from trees grown specifically for harvest, not from old-growth forests.

11 SOFT, NATURAL FIBER BEDDING is made from bamboo, a renewable resource.

12 CEILING FANS circulate air and help keep rooms cooler in warm weather.

13 In the bathrooms, you use BIODEGRADABLE SOAPS AND SHAMPOOS that won't add chemicals to streams, rivers, and oceans. DUAL-FLUSH TOILETS choose the amount of water you need for flushing. BIODEGRADABLE TOILET PAPER is made from recycled paper. Your shower curtain is made of HEMP, a renewable resource.

14 Energy-saving light switches called OCCUPANT SENSORS automatically turn lights on when you enter the room and off when you leave. COMPACT FLUORESCENT BULBS in all the light fixtures use 75% less energy and last ten times longer than standard bulbs.

15 To water your garden, you use the rainwater that collects in OUTDOOR HOLDING TANKS.

16 The FRONT-LOADING WASHING MACHINE uses less water than a top-loading one.

17 The kitchen COUNTERTOP is made of reclaimed granite salvaged from discarded granite products. The APPLIANCES are certified energy savers. AERATORS conserve water by reducing faucet flow.

18 Your whole family's stylish clothing is made from RENEWABLE, NATURAL FIBERS, such as organically grown cotton.

19 The dog and cat eat ORGANIC PET FOOD. The pets use HEMP collars, beds, and toys. The KITTY LITTER comes from recycled paper.

20 SOLAR GARDEN LIGHTS store energy for nighttime use.

21 Your family's new HYBRID CAR emits very little CO2.

22 RECYCLING BINS make it easy for you to sort glass, plastic, aluminum, and paper.

Volunteering

A volunteer is a PERSON who freely GIVES of his or her TIME and EFFORTS to HELP OTHERS or the community.

Not sure how you can make a difference in the world? One great way to help out is to volunteer. There are tons of places and organizations looking for volunteers to help them with their efforts. You can also design and organize your own project for your community.

Think about what interests you. Do you like to cook? Maybe you can organize a bake sale to raise money for a charity. Perhaps you love animals. Volunteer at a zoo. There are tons of options.

Here are some other fun ways to volunteer:

- **Renew a park,** school, or community area by planting flowers or trees.

- **Help deliver food** to seniors and others who may be housebound.

- **Distribute food** at local home-less shelters or soup kitchens.

- **Offer to walk** a senior citizen's dog.

- **Donate toys** and goods to organizations for needy children.

- **Tutor children or adults** in reading and other subjects.

- **Sponsor a food drive** for an area food bank or shelter.

- **Recycle old clothing** by donating to shelters or orphanages.

- **Clean up your community** by picking up trash.

Grab a friend, gather your family, or volunteer on your own to help make the world a better place. Volunteering will not only help others and the world around you, it will be a fantastic experience for you, too.

COOL CLICK

If you're not sure how to volunteer, go online for lots of opportunities and ideas.
hud.gov/kids/kidsvlta.html

Try This!

FOOD FOR YOUR GARDEN!

Grow a healthy garden and reduce waste by using leftovers to make your own compost, which is organic material that adds nutrients to the soil.

RECYCLE THE NATURAL WAY

By composting you reduce the need for chemical fertilizers in your yard, and you send less waste to landfills. Yard trimmings and food scraps make up about 25 percent of the trash from cities and towns in the United States. So put that banana peel to good use. Turn it—and a lot of other things in your trash can—into environmentally helpful compost. By making natural fertilizer you will help the environment *and* have a great excuse to play with your food!

COMPOST THESE

"BROWN" MATERIALS
Dead leaves
Eggshells
Twigs
Shredded newspaper
Nutshells

"GREEN" MATERIALS
Grass clippings
Fruit and vegetable scraps
Coffee grounds
Tea bags

GROW VEGGIES AND FLOWERS

HOW TO MAKE COMPOST

1. Choose a dry, shady spot to create your compost pile.

2. Use a bin with a tight-fitting lid and plenty of airholes to hold your compost ingredients. In the bin, start with a 6-inch (15-cm) layer of dry "brown" material (see examples in list above, right). Break down large pieces before you place them in the bin.

3. Add a 3-inch (8-cm) layer of "green" materials (see list). Add a little bit of soil to this layer.

4. Mix the brown and green layers.

5. Finish with another 3-inch (8-cm) layer of brown materials.

6. Add water until the contents are moist. If you accidentally add too much water, just add more brown materials to the bin. Mix your compost pile every week or two.

7. After one to four months, the compost will be almost ready. When it is dark brown and moist, and you can't identify the original ingredients, wait two more weeks. Then add your finished compost to your garden.

For more about helping Earth, go online.
preserveourplanet.com

COOL CLICK

It's easy to protect the planet! These 30 tips help save limited resources such as water, energy, and animals; prevent landfill waste; or decrease harmful gases, such as CO_2, which contribute to global warming. So get green and give these tips a try.

EARTH'S FIRST-AID KIT

MAKE SURE TO ASK YOUR PARENTS BEFORE TRYING ANY OF THESE TIPS!

1 BUY METAL OR CERAMIC BOWLS FOR YOUR PET.

PLASTIC BOWLS ARE MADE FROM OIL, A LIMITED RESOURCE.

Check out the Web link below for more green tips.

kids.nationalgeographic.com

2 SET THE THERMOSTAT TO NO LOWER THAN 78°F (26°C) IN THE SUMMER AND NO HIGHER THAN 68°F (20°C) IN THE WINTER.

3 SET OUT CANS AND BOTTLES FOR NEIGHBORHOOD PICKUP OR EXCHANGE THEM FOR CASH AT A RECYCLING CENTER.

4 TAKE A REUSABLE BAG (SUCH AS ONE MADE OUT OF CLOTH) TO THE STORE INSTEAD OF USING PAPER OR PLASTIC.

5 CHOOSE LOCALLY GROWN FOOD. TRANSPORTING FOOD LONG DISTANCES WASTES FUEL AND CREATES EXTRA CO_2.

6 TURN OFF THE TV OR VIDEO GAME CONSOLE AND PLAY OUTSIDE.

7 REPLACE INCANDESCENT LIGHTBULBS WITH COMPACT FLUORESCENT ONES. THEY LAST UP TO TEN TIMES LONGER AND CAN USE A QUARTER OF THE ENERGY.

8 SCRAPE LEFTOVERS OFF THE DISHES INSTEAD OF RINSING THEM. (WASH THE DISHES SOON AFTER.)

9 KEEP THOSE FANS BUZZING IN SUMMER INSTEAD OF TURNING ON THE AIR CONDITIONER.

10 BUY A LITTLE BIT LESS. DO YOU REALLY NEED IT? CAN YOU RENT OR BORROW IT? CAN YOU FIND IT USED?

11 CARPOOL.

12 TURN OVER USED PAPER AND USE IT FOR ARTWORK OR SCRAP PAPER.

13 CHOOSE RECHARGEABLE BATTERIES. THEN RECYCLE THEM WHEN THEY DIE.

14 RIDE A BIKE OR WALK INSTEAD OF USING THE CAR.

15 CLOSE YOUR CURTAINS TO KEEP OUT DAYTIME SUMMER HEAT OR KEEP IN NIGHTTIME WINTER WARMTH.

16 PARTICIPATE IN CLEANUP DAYS AT A BEACH OR PARK.

17 ASK MOM OR DAD TO TURN OFF THE CAR INSTEAD OF LETTING IT IDLE WHILE YOU'RE WAITING.

18 PLANT A DECIDUOUS (LEAFY) TREE THAT LOSES ITS LEAVES IN FALL ON THE SOUTH SIDE OF YOUR HOME. ITS SHADE WILL COOL YOUR HOUSE IN THE SUMMER. AFTER THE TREE'S LEAVES FALL, SUNLIGHT WILL HELP WARM YOUR HOUSE IN WINTER.

19 PLUG ELECTRONICS INTO A POWER STRIP AND FLIP OFF THE SWITCH WHEN THE GADGETS AREN'T IN USE. (MAKE SURE THIS WON'T MESS UP CLOCKS AND RECORDINGS.)

20 REUSE CREATIVELY! FOR INSTANCE, USE EMPTY YOGURT CONTAINERS AS PAINT CUPS OR PLANT POTS.

21 PLACE YOUR DESK NEXT TO A WINDOW AND USE NATURAL LIGHT INSTEAD OF A LAMP.

22 USE THOSE OUTDOOR TRASH CANS! NEVER LITTER.

EARTH'S FIRST-AID KIT

23 SHARE THESE GREEN TIPS WITH YOUR FAMILY AND FRIENDS.

24 TURN OFF THE WATER WHILE BRUSHING YOUR TEETH.

25 TAKE SHORT SHOWERS INSTEAD OF BATHS. AIM FOR FIVE MINUTES— BUT STILL GET CLEAN!

26 CREATE A LENDING LIBRARY. SHARE ITEMS SUCH AS BOOKS, DVDS, OR VIDEO GAMES WITH YOUR FRIENDS AND NEIGHBORS.

27 SEND AN E-CARD INSTEAD OF A PAPER CARD.

28 SWITCH OFF THE LIGHT EVERY TIME YOU LEAVE A ROOM.

29 PACK YOUR LUNCH WITH REUSABLE UTENSILS, A CLOTH NAPKIN, AND A CUP. CARRY LUNCH IN A METAL OR FABRIC LUNCH CONTAINER FOR A ZERO-WASTE LUNCH.

30 "ADOPT" AN ENDANGERED ANIMAL THROUGH A CHARITY.

WRITE A LETTER THAT GETS RESULTS

Knowing how to write a good letter is a useful skill. It will come in handy anytime you want to persuade someone to understand your point of view. Whether you're emailing your Congressman, or writing a letter for a school project or to your grandma, a great letter will help you get your message across. Most important, a well-written letter leaves a good impression.

Check out the example below for the elements of a good letter.

Your address

Date

Salutation
Always use "Dear" followed by the person's name; use Mr. or Mrs. or Dr. as appropriate.

Introductory paragraph
Give the reason you're writing the letter.

Body
The longest part of the letter, which provides evidence that supports your position. Be persuasive!

Closing paragraph
Sum up your argument

Complimentary closing
Sign off with "Sincerely" or "Thank you"

Your Signature

Sadie Donnelly
1128 Albermarle Street
Los Angeles, CA 90045

March 31, 2011

Dear Mr. School Superintendent,

I am writing to you about all the trash I see at our school at lunchtime and to offer a solution.

I see the trash on the ground, blowing around the yard, getting stuck on the fences, and sometimes overflowing the trash cans. Usually, there are also plastic bags, paper bags, food containers, water bottles, and juice boxes from student and teacher lunches.

I am suggesting that one day a week the whole school have a No Trash Lunch Day. My idea is to have students and teachers bring their food and drinks in reusable containers. We would take the containers home to clean and use again another day.

Above all, I think our school could help the environment and cut back on how much of this trash goes to the landfills and pollutes the ocean. Let's see No Trash Lunch Day at our school soon. Thank you.

Sincerely,

Sadie Donnelly

COMMONLY USED COMPLIMENTARY CLOSINGS

Sincerely,
Sincerely yours,
Thank you,
Regards,
Best wishes,
Respectfully,

YOU CAN MAKE A DIFFERENCE

Want to do more to make the world a better place? Have a question or an opinion? Do something about it. Turn your passion for a cause into meaningful action.

DIG DEEPER! Look to newspaper or magazine articles, books, the Internet, and anything else you can get your hands on. Learn about the issue or organization that most inspires you.

GET INVOLVED! The following organizations can connect you to opportunities so you can make a difference.
dosomething.org
volunteermatch.org
globalvolunteers.org

MAKE YOUR VOICE HEARD! Email, call, or write to politicians or government officials.
congress.org

GO ONLINE TO HELP CARE FOR THE EARTH.
Learn more about environmental issues:
earthday.net
ecokids.ca/pub/kids_home.cfm
treepeople.org
meetthegreens.org
kidsplanet.org/defendit/new/

Collect pennies to help save wild species and wild places:
togethergreen.org/p4p

Start an environmental club at your school:
greenguideforkids.blogspot.com/
search/label/activities

Learn how to start a kitchen compost bin.
meetthegreens.org/episode4/
kitchen-composting.html

Reduce paper waste by receiving fewer catalogs.
catalogchoice.org

Learn how to green your school.
nrdc.org/greensquad

LETTER-WRITING TIPS

Before you start writing, think about what you would like to write about.

Use your own words.

Use stationary that is appropriate for the recipient; for example, plain, nice paper for a Congressman and maybe a pretty card for Grandma.

When hand-writing, make sure you write neatly.

Follow the elements of a well-written letter.

Be creative!

Before you send the letter, read it again, and check for spelling errors.

Write neatly on the envelope so that the postal worker can read it easily.

Don't forget the stamp for snail mail.

Want to find out more about how to help look after the planet? See these websites.
epa.gov/kids
childrenoftheearth.org

COOL CLICKS

GO GREEN!
Save paper and send your letter by email. If you have to print it out, try to use recycled paper.

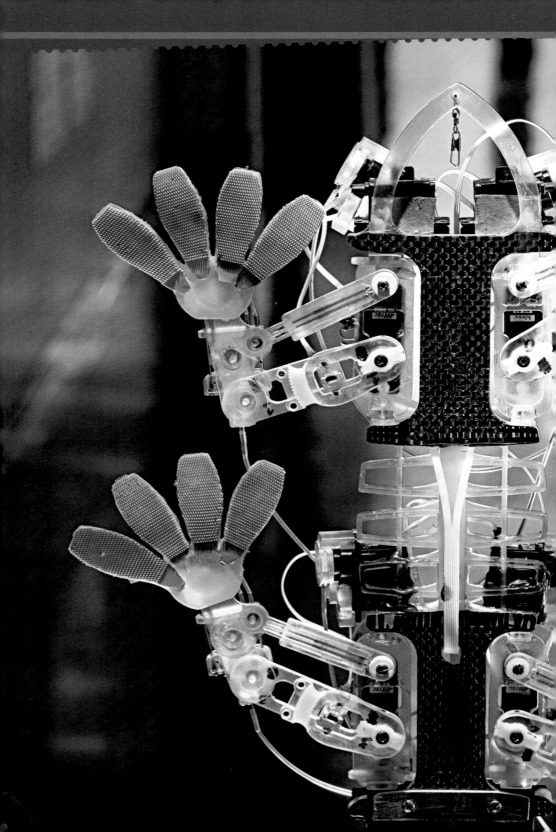

Super Science

A gecko-like robot called Stickybot uses its sticky feet to climb a glass wall.

The Three Domains of Life

Biologists divide all living organisms into three domains: Bacteria, Archaea, and Eukarya. Archaean and Bacterial cells do not have nuclei; they are so different from each other that they belong to different domains. Since human cells have a nucleus, humans belong to the Eukarya domain, which is divided into fungi, protists, plants, and animals.

1

BACTERIA

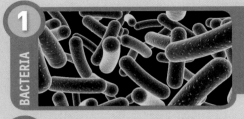

Domain Bacteria: These single-celled microorganisms are found almost everywhere in the world. Bacteria are small and do not have nuclei. They can be shaped like rods, spirals, or spheres. Some bacteria are helpful to humans, and some are harmful.

2

ARCHAEA

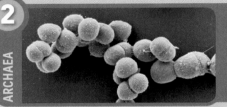

Domain Archaea: These single-celled micro-organisms are often found in extremely hostile environments. Like Bacteria, Archaea do not have nuclei. but they have some genes in common with Eukarya. For this reason, scientists think the Archaea living today most closely resemble the earliest forms of life on Earth.

3

EUKARYA

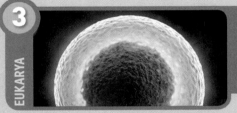

Domain Eukarya: This diverse group of life-forms is more complicated than Bacteria and Archaea, as Eukarya have one or more cells with nuclei. These are the tiny cells that make up your whole body. Eukarya are divided into four groups: fungi, protists, plants, and animals.

What is a domain? Scientifically speaking, a domain is a major taxonomic division into which natural objects are classified (see p. 20 for "What is Taxonomy?").

FYI

FUNGI

Kingdom Fungi (about 100,000 species): Mainly multicellular organisms, fungi cannot make their own food. Mushrooms and yeast are fungi.

PROTISTS

Protists (about 250,000 species): Once considered a kingdom, this group is a "grab bag" that includes unicellular and multicellular organisms of great variety.

PLANTS

Kingdom Plantae (about 300,000 species): Plants are multicellular, and many can make their own food using photosynthesis (see p. 316 for "Photosynthesis").

ANIMALS

Kingdom Animalia (about a million species): Most animals, which are multicellular, have their own organ systems. Animals do not make their own food.

WHAT IS LIFE?

This seems like such an easy question to answer. Everybody knows singing birds are alive and rocks are not. But when we start studying bacteria and other microscopic creatures, things get more complicated.

SO WHAT EXACTLY IS LIFE?

Most scientists agree that something is alive if it has the following characteristics: it can reproduce, grow in size to become more complex in structure, take in nutrients to survive, give off waste products, and respond to external stimuli, such as increased sunlight or changes in temperature.

KINDS OF LIFE

Biologists classify living organisms by how they get their energy. Organisms such as algae, green plants, and some bacteria use sunlight as an energy source. Human beings, fungi, and some Archaea use chemicals to provide energy. When we eat food, chemical reactions within our digestive system turn our food into fuel.

Living things inhabit land, sea, and air. In fact, life also thrives deep beneath the oceans, embedded in rocks miles below the Earth's crust, in ice, and in other extreme environments. The life-forms that thrive in these challenging environments are called extremophiles. Some of these draw directly upon the chemicals surrounding them for energy. Since these are very different forms of life than what we're used to, we may not think of them as alive, but they are.

HOW IT ALL WORKS

To try and understand how a living organism works, it helps to look at one example of its simplest form—the single-celled bacterium called *Streptococcus*. There are many kinds of these tiny organisms, and some are responsible for human illnesses. What makes us sick or uncomfortable are the toxins the bacteria give off in our bodies.

A single *Streptococcus* bacterium is so small that at least 500 of them could fit on the dot above the letter *i*. These bacteria are some of the simplest forms of life we know. They have no moving parts, no lungs, no brain, no heart, no liver, no leaves or fruit. And yet this life-form reproduces, grows in size by producing long chain structures, takes in nutrients, and gives off waste products. This tiny life-form is alive, just as you are alive.

Just what makes something alive is a question scientists grapple with when they study viruses. Viruses, such as the ones that cause the common cold and smallpox, can grow and reproduce but they can only grow within host cells, as in those that make up your body. Since viruses lack cells and cannot metabolize nutrients for energy or reproduce without a host, scientists ask if they are even alive. And don't go looking for them without a strong microscope—viruses are a hundred times smaller than bacteria.

Scientists think life began on Earth some 4.1 to 3.9 billion years ago, but no fossils exist from that time. The earliest fossils ever found are from the primitive life that existed 3.6 billion years ago. Other life-forms soon followed, and some of these are shown below. Scientists continue to study how life evolved on Earth and whether or not it is possible that life exists on other planets.

MICROSCOPIC ORGANISMS

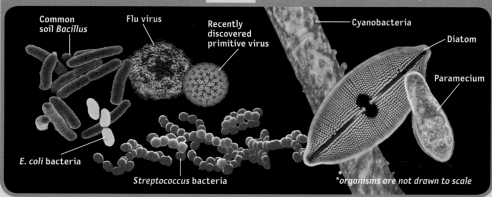

Common soil *Bacillus*

Flu virus

Recently discovered primitive virus

Cyanobacteria

Diatom

Paramecium

E. coli bacteria

Streptococcus bacteria

*organisms are not drawn to scale

THE UNIVERSE BEGAN WITH A BIG BANG

Clear your mind for a minute and try to imagine this: All the things you see in the universe today—all the stars, galaxies, and planets—are not actually out there. Everything that now exists is concentrated in a single, incredibly dense point that scientists call a singularity. Then, suddenly, the elements that make up the universe flash into existence. That actually happened about 13.7 billion years ago, in the moment we call the big bang.

For centuries scientists, religious scholars, poets, and philosophers have wondered how the universe came to be. Was it always there? Will it always be the same, or will it change? If it had a beginning, will it someday end, or will it go on forever?

These are huge questions. But today, because of recent observations of space and what it's made of, we think we may have some of the answers. We know the big bang created not only matter but also space itself. And scientists think that in the very distant future, stars will run out of fuel and burn out. Once again the universe will become dark.

Everything we can see or detect around us in the universe began with the big bang. After the big bang, the universe expanded.

COOL CLICK

Go online for more information on the origins of the universe.
science.nationalgeographic.com/science/space/universe/origins-universe-article.html

PROGRESS OF LIFE ON EARTH

About 3.5 billion years ago
Earth was covered by one gigantic reddish ocean. The color came from hydrocarbons.

The first life-forms on Earth were Archaea that were able to live without oxygen. They released large amounts of methane gas into an atmosphere that would have been poisonous to us.

About 3 billion years ago
something new appeared in the global ocean. Erupting volcanoes linked together to form larger landmasses. And a new form of life appeared—cyanobacteria, the first living things that used energy from the sun.

Some 2 billion years ago
the cyanobacteria algae filled the air with oxygen, killing off the methane-producing Archaea. Colored pools of greenish-brown plant life floated on the oceans. The oxygen revolution that would someday make human life possible was now under way.

About 530 million years ago,
the Cambrian explosion occurred. It's called an explosion because it's the time when most major animal groups first appeared in our fossil records. Back then, Earth was made up of swamps, seas, a few active volcanoes, and oceans teeming with strange life.

More than 450 million years ago,
life began moving from the oceans onto dry land. About 200 million years later dinosaurs began to appear. They would dominate life on Earth for more than 150 million years.

Our New Solar System

JUST THE FACTS

- Our solar system is made up of planets, dwarf planets, asteroids, and comets orbiting around a star we call the sun.
- Our star system formed 4.6 billion years ago from a nebular cloud, a large, spinning cloud of gas and dust.
- Our solar system is divided into three different categories of planets, based on size and density: terrestrial, dwarf, and Jovian.
- The terrestrial planets—Mercury, Venus, Earth, and Mars—orbit closest to the sun and are small, dense, and rocky.
- Ceres, a dwarf planet, lies in the asteroid belt, beyond the terrestrial planets.
- The gas giants—Jupiter, Saturn, Uranus, and Neptune—are large, surrounded by rings and multiple moons, and made out of gases. These are called the Jovian planets.
- The Kuiper belt, an area filled with comets and other solar system debris, lies past the gas planets. In the Kuiper belt are more dwarf planets, including Pluto, Eris, Haumea, and Makemake.

DAYS ARE LONGER THAN YEARS ON THE PLANET MERCURY

Solar System Glossary

DWARF PLANET
Generally smaller than Mercury, a dwarf planet orbits the sun along with other objects near it. Its gravity has pulled it into a round (or nearly round) shape.

COMET
A body of rock, dust, and gaseous ice in an elongated orbit around the sun. Near the sun, heat diffuses gas and dust to form a streaming "tail" from the comet's nucleus.

ASTEROID
A rocky body, measuring from less than 1 mile (1.6 km) to 600 miles (966 km) in diameter, in orbit around the sun. Most asteroids are found between the orbits of Mars and Jupiter.

ECLIPSE
An event caused by the passage of one astronomical body in front of another astronomical body, briefly blocking light from the farthest one.

PLANET
A planet orbits a star. Gravity has pulled it into a round (or nearly round) shape, and it has cleared its neighborhood of other objects.

THE SUN

The sun is a star that is about 4.6 billion years old. As the anchor that holds our solar system together, it provides the energy necessary for life to flourish on Earth. It accounts for 99 percent of the matter in the solar system. The rest of the planets, moons, asteroids, and comets added together amount to the remaining one percent.

Even though a million Earths could fit inside the sun, it is still considered an average-size star. Betelgeuse (BET-el-jooz), the star on the shoulder of the constellation known as Orion, is almost 400 times larger.

A BIG BALL OF GAS

Like other stars the sun is a giant ball of hydrogen gas radiating heat and light through nuclear fusion—a process by which the sun converts about four million tons (3,628,739 t) of matter to energy every second.

Also like other stars the sun revolves around its galaxy. Located halfway out in one of the arms of the Milky Way galaxy, the sun takes 225 to 250 million years to complete one revolution around the galaxy.

The sun is composed of about 74 percent hydrogen, 25 percent helium, and one percent trace elements like iron, carbon, lead, and uranium. These trace elements provide us with amazing insight into the history of our star. They're the heavier elements that are produced when stars explode. Since these elements are relatively abundant in the sun, scientists know it was forged from materials that came together in two previous star explosions. All of the elements found in the sun, on Earth, and in our bodies were recycled from those two exploding stars.

OUR AMAZING SUN

When viewed from space by astronauts, the sun burns white in color. But when we see it from Earth, through our atmosphere, it looks yellow.

Solar flares—explosions of charged particles—sometimes erupt from the sun's surface. They create beautiful aurora displays on Earth, Jupiter, Saturn, and even distant Uranus and Neptune.

We know that the sun makes life possible here on Earth. We couldn't survive without it.

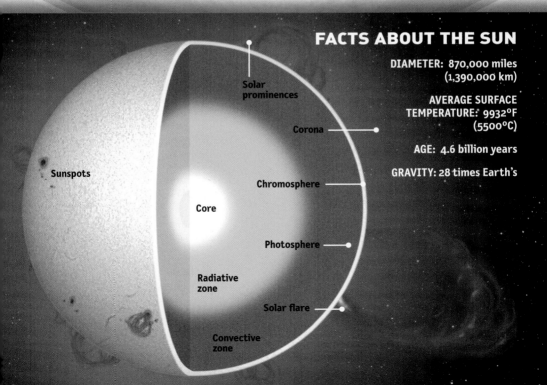

FACTS ABOUT THE SUN

DIAMETER: 870,000 miles (1,390,000 km)

AVERAGE SURFACE TEMPERATURE: 9932°F (5500°C)

AGE: 4.6 billion years

GRAVITY: 28 times Earth's

Solar prominences

Corona

Chromosphere

Photosphere

Solar flare

Sunspots

Core

Radiative zone

Convective zone

PLANETS

Ceres

Mars

Earth

Venus

Mercury

Jupiter

Sun

MERCURY
Average distance from the sun:
35,980,000 miles (57,900,000 km)
Position from the sun in orbit: first
Equatorial diameter: 3,030 miles (4,878 km)
Mass (Earth = 1): 0.055   Density (Water = 1): 5.43
Length of day: 58 Earth days
Length of year: 88 Earth days
Surface temperatures: -300°F (-184°C) to 800°F (427°C)
Known moons: 0

VENUS
Average distance from the sun:
67,230,000 miles (108,200,000 km)
Position from the sun in orbit: second
Equatorial diameter: 7,520 miles (12,100 km)
Mass (Earth = 1): 0.815   Density (Water = 1): 5.25
Length of day: -243 Earth days (retrograde)
Length of year: 225 Earth days
Average surface temperature: 864°F (462°C)
Known moons: 0

EARTH
Average distance from the sun:
93,000,000 miles (149,600,000 km)
Position from the sun in orbit: third
Equatorial diameter: 7,900 miles (12,750 km)
Mass (Earth = 1): 1   Density (Water = 1): 5.52
Length of day: 24 hours
Length of year: 365 days
Surface temperatures: -126°F (-88°C) to 136°F (58°C)
Known moons: 1

MARS
Average distance from the sun:
141,633,000 miles (227,936,000 km)
Position from the sun in orbit: fourth
Equatorial diameter: 4,333 miles (6,794 km)
Mass (Earth = 1): 0.107   Density (Water = 1): 3.93
Length of day: 25 Earth hours
Length of year: 1.88 Earth years
Surface temperatures: -270°F (-168°C) to 80°F (27°C)
Known moons: 2

CERES (DWARF PLANET)
Position from the sun in orbit: fifth
Length of day: 9.1 Earth hours
Length of year: 4.6 Earth years
Known moons: 0

JUPITER
Average distance from the sun:
483,682,000 miles (778,412,000 km)
Position from the sun in orbit: sixth
Equatorial diameter: 86,880 miles (139,800 km)
Mass (Earth = 1): 318   Density (Water = 1): 1.3
Length of day: 9.9 Earth hours
Length of year: 11.9 Earth years
Average surface temperature: -235°F (-148°C)
Known moons: at least 63

WINTER
lasts for
21
years on
URANUS.

This artwork shows the 13 planets and dwarf planets that astronomers now recognize in our solar system. The relative sizes and positions of the planets are shown but not the relative distances between them. Many of the planets closest to Earth can be seen without a telescope in the night sky.

Saturn

Uranus

Neptune   Pluto   Haumea

Makemake

Eris

SATURN
Average distance from the sun:
886,526,000 miles (1,426,725,000 km)
Position from the sun in orbit: seventh
Equatorial diameter: 72,370 miles (116,460 km)
Mass (Earth = 1): 95   Density (Water = 1): 0.71
Length of day: 10 Earth hours
Length of year: 29.46 Earth years
Average surface temperature: -218°F (-139°C)
Known moons: at least 60

URANUS
Average distance from the sun:
1,784,000,000 miles (2,870,970,000 km)
Position from the sun in orbit: eighth
Equatorial diameter: 31,500 miles (50,724 km)
Mass (Earth = 1): 15   Density (Water = 1): 1.24
Length of day: 17.9 Earth hours
Length of year: 84 Earth years
Average surface temperature: -323°F (-197°C)
Known moons: 27

NEPTUNE
Average distance from the sun:
2,795,000,000 miles (4,498,250,000 km)
Position from the sun in orbit: ninth
Equatorial diameter: 30,775 miles (49,528 km)
Mass (Earth = 1): 17   Density (Water = 1): 1.67
Length of day: 19 Earth hours
Length of year: 164.8 Earth years
Average surface temperature: -353°F (-214°C)
Known moons: 13

PLUTO (DWARF PLANET)
Position from the sun in orbit: tenth
Length of day: 6.4 Earth days
Length of year: 248 Earth years
Known moons: 3

HAUMEA (DWARF PLANET)
Position from the sun in orbit: eleventh
Length of day: 4 Earth hours
Length of year: 284 Earth years
Known moons: 2

MAKEMAKE (DWARF PLANET)
Position from sun in orbit: twelfth
Length of day: unknown
Length of year: 307 Earth years
Known Moons: 0

ERIS (DWARF PLANET)
Position from the sun in orbit: thirteenth
Length of day: less than 8 Earth hours
Length of year: 557 Earth years
Known moons: 1

FOR THE DEFINITIONS OF *PLANET* AND *DWARF PLANET* SEE P. 122.

HOW PLANETS FORM

Planets arise as a natural result of the star-formation process. Stars are born from large clouds of gas and dust. That gas and dust spins in space, flattening into a disk the way pizza dough does when a baker tosses it. The center of the disk becomes a star, while the rest of the disk may form planets.

Within the disk dusty bits of carbon and silicon begin to clump together. Those clumps eventually get bigger and become rocky objects called protoplanets, which smack into each other and stick together to make planets.

The asteroids in our solar system are leftover plantesimals, or small planets from the early solar system. Jupiter's gravity stirred them up and prevented them from sticking together. Astronomers have found evidence of asteroids in other star systems.

If a rocky planet grows large enough, it can collect and hold on to surrounding hydrogen gas. That's how the gas giants of our outer solar system grew so big.

Time Line of EARTH

IF THE AGE OF THE EARTH and solar system were compared with the length of time in a year, here's how long things would take to form and develop:

JANUARY 1
On New Year's Day, the solar system begins condensing out of a swirling cloud of stardust.

JANUARY 7
The nuclear fires of the sun ignite.

JANUARY 28
A truly memorable day—Earth forms.

FEBRUARY
Through the month of February, Earth continues to shrink and cool.

MARCH 10
Escaped water vapor returns to Earth as rain, and oceans form.

APRIL 15
Somewhere in Earth's warm, blue-green waters life begins.

MAY 22
Oxygen starts to form in the atmosphere.

JULY TO AUGUST
Life continues to develop.

SEPTEMBER 14
Somewhere in the oceanic depths, single-cell plants begin sexual reproduction.

OCTOBER
Multicell creatures and plants burst onto the scene.

DECEMBER 2
Some animals and plants begin to live on land.

DECEMBER 13
Dinosaurs appear.

DECEMBER 25
Dinosaurs disappear.

DECEMBER 31
At 5:00 in the evening, Lucy, one of the earliest known human ancestors, is born in Africa.

Bet you didn't know

THERE IS NO SOUND IN SPACE.

The Life Cycle of a Star

Poets might say that the stars are forever, but scientists know that's not true. All stars eventually die when they run out of fuel.

You might think a more massive star would live longer because it has more fuel to burn. But the heavier a star is, the faster it burns through its fuel, and the shorter its lifetime is. The most massive stars will live for only a few million years, while the smallest can live for trillions of years.

All stars spend most of their lives fusing hydrogen and turning it into helium in their cores. This nuclear fusion creates the energy we see as starlight. Eventually, the star's core runs out of hydrogen. This is the end for low-mass stars like the sun.

When higher-mass stars run out of hydrogen, they can start fusing the helium in their cores, creating carbon and oxygen. The largest stars can keep fusing heavier and heavier elements until their core is full of hot, dense iron. That's when the star dies, because no energy comes from fusing iron.

Black Holes

A black hole really seems like a hole in space. Most black holes form when the core of a massive star collapses, falling into oblivion. A black hole has a stronger gravitational pull than anything else in the known universe. It's like a bottomless pit, swallowing anything that gets close enough to it to be pulled in. It's black because it pulls in light.

Black holes come in different sizes. The smallest one known has a mass about three times that of the sun. The biggest one scientists have found so far has a mass about three billion times greater than the sun's. Really big black holes at the centers of galaxies probably form by swallowing enormous amounts of gas over time. One of NASA's spacecraft has found thousands of possible black holes in the Milky Way, but there are probably more. The nearest one to Earth is about 1,600 light-years away.

What Is the Milky Way?

Our galaxy, the Milky Way, appears to be a band of stars in the sky, but it's actually a disk. Its 400 billion stars are clumped into lines called spiral arms because they spiral outward. When we look up at the night sky, we're seeing the edge of the disk, like the side of a Frisbee. It appears to us as a hazy band of white light.

Earth is located about halfway between the center of the Milky Way and its outer edge, in one of the spiral arms. Light from the galaxy's center takes 25,000 years to reach us.

Our solar system orbits the galactic center once every 250 million years. The last time we were on this side of the Milky Way, the earliest dinosaurs were just starting to emerge.

At the galaxy's center, frequent star explosions fry huge sections of space. Those explosions would wipe out any life on nearby planets. We're lucky that Earth is located where it is, far away from the center.

SKY DREAMS

Long ago, people looking at the sky noticed that some stars made shapes and patterns. By playing connect-the-dots, they imagined people and animals in the sky. Their legendary heroes and monsters were pictured in the stars.

Today, we call the star patterns identified by the ancient Greeks and Romans constellations. There are 88 constellations in all. Some are only visible when you're north of the Equator, and some only when you're south of it.

European ocean voyagers named the constellations that are visible in the Southern Hemisphere, such as the Southern Cross. In the 16th-century age of exploration, their ships began visiting southern lands. Astronomers used the star observations of these navigators to fill in the blank spots on their celestial maps.

Constellations aren't fixed in the sky. The star arrangement that makes up each one would look different from another location in the universe. Constellations also change over time because every star we see is moving through space. Over thousands of years, the stars in the Big Dipper (right), which is part of the larger constellation Ursa Major (the Great Bear), will move so far apart that the dipper pattern will disappear.

A constellation wheel depicting imagined people and animals in star patterns

CONSTELLATIONS

The Big Dipper is also commonly known as the Great Bear.

Some Major Constellations and When to See Them in the Northern Hemisphere

ALWAYS
Big Dipper, the Great Bear
Cassiopeia, the Queen
Perseus, Medusa's Killer
Cepheus, the King

AUTUMN
Cygnus, the Swan
Lyra, the Lyre
Pegasus, the Winged Horse
Aquila, the Eagle

WINTER
Orion, the Hunter
Andromeda, the Chained Maiden
Taurus, the Bull
Canis Major, the Great Dog

SPRING
Gemini, the Twins
Leo, the Lion
Virgo, the Virgin

SUMMER
Bootes, the Herdsman
Sagittarius, the Archer
Scorpio, the Scorpion

THE SIGNS AND CONSTELLATIONS OF THE ZODIAC

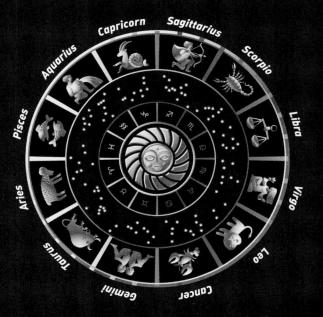

COOL inventions

COOL CAMERA

You're having a blast at your buddy's birthday party. But when it's time to bring out the cake, everyone crowds around, blocking your view. No worries. Throw the Triops into the air, and this clever camera captures the view from above. Triops can take three pictures at once, each from a different angle. So how does the Triops know when to take the photo? A motion sensor recognizes when you've tossed the camera upward and activates at the highest point. You can also record sounds—for instance, a whistle or finger snap—and command the Triops to start shooting whenever it hears that noise. That's one smart camera.

LAND ROCKET

Imagine traveling faster than the speed of sound. The Bloodhound SuperSonic Car (SSC) will be the first car to attempt to break the 1,000-mile-an-hour (1,609-kph) barrier. (The current record is 763 miles an hour (1,228 kph).) A concept for now, the rocket-shaped car gets its initial push to 350 miles an hour (563 kph) from a jet engine. Then a rocket fires up, blasting the SSC past 1,000 miles an hour. The SSC has three sets of brakes: flaps that rise from the body to create drag, a parachute that flies out the back, and a set of wheel brakes to bring the car to a complete halt. So just what does it mean to be going 1,000 miles an hour? It's the same as shooting down four American football fields in one second. In other words, it's blink-of-an-eye fast.

POWER SUIT

Strap on the XOS Exoskeleton, and suddenly you can have superhuman strength and endurance. This computerized metal suit, a prototype right now, allows you to lift objects weighing hundreds of pounds over and over again—without even breathing hard. Sensors in the robot measure the movements of your hands, arms, and legs, some as often as several thousand times each second. In this way the powered suit instantly copies your every movement. A firefighter wearing an XOS could effortlessly move heavy wreckage or carry multiple people away from danger. And you could use the suit to help your parents move the piano or lift furniture, or do anything else that, um, *suits* you.

TALK TO THE MIRROR

You're at the mall when you spot the perfect skirt in a store window. But will it look good on you? With Social Retailing, you can try it on in a flash. Bonus: You don't even have to shimmy out of what you're wearing to see how it looks. A full-size image of the dress flashes on a special mirror. You step in the right position to see the dress on your mirror image. Still not sure? Get your best friend—who's at home—to weigh in over the Internet. Beam contact info from your cell phone to the mirror. Your pal can then click on a special website to see a live video of you modeling the outfit. She can send you a text message that appears on the mirror, like "Looks awesome." Sold!

SELECT OUTFIT HERE.

NOW TRY IT ON.

MEET THE NAT GEO EXPLORER

ENRIC SALA

A marine ecologist who studies underwater systems, Sala doesn't mind making waves to protect the oceans. Sala's focus is unlike traditional marine scientists who generally study individual species. "It's the only way to understand the full impact humans have on these places," says Sala.

How did you become an explorer?
I think the first time I got in the water of the Mediterranean when I was a kid, I wanted to emulate my heroes, famous undersea explorer Jacques Cousteau and his divers on his ship, the *Calypso*. When I grew up and became a marine biologist, I led expeditions to many wild places around the world, but one only needs curiosity to become an explorer.

What was your closest call in the field?
I was once diving deep in the Mediterranean and the hose of my oxygen tank exploded. Air came out of the hose violently, making a very loud noise, and the tank was being emptied very fast. Fortunately, I was diving with a good buddy, and we were trained for such emergencies. I turned the air valve on my tank off, and we shared the air from his tank as we came back to the surface calmly and safely.

How would you suggest kids follow in your footsteps?
I urge kids to go out to nature and find out about the wonderful animals and plants that live there. There are natural wonders on every square inch of our planet! If they like nature, kids should ask their parents to take them camping, climbing, walking in the woods, or snorkeling. And if you want to be an explorer, choose what you like, study hard, and don't stop until you make it.

In 1930, a woman added PIECES OF A SEMI-SWEET CHOCOLATE CANDY BAR to her butter cookie DOUGH, making the FIRST CHOCOLATE CHIP COOKIE RECIPE.

What kind of scientist would you be?

Here are some of the types of scientists who help our world:

PHYSICAL SCIENCE
Physicists study matter and energy and how they are related.
Chemists study the composition, properties, reactions, and structure of matter.
Astronomers study stars, planets, and galaxies.

EARTH SCIENCE
Geologists specialize in the history of Earth.
Oceanographers study and explore the ocean.
Paleontologists specialize in fossils.

Meteorologists study weather and climate.
Geographers study Earth's surface.

LIFE SCIENCE
Botanists specialize in plants.
Microbiologists study microscopic forms of life.
Zoologists study animals and animal life.
Geneticists study heredity and variations in organisms.
Medical doctors diagnose, treat, and prevent injury, illness, and disease.

Science Pioneers

Isaac Newton (1642–1727)

One of the most influential scientists ever, Newton developed the three laws of motion and defined how gravity works.

Benjamin Franklin (1706–1790)

A pioneer in the study of electricity, this Founding Father of the United States was a creator of numerous inventions, including bifocal lenses, the Franklin stove (heat-circulating stove), the odometer (measures speed), and the lightning rod.

Eli Whitney (1765–1825)

This inventor created the cotton gin, which made cotton a profitable crop and helped revolutionize agriculture.

Michael Faraday (1791–1867)

With his invention of the generator in 1831, Faraday changed the use of electricity around the world.

Florence Nightingale (1820–1910)

An English nurse, writer, and statistician, Nightingale's changes to battlefield hospitals revolutionized the modern nursing field.

Alexander Graham Bell (1847–1922)

Considered the inventor of the telephone, Bell was also one of the founding members of the National Geographic Society.

Carlos Finlay (1833–1915)

Born in Cuba, this scientist and physician is best known for his pioneering work in preventing yellow fever, a deadly disease spread by mosquitoes.

Albert Einstein (1879–1955)

A German-born physicist, Einstein is best known for his theory of relativity and his most well-known equation, $E=mc^2$, which relates energy, mass, and the speed of light.

Alfred J. Gross (1918–2000)

This Toronto, Canada, native made his mark on wireless communication by inventing the first walkie-talkie, CB radio, pager, and cellular telephone. It's thanks to this man that you can text your BFF!

BACK-TO-SCHOOL SCIENTIFIC DISCOVERY

2.5 MONTHS IS THE APPROXIMATE LENGTH OF TIME IT TAKES FOR JELL-O TO RETURN TO EARTH AFTER BEING TOSSED ONTO THE CEILING.

NATURE'S SOLUTIONS

PEOPLE LIKE TO MAKE THINGS WORK BETTER, FASTER, AND CLEANER. LUCKILY, THEY CAN TURN TO NATURE FOR SOME GREAT IDEAS.

We can learn a lot from nature because it doesn't waste energy or harm the Earth. So people are studying nature to solve common problems.

LESSONS FROM LEAVES

Problem: How can we keep the outside of buildings clean?

Solution: Study how rainwater rolls off a leaf.

A lotus leaf is covered with tiny bumps, which keep the leaf clean and dry. The bumps keep rainwater from touching the leaf. They also make the drops of rain bead up into a ball of water, which rolls right off the leaf. Dust and dirt roll off, too.

Engineers studied the lotus leaf to create special paint that can clean itself! Dirt rolls off the paint just as it rolls off the leaf. Thanks to the lotus, we may soon be able to keep ice off airplane wings. We may even learn new ways to keep clothes dry.

BIRD BEAKS AND BULLET TRAINS

Problem: How can we build quieter and better trains?

Solution: Copy the shape of a bird's beak.

Kingfisher birds eat fish. Their long beaks help them dive into water and catch prey without making a splash. This gave a Japanese engineer an idea that helped make one of the fastest trains in the world.

The bullet train is fast, but when it came out of tunnels, it made a lot of noise. The engineer thought about the bird. He changed the front end of the train, giving it a pointed shape like the bird's beak. Now the train is quieter and uses less power, too!

KEEPING CLEAN Engineers used what they knew about lotus leaves to make a new type of paint.

SLEEK SHAPE The shape of a kingfisher's beak inspired the front end of this bullet train.

5 WAYS
You Use Satellites

Psst! Want in on a secret? Spaceships control our world! Well, not exactly. But much of the technology you use—TVs, telephones, email—relies on tons of satellites whizzing around Earth. Here's a look at five ways you use satellites.

1 TELEVISION If you've watched TV, then you've used a satellite. Broadcast stations send images from Earth up to satellites as radio waves. The satellite bounces those signals, which can only travel straight, back down to a satellite dish at a point on Earth closer to your house. Satellite transmission works sort of like a shot in a game of pool when you ricochet your ball off the side of the pool table at an angle that sinks it into the right pocket.

2 WEATHER News flash! A severe thunderstorm with dangerous lightning is approaching your town. How do weather forecasters know what's coming so they can warn the public? They use satellites equipped with cameras and infrared sensors to watch clouds. Computers use constantly changing satellite images to track the storm.

3 TELEPHONE As you talk back and forth with a relative overseas on a landline, you might experience a delay of a quarter second—the time it takes for your voices to be relayed by a satellite bounce.

4 EMAIL Satellites also bridge long distances over the Internet by transmitting emails. Communications satellites for phones and the Internet use a geostationary orbit. That means that a satellite's speed matches Earth's rotation exactly, keeping the satellite in the same spot above Earth.

5 GPS Driving you to a party at a friend's house, your dad turns down the wrong street. You're lost. No problem if the car has a global positioning system (GPS) receiver. GPS is a network of satellites. The receiver collects information from the satellites and plots its distance from at least three of them. It can show where you are on a digital map. Thanks to satellites, you will make it to the party on time.

HOW A BASIC CELL CALL REACHES A FRIEND

You punch in a phone number and press SEND.

Your cell (mobile) phone sends a coded message—a radio signal—to a tall cellular tower. The tower transfers the radio signal to a land-line wire, and the signal travels underground.

The underground signal reaches a switching center where a computer figures out where the call needs to go next.

Through landlines the message reaches the cell tower nearest the call's destination.

Switched back to a radio signal, the call reaches the person you dialed. Let the talking begin!

WHAT IS THE "CELL" IN CELL PHONE?

Each cellular, or mobile, tower serves a small area—about ten square miles (26 sq km). That area is called a cell. Whichever cell you are in when you make your call is the cell that picks up your data and sends it on.

IM Lingo

NEED A CHEAT SHEET FOR IM? There are so many short-cuts for instant messaging that sometimes they can be hard to remember! Check out this quick guide to IM lingo to help you keep up with your friends. **GTG! GL!** (Got to go! Good luck!)

AFK Away from keyboard
ATM At the moment
ASAP As soon as possible
B4 Before
BBS Be back soon
BC Because
BFF Best friends forever
BRB Be right back
BTW By the way
CUL8R See you later
FYI For your information
G2G Got to go
GL Good luck
GR8 Great
HAND Have a nice day
HT Hi there
HTH Hope this helps
HW Homework
IDK I don't know

IM Instant message
IMO In my opinion
IMS I am sorry
JIC Just in case
JIT Just in time
JK Just kidding
JMS Just making sure
JTLYK Just to let you know
K Okay
L8R Later
LOL Laughing out loud
NVM Never mind
NM Not much
MSG Message
NP No problem
NW No way
OIC Oh I see
OMG Oh my gosh
OTOH On the other hand

OTP On the phone
PLS Please
PPL People
QT Cutie
SRY Sorry
SYL See you later
TAFN That's all for now
TBH To be honest
THX Thanks
TIA Thanks in advance
TMI Too much information
TTYL Talk to you later
TY Thank you
WB Welcome back
WFM Works for me
WU? What's up?
YT? You there?
YTB You're the best
YW You're welcome

EMOTICONS These keyboard symbols represent faces and express your moods.

:) Smile   **:(** Sad   **;)** Wink   **:D** Big Smile   **:p** Sticking your tongue out
:-* Kiss   **:O** Gasp   **:|** Straight-faced / emotionless   **:X** Denotes something bad
:'D Laughing so hard you're crying   **:'(** Crying   **:S** Confused

5 TIPS for Staying Safe on the Internet

 Always get your parents' permission before posting messages or pictures on the Internet.

 Make sure you know who you are "chatting" with. Sometimes people pretend to be different from who they really are. And definitely do not give out personal details.

 Make sure to mind your manners. Just because you are online doesn't mean that you can be rude or mean.

 Don't reply to emails from people you don't know.

 If something makes you feel scared, uncomfortable, or confused while online, make sure you tell your parent or a trusted adult. Don't be scared to ask for help.

Common Conversions

TO CHANGE	TO	MULTIPLY BY	TO CHANGE	TO	MULTIPLY BY
acres	hectares	0.40	metric tons	tons (short)	1.10
centimeters	inches	0.39	miles	kilometers	1.61
cubic inches	milliliters	16.39	millimeters	inches	0.04
cubic feet	cubic meters	0.03	millimeters	cubic inches	0.06
cubic meters	cubic feet	35.31	millimeters	ounces (liquid)	0.03
cubic meters	cubic yards	1.31	ounces	grams	28.35
cubic yards	cubic meters	0.76	ounces (liquid)	milliliters	29.57
feet	meters	0.30	pints (dry)	liters	0.55
gallons (U.S.)	liters	3.79	pints (liquid)	liters	0.47
grams	ounces	0.04	pounds	kilograms	0.45
hectares	acres	2.47	quarts (dry)	liters	1.10
inches	millimeters	25.40	quarts (liquid)	liters	0.95
inches	centimeters	2.54	square inches	square centimeters	6.45
kilograms	pounds	2.20	square feet	square meters	0.09
kilometers	miles	0.62	square centimeters	square inches	0.16
liters	gallons	0.26	square kilometers	square miles	0.39
liters	pints (dry)	1.812	square meters	square feet	10.76
liters	pints (liquid)	2.11	square meters	square yards	1.20
liters	quarts (dry)	0.91	square miles	square kilometers	2.59
liters	quarts (liquid)	1.06	square yards	square meters	0.86
meters	feet	3.28	tons (short)	metric tons	0.91
meters	yards	1.09	yards	meters	0.91

The Periodic Table of Elements

Legend

Li : Solid
Br : Liquid
O : Gas
Sg : Unknown

Metals
- Alkali Metals
- Alkaline Earth Metals
- Lanthanoids
- Actinoids
- Transition Metals
- Poor Metals

Nonmetals
- Other Nonmetals
- Noble Gases

Main table (atomic number, symbol, name, atomic mass)

#	Symbol	Name	Atomic Mass
1	H	Hydrogen	1.00794
2	He	Helium	4.002603
3	Li	Lithium	6.941
4	Be	Beryllium	9.012182
5	B	Boron	10.811
6	C	Carbon	12.0107
7	N	Nitrogen	14.0067
8	O	Oxygen	15.9994
9	F	Fluorine	18.9984032
10	Ne	Neon	20.1797
11	NA	Sodium	22.98976928
12	Mg	Magnesium	24.3050
13	Al	Aluminium	26.9815386
14	Si	Silicon	28.0855
15	P	Phosphorus	30.973762
16	S	Sulfur	32.065
17	Cl	Chlorine	35.453
18	Ar	Argon	39.948
19	K	Potassium	39.0983
20	Ca	Calcium	40.078
21	Sc	Scandium	44.955912
22	Ti	Titanium	47.867
23	V	Vanadium	50.9415
24	Cr	Chromium	51.9961
25	Mn	Manganese	54.938045
26	Fe	Iron	55.845
27	Co	Cobalt	58.933195
28	Ni	Nickel	58.6934
29	Cu	Copper	63.546
30	Zn	Zinc	65.38
31	Ga	Gallium	69.723
32	Ge	Germanium	72.64
33	As	Arsenic	74.92160
34	Se	Selenium	78.96
35	Br	Bromine	79.904
36	Kr	Krypton	83.798
37	Rb	Rubidium	85.4678
38	Sr	Strontium	87.62
39	Y	Yttrium	88.90585
40	Zr	Zirconium	91.224
41	Nb	Niobium	92.90638
42	Mo	Molybdenum	95.96
43	Tc	Technetium	(97.9072)
44	Ru	Ruthenium	101.07
45	Rh	Rhodium	102.90550
46	Pd	Palladium	106.42
47	Ag	Silver	107.8682
48	Cd	Cadmium	112.411
49	In	Indium	114.818
50	Sn	Tin	118.710
51	Sb	Antimony	121.760
52	Te	Tellurium	127.60
53	I	Iodine	126.90447
54	Xe	Xenon	131.293
55	Cs	Caesium	132.9054519
56	Ba	Barium	137.327
72	Hf	Hafnium	178.49
73	Ta	Tantalum	180.94788
74	W	Tungsten	183.84
75	Re	Rhenium	186.207
76	Os	Osmium	190.23
77	Ir	Iridium	192.217
78	Pt	Platinum	195.084
79	Au	Gold	196.966569
80	Hg	Mercury	200.59
81	Tl	Thallium	204.3833
82	Pb	Lead	207.2
83	Bi	Bismuth	208.98040
84	Po	Polonium	(208.9824)
85	At	Astatine	(209.9871)
86	Rn	Radon	(222.0176)
87	Fr	Francium	(223)
88	Ra	Radium	(226)
104	Rf	Rutherfordium	(261)
105	Db	Dubnium	(262)
106	Sg	Seaborgium	(266)
107	Bh	Bohrium	(264)
108	Hs	Hassium	(277)
109	Mt	Meitnerium	(268)
110	Ds	Darmstadtium	(271)
111	Rg	Roentgenium	(272)
112	Uub	Ununbium	(285)
113	Uut	Ununtrium	(284)
114	Uuq	Ununquadium	(289)
115	Uup	Ununpentium	(288)
116	Uuh	Ununhexium	(292)
117	Uus	Ununseptium	(294)
118	Uuo	Ununoctium	(294)

Lanthanoids (57–71)

#	Symbol	Name	Atomic Mass
57	La	Lanthanum	138.90547
58	Ce	Cerium	140.116
59	Pr	Praseodymium	140.90765
60	Nd	Neodymium	144.242
61	Pm	Promethium	(145)
62	Sm	Samarium	150.36
63	Eu	Europium	151.25
64	Gd	Gadolinium	157.25
65	Tb	Terbium	158.92535
66	Dy	Dysprosium	162.500
67	Ho	Holmium	164.93032
68	Er	Erbium	167.259
69	Tm	Thulium	168.93421
70	Yb	Ytterbium	173.054
71	Lu	Lutetium	174.9668

Actinoids (89–103)

#	Symbol	Name	Atomic Mass
89	Ac	Actinium	(227)
90	Th	Thorium	232.03806
91	Pa	Protactinium	231.03588
92	U	Uranium	238.02891
93	Np	Neptunium	(237)
94	Pu	Plutonium	(244)
95	Am	Americium	(243)
96	Cm	Curium	(247)
97	Bk	Berkelium	(247)
98	Cf	Californium	(251)
99	Es	Einsteinium	(252)
100	Fm	Fermium	(257)
101	Md	Mendelevium	(258)
102	No	Nobelium	(259)
103	Lr	Lawrencium	(262)

Body Systems

60,000 miles (96,560 km) of blood vessels *run through* your body.

The human body is a complicated mass of systems—nine systems, to be exact. Each system has a unique and critical purpose in the body, and we wouldn't be able to survive without all of them.

The **NERVOUS** system controls the body.

The **MUSCULAR** system makes movement possible.

The **SKELETAL** system supports the body.

The **CIRCULATORY** system moves blood throughout the body.

The **RESPIRATORY** system provides the body with oxygen.

The **DIGESTIVE** system breaks down food into nutrients and gets rid of waste.

The **IMMUNE** system protects the body against disease and infection.

The **ENDOCRINE** system regulates the body's functions.

The **REPRODUCTIVE** system enables people to produce offspring.

Is it bedtime?

Most people think we yawn because we are tired. But that may not be true. We don't know for certain why we yawn, but there are many theories. Some scientists believe that we yawn when there is a change in activity. Other research has shown that we might yawn to cool off our brain by breathing in cool air. We also seem to yawn when we are bored or stressed, or even because we see someone else yawning. So you might be yawning for many reasons—not necessarily because it's time for bed.

What Being a LEFTY or a RIGHTY Says About You

RIGHTIES

Some studies show that right-handers are more talkative and outgoing than lefties. Other research has revealed that righties are more coordinated. They also tend to learn better verbally—they can listen to directions to a friend's house and understand how to get there. Right-handers also may be better pitchers and basketball guards. Just ask righty Michael Jordan!

Being right-handed or left-handed may say a lot about you. Although scientists aren't sure what causes people to favor one hand over the other (they think it has to do with brain wiring), many do believe that lefties and righties may have distinct personality traits. Here's some handy information!

IF THESE PERSONALITY PROFILES DON'T MATCH YOU, THAT'S OK. THESE ARE JUST FOR FUN!

LEFTIES

Several studies suggest that lefties are highly creative and artistic. In fact many performers—including Mary-Kate Olsen, Jim Carrey, and Paul McCartney of the Beatles—are left-handed. Lefties also seem to have an edge in tennis, fencing, and other individual sports. And they may learn better visually. For instance, if someone draws them a map, they understand exactly how to get there.

AMBIDEXTROUS

Surprise! Most scientists think that no one is truly ambidextrous, or able to use both hands equally. But if you have a dominant hand and can still write or throw accurately with the other, you're what scientists call mixed-handed. Studies show mixed-handers tend to have better memories of everyday experiences, such as what they had for lunch a week ago. Mixed-handers also may be more open-minded.

Your Amazing
eyes

Discover the magic of your body's built-in cameras.

You carry around a pair of cameras in your head so incredible they can work in bright sunshine or at night. Only about an inch (2.5 cm) in diameter, they can bring you the image of a tiny ant or a twinkling star trillions of miles away. They can change focus almost instantly and stay focused even when you're shaking your head or jumping up and down. These cameras are your eyes.

A CRUCIAL PART OF YOUR EYE IS AS FLIMSY AS A WET TISSUE.

A dragonfly darts toward your head! Light bounces off the insect, enters your eye, passes through your pupil (the black circle in the middle of your iris), and goes to the lens. The lens focuses the light onto your retina—a thin lining on the back of your eye that is vital but as flimsy as a wet tissue. Your retina acts like film in a camera, capturing the picture of this dragonfly. The picture is sent to your brain, which instantly sends you a single command—*duck!*

YOU BLINK MORE THAN 10,000 TIMES A DAY.

Your body has many ways to protect and care for your eyes. Each eye sits on a cushion of fat, almost completely surrounded by protective bone. Your eyebrows help prevent sweat from dripping into your eyes. Your eyelashes help keep dust and other small particles out. Your eyelids act as built-in windshield wipers, spreading tear fluid with every blink to keep your eyes moist and wash away bacteria and other particles. And if anything ever gets too close to your eyes, your eyelids slam shut with incredible speed—$^2/_5$ of a second—to protect them!

YOUR EYES SEE EVERYTHING UPSIDE DOWN AND BACKWARD!

As amazing as your eyes are, the images they send your brain are a little quirky: They're upside down, backward, and two-dimensional! Your brain automatically flips the images from your retinas right side up and combines the images from each eye into a three-dimensional picture. There is a small area of each retina, called a blind spot, that can't record what you're seeing. Luckily your brain makes adjustments for this, too.

YOUR PUPILS CHANGE SIZE WHENEVER THE LIGHT CHANGES.

Your black pupils may be small, but they have an important job—they grow or shrink to let just the right amount of light enter your eyes to let you see.

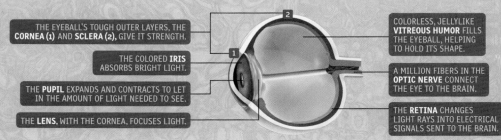

THE EYEBALL'S TOUGH OUTER LAYERS, THE **CORNEA (1)** AND **SCLERA (2)**, GIVE IT STRENGTH.

THE COLORED **IRIS** ABSORBS BRIGHT LIGHT.

THE **PUPIL** EXPANDS AND CONTRACTS TO LET IN THE AMOUNT OF LIGHT NEEDED TO SEE.

THE **LENS**, WITH THE CORNEA, FOCUSES LIGHT.

COLORLESS, JELLYLIKE **VITREOUS HUMOR** FILLS THE EYEBALL, HELPING TO HOLD ITS SHAPE.

A MILLION FIBERS IN THE **OPTIC NERVE** CONNECT THE EYE TO THE BRAIN.

THE **RETINA** CHANGES LIGHT RAYS INTO ELECTRICAL SIGNALS SENT TO THE BRAIN.

The FIVE Senses

Do you love the feel of your favorite stuffed animal or the smell and taste of your favorite food? Maybe you love to look at beautiful flowers or listen to the latest band. If you enjoy doing any of these things, then you better thank your senses, all five of them! The five senses and their related organs help you to experience the world around you. Using our sense organs, we take in information from the world. This information is then sent to our brain, which tells us how to respond. These five senses are:

TASTE
Different parts of the tongue can detect different kinds of tastes using taste buds, or receptors, on the tongue. These tastes include: sweet, sour, salty, bitter, and umami. The inability to taste is called ageusia.

1 SIGHT
The ability to see comes from the brain and the eye's capacity to detect light waves. Vision allows the eyes to detect color, light, and depth. The inability to see is called blindness.

4 HEARING
Hearing is the sense of sound perception. The inner ear detects vibrations. The inability to hear is called deafness.

2 SMELL
Sense of smell, called olfaction, is the work of the nose and the brain. When chemicals in the air enter the nose, our brain perceives a smell. The inability to smell is called anosmia.

5 TOUCH
The skin is the largest sensory organ of the body, and it is responsible for the sense of touch. The skin is sensitive to different kinds of stimuli, such as pain, pressure, and temperature. The inability to feel anything if touched is called tactile anesthesia.

weird but true

Girls have more taste buds than **boys** do.

VISION USES ONE-THIRD OF ALL YOUR BRAINPOWER.

Your Amazing brain

Inside your body's supercomputer

You carry around a three-pound (1-kg) mass of wrinkly material in your head that controls every single thing you will ever do. From enabling you to think, learn, create, and feel emotions to controlling every blink, breath, and heartbeat—this fantastic control center is your brain. It is a structure so amazing that a famous scientist once called it "the most complex thing we have yet discovered in our universe."

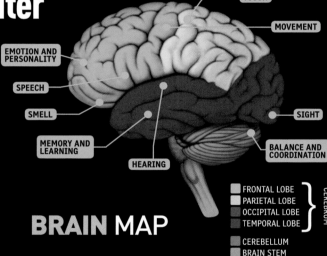

BRAIN MAP

- TOUCH
- MOVEMENT
- EMOTION AND PERSONALITY
- SPEECH
- SMELL
- MEMORY AND LEARNING
- HEARING
- SIGHT
- BALANCE AND COORDINATION

CEREBRUM
- FRONTAL LOBE
- PARIETAL LOBE
- OCCIPITAL LOBE
- TEMPORAL LOBE

- CEREBELLUM
- BRAIN STEM

THE BIG QUESTION

WHAT TAKES UP TWO-THIRDS OF YOUR BRAIN'S WEIGHT AND ALLOWS YOU TO SWIM, EAT, AND SPEAK?

The huge hunk of your brain called the cerebrum. It's definitely the biggest part of the brain. It houses the centers for memory, the senses, movement, and emotion, among other things.

The cerebrum is made up of two hemispheres—the right and the left. Each side controls the muscles of the opposite side of the body.

How to Decode Your Dreams

YOUR BRAIN MAY BE TELLING YOU SOMETHING

How many times have you told someone, "I had the craziest dream last night"? Lots of times, huh? You can have up to six dreams a night. Some of them are sure to be wild!

Dreams are created by the part of your brain that stores memories, emotions, and thoughts. At night your brain blends what's stored in your mind with what you've been thinking about lately. The result can be wild but realistic dreams.

Dreams hardly ever become reality, but they may contain hints about what's going on in your life. "Dreams help us get in touch with our deeper feelings," says dream researcher Alan Siegel. "They can tell us a lot about ourselves and may even help us figure out problems."

Scientists have discovered that many dreams contain common themes that have meaning. Here are eight types of dreams that may tell you a lot about yourself and what's happening in your life!

THE THEME Being chased

WHAT IT MEANS The scary thing that's chasing you is probably a symbol of a real-life problem you don't want to deal with. But this dream is telling you it's time to stop running from the problem, and start facing it.

THE THEME Showing up in pajamas

WHAT IT MEANS Your brain may be helping you recover from a real-life embarrassing moment. If no one's making a big deal about the pj's, chances are your friends think you're cool no matter what. If they *are* laughing? It may be time for some new friends.

THE THEME Flying

WHAT IT MEANS It's likely you're flying high in real life as well. Maybe your friends see you as a leader, or your parents have given you more freedom.

THE THEME Being lost

WHAT IT MEANS You're probably feeling a little lost in life. Are you currently facing a tough decision? You might be afraid of making the wrong choice. Think carefully about your options to find your way out of this dilemma.

THE THEME Falling

WHAT IT MEANS You might have too much going on. It's time to slow down and take a break from whatever is stressing you out. And the soft landing? A sign that you'll soon get over this tough time.

THE THEME Not being able to move

WHAT IT MEANS You're probably feeling "stuck" in life. (Maybe your parents just grounded you.) You need to think about how you got into this sticky situation and then try to make smarter choices in the future.

THE THEME Losing something

WHAT IT MEANS You may be looking for an ego boost. Perhaps you want to try out a new sport or hobby, and you're not sure if you can do it. Search deep inside yourself for that confidence. It's there—you just have to find it!

THE THEME Being unprepared or late

WHAT IT MEANS You're worrying big-time about an upcoming event or project. If you're prepared, it's just a sign that you're nervous. That's normal. But if you've been slacking, take this dream as a hint, and get to work!

ZZzz!

A dream usually lasts from 10 to 40 minutes.

Your brain waves can be more active when you're dreaming than when you're awake.

You'll spend about six years of your life dreaming.

Exercise for Health

Why should you exercise? You will ...
- be stronger.
- be less likely to be overweight.
- decrease chances of getting sick.
- feel happier.

Exercise without even knowing it!

STAY OUT OF THE CAR—Walk or bike short distances instead of riding in a car.

GET OUT THERE—Help with yard work and housework; they're great calorie burners.

STEP IT UP—Take the stairs instead of elevators or escalators.

STICK TOGETHER—Gather your family and go for a run, walk, or bike ride.

Warm Up
Spend about five minutes before exercising doing light activity, such as walking or stretching.

Exercise
Try to do about 15 to 45 minutes of exercise each day. Some great ideas for exercise include walking, running, swimming, biking, skateboarding, or group sports, such as basket-ball, soccer, baseball, volleyball, or hockey.

Cool Down
Don't hurt yourself—make sure you cool down after vigorous exercise by doing five minutes of light activity.

Eat healthy and try new foods.

COOL CLICK

To learn more about nutrition and the food pyramid, go online to this U.S. Department of Agriculture's website.
mypyramid.gov

Grains Make half your grains whole	**Vegetables** Vary your veggies	**Fruits** Focus on fruits	**Milk** Get your calcium-rich foods	**Meat & Beans** Go lean with protein

◊ **Oils** Oils are not a food group, but you need some for good health. Get your oils from fish, nuts, and liquid oils such as corn oil, soybean oil, and canola oil.

★ **Find your balance between food and fun** ★ **Fats and sugars — know your limits**

Try This! MEMORY MOBILE

YOU WILL NEED

- POSTER BOARD IN GREEN, YELLOW, BLUE, AND ORANGE (OR THE COLORS OF YOUR CHOICE)
- INDIVIDUAL PORTRAITS OF YOU, YOUR PARENTS, GRANDPARENTS, AND GREAT-GRANDPARENTS
- TWIGS (OR DOWELS) OF THESE LENGTHS: ONE 10-INCH (25-CM), ONE 16-INCH (40-CM), TWO 8-INCH (20-CM), FOUR 5-INCH (12-CM)
- STRING
- WHITE GLUE

WHAT TO DO

1. Cut squares out of the poster board in these sizes: green, one 3-inch square; yellow, two 2 ½-inch squares; blue, four 2 ½-inch squares; orange, eight 2-inch squares.

2. Ask for your parents' permission to use the photos. Use copies of all originals. Cut your photo to a 2½-inch square. Cut photos of your parents and grandparents to 2-inch squares; cut photos of your great-grandparents to 1½-inch squares. Center the photos on the correct color squares (as shown). Glue in place and let dry.

3. Poke a small hole ⅛ inch from the top and bottom of each square. (Great-grandparent squares need holes only on top.) The holes should be centered. Write each person's name and something interesting about him or her on the back of each square.

4. Lay out the twigs in rows, as shown: row one, 10-inch twig; row two, 16-inch twig; row three, both 8-inch twigs, equally spaced; row four, all 5-inch twigs, equally spaced. Leave about 4½ inches between rows.

5. Position the photo squares as shown. Your mom's family goes on the left side, and your dad's on the right. Arrange each couple with the woman on the left and the man on the right.

6. Cut 22 6-inch-long pieces of string. Thread one piece through each of the holes in the photo squares. Tie to the twigs above and below each square. Hold up the mobile and adjust the photos until it balances. Hint: Add little pieces of paper to the backs of the squares if you need to add weight to one side.

7. Cut a 2-foot-long piece of string and tie the ends to the top twig as shown, then hang.

8. You can redesign the mobile to include siblings and stepfamily. Be sure to balance the photos.

BE THE FAMILY DETECTIVE

Do you have the same nose as a family member? Do you know where your hair color or last name comes from? Asking questions about these things can turn you into an instant expert on your family. First, work with your parents to create the family tree mobile. As you hang each picture, ask questions about the people in the photos. You might discover how being close to your family can add to your happiness.

FOODERSTITIONS

Will you ace your math test? Are you getting an iPod for your birthday? The secrets to your future may lie in your food. But be sure to study for that test no matter what— these activities are just for fun.

TWIST OF FATE

Want to know who your next friend will be? Twist an apple stem, reciting one letter of the alphabet with each turn. The letter you say when the stem breaks off could be the first initial of your new friend's name.

ASK A BANANA A QUESTION

Need an answer fast? Pick up a banana, and ask it a yes-or-no question. Make one slice near the end of the banana. If the lines in the center form a Y, the answer is yes. If not, the answer is no.

ASK FOR A PARENT'S HELP BEFORE USING A KNIFE OR BOILING WATER.

TELL YOUR FORTUNE WITH TEA LEAVES

FORTUNE-TELLERS HAVE read tea leaves for hundreds of years. They believe that patterns you see in your tea leaves are symbols of what may happen in your future. Now discover what your tea could be telling you.

BREW A POT OF HOT TEA using loose tea leaves or leaves emptied from tea bags. Pour yourself a cup, then drink the tea or slowly pour out the liquid, keeping the leaves inside the cup.

WHAT PATTERN DO YOU SEE in your tea leaves? Use the chart at right to find out what some common symbols mean. If yours isn't listed here, go online for a longer list of symbols and their meanings.

tasseography.com/symbol.htm

TEA LEAF SYMBOLS

PATTERN ... MEANING	
CRESCENT MOON	GOOD LUCK
DOG	GOOD FRIEND
CAT	DISHONESTY
HOUSE	SECURITY
HEART	LOVE
KITE	A WISH THAT MAY COME TRUE

The Straight Scoop

3 TRICKS THAT WILL PUT YOU IN A GREAT MOOD

Make your own decisions.
WHY IT WORKS
You'll feel confident and in control when you make thoughtful, individual choices.
HOW TO DO IT
• Decide your family's dinner menu for a week. Go through cookbooks and select your favorite recipes.
• Redecorate your room (with permission). Make it scream "you" by choosing a theme and your favorite colors.

Chill out.
WHY IT WORKS
Relaxing can zap stress and put you in a positive mood.
HOW TO DO IT
• Turn off the TV, and pick up a book, letting the story launch you into another world.
• Do at least one quiet activity a week, such as listening to music or stargazing.

Laugh.
WHY IT WORKS
Laughter releases endorphins, chemicals in your brain that make you feel good.
HOW TO DO IT
• Tell a new joke every day. For ideas, go online.
kids.nationalgeographic.com/ Activities/JustJoking
• Make a hilarious video with your friends.

STOP! Freeze right there! Now, without moving a muscle, check out your posture. If you're like a lot of people, you are sitting sort of slumped over.

Ergonomics refers to the study of the relationship between people and their surroundings. For example, if you are slumping at the computer or are hunched over carrying a really heavy backpack, you have poor ergonomics. When you don't practice good ergonomics, that's when the pain sets in, so be sure to take good care of yourself, and follow these tips to good health.

Good Ideas for Gaming and Computer Use
• Sit up straight with your shoulders back.
• Make sure your feet are on the ground.
• Take frequent breaks; walk around and stretch.

Better Backpack Strategies
• Carry less. Buying an extra set of books to keep at home is less expensive than doctor visits.
• Tighten straps so the weight is close to your body, and don't let the backpack ride below the waist.
• Put the heaviest items closest to your back, and the pack will be less likely to pull you out of balance.
• Kids should not carry backpacks that weigh more than 10 to 15 percent of their body weight. So students weighing 100 pounds (45 kg) should not carry more than 10 to 15 pounds (5 to 7 kg) in their packs.

147

SENSATIONAL SCIENCE PROJECTS

You can learn a lot about science from books, but to really experience it firsthand, you need to get into the lab and "do" some science. Whether you're entering a science fair or just want to learn more on your own, there are many scientific projects you can do. So put on your goggles and lab coat, and start experimenting.

Most likely, the topic of the project will be up to you. So remember to choose something that is interesting to you.

THE BASIS OF ALL SCIENTIFIC INVESTIGATION AND DISCOVERY IS THE SCIENTIFIC METHOD. CONDUCT THE EXPERIMENT USING THESE STEPS:

1 Observation/Research—Ask a question or identify a problem.

2 Hypothesis—Once you've asked a question, do some thinking and come up with some possible answers.

3 Experimentation—How can you determine if your hypothesis is correct? You test it. You perform an experiment. Make sure the experiment you design will produce an answer to your question.

4 Analysis—Gather your results, and use a consistent process to carefully measure the results.

5 Conclusion—Do the results support your hypothesis?

6 Report Your Findings—Communicate your results in the form of a paper that summarizes your entire experiment.

Bonus!
Take your project one step further. Your school may have an annual science fair, but there are also local, state, regional, and national science fair competitions. Compete with other students for awards, prizes, and scholarships!

EXPERIMENT DESIGN
There are three types of experiments you can do.

A Model Kit—a display, such as an "erupting volcano" model. Simple and to the point.

The Demonstration—shows the scientific principles in action, such as a tornado in a wind tunnel.

The Investigation—the home run of science projects, and just the type of project for science fairs. This kind demonstrates proper scientific experimentation and uses the scientific method to reveal answers to questions.

SURFING THE INTERNET

ALMOST ANY AND ALL
information can be found on the Internet, whether it's used for work, study, or fun!

Be Specific
To come up with the most effective keywords, write down what you're looking for in the form of a question, and then circle the most important words in that sentence. Those are the keywords to use in your search. And for best results use words that are specific rather than general.

Research
Research on the Internet involves "looking up" information using a search engine (see list below). Type one or two keywords—words that describe what you want to know more about—and the search engine will provide a list of websites that contain information pertinent to your topic.

Trustworthy Sources
When conducting Internet research, be sure the website you use is reliable and the information it provides can be trusted. Sites produced by well-known, established organizations, companies, publications, educational institutions, or the government are your best bet.

Don't Copy
Avoid Internet plagiarism. Take careful notes and cite the websites you use to conduct research (see p. 301 for "Don't Be A Copycat").

HELPFUL AND SAFE SEARCH ENGINES FOR KIDS

Google Safe Search	squirrelnet.com/search/Google_SafeSearch.asp
Yahooligans	yahooligans.com
Superkids	super-kids.com
Ask Jeeves Kids	ajkids.com
Kids Click	kidsclick.org

COOL CLICKS

Looking for a good science fair project idea? Go online. sciencebuddies.org. Or read about a science fair success. kids.nationalgeographic.com/Stories/SpaceScience/Snowfences

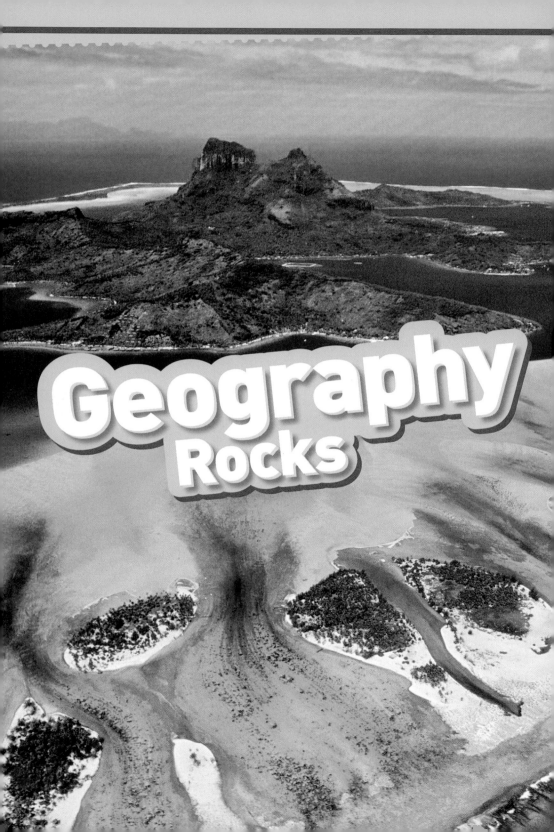

Geography
Rocks

The barrier reef around Mount Otemanu
in Bora-Bora, French Polynesia

THE POLITICAL WORLD

Earth's land area is made up of seven continents, but people have divided much of the land into smaller political units called countries. Australia is a continent with a single country, and Antarctica is set aside for scientific research. But the other five continents include almost 200 independent countries. The political map shown here depicts boundaries—imaginary lines created by treaties—that separate countries. Some boundaries, such as the one between the United States and Canada, are very stable and have been recognized for many years.

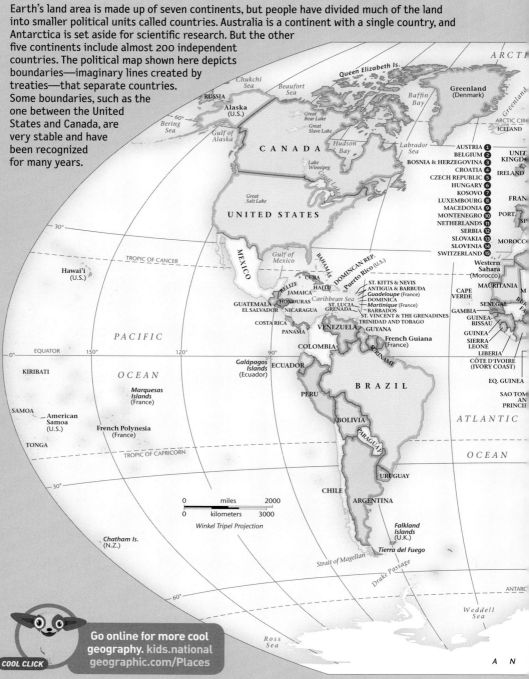

AUSTRIA ❶
BELGIUM ❷
BOSNIA & HERZEGOVINA ❸
CROATIA ❹
CZECH REPUBLIC ❺
HUNGARY ❻
KOSOVO ❼
LUXEMBOURG ❽
MACEDONIA ❾
MONTENEGRO ❿
NETHERLANDS ⓫
SERBIA ⓬
SLOVAKIA ⓭
SLOVENIA ⓮
SWITZERLAND ⓯

Winkel Tripel Projection

Go online for more cool geography. kids.national geographic.com/Places

COOL CLICK

Other boundaries, like the one between Ethiopia and Eritrea in northeast Africa, are relatively new and still disputed. Countries come in all shapes and sizes. Russia and Canada are giants; others, like Luxembourg, are small. Some countries are long and skinny—look at Chile in South America! Still other countries—like Indonesia and Japan in Asia—are made up of groups of islands. The political map is a clue to the diversity that makes Earth so fascinating.

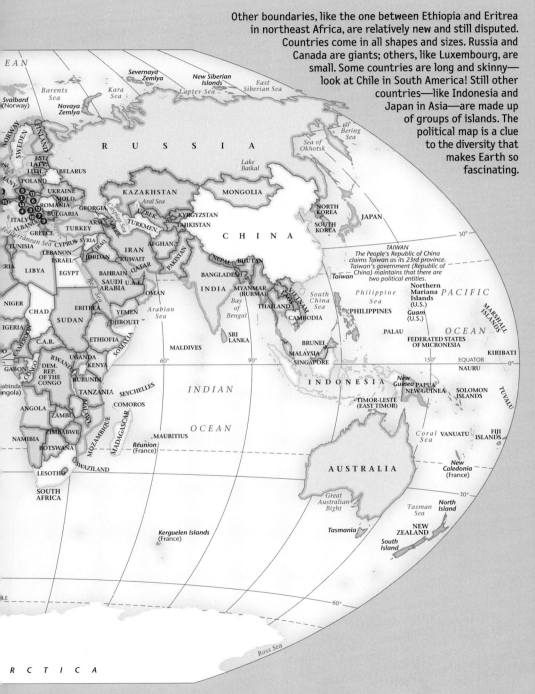

TAIWAN
The People's Republic of China claims Taiwan as its 23rd province. Taiwan's government (Republic of China) maintains that there are two political entities.

THE PHYSICAL WORLD

Earth is dominated by large landmasses called continents—seven in all—and by an interconnected global ocean that is divided into four parts by the continents. More than 70 percent of Earth's surface is covered by oceans, and the remaining 30 percent is made up of land areas.

Different landforms give variety to the surface of the continents. The Rockies and Andes mark the western edge of the Americas, and the Himalaya mountains tower above southern Asia. The Plateau of Tibet forms the rugged core of

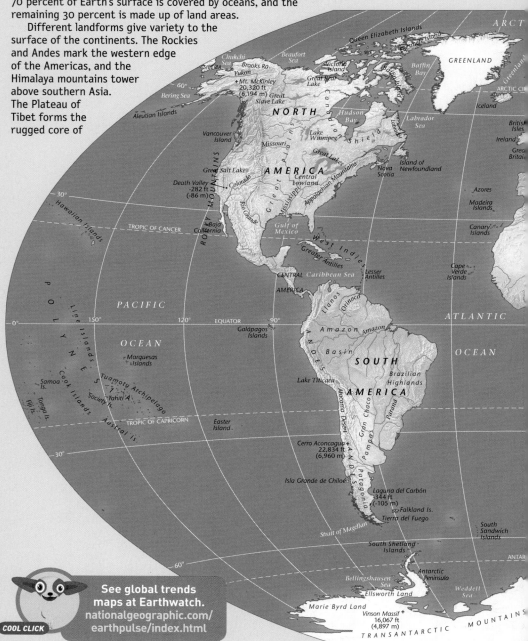

See global trends maps at Earthwatch.
nationalgeographic.com/
earthpulse/index.html

COOL CLICK

Asia, while the Northern European Plain extends from the North Sea to the Ural Mountains. Much of Africa is a plateau, and dry plains cover large areas of Australia. Beneath massive ice sheets, mountains rise more than 16,000 feet (4,877 m) in Antarctica. Mountains and trenches make the ocean floors as varied as any continent. A chain called the Mid-Atlantic Ridge runs the length of the Atlantic Ocean. In the western Pacific, trenches drop deep into the ocean floor.

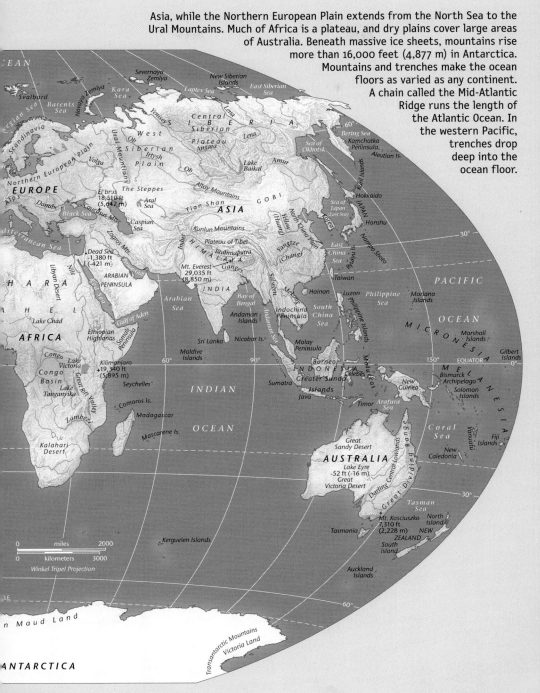

155

KINDS OF MAPS

Maps are special tools that geographers use to tell a story about Earth. Maps can be used to show just about anything related to places. Some maps show physical features, such as mountains or vegetation. Maps can also show climates or natural hazards and other things we cannot easily see. Other maps illustrate different features on Earth—political boundaries, urban centers, and economic systems.

AN IMPERFECT TOOL

Maps are not perfect. A globe is a scale model of Earth with accurate relative sizes and locations. Because maps are flat, they involve distortions of size, shape, and direction. Also, cartographers—people who create maps—make choices about what information to include. By studying different types of maps you can learn different thematic information about the Earth. Three commonly found kinds of maps are shown on this page.

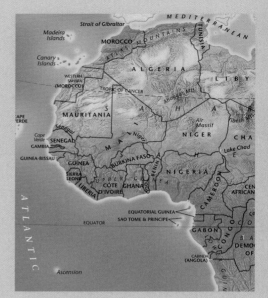

PHYSICAL MAPS. Earth's natural features—landforms, water bodies, and vegetation—are shown on physical maps. The map above uses color and shading to illustrate mountains, lakes, rivers, and deserts of western Africa. Country names and borders are added for reference, but they are not natural features.

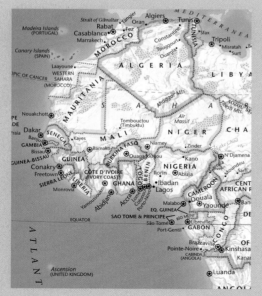

POLITICAL MAPS. These maps represent characteristics of the landscape created by humans, such as boundaries, cities, and place names. Natural features are added only for reference. On the map above, capital cities are represented with a star inside a circle, while other cities are shown with black dots.

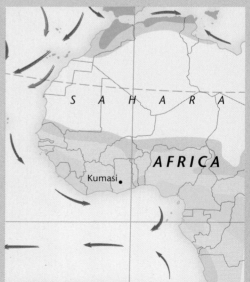

THEMATIC MAPS. Patterns related to a particular topic, or theme, such as population distribution, appear on these maps. The map above displays the region's climate zones, which range from tropical wet (bright green) to tropical wet and dry (light green) to semiarid (dark yellow) to arid or desert (light yellow).

KINDS OF PHYSICAL FEATURES

The world is full of a wondrous selection of natural physical features. If you take a look around, you'll be amazed by the beauty of our world. From roaring rivers to parched deserts, from underwater canyons to jagged mountains, Earth is covered with beautiful and diverse environments.

Here are some examples of the most common types of geographic features found around the world.

RIVER

As a river moves through flatlands, it twists and turns. The Rio Los Amigos (above) winds through a rain forest in Peru.

CANYON

Steep-sided valleys called canyons are created mainly by running water. Buckskin Gulch (above) is the deepest slot canyon in the American Southwest.

DESERT

Deserts are land features created by climate, specifically by a lack of water. A camel caravan (above) crosses the Sahara, in northern Africa.

OASIS

Occasionally water rises from deep below a desert, creating a refuge that supports trees and sometimes crops, as in this oasis in Africa.

MOUNTAIN

Mountains are Earth's tallest landforms, and Mount Everest (above) rises highest of all, at 29,035 feet (8,850 m) above sea level.

GLACIER

Glaciers—"rivers" of ice— such as Alaska's Hubbard Glacier (above) move slowly from mountains to the sea.

VALLEY

Valleys, cut by running water or moving ice, may be broad and flat or narrow and steep, such as the Indus River Valley in Ladakh, India (above).

WATERFALL

Waterfalls form when a river reaches an abrupt change in elevation. Kaitur Falls (above), in Guyana, descends 800 feet (244 m).

A GREEN MAP

Check out green action around the globe.

Maps can show all sorts of information. This thematic map shows how protecting the planet is a concern all around the world—it's a global issue. Everyone needs to pitch in, no matter where they live. Take a look at what's happening around the world in the mission to save Earth.

ALASKA
(U.S.)

CANADA

NORTH
AMERICA

UNITED STATES

New
York
City

HAWAI'I
(U.S.)

SOUTH
AMERICA

BRAZIL

ARGENTINA

ANTARCTICA

CANADA

Look for the logo: Canada has had a certification program for "green" products in place for more than 22 years, and now parents can buy "green" products for their kids by looking for the EcoLogo.

UNITED STATES

As of 2009, 200 miles (322 km) of bicycle lanes were available in New York City.

BRAZIL & ARGENTINA

Many cars and trucks in Brazil and Argentina run on biodiesel fuel—an eco-friendly blend of diesel fuel and alcohols made from plants, such as algae or sugarcane (below).

IRELAND

In Ireland shoppers must pay an extra 33 cents for each plastic shopping bag they take home.

GERMANY

Germany produces more electricity from wind power than any other European country. Unlike coal or oil, wind power is clean and renewable.

CHINA

One day a week residents of Beijing, China, are encouraged not to drive, and everyone walks, bicycles, or rides public transportation.

JAPAN

Many office buildings in Japan are no cooler than 82.4°F (28°C) in the summer. To keep comfy, employees are encouraged to trade in their suits for short sleeves.

PAKISTAN

Pakistan is beginning to provide some citizens with energy produced by wind.

PHILIPPINES

More than a fourth of the electricity in the Philippines is from clean, renewable geothermal energy, which comes from heat beneath Earth's surface.

ASIA

EUROPE

RELAND

GERMANY

Beijing

JAPAN

CHINA

PAKISTAN

AFRICA

KENYA

PHILIPPINES

MALAYSIA

AUSTRALIA

MALAYSIA

Many Malaysians will be required to use rainwater for things such as watering plants and flushing toilets. Treated water is saved for drinking and cooking.

KENYA

In Kenya, a woman named Wangari Maathai started a project that has planted more than 40 million trees so far.

AUSTRALIA

Incandescent lightbulbs have been banned in Australia as of 2010. Residents are replacing them with energy-efficient compact fluorescent bulbs (right).

AFRICA

PHYSICAL

Land area
11,608,000 sq mi
(30,065,000 sq km)

Highest point
Kilimanjaro,
Tanzania
19,340 ft
(5,895 m)

Lowest point
Lake Assal,
Djibouti
-512 ft (-156 m)

Longest river
Nile
4,241 mi (6,825 km)

Largest lake
Victoria
26,800 sq mi
(69,500 sq km)

POLITICAL

Population
998,705,000

Largest country
Sudan
967,500 sq mi
(2,505,813 sq km)

**Largest
metropolitan area**
Cairo, Egypt
Pop. 11,893,000

**Most densely
populated country**
Mauritius
1,619 people per sq mi
(625 per sq km)

Economy
Farming: fruit, grains
Industry: chemicals,
   mining, cement
Services

Maasai women
in native costume

The massive continent of Africa, where humankind is believed to have begun millions of years ago, is second only to Asia in size. The 53 independent countries of Africa are home to a wide variety of cultures and traditions. In many areas traditional tribal life is still very common, such as with the Maasai people.

From Arabic and Nubian, to Zulu and Sandawe, this vast continent also has a wealth of languages—some 1,600—more than any other continent.

Although rich in natural resources, from oil to coal to gemstones and precious metals, Africa is the poorest continent, long plagued by outside interference, corruption, and disease.

Africa spans nearly as far from west to east as it does from north to south. The Sahara—the world's largest desert—covers Africa's northern third, while to the south lie bands of grassland, tropical rain forest, and more desert. The rain forests of Africa are home to half of the continent's animal species. Wild creatures, such as lions, roam sub-Saharan Africa, and water-loving hippos live near the great lakes of this large continent.

The first great civilization in Africa arose 6,000 years ago on the banks of the lower Nile. Today, though still largely rural, Africans increasingly migrate to booming cities such as Cairo, Egypt; Lagos, Nigeria; and Johannesburg, South Africa.

MORE THAN 12,000 SQUARE MILES (31,080 SQ KM)	SURFACE AREA OF THE CENTRAL AFRICAN FRESHWATER LAKE, LAKE TANGANYIKA
3,475,000 SQUARE MILES (9,000,209 SQ KM)	AREA OF THE SAHARA, LARGEST HOT DESERT ON EARTH
14.7	PERCENT OF THE WORLD'S POPULATION THAT LIVES IN AFRICA

FEMALE LIONS HUNT MORE THAN MALES • A MALE'S BIG MANE INTIMIDATES

7 COOL THINGS ABOUT AFRICA

1. Africa could hold the land occupied by China, Europe, and the United States—with room to spare!

2. The Great Pyramid of Khufu in Egypt was the world's tallest man-made structure for more than 4,400 years and is still standing.

3. South Africa is the world's largest producer of platinum.

4. The venomous gaboon viper of Central Africa can have fangs that reach two inches (5 cm) long, the longest of any snake.

5. Africa has more countries than any other continent.

6. Almost half of the population of Africa is under the age of 15.

7. Africa is almost an island. Its only connection to other land is the tiny Sinai Peninsula in Egypt.

female lion

THER MALES • LION CUBS DEPEND ON ADULTS FOR FOOD FOR 16 MONTHS

ANTARC

PHYSICAL

Land area
5,100,000 sq mi
(13,209,000 sq km)

Highest point
Vinson Massif
16,067 ft (4,897 m)

Lowest point
Bentley Subglacial
Trench
-8,383 ft (-2,555 m)

Coldest place
Plateau Station, annual
average temperature
-70°F (-56.7°C)

**Average precipitation
on the polar plateau**
Less than 2 in (5 cm)
a year

POLITICAL

Population
There are no indig-
enous inhabitants,
but there are both
permanent and
summer-only staffed
research stations.

**Number of
independent countries**
0

**Number of countries
claiming land**
7

**Number of countries
operating year-round
research stations**
19

**Number of year-round
research stations**
45

This frozen continent may be an interesting place to see, but unless you're a penguin, you probably wouldn't want to hang out in Antarctica for long. The fact that it's the coldest, windiest, and driest continent helps explain why humans never colonized this ice-covered land surrounding the South Pole.

No country actually owns Antarctica. Dozens of countries work together to study and care for its barren landscape. Photographers and tourists visit. Scientists live there temporarily to study such things as weather, environment, and wildlife.

Visitors can observe several species of penguins that breed in Antarctica, including the Emperor penguin. Antarctica's shores also serve as breeding grounds for six kinds of seals. And the surrounding waters provide food for whales.

People and animals share Antarctica. But there are still places on this vast, icy continent that have yet to be explored.

2 PERCENT — AMOUNT OF ANTARCTICA THAT IS ICE-FREE

3 MILES (4.8 KM) — DEPTH OF THICKEST ICE COVERING THE CONTINENT

OVER 25,000 — AVERAGE NUMBER OF TOURISTS WHO VISIT ANTARCTICA ANNUALLY

emperor penguins
with chicks

EMPEROR PENGUINS ARE THE LARGEST PENGUIN SPECIES • A

TICA

7 COOL THINGS ABOUT ANTARCTICA

1. Summer in Antarctica lasts from November until February.

2. For nine months of the year, intense cold makes it too dangerous for planes to fly.

3. All water at the South Pole is melted ice, some of the purest and coldest water on Earth.

4. The largest land animal in Antarctica is a wingless insect (penguins are marine animals).

5. Roald Amundsen and his team were the first people to reach the South Pole, in 1911.

6. Antarctica is often called the "white continent" because it's ice-covered.

7. The continent was discovered in 1820 by a Russian expedition, but it took nearly 100 years before scientific exploration took off.

PEROR PENGUIN CAN HOLD ITS BREATH FOR UP TO 20 MINUTES

ASIA

the bustling commercial district of Shinjuku, Tokyo, Japan

PHYSICAL

Land area
17,208,000 sq mi
(44,570,000 sq km)

Highest point
Mount Everest,
China-Nepal
29,035 ft (8,850 m)

Lowest point
Dead Sea, Israel-
Jordan
-1,365 ft (-416 m)

Longest river
Yangtze (Chang), China
3,964 mi (6,380 km)

**Largest lake entirely
in Asia**
Lake Baikal
12,200 sq mi
(31,500 sq km)

POLITICAL

Population
4,117,435,000

**Largest metropolitan
area**
Tokyo, Japan
Pop. 35,676,000

**Largest country
entirely in Asia**
China 3,705,405 sq mi
(9,596,960 sq km)

**Most densely
populated country**
Singapore
19,389 people
per sq mi
(7,486 per sq km)

Economy
Farming: rice, wheat
Industry: petroleum,
  electronics
Services

A TYPICAL PANDA SPENDS 12 HOURS EACH DAY EATING

7 COOL THINGS ABOUT ASIA

1. Asia is home to many endangered species, including the giant panda, the Sumatran rhino, and the orangutan.

2. Dragons are considered good luck in China.

3. Legend has it that the Hanging Gardens of Babylon, one of the Seven Wonders of the Ancient World (see p. 217), was planted on an artificial mountain, but many experts say it never really existed.

4. Popular pizza toppings in Japan include seaweed and octopus.

5. Nepal's flag is the only national flag in the world that is not rectangular in shape.

6. Jerusalem, in Israel, has holy sites related to Islam, Christianity, and Judaism.

7. Tae kwon do originated about 2,000 years ago in Korea, which is now North and South Korea.

From Turkey to the eastern tip of Russia, Asia sprawls across nearly 180 degrees of longitude—almost half the globe! It boasts the highest (Mount Everest) and the lowest (the Dead Sea) places on Earth's surface.

Home to more than 40 countries, Asia is the world's largest continent. Then there are Asia's people—more than four billion of them. Three out of five people on the planet are found here—that's more than live on all the other continents combined. Asia has both the most farmers and the most million-plus cities, including Tokyo, Japan; Jakarta, Indonesia; and Seoul, South Korea. Contemporary, commercial, and sacred cities cover the vast lands of Asia.

The world's first civilization arose in Sumer, in what is now Iraq. Rich cultures also emerged along rivers in present-day India and China, strongly influencing the world ever since. Asia is also home to a large number of religions, and languages, such as Turkish, Persian, Mongolian, Indonesian, and Nepali.

As the economy of Asia continues to grow rapidly, so does its cultural influence.

giant panda

Buddhist prayer flags in Tibet, China

ONE-THIRD	PORTION OF THE WORLD'S POPULATION THAT LIVES IN CHINA AND INDIA
1,500	NUMBER OF SPECIES OF PLANTS AND ANIMALS THAT LIVE IN LAKE BAIKAL IN RUSSIA
8.6	PERCENT OF EARTH'S TOTAL SURFACE AREA THAT ASIA COVERS

HERE ARE ONLY 1,000 TO 2,000 PANDAS LEFT IN THE WILD

AUSTRA
NEW ZEALAND, AN

PHYSICAL

Land area
3,278,000 sq mi
(8,490,000 sq km)

Highest point
Mount Wilhelm,
Papua New Guinea
14,793 ft (4,509 m)

Lowest point
Lake Eyre, Australia
-52 ft (-16 m)

Longest river
Murray-Darling,
Australia 2,310 mi
(3,718 km)

Largest lake
Lake Eyre, Australia
3,430 sq mi
(8,884 sq km)

POLITICAL

Population
35,845,000

**Largest metropolitan
area**
Sydney, Australia
Pop. 4,327,000

Largest country
Australia
2,969,906 sq mi
(7,692,024 sq km)

**Most densely populated
country**
Nauru
1,204 people per sq mi
(465 per sq km)

Economy
Farming: livestock,
   wheat, fruit
Industry: mining, wool,
   oil
Services

This vast region includes Australia—the world's smallest and flattest continent—New Zealand, and a fleet of mostly tiny islands scattered across the Pacific Ocean. Apart from Australia, New Zealand, and Papua New Guinea, Oceania's other 11 independent countries cover about 25,000 square miles (65,000 sq km), an area only slightly larger than half of New Zealand's North Island. Twenty-one other island groups are dependencies of the United States, France, Australia, New Zealand, or the United Kingdom.

Aborigine in
ceremonial makeup

   Although heavily influenced by Anglo-Western culture, Australia has a strong indigenous population of Aborigines. "Aussies," as Australians like to call themselves, nicknamed their continent "the land down under." That's because the entire continent lies south of, or "under," the Equator. Most Australians live in cities along the coast. But Australia also has huge cattle and sheep ranches. Many ranch children live far from school. They get their lessons by mail or over the Internet or radio. Their doctors even visit by airplane!

Bay of Islands,
North Island, New Zealand

SOMETIMES CALLED KOALA BEARS, KOALAS ARE MARSUPIALS N

IA,
OCEANIA

a young koala

7 COOL THINGS ABOUT AUSTRALIA, NEW ZEALAND, AND OCEANIA

1. The entire continent of Australia is three times larger than the largest island (Greenland) in the world.

2. A kiwi is not just a fruit, it's a bird native to New Zealand and a slang term for a New Zealander.

3. Tonga, a country in the South Pacific, has 170 islands, but only 36 are inhabited.

4. Sheep outnumber people in Australia and New Zealand.

5. The vast interior of Australia, called the outback, consists mainly of desert plains.

6. Off the coast of Australia, the Great Barrier Reef is the longest coral reef system in the world.

7. The light from thousands of glowworms makes the ceilings in the grottoes of New Zealand's Waitomo Caves look like starry night skies.

50,000 TO 60,000 YEARS OLD	AGE OF THE FIRST ABORIGINAL CULTURES IN AUSTRALIA
54	SPECIES OF KANGAROOS
MORE THAN 20,000 MILES (32,187 KM)	LENGTH OF AUSTRALIAN COASTLINE

EARS • KOALAS FEED ON EUCALYPTUS TREES, MAINLY AT NIGHT

EUROPE

PHYSICAL

Land area
3,841,000 sq mi
(9,947,000 sq km)

Highest point
El'brus, Russia
18,510 ft (5,642 m)

Lowest point
Caspian Sea
-92 ft (-28 m)

Longest river
Volga, Russia
2,290 mi
(3,685 km)

**Largest lake
entirely in Europe**
Ladoga, Russia
6,835 sq mi
(17,703 sq km)

POLITICAL

Population
737,725,000

**Largest metropolitan
area**
Moscow, Russia
Pop. 10,452,000

**Largest country
entirely in Europe**
Ukraine
233,090 sq mi
(603,700 sq km)

**Most densely
populated country**
Monaco
48,231 people per sq mi
(18,622 per sq km)

Economy
Farming: vegetables,
fruit, grains
Industry: chemicals,
machinery
Services

A cluster of islands and peninsulas jutting west from Asia, Europe is bordered by the Atlantic and Arctic Oceans and more than a dozen seas, which are linked to inland areas by canals and navigable rivers such as the Rhine and the Danube. The continent boasts a bounty of landscapes. Sweeping west from the Ural Mountains in Russia and Kazakhstan is the fertile Northern European Plain. Rugged uplands form part of the western coast. The Alps shield Mediterranean lands from frigid northern winds.

Geographically small, Europe is home to more than 700 million people in almost 50 countries, representing a mosaic of cultures, languages, and borders. Some of the most widely spoken languages in Europe include German, French, Italian, Spanish, Polish, Russian, and Dutch.

Europe's colonial powers built vast empires, while its inventors and thinkers revolutionized world industry, economy, and politics.

In the 21st century, Europe seeks to create peace and prosperity—built on freedom and diversity—that embraces all of its countries. Today, the 27-member European Union faces the sometimes difficult challenge of working together.

Neuchwanstein Castle in the Bavaria region of Germany

reindeer herder from the indigenous Sami culture of Northern Europe

143,200 SQUARE MILES (370,886 SQ KM) — AREA OF CASPIAN SEA, LARGEST LAKE ON EARTH

5,354 FEET (1,632 M) — DEPTH OF THE DEEPEST CAVE IN EUROPE, AUSTRIA'S LAMPRECHTSOFEN-VOGELSCHACHT

798 — PEOPLE LIVING IN VATICAN CITY, THE SMALLEST COUNTRY IN THE WORLD

Eiffel Tower in Paris, France

7 COOL THINGS ABOUT EUROPE

1. Europe is home to about 25 percent of the world's total population.

2. The first circus was held in Rome, Italy.

3. More chocolate is consumed in Switzerland than anywhere else in the world—22 pounds (10 kg) of chocolate per person each year.

4. The first subway in the world opened in 1863 in London, England, in the United Kingdom.

5. France produces more than 360 kinds of cheese.

6. The first jet plane was flown in Germany.

7. About 85 percent of homes in Iceland are warmed using underground heat from geo-thermal hot springs.

,828 KM) A YEAR • REPORTS OF "FLYING REINDEER" DATE TO A.D. 1052

NORTH AMERICA

PHYSICAL

Land area
9,449,000 sq mi
(24,474,000 sq km)

Highest point
Mount McKinley
(Denali), Alaska
20,320 ft (6,194 m)

Lowest point
Death Valley,
California
-282 ft (-86 m)

Longest river
Mississippi-Missouri,
United States
3,710 mi (5,971 km)

Largest lake
Lake Superior, U.S.-
Canada; 31,700 sq mi
(82,100 sq km)

POLITICAL

Population
534,232,000

**Largest metropolitan
area**
New York,
United States
Pop. 19,541,453

Largest country
Canada 3,855,101 sq mi
(9,984,670 sq km)

**Most densely
populated country**
Barbados
1,691 people
per sq mi
(653 per sq km)

Economy
Farming: cattle,
    grains, cotton,
    sugar
Industry: machinery,
    metals, mining
Services

From the Great Plains of the United States and Canada to the rain forest of Panama, the third-largest continent stretches 5,500 miles (8,850 km), spanning natural environments that support wildlife from polar bears to jaguars.

North America can be divided into four large regions: the Great Plains, the mountainous west, the Canadian Shield of the northeast, and the eastern region.

Before Columbus even "discovered" the New World, it was a land of abundance for its inhabitants. Cooler, less seasonal, and more thickly forested than today, it contained a wide variety of species. Living off the land, Native Americans spread across these varied landscapes. Although some native groups remain, the majority of North Americans today are actually descendants of immigrants.

North America is home to many large industrialized cities, including two of the largest metropolitan areas in the world: Mexico City, Mexico, and New York City, New York, U.S.A.

While abundant resources and fast-changing technologies have brought prosperity to Canada and the United States, other North American countries wrestle with the most basic needs. Promise and problems abound across this contrasting realm of 23 countries and more than 530 million people.

Native American in ceremonial dress

2 BILLION YEARS	AGE OF THE GRAND CANYON'S OLDEST ROCKS
9 MILLION	APPROXIMATE NUMBER OF CANADIANS WHO SPEAK FRENCH
-87°F (-66°C)	COLDEST TEMPERATURE RECORDED IN NORTH AMERICA (IN GREENLAND)

SOLITARY ANIMALS, BLACK BEARS ROAM LARGE TERRITORIE

black bear

7 COOL THINGS ABOUT NORTH AMERICA

1. Mexico is the most populous Spanish-speaking country in the world.

2. Greenland is the largest island in the world (excluding Australia).

3. The beaver is a national symbol of Canada.

4. The United States grows nearly all of the world's popcorn.

5. About 35 species of sharks live off the coast of Cuba.

6. According to the Happy Planet Index, Costa Rica is rated as the "greenest" and happiest country in the world.

7. An Aztec emperor in what is now Mexico introduced hot chocolate to Europeans.

CN Tower in Toronto, Ontario, Canada

THEY SPEND THE WINTER HIBERNATING IN THEIR DENS

SOUTH AMERICA

PHYSICAL

Land area
6,880,000 sq mi
(17,819,000 sq km)

Highest point
Cerro Aconcagua,
Argentina
22,834 ft (6,960 m)

Lowest point
Laguna del Carbón,
Argentina
-344 ft (-105 m)

Longest river
Amazon
4,000 mi (6,437 km)

Largest lake
Lake Titicaca, Bolivia-
Peru; 3,200 sq mi
(8,290 sq km)

POLITICAL

Population
386,030,000

**Largest metropolitan
area**
São Paulo, Brazil
Pop. 18,845,000

Largest country
Brazil
3,300,171 sq mi
(8,547,403 sq km)

**Most densely
populated country**
Ecuador
124 people per sq mi
(48 per sq km)

Economy
Farming: cattle,
   coffee, fruit
Industry: mining, oil,
   manufacturing
Services

A golden lion tamarin
dad holds a tasty locust.

3	NUMBER OF SOUTH AMERICAN COUN-TRIES THE EQUATOR RUNS THROUGH (ECUADOR, COLOMBIA, AND BRAZIL)
2 MILLION SQUARE MILES (5.2 MILLION SQ KM)	SIZE OF THE AMAZON RAIN FOREST
3,212 FEET (979 M)	HEIGHT OF VENEZUELA'S ANGEL FALLS, THE WORLD'S TALLEST WATERFALL

GOLDEN LION TAMARIN MOMS USUALLY GIVE BIRTH TO TWINS

The twelve countries of South America stretch from the warm waters of the Caribbean to the frigid ocean around Antarctica. Draining a third of the continent, the mighty Amazon carries more water than the world's next ten biggest rivers combined. Its basin contains the planet's largest rain forest. The Andes tower along the continent's western edge from Colombia to southern Chile.

The gold-seeking Spaniards conquered the Amerindians when they arrived in 1532. Along with the Portuguese, they ruled most of the continent for almost 300 years. The conquest of South America by Europeans took a heavy toll on its indigenous peoples.

Centuries of ethnic blending have woven Amerindian, European, African, and Asian heritage into South America's rich cultural fabric. The continent's mix of colonial and indigenous languages demonstrates this unique blend.

Despite its relatively small population and wealth of natural resources, South America today is burdened by economic, social, and environmental problems. But with the majestic Andean mountain chain, the mighty Amazon River, and the most extensive rain forest on Earth, South America has nearly unlimited potential.

South America's most popular sport is football, called soccer in the United States.

Machu Picchu, Peru—a mountaintop city built by an Inca ruler

7 COOL THINGS ABOUT SOUTH AMERICA

1. One-fifth of the world's birds come from the Amazon rain forest—more than 1,200 different species.

2. Marine iguanas are found only in Ecuador's Galápagos Islands.

3. The world's largest soccer stadium, which seats 200,000 people, is in Rio de Janeiro, Brazil.

4. Pink dolphins live in the Amazon River.

5. South America's beautiful Iguazú Falls are the result of a volcanic eruption.

6. The guinea pig was first domesticated in South America.

7. Many of the most important dinosaur fossils have been found in South America.

GOLDEN LION TAMARINS ARE KNOWN FOR THEIR LONG FINGERS.

COUNTRIES OF THE WORLD

The following pages present a general overview of all 194 independent countries recognized by the National Geographic Society, including the newest nation, Kosovo, which gained independence in 2008.

Flags of each independent country symbolize diverse cultures and histories. The statistical data provide highlights of geography and demography. They are a brief overview of each country. They present general characteristics and are not intended to be comprehensive. For example, not every language spoken in a specific country can be listed. Thus, languages shown are the most representative of that area. This is also true of the religions mentioned.

A country is defined as a political body with its own independent government, geographical space, and, in most cases, laws, military, and taxes.

Disputed areas such as Northern Cyprus and Taiwan, and dependencies of independent nations, such as Bermuda and Puerto Rico, are not included in this listing.

Note the color key at the bottom of the pages and the locator map below, which assign a color to each country based on the continent on which it is located. All information is based on 2007 to 2009 data—the most recent information available at press time.

Color Key by Continent

Afghanistan

Area: 251,773 sq mi (652,090 sq km)
Population: 28,396,000
Capital: Kabul, pop. 3,324,000
Currency: afghani
Religions: Sunni Muslim, Shiite Muslim
Languages: Afghan Persian (Dari), Pashtu, Turkic languages (primarily Uzbek and Turkmen), Baluchi, 30 minor languages (including Pashai)

Andorra

Area: 181 sq mi (468 sq km)
Population: 86,000
Capital: Andorra la Vella, pop. 24,000
Currency: euro
Religion: Roman Catholic
Languages: Catalan, French, Castilian, Portuguese

Albania

Area: 11,100 sq mi (28,748 sq km)
Population: 3,196,000
Capital: Tirana, pop. 406,000
Currency: lek
Religions: Muslim, Albanian Orthodox, Roman Catholic
Languages: Albanian, Greek, Vlach, Romani, Slavic dialects

Angola

Area: 481,354 sq mi (1,246,700 sq km)
Population: 17,074,000
Capital: Luanda, pop. 4,007,000
Currency: kwanza
Religions: indigenous beliefs, Roman Catholic, Protestant
Languages: Portuguese, Bantu, and other African languages

Algeria

Area: 919,595 sq mi (2,381,741 sq km)
Population: 35,370,000
Capital: Algiers, pop. 3,355,000
Currency: Algerian dinar
Religion: Sunni Muslim
Languages: Arabic, French, Berber dialects

Antigua and Barbuda

Area: 171 sq mi (442 sq km)
Population: 88,000
Capital: St. John's, pop. 26,000
Currency: East Caribbean dollar
Religions: Anglican, Seventh-day Adventist, Pentecostal, Moravian, Roman Catholic, Methodist, Baptist, Church of God, other Christian
Languages: English, local dialects

Argentina

Area: 1,073,518 sq mi
(2,780,400 sq km)
Population: 40,276,000
Capital: Buenos Aires,
pop. 12,795,000
Currency: Argentine peso
Religion: Roman Catholic
Languages: Spanish, English, Italian, German, French

Armenia

Area: 11,484 sq mi
(29,743 sq km)
Population: 3,097,000
Capital: Yerevan, pop. 1,102,000
Currency: dram
Religions: Armenian Apostolic, other Christian
Language: Armenian

Australia

Area: 2,969,906 sq mi
(7,692,024 sq km)
Population: 21,852,000
Capital: Canberra, pop. 378,000
Currency: Australian dollar
Religions: Roman Catholic, Anglican
Language: English

Austria

Area: 32,378 sq mi (83,858 sq km)
Population: 8,374,000
Capital: Vienna, pop. 2,315,000
Currency: euro
Religions: Roman Catholic, Protestant, Muslim
Language: German

Azerbaijan

Area: 33,436 sq mi
(86,600 sq km)
Population: 8,781,000
Capital: Baku, pop. 1,892,000
Currency: Azerbaijani manat
Religion: Muslim
Language: Azerbaijani (Azeri)

Bahamas

Area: 5,382 sq mi (13,939 sq km)
Population: 341,000
Capital: Nassau, pop. 240,000
Currency: Bahamian dollar
Religions: Baptist, Anglican, Roman Catholic,
Pentecostal, Church of God
Languages: English, Creole

Bahrain

Area: 277 sq mi (717 sq km)
Population: 1,217,000
Capital: Manama, pop. 157,000
Currency: Bahraini dinar
Religions: Shiite Muslim, Sunni Muslim, Christian
Languages: Arabic, English, Farsi, Urdu

Bangladesh

Area: 56,977 sq mi (147,570 sq km)
Population: 162,221,000
Capital: Dhaka, pop. 13,485,000
Currency: taka
Religions: Muslim, Hindu
Languages: Bangla (Bengali), English

Barbados

Area: 166 sq mi (430 sq km)
Population: 281,000
Capital: Bridgetown, pop. 116,000
Currency: Barbadian dollar
Religions: Anglican, Pentecostal, Methodist, other
Protestant, Roman Catholic
Language: English

Belarus

Area: 80,153 sq mi
(207,595 sq km)
Population: 9,662,000
Capital: Minsk, pop. 1,806,000
Currency: Belarusian ruble
Religions: Eastern Orthodox, other (includes Roman
Catholic, Protestant, Jewish, Muslim)
Languages: Belarusian, Russian

● Asia ● Europe ● North America ● South America

Belgium

Area: 11,787 sq mi (30,528 sq km)
Population: 10,792,000
Capital: Brussels, pop. 1,743,000
Currency: euro
Religions: Roman Catholic, other (includes Protestant)
Languages: Dutch, French

Belize

Area: 8,867 sq mi (22,965 sq km)
Population: 329,000
Capital: Belmopan, pop. 16,000
Currency: Belizean dollar
Religions: Roman Catholic, Protestant (includes Pentecostal, Seventh-day Adventist, Mennonite, Methodist)
Languages: Spanish, Creole, Mayan dialects, English, Garifuna (Carib), German

Benin

Area: 43,484 sq mi (112,622 sq km)
Population: 8,935,000
Capitals: Porto-Novo, pop. 257,000; Cotonou, pop. 762,000
Currency: Communauté Financière Africaine franc
Religions: Christian, Muslim, Vodoun
Languages: French, Fon, Yoruba, tribal languages

Bhutan

Area: 17,954 sq mi (46,500 sq km)
Population: 683,000
Capital: Thimphu, pop. 83,000
Currencies: ngultrum; Indian rupee
Religions: Lamaistic Buddhist, Indian- and Nepalese-influenced Hindu
Languages: Dzongkha, Tibetan dialects, Nepalese dialects

Bolivia

Area: 424,164 sq mi (1,098,581 sq km)
Population: 9,863,000
Capitals: La Paz, pop. 1,590,000; Sucre, pop. 243,000
Currency: boliviano
Religions: Roman Catholic, Protestant (includes Evangelical Methodist)
Languages: Spanish, Quechua, Aymara

Bosnia and Herzegovina

Area: 19,741 sq mi (51,129 sq km)
Population: 3,843,000
Capital: Sarajevo, pop. 377,000
Currency: konvertibilna marka (convertible mark)
Religions: Muslim, Orthodox, Roman Catholic
Languages: Bosnian, Croatian, Serbian

Botswana

Area: 224,607 sq mi (581,730 sq km)
Population: 1,991,000
Capital: Gaborone, pop. 224,000
Currency: pula
Religions: Christian, Badimo
Languages: Setswana, Kalanga

Brazil

Area: 3,300,171 sq mi (8,547,403 sq km)
Population: 191,481,000
Capital: Brasília, pop. 3,594,000
Currency: real
Religions: Roman Catholic, Protestant
Language: Portuguese

Brunei

Area: 2,226 sq mi (5,765 sq km)
Population: 383,000
Capital: Bandar Seri Begawan, pop. 22,000
Currency: Bruneian dollar
Religions: Muslim, Buddhist, Christian, other (includes indigenous beliefs)
Languages: Malay, English, Chinese

Bulgaria

Area: 42,855 sq mi (110,994 sq km)
Population: 7,590,000
Capital: Sofia, pop. 1,186,000
Currency: lev
Religions: Bulgarian Orthodox, Muslim
Languages: Bulgarian, Turkish, Roma

Burkina Faso

Area: 105,869 sq mi (274,200 sq km)
Population: 15,757,000
Capital: Ouagadougou, pop. 1,148,000
Currency: Communauté Financière Africaine franc
Religions: Muslim, indigenous beliefs, Christian
Languages: French, native African languages

Burundi

Area: 10,747 sq mi (27,834 sq km)
Population: 8,303,000
Capital: Bujumbura, pop. 430,000
Currency: Burundi franc
Religions: Roman Catholic, indigenous beliefs, Muslim, Protestant
Languages: Kirundi, French, Swahili

Cambodia

Area: 69,898 sq mi (181,035 sq km)
Population: 14,805,000
Capital: Phnom Penh, pop. 1,465,000
Currency: riel
Religion: Theravada Buddhist
Language: Khmer

Cameroon

Area: 183,569 sq mi (475,442 sq km)
Population: 18,879,000
Capital: Yaoundé, pop. 1,610,000
Currency: Communauté Financière Africaine franc
Religions: indigenous beliefs, Christian, Muslim
Languages: 24 major African language groups, English, French

Canada

Area: 3,855,101 sq mi (9,984,670 sq km)
Population: 33,707,000
Capital: Ottawa, pop. 1,143,000
Currency: Canadian dollar
Religions: Roman Catholic, Protestant (includes United Church, Anglican), other Christian
Languages: English, French

Cape Verde

Area: 1,558 sq mi (4,036 sq km)
Population: 509,000
Capital: Praia, pop. 125,000
Currency: Cape Verdean escudo
Religions: Roman Catholic (infused with indigenous beliefs), Protestant (mostly Church of the Nazarene)
Languages: Portuguese, Crioulo

MOST POPULOUS COUNTRIES (mid-2009 data)		MOST CROWDED COUNTRIES Population Density (people per sq mi/sq km; mid-2009 data)	
1. China	1,362,069,000	1. Monaco	48,231/18,622
2. India	1,171,029,000	2. Singapore	19,389/7,486
3. United States	306,805,000	3. Vatican City	4,698/1,814
4. Indonesia	243,306,000	4. Bahrain	4,543/1,754
5. Brazil	191,481,000	5. Malta	3,393/1,310
6. Pakistan	180,808,000	6. Bangladesh	2,919/1,127
7. Nigeria	152,616,000	7. Maldives	2,738/1,057
8. Bangladesh	162,221,000	8. Barbados	1,691/653

● Asia ● Europe ● North America ● South America

Central African Republic

Area: 240,535 sq mi (622,984 sq km)
Population: 4,511,000
Capital: Bangui, pop. 672,000
Currency: Communauté Financière Africaine franc
Religions: indigenous beliefs, Protestant, Roman Catholic, Muslim
Languages: French, Sangho, tribal languages

Comoros

Area: 719 sq mi (1,862 sq km)
Population: 676,000
Capital: Moroni, pop. 46,000
Currency: Comoran franc
Religion: Sunni Muslim
Languages: Arabic, French, Shikomoro

Chad

Area: 495,755 sq mi (1,284,000 sq km)
Population: 10,329,000
Capital: N'Djamena, pop. 987,000
Currency: Communauté Financière Africaine franc
Religions: Muslim, Catholic, Protestant, animist
Languages: French, Arabic, Sara, over 120 languages and dialects

Congo

Area: 132,047 sq mi (342,000 sq km)
Population: 3,683,000
Capital: Brazzaville, pop. 1,332,000
Currency: Communauté Financière Africaine franc
Religions: Christian, animist
Languages: French, Lingala, Monokutuba, local languages

Chile

Area: 291,930 sq mi (756,096 sq km)
Population: 16,970,000
Capital: Santiago, pop. 5,719,000
Currency: Chilean peso
Religions: Roman Catholic, Evangelical
Language: Spanish

Costa Rica

Area: 19,730 sq mi (51,100 sq km)
Population: 4,509,000
Capital: San José, pop. 1,284,000
Currency: Costa Rican colon
Religions: Roman Catholic, Evangelical
Languages: Spanish, English

China

Area: 3,705,405 sq mi (9,596,960 sq km)
Population: 1,362,069,000
Capital: Beijing, pop. 11,106,000
Currency: renminbi (yuan)
Religions: Taoist, Buddhist, Christian
Languages: Standard Chinese or Mandarin, Yue, Wu, Minbei, Minnan, Xiang, Gan, Hakka dialects

Côte d'Ivoire (Ivory Coast)

Area: 124,503 sq mi (322,462 sq km)
Population: 21,395,000
Capitals: Abidjan, pop. 3,801,000; Yamoussoukro, pop. 669,000
Currency: Communauté Financière Africaine franc
Religions: Muslim, indigenous beliefs, Christian
Languages: French, Dioula, other native dialects

Colombia

Area: 440,831 sq mi (1,141,748 sq km)
Population: 45,065,000
Capital: Bogotá, pop. 7,764,000
Currency: Colombian peso
Religion: Roman Catholic
Language: Spanish

Croatia

Area: 21,831 sq mi (56,542 sq km)
Population: 4,433,000
Capital: Zagreb, pop. 689,000
Currency: kuna
Religions: Roman Catholic, Orthodox
Language: Croatian

COLOR KEY ● Africa ● Australia, New Zealand, and Oceania

Cuba

Area: 42,803 sq mi (110,860 sq km)
Population: 11,225,000
Capital: Havana, pop. 2,178,000
Currency: Cuban peso
Religions: Roman Catholic, Protestant, Jehovah's Witness, Jewish, Santeria
Language: Spanish

Cyprus

Area: 3,572 sq mi (9,251 sq km)
Population: 1,072,000
Capital: Nicosia, pop. 233,000
Currencies: euro; new Turkish lira in Northern Cyprus
Religions: Greek Orthodox, Muslim, Maronite, Armenian Apostolic
Languages: Greek, Turkish, English

Czech Republic (Czechia)

Area: 30,450 sq mi (78,866 sq km)
Population: 10,511,000
Capital: Prague, pop. 1,162,000
Currency: koruny
Religion: Roman Catholic
Language: Czech

Democratic Republic of the Congo

Area: 905,365 sq mi (2,344,885 sq km)
Population: 68,693,000
Capital: Kinshasa, pop. 7,851,000
Currency: Congolese franc
Religions: Roman Catholic, Protestant, Kimbanguist, Muslim, syncretic sects, indigenous beliefs
Languages: French, Lingala, Kingwana, Kikongo, Tshiluba

Denmark

Area: 16,640 sq mi (43,098 sq km)
Population: 5,529,000
Capital: Copenhagen, pop. 1,086,000
Currency: Danish krone
Religions: Evangelical Lutheran, other Protestant, Roman Catholic
Languages: Danish, Faroese, Greenlandic, German, English as second language

Djibouti

Area: 8,958 sq mi (23,200 sq km)
Population: 864,000
Capital: Djibouti, pop. 583,000
Currency: Djiboutian franc
Religions: Muslim, Christian
Languages: French, Arabic, Somali, Afar

Dominica

Area: 290 sq mi (751 sq km)
Population: 72,000
Capital: Roseau, pop. 14,000
Currency: East Caribbean dollar
Religions: Roman Catholic, Seventh-day Adventist, Pentecostal, Baptist, Methodist, other Christian
Languages: English, French patois

Dominican Republic

Area: 18,704 sq mi (48,442 sq km)
Population: 10,090,000
Capital: Santo Domingo, pop. 2,154,000
Currency: Dominican peso
Religion: Roman Catholic
Language: Spanish

Ecuador

Area: 109,483 sq mi (283,560 sq km)
Population: 13,625,000
Capital: Quito, pop. 1,697,000
Currency: U.S. dollar
Religion: Roman Catholic
Languages: Spanish, Quechua, other Amerindian languages

COOL CLICK

For more country facts, visit the CIA World Factbook online. https://www.cia.gov/library/publications/the-world-factbook/index.html

Egypt

Area: 386,874 sq mi
(1,002,000 sq km)
Population: 78,629,000
Capital: Cairo, pop. 11,893,000
Currency: Egyptian pound
Religions: Muslim (mostly Sunni), Coptic Christian
Languages: Arabic, English, French

Ethiopia

Area: 437,600 sq mi
(1,133,380 sq km)
Population: 82,825,000
Capital: Addis Ababa,
pop. 3,102,000
Currency: birr
Religions: Christian, Muslim, traditional
Languages: Amharic, Oromigna, Tigrinya, Guaragigna

El Salvador

Area: 8,124 sq mi (21,041 sq km)
Population: 7,339,000
Capital: San Salvador,
pop. 1,433,000
Currency: U.S. dollar
Religions: Roman Catholic, Protestant
Languages: Spanish, Nahua

Fiji Islands

Area: 7,095 sq mi (18,376 sq km)
Population: 844,000
Capital: Suva, pop. 224,000
Currency: Fijian dollar
Religions: Christian (Methodist, Roman Catholic,
Assembly of God), Hindu (Sanatan), Muslim (Sunni)
Languages: English, Fijian, Hindustani

Equatorial Guinea

Area: 10,831 sq mi (28,051 sq km)
Population: 676,000
Capital: Malabo, pop. 96,000
Currency: Communauté
Financière Africaine franc
Religions: Christian (predominantly Roman Catholic),
pagan practices
Languages: Spanish, French, Fang, Bubi

Finland

Area: 130,558 sq mi
(338,145 sq km)
Population: 5,339,000
Capital: Helsinki, pop. 1,115,000
Currency: euro
Religion: Lutheran Church of Finland
Languages: Finnish, Swedish

Eritrea

Area: 46,774 sq mi (121,144 sq km)
Population: 5,073,000
Capital: Asmara, pop. 600,000
Currency: nakfa
Religions: Muslim, Coptic Christian, Roman Catholic,
Protestant
Languages: Afar, Arabic, Tigre, Kunama, Tigrinya, other
Cushitic languages

France

Area: 210,026 sq mi
(543,965 sq km)
Population: 62,621,000
Capital: Paris, pop. 9,902,000
Currency: euro
Religions: Roman Catholic, Muslim
Language: French

Estonia

Area: 17,462 sq mi (45,227 sq km)
Population: 1,340,000
Capital: Tallinn, pop. 397,000
Currency: Estonian kroon
Religions: Evangelical Lutheran, Orthodox
Languages: Estonian, Russian

Gabon

Area: 103,347 sq mi (267,667 sq km)
Population: 1,475,000
Capital: Libreville, pop. 576,000
Currency: Communauté Financière
Africaine franc
Religions: Christian, animist
Languages: French, Fang, Myene, Nzebi, Bapounou/
Eschira, Bandjabi

COLOR KEY   ● Africa   ● Australia, New Zealand, and Oceania

Gambia

Area: 4,361 sq mi (11,295 sq km)
Population: 1,609,000
Capital: Banjul, pop. 407,000
Currency: dalasi
Religions: Muslim, Christian
Languages: English, Mandinka, Wolof, Fula, other indigenous vernaculars

Georgia

Area: 26,911 sq mi (69,700 sq km)
Population: 4,611,000
Capital: T'bilisi, pop. 1,099,000
Currency: lari
Religions: Orthodox Christian, Muslim, Armenian-Gregorian
Languages: Georgian, Russian, Armenian, Azeri, Abkhaz

Germany

Area: 137,847 sq mi (357,022 sq km)
Population: 81,980,000
Capital: Berlin, pop. 3,405,000
Currency: euro
Religions: Protestant, Roman Catholic, Muslim
Language: German

Ghana

Area: 92,100 sq mi (238,537 sq km)
Population: 23,837,000
Capital: Accra, pop. 2,120,000
Currency: Ghana cedi
Religions: Christian (Pentecostal/Charismatic, Protestant, Roman Catholic, other), Muslim, traditional beliefs
Languages: Asante, Ewe, Fante, Boron (Brong), Dagomba, Dangme, Dagarte (Dagaba), Akyem, Ga, English

Greece

Area: 50,949 sq mi (131,957 sq km)
Population: 11,277,000
Capital: Athens, pop. 3,242,000
Currency: euro
Religion: Greek Orthodox
Languages: Greek, English, French

Grenada

Area: 133 sq mi (344 sq km)
Population: 106,000
Capital: St. George's, pop. 32,000
Currency: East Caribbean dollar
Religions: Roman Catholic, Anglican, other Protestant
Languages: English, French patois

Guatemala

Area: 42,042 sq mi (108,889 sq km)
Population: 14,027,000
Capital: Guatemala City, pop. 1,025,000
Currency: quetzal
Religions: Roman Catholic, Protestant, indigenous Maya beliefs
Languages: Spanish, 23 official Amerindian languages

5 cool things about GUATEMALA

1. Some think the word "Guatemala" means "land of trees" in the Maya-Toltec language.

2. Men in Guatemala work an average of 10 hours, 29 minutes per day.

3. The white stripe between two blue stripes on the flag symbolizes the land of Guatemala, which is located between two oceans, the Atlantic and Pacific.

4. Maya ruins, like this one (right), dating back to 700 B.C., can be found all over the country.

5. Antigua, one of the country's most famous cities, is nestled between three volcanoes.

Guinea

Area: 94,926 sq mi (245,857 sq km)
Population: 10,058,000
Capital: Conakry, pop. 1,494,000
Currency: Guinean franc
Religions: Muslim, Christian, indigenous beliefs
Languages: French, ethnic languages

Guinea-Bissau

Area: 13,948 sq mi (36,125 sq km)
Population: 1,611,000
Capital: Bissau, pop. 330,000
Currency: Communauté Financière Africaine franc
Religions: indigenous beliefs, Muslim, Christian
Languages: Portuguese, Crioulo, African languages

Guyana

Area: 83,000 sq mi (214,969 sq km)
Population: 773,000
Capital: Georgetown, pop. 133,000
Currency: Guyanese dollar
Religions: Christian, Hindu, Muslim
Languages: English, Amerindian dialects, Creole, Hindustani, Urdu

Haiti

Area: 10,714 sq mi (27,750 sq km)
Population: 9,242,000
Capital: Port-au-Prince, pop. 2,002,000
Currency: gourde
Religions: Roman Catholic, Protestant (Baptist, Pentecostal, other)
Languages: French, Creole

Honduras

Area: 43,433 sq mi (112,492 sq km)
Population: 7,466,000
Capital: Tegucigalpa, pop. 947,000
Currency: lempira
Religions: Roman Catholic, Protestant
Languages: Spanish, Amerindian dialects

Hungary

Area: 35,919 sq mi (93,030 sq km)
Population: 10,024,000
Capital: Budapest, pop. 1,675,000
Currency: forint
Religions: Roman Catholic, Calvinist, Lutheran
Language: Hungarian

Iceland

Area: 39,769 sq mi (103,000 sq km)
Population: 321,000
Capital: Reykjavík, pop. 192,000
Currency: Icelandic krona
Religion: Lutheran Church of Iceland
Languages: Icelandic, English, Nordic languages, German

India

Area: 1,269,221 sq mi (3,287,270 sq km)
Population: 1,171,029,000
Capital: New Delhi, pop. 15,926,000 (part of Delhi metropolitan area)
Currency: Indian rupee
Religions: Hindu, Muslim
Languages: Hindi, 21 other official languages, Hindustani (popular Hindi/Urdu variant in the north)

Indonesia

Area: 742,308 sq mi (1,922,570 sq km)
Population: 243,306,000
Capital: Jakarta, pop. 9,143,000
Currency: Indonesian rupiah
Religions: Muslim, Protestant, Roman Catholic
Languages: Bahasa Indonesia (modified form of Malay), English, Dutch, Javanese, local dialects

Iran

Area: 636,296 sq mi (1,648,000 sq km)
Population: 73,244,000
Capital: Tehran, pop. 7,875,000
Currency: Iranian rial
Religions: Shiite Muslim, Sunni Muslim
Languages: Persian, Turkic, Kurdish, Luri, Baluchi, Arabic

COLOR KEY ● Africa ● Australia, New Zealand, and Oceania

Iraq

Area: 168,754 sq mi
(437,072 sq km)
Population: 30,047,000
Capital: Baghdad, pop. 5,500,000
Currency: Iraqi dinar
Religions: Shiite Muslim, Sunni Muslim
Languages: Arabic, Kurdish, Assyrian, Armenian

Ireland

Area: 27,133 sq mi
(70,273 sq km)
Population: 4,528,000
Capital: Dublin, pop. 1,060,000
Currency: euro
Religions: Roman Catholic, Church of Ireland
Languages: Irish (Gaelic), English

Israel

Area: 8,550 sq mi (22,145 sq km)
Population: 7,634,000
Capital: Jerusalem, pop. 736,000
Currency: new Israeli sheqel
Religions: Jewish, Muslim
Languages: Hebrew, Arabic, English

5 cool things about ISRAEL

1. Israel is the world's only predominantly Jewish state.

2. Less than 5 percent of the population lives in a rural cooperative settlement, either a *kibbutz* or a *moshav*.

3. The Dead Sea is so salty and heavy that everyone floats, even a nonswimmer!

4. Israel became an independent country in 1948, only 63 years ago.

5. Israeli currency notes have Braille on them so the blind can identify them.

Italy

Area: 116,345 sq mi
(301,333 sq km)
Population: 60,274,000
Capital: Rome, pop. 3,340,000
Currency: euro
Religions: Roman Catholic, Protestant, Jewish, Muslim
Languages: Italian, German, French, Slovene

5 cool things about ITALY

1. With more than 40 million visitors annually, Italy is the third most visited country in Europe.

2. Eyeglasses and the thermometer are both Italian inventions.

3. Italy has more hotel rooms than any other nation in Europe.

4. Italy's national dish is pasta.

5. Italy has more than 3,000 museums.

Jamaica

Area: 4,244 sq mi
(10,991 sq km)
Population: 2,702,000
Capital: Kingston, pop. 581,000
Currency: Jamaican dollar
Religions: Protestant (Church of God, Seventh-day Adventist, Pentecostal, Baptist, Anglican, other)
Languages: English, English patois

Japan

Area: 145,902 sq mi (377,887 sq km)
Population: 127,568,000
Capital: Tokyo, pop. 35,676,000
Currency: yen
Religions: Shinto, Buddhist
Language: Japanese

Jordan

Area: 34,495 sq mi
(89,342 sq km)
Population: 5,915,000
Capital: Amman, pop. 1,064,000
Currency: Jordanian dinar
Religions: Sunni Muslim, Christian
Languages: Arabic, English

Kuwait

Area: 6,880 sq mi
(17,818 sq km)
Population: 2,985,000
Capital: Kuwait City,
pop. 2,061,000
Currency: Kuwaiti dinar
Religions: Sunni Muslim, Shiite Muslim
Languages: Arabic, English

Kazakhstan

Area: 1,049,155 sq mi
(2,717,300 sq km)
Population: 15,880,000
Capital: Astana, pop. 594,000
Currency: tenge
Religions: Muslim, Russian Orthodox
Languages: Kazakh (Qazaq), Russian

Kyrgyzstan

Area: 77,182 sq mi
(199,900 sq km)
Population: 5,304,000
Capital: Bishkek, pop. 837,000
Currency: som
Religions: Muslim, Russian Orthodox
Languages: Kyrgyz, Uzbek, Russian

Kenya

Area: 224,081 sq mi (580,367 sq km)
Population: 39,070,000
Capital: Nairobi, pop. 3,011,000
Currency: Kenyan shilling
Religions: Protestant, Roman Catholic, Muslim, indigenous beliefs
Languages: English, Kiswahili, many indigenous languages

Laos

Area: 91,429 sq mi
(236,800 sq km)
Population: 6,320,000
Capital: Vientiane, pop. 746,000
Currency: kip
Religions: Buddhist, animist
Languages: Lao, French, English, various ethnic languages

Kiribati

Area: 313 sq mi (811 sq km)
Population: 99,000
Capital: Tarawa, pop. 42,000
Currency: Australian
dollar
Religions: Roman Catholic, Protestant
(Congregational)
Languages: I-Kiribati, English

Latvia

Area: 24,938 sq mi
(64,589 sq km)
Population: 2,256,000
Capital: Riga, pop. 722,000
Currency: Latvian lat
Religions: Lutheran, Roman Catholic, Russian Orthodox
Languages: Latvian, Russian, Lithuanian

Kosovo

Area: 4,203 sq mi (10,887 sq km)
Population: 2,222,000
Capital: Pristina, pop. 600,000
Currency: euro
Religions: Muslim, Serbian Orthodox, Roman Catholic
Languages: Albanian, Serbian, Bosnian, Turkish, Roma

Lebanon

Area: 4,036 sq mi (10,452 sq km)
Population: 3,876,000
Capital: Beirut, pop. 1,857,000
Currency: Lebanese pound
Religions: Muslim, Christian
Languages: Arabic, French, English, Armenian

COLOR KEY ● Africa ● Australia, New Zealand, and Oceania

Lesotho

Area: 11,720 sq mi (30,355 sq km)
Population: 2,135,000
Capital: Maseru, pop. 212,000
Currencies: loti; South African rand
Religions: Christian, indigenous beliefs
Languages: Sesotho, English, Zulu, Xhosa

Liberia

Area: 43,000 sq mi (111,370 sq km)
Population: 3,955,000
Capital: Monrovia, pop. 1,165,000
Currency: Liberian dollar
Religions: Christian, indigenous beliefs, Muslim
Languages: English, some 20 ethnic languages

Libya

Area: 679,362 sq mi (1,759,540 sq km)
Population: 6,283,000
Capital: Tripoli, pop. 2,189,000
Currency: Libyan dinar
Religion: Sunni Muslim
Languages: Arabic, Italian, English

Liechtenstein

Area: 62 sq mi (160 sq km)
Population: 36,000
Capital: Vaduz, pop. 5,000
Currency: Swiss franc
Religions: Roman Catholic, Protestant
Languages: German, Alemannic dialect

Lithuania

Area: 25,212 sq mi (65,300 sq km)
Population: 3,339,000
Capital: Vilnius, pop. 553,000
Currency: litas
Religions: Roman Catholic, Russian Orthodox
Languages: Lithuanian, Russian, Polish

Luxembourg

Area: 998 sq mi (2,586 sq km)
Population: 498,000
Capital: Luxembourg, pop. 84,000
Currency: euro
Religions: Roman Catholic, Protestant, Jewish, Muslim
Languages: Luxembourgish, German, French

Macedonia

Area: 9,928 sq mi (25,713 sq km)
Population: 2,049,000
Capital: Skopje, pop. 480,000
Currency: Macedonian denar
Religions: Macedonian Orthodox, Muslim
Languages: Macedonian, Albanian, Turkish

Madagascar

Area: 226,658 sq mi (587,041 sq km)
Population: 19,464,000
Capital: Antananarivo, pop. 1,697,000
Currency: Madagascar ariary
Religions: indigenous beliefs, Christian, Muslim
Languages: English, French, Malagasy

Malawi

Area: 45,747 sq mi (118,484 sq km)
Population: 14,214,000
Capital: Lilongwe, pop. 732,000
Currency: Malawian kwacha
Religions: Christian, Muslim
Languages: Chichewa, Chinyanja, Chiyao, Chitumbuka

COOL CLICK

Want to see interactive maps and videos of the countries? Go online to National Geographic.
travel.nationalgeographic.com/places/countries/index.html

● Asia ● Europe ● North America ● South America

Malaysia

Area: 127,355 sq mi (329,847 sq km)
Population: 28,295,000
Capital: Kuala Lumpur, pop. 1,448,000
Currency: ringgit
Religions: Muslim, Buddhist, Christian, Hindu
Languages: Bahasa Malaysia, English, Chinese, Tamil, Telugu, Malayalam, Panjabi, Thai, indigenous languages

Maldives

Area: 115 sq mi (298 sq km)
Population: 315,000
Capital: Male, pop. 111,000
Currency: rufiyaa
Religion: Sunni Muslim
Languages: Maldivian Dhivehi, English

Mali

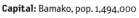

Area: 478,841 sq mi (1,240,192 sq km)
Population: 13,010,000
Capital: Bamako, pop. 1,494,000
Currency: Communauté Financière Africaine franc
Religions: Muslim, indigenous beliefs
Languages: Bambara, French, numerous African languages

Malta

Area: 122 sq mi (316 sq km)
Population: 414,000
Capital: Valletta, pop. 199,000
Currency: euro
Religion: Roman Catholic
Languages: Maltese, English

Marshall Islands

Area: 70 sq mi (181 sq km)
Population: 54,000
Capital: Majuro, pop. 28,000
Currency: U.S. dollar
Religions: Protestant, Assembly of God, Roman Catholic
Language: Marshallese

Mauritania

Area: 397,955 sq mi (1,030,700 sq km)
Population: 3,291,000
Capital: Nouakchott, pop. 673,000
Currency: ouguiya
Religion: Muslim
Languages: Arabic, Pulaar, Soninke, French, Hassaniya, Wolof

Mauritius

Area: 788 sq mi (2,040 sq km)
Population: 1,276,000
Capital: Port Louis, pop. 150,000
Currency: Mauritian rupee
Religions: Hindu, Roman Catholic, Muslim, other Christian
Languages: Creole, Bhojpuri, French

Mexico

Area: 758,449 sq mi (1,964,375 sq km)
Population: 109,610,000
Capital: Mexico City, pop. 19,026,000
Currency: Mexican peso
Religions: Roman Catholic, Protestant
Languages: Spanish, Mayan, Nahuatl, other indigenous

Micronesia

Area: 271 sq mi (702 sq km)
Population: 111,000
Capital: Palikir, pop. 7,000
Currency: U.S. dollar
Religions: Roman Catholic, Protestant
Languages: English, Trukese, Pohnpeian, Yapese, other indigenous languages

Moldova

Area: 13,050 sq mi (33,800 sq km)
Population: 4,133,000
Capital: Chisinau, pop. 592,000
Currency: Moldovan leu
Religion: Eastern Orthodox
Languages: Moldovan, Russian, Gagauz

COLOR KEY   ● Africa   ● Australia, New Zealand, and Oceania

Monaco

Area: 0.8 sq mi (2.0 sq km)
Population: 35,000
Capital: Monaco, pop. 34,000
Currency: euro
Religion: Roman Catholic
Languages: French, English, Italian, Monegasque

Montenegro

Area: 5,415 sq mi (14,026 sq km)
Population: 628,000
Capital: Podgorica, pop. 142,000
Currency: euro
Religions: Orthodox, Muslim, Roman Catholic
Languages: Serbian (Ijekavian dialect), Bosnian, Albanian, Croatian

Mongolia

Area: 603,909 sq mi (1,564,116 sq km)
Population: 2,708,000
Capital: Ulaanbaatar, pop. 884,000
Currency: togrog/tugrik
Religions: Buddhist Lamaist, Shamanist, Christian
Languages: Khalkha Mongol, Turkic, Russian

Morocco

Area: 274,461 sq mi (710,850 sq km)
Population: 31,495,000
Capital: Rabat, pop. 1,705,000
Currency: Moroccan dirham
Religion: Muslim
Languages: Arabic, Berber dialects, French

Mongolia

HUNTING WITH GOLDEN EAGLES

Galloping on horseback across a rocky plain, a man rides with a golden eagle perched on his arm. The bird's owner, named Baitolda (BUY-tol-dah), is a member of a group of Kazakh (KAH-zahk) people who have trained eagles for hundreds of years. For these Kazakhs, who live in the remote Altay Mountains of Mongolia, a country in Asia, these birds are both hunting companions and honored family members.

On the Move

Baitolda is one of about 150,000 Kazakhs in Mongolia who still live a traditional nomadic life-style. When the seasons change, families load up camels and sometimes trucks, and trek through the mountains on horseback to find pastures for their sheep and goats. In winter families return to permanent houses built from bricks of mud.

During the journey, Baitolda's eagle rides on his arm and has a perch inside the family's sturdy tent (called a yurt, or *ger* in Mongolia). But the eagle also earns her keep. The foxes and hares she catches provide fur for the family's clothing— a necessity in temperatures that can dip to minus 40°F (-40°C).

When an eagle turns eight, Kazakhs traditionally release the bird back into the wild to live free.

Mozambique

Area: 308,642 sq mi
(799,380 sq km)
Population: 21,971,000
Capital: Maputo, pop. 1,445,000
Currency: metical
Religions: Roman Catholic, Muslim, Zionist Christian
Languages: Emakhuwa, Xichangana, Portuguese, Elomwe, Cisena, Echuwabo, other local languages

Namibia

Area: 318,261 sq mi
(824,292 sq km)
Population: 2,171,000
Capital: Windhoek, pop. 313,000
Currencies: Namibian dollar;
South African rand
Religions: Lutheran, other Christian, indigenous beliefs
Languages: Afrikaans, German, English

Myanmar (Burma)

Area: 261,218 sq mi (676,552 sq km)
Population: 50,020,000
Capitals: Nay Pyi Taw, pop. 200,000;
Yangon (Rangoon), pop. 4,088,000
Currency: kyat
Religions: Buddhist, Christian, Muslim
Languages: Burmese, minority ethnic languages

Nauru

Area: 8 sq mi (21 sq km)
Population: 10,000
Capital: Yaren, pop. NA
Currency: Australian dollar
Religions: Protestant, Roman Catholic
Languages: Nauruan, English

CLIMBING MOUNT EVEREST IS A WAY OF LIFE FOR THE SHERPA PEOPLE OF Nepal

The highest mountain in the world loomed in front of 16-year-old Temba Tsheri Sherpa. One of the youngest people ever to summit the 29,035-foot (8,850-m) Everest, Temba is a Sherpa—a member of an ethnic group that lives mainly in the country of Nepal, in the Himalaya mountains.

Living in mountain villages as high as 14,000 feet (4,267 m), with no roads or cars, Sherpas hike everywhere and lug everything on their backs—even TVs and refrigerators.

The Sky's the Limit

Temba's courage comes partly from his religious beliefs. As followers of a religion called Tibetan Buddhism, the Sherpa believe in being peaceful, honoring all people, and accepting suffering without complaint.

Temba's trek continues his people's history of climbing feats. The tradition began nearly a hundred years ago when Sherpas started carrying supplies for visiting mountaineers.

Today, Sherpas still hike everywhere. Without his heritage, Temba might have given up. But finally he took the last step and stood on the summit of Everest—the top of the world. Temba knew his success was a triumph for his people.

COLOR KEY ● Africa ● Australia, New Zealand, and Oceania

Nepal

Area: 56,827 sq mi
(147,181 sq km)
Population: 27,504,000
Capital: Kathmandu, pop. 895,000
Currency: Nepalese rupee
Religions: Hindu, Buddhist, Muslim, Kirant
Languages: Nepali, Maithali, Bhojpuri, Tharu, Tamang, Newar, Magar

Netherlands

Area: 16,034 sq mi
(41,528 sq km)
Population: 16,527,000
Capital: Amsterdam, pop. 1,031,000
Currency: euro
Religions: Roman Catholic, Dutch Reformed, Calvinist, Muslim
Languages: Dutch, Frisian

New Zealand

Area: 104,454 sq mi
(270,534 sq km)
Population: 4,371,000
Capital: Wellington, pop. 366,000
Currency: New Zealand dollar
Religions: Anglican, Roman Catholic, Presbyterian, other Christian
Languages: English, Maori

Nicaragua

Area: 50,193 sq mi
(130,000 sq km)
Population: 5,669,000
Capital: Managua, pop. 920,000
Currency: gold cordoba
Religions: Roman Catholic, Evangelical
Language: Spanish

Niger

Area: 489,191 sq mi (1,267,000 sq km)
Population: 15,290,000
Capital: Niamey, pop. 915,000
Currency: Communauté Financière Africaine franc
Religions: Muslim, other (includes indigenous beliefs and Christian)
Languages: French, Hausa, Djerma

Nigeria

Area: 356,669 sq mi
(923,768 sq km)
Population: 152,616,000
Capital: Abuja, pop. 1,579,000
Currency: naira
Religions: Muslim, Christian, indigenous beliefs
Languages: English, Hausa, Yoruba, Igbo (Ibo), Fulani

North Korea

Area: 46,540 sq mi
(120,538 sq km)
Population: 22,665,000
Capital: Pyongyang, pop. 3,301,000
Currency: North Korean won
Religions: Buddhist, Confucianist, some Christian and syncretic Chondogyo
Language: Korean

Norway

Area: 125,004 sq mi
(323,758 sq km)
Population: 4,827,000
Capital: Oslo, pop. 834,000
Currency: Norwegian krone
Religion: Church of Norway (Lutheran)
Languages: Bokmal Norwegian, Nynorsk Norwegian, Sami

Oman

Area: 119,500 sq mi
(309,500 sq km)
Population: 3,108,000
Capital: Muscat, pop. 621,000
Currency: Omani rial
Religions: Ibadhi Muslim, Sunni Muslim, Shiite Muslim, Hindu
Languages: Arabic, English, Baluchi, Urdu, Indian dialects

Pakistan

Area: 307,374 sq mi
(796,095 sq km)
Population: 180,808,000
Capital: Islamabad, pop. 780,000
Currency: Pakistani rupee
Religions: Sunni Muslim, Shiite Muslim
Languages: Punjabi, Sindhi, Siraiki, Pashtu, Urdu, Baluchi, Hindko, English

Palau

Area: 189 sq mi (489 sq km)
Population: 21,000
Capital: Melekeok, pop. NA
Currency: U.S. dollar
Religions: Roman Catholic, Protestant, Modekngei, Seventh-day Adventist
Languages: Palauan, Filipino, English, Chinese

Philippines

Area: 115,831 sq mi (300,000 sq km)
Population: 92,227,000
Capital: Manila, pop. 11,100,000
Currency: Philippine peso
Religions: Roman Catholic, Muslim, other Christian
Languages: Filipino (based on Tagalog), English

Panama

Area: 29,157 sq mi (75,517 sq km)
Population: 3,454,000
Capital: Panama City, pop. 1,280,000
Currencies: balboa; U.S. dollar
Religions: Roman Catholic, Protestant
Languages: Spanish, English

Poland

Area: 120,728 sq mi (312,685 sq km)
Population: 38,146,000
Capital: Warsaw, pop. 1,707,000
Currency: zloty
Religion: Roman Catholic
Language: Polish

Papua New Guinea

Area: 178,703 sq mi (462,840 sq km)
Population: 6,610,000
Capital: Port Moresby, pop. 299,000
Currency: kina
Religions: indigenous beliefs, Roman Catholic, Lutheran, other Protestant
Languages: Melanesian Pidgin, 820 indigenous languages

Portugal

Area: 35,655 sq mi (92,345 sq km)
Population: 10,639,000
Capital: Lisbon, pop. 2,811,000
Currency: euro
Religion: Roman Catholic
Languages: Portuguese, Mirandese

Paraguay

Area: 157,048 sq mi (406,752 sq km)
Population: 6,349,000
Capital: Asunción, pop. 1,870,000
Currency: guarani
Religions: Roman Catholic, Protestant
Languages: Spanish, Guarani

Qatar

Area: 4,448 sq mi (11,521 sq km)
Population: 1,409,000
Capital: Doha, pop. 386,000
Currency: Qatari rial
Religions: Muslim, Christian
Languages: Arabic, English commonly a second language

Peru

Area: 496,224 sq mi (1,285,216 sq km)
Population: 29,165,000
Capital: Lima, pop. 8,007,000
Currency: nuevo sol
Religion: Roman Catholic
Languages: Spanish, Quechua, Aymara, minor Amazonian languages

Romania

Area: 92,043 sq mi (238,391 sq km)
Population: 21,474,000
Capital: Bucharest, pop. 1,940,000
Currency: new leu
Religions: Eastern Orthodox, Protestant, Roman Catholic
Languages: Romanian, Hungarian

COLOR KEY ● Africa ● Australia, New Zealand, and Oceania

Russia

Area: 6,592,850 sq mi
(17,075,400 sq km)
Population: 141,839,000
Capital: Moscow, pop. 10,452,000
Currency: ruble
Religions: Russian Orthodox, Muslim
Languages: Russian, many minority languages

Note: Russia is in both Europe and Asia, but its capital is in Europe, so it is classified here as a European country.

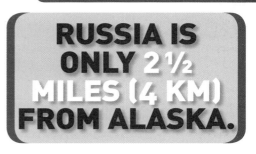

RUSSIA IS ONLY 2½ MILES (4 KM) FROM ALASKA.

Rwanda

Area: 10,169 sq mi
(26,338 sq km)
Population: 9,877,000
Capital: Kigali, pop. 852,000
Currency: Rwandan franc
Religions: Roman Catholic, Protestant,
Adventist, Muslim
Languages: Kinyarwanda, French, English, Kiswahili

San Marino

Area: 24 sq mi (61 sq km)
Population: 31,000
Capital: San Marino, pop. 4,000
Currency: euro
Religion: Roman Catholic
Language: Italian

Samoa

Area: 1,093 sq mi (2,831 sq km)
Population: 190,000
Capital: Apia, pop. 43,000
Currency: tala
Religions: Congregationalist, Roman Catholic,
Methodist, Church of Latter-day Saints, Assembly
of God, Seventh-day Adventist
Languages: Samoan (Polynesian), English

São Tomé and Principe

Area: 386 sq mi (1,001 sq km)
Population: 163,000
Capital: São Tomé, pop. 58,000
Currency: dobra
Religions: Roman Catholic, Evangelical
Language: Portuguese

MEET THE NAT GEO EXPLORER

SPENCER WELLS

A leading population geneticist and director of the Genographic
Project (genographic.nationalgeographic.com), Wells is studying
humankind's family tree.

What was your closest call in the field?
I've had a few, but the most physically difficult experience was when I lived with Chukchi
reindeer herders in Russia's Far East, inside the Arctic Circle. The temperatures fell as low
as -94°F (-70°C), which freezes unprotected skin and can kill you in minutes.

How would you suggest kids follow in your footsteps?
Find something in school you are passionate about, focus on it, and study hard. Don't let
people tell you that it's not a practical subject to study—if you are excited enough about
it, you will find a way to do it for a living. Take risks. Challenging yourself will give you
confidence, and you'll learn something that may be useful in your future work.

● Asia   ● Europe   ● North America   ● South America

Saudi Arabia

Area: 756,985 sq mi
(1,960,582 sq km)
Population: 28,687,000
Capital: Riyadh, pop. 4,462,000
Currency: Saudi riyal
Religion: Muslim
Language: Arabic

Senegal

Area: 75,955 sq mi
(196,722 sq km)
Population: 12,534,000
Capital: Dakar, pop. 2,603,000
Currency: Communauté
Financière Africaine franc
Religions: Muslim, Christian (mostly Roman Catholic)
Languages: French, Wolof, Pulaar, Jola, Mandinka

Serbia

Area: 29,913 sq mi (77,474 sq km)
Population: 7,322,000
Capital: Belgrade, pop. 1,100,000
Currency: Serbian dinar
Religions: Serbian Orthodox, Roman Catholic, Muslim
Languages: Serbian, Hungarian

Seychelles

Area: 176 sq mi (455 sq km)
Population: 87,000
Capital: Victoria, pop. 26,000
Currency: Seychelles rupee
Religions: Roman Catholic, Anglican, other Christian
Languages: Creole, English

Sierra Leone

Area: 27,699 sq mi (71,740 sq km)
Population: 5,696,000
Capital: Freetown, pop. 826,000
Currency: leone
Religions: Muslim, indigenous beliefs, Christian
Languages: English, Mende, Temne, Krio

Singapore

Area: 255 sq mi (660 sq km)
Population: 5,113,000
Capital: Singapore, pop. 4,790,000
Currency: Singapore dollar
Religions: Buddhist, Muslim, Taoist, Roman Catholic, Hindu, other Christian
Languages: Mandarin, English, Malay, Hokkien, Cantonese, Teochew, Tamil

Slovakia

Area: 18,932 sq mi
(49,035 sq km)
Population: 5,417,000
Capital: Bratislava, pop. 424,000
Currency: Slovak koruna
Religions: Roman Catholic, Protestant, Greek Catholic
Languages: Slovak, Hungarian

Slovenia

Area: 7,827 sq mi
(20,273 sq km)
Population: 2,043,000
Capital: Ljubljana, pop. 244,000
Currency: euro
Religion: Roman Catholic, Muslim, Orthodox
Languages: Slovene, Serbo-Croatian

Solomon Islands

Area: 10,954 sq mi
(28,370 sq km)
Population: 519,000
Capital: Honiara, pop. 66,000
Currency: Solomon Islands dollar
Religions: Church of Melanesia, Roman Catholic, South Seas Evangelical, other Christian
Languages: Melanesian pidgin, 120 indigenous languages

Somalia

Area: 246,201 sq mi
(637,657 sq km)
Population: 9,133,000
Capital: Mogadishu, pop. 1,450,000
Currency: Somali shilling
Religion: Sunni Muslim
Languages: Somali, Arabic, Italian, English

COLOR KEY ● Africa ● Australia, New Zealand, and Oceania

South Africa

Area: 470,693 sq mi (1,219,090 sq km)
Population: 50,674,000
Capitals: Pretoria (Tshwane), pop. 1,336,000; Bloemfontein, pop. 417,000; Cape Town, pop. 3,211,000
Currency: rand
Religions: Zion Christian, Pentecostal, Catholic, Methodist, Dutch Reformed, Anglican, other Christian
Languages: IsiZulu, IsiXhosa, Afrikaans, Sepedi, English

South Korea

Area: 38,321 sq mi (99,250 sq km)
Population: 48,747,000
Capital: Seoul, pop. 9,799,000
Currency: South Korean won
Religions: Christian, Buddhist
Languages: Korean, English

Spain

Area: 195,363 sq mi (505,988 sq km)
Population: 46,916,000
Capital: Madrid, pop. 5,567,000
Currency: euro
Religion: Roman Catholic
Languages: Castilian Spanish, Catalan, Galician, Basque

Sri Lanka

Area: 25,299 sq mi (65,525 sq km)
Population: 20,502,000
Capital: Colombo, pop. 656,000
Currency: Sri Lankan rupee
Religions: Buddhist, Muslim, Hindu, Christian
Languages: Sinhala, Tamil

St. Kitts and Nevis

Area: 104 sq mi (269 sq km)
Population: 50,000
Capital: Basseterre, pop. 13,000
Currency: East Caribbean dollar
Religions: Anglican, other Protestant, Roman Catholic
Language: English

St. Lucia

Area: 238 sq mi (616 sq km)
Population: 172,000
Capital: Castries, pop. 14,000
Currency: East Caribbean dollar
Religions: Roman Catholic, Seventh-day Adventist, Pentecostal
Languages: English, French patois

St. Vincent and the Grenadines

Area: 150 sq mi (389 sq km)
Population: 110,000
Capital: Kingstown, pop. 26,000
Currency: East Caribbean dollar
Religions: Anglican, Methodist, Roman Catholic
Languages: English, French patois

Sudan

Area: 967,500 sq mi (2,505,813 sq km)
Population: 42,272,000
Capital: Khartoum, pop. 4,762,000
Currency: Sudanese pound
Religions: Sunni Muslim, indigenous beliefs, Christian
Languages: Arabic, Nubian, Ta Bedawie, many diverse dialects of Nilotic, Nilo-Hamitic, Sudanic languages

Suriname

Area: 63,037 sq mi (163,265 sq km)
Population: 502,000
Capital: Paramaribo, pop. 252,000
Currency: Suriname dollar
Religions: Hindu, Protestant (predominantly Moravian), Roman Catholic, Muslim, indigenous beliefs
Languages: Dutch, English, Sranang Tongo, Hindustani, Javanese

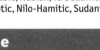

COOL CLICK

The United Nations has a great website with information, games, and more. Check it out online.
cyberschoolbus.un.org

Swaziland

Area: 6,704 sq mi (17,363 sq km)
Population: 1,185,000
Capitals: Mbabane, pop. 78,000; Lobamba NA
Currency: lilangeni
Religions: Zionist, Roman Catholic, Muslim
Languages: English, siSwati

Tanzania

Area: 364,900 sq mi (945,087 sq km)
Population: 43,739,000
Capitals: Dar es Salaam, pop. 2,930,000; Dodoma, pop. 183,000
Currency: Tanzanian shilling
Religions: Muslim, indigenous beliefs, Christian
Languages: Kiswahili, Kiunguja (Kiswahili in Zanzibar), English, Arabic, local languages

Sweden

Area: 173,732 sq mi (449,964 sq km)
Population: 9,288,000
Capital: Stockholm, pop. 1,264,000
Currency: Swedish krona
Religion: Lutheran
Languages: Swedish, Sami, Finnish

Thailand

Area: 198,115 sq mi (513,115 sq km)
Population: 67,764,000
Capital: Bangkok, pop. 6,706,000
Currency: baht
Religions: Buddhist, Muslim
Languages: Thai, English, ethnic dialects

Switzerland

Area: 15,940 sq mi (41,284 sq km)
Population: 7,754,000
Capital: Bern, pop. 337,000
Currency: Swiss franc
Religions: Roman Catholic, Protestant, Muslim
Languages: German, French, Italian, Romansh

Timor-Leste (East Timor)

Area: 5,640 sq mi (14,609 sq km)
Population: 1,134,000
Capital: Díli, pop. 159,000
Currency: U.S. dollar
Religion: Roman Catholic
Languages: Tetum, Portuguese, Indonesian, English, indigenous languages

Syria

Area: 71,498 sq mi (185,180 sq km)
Population: 21,906,000
Capital: Damascus, pop. 2,467,000
Currency: Syrian pound
Religions: Sunni, other Muslim (includes Alawite, Druze), Christian
Languages: Arabic, Kurdish, Armenian, Aramaic, Circassian

Togo

Area: 21,925 sq mi (56,785 sq km)
Population: 6,619,000
Capital: Lomé, pop. 1,451,000
Currency: Communauté Financière Africaine franc
Religions: indigenous beliefs, Christian, Muslim
Languages: French, Ewe, Mina, Kabye, Dagomba

Tajikistan

Area: 55,251 sq mi (143,100 sq km)
Population: 7,450,000
Capital: Dushanbe, pop. 553,000
Currency: somoni
Religions: Sunni Muslim, Shiite Muslim
Languages: Tajik, Russian

Tonga

Area: 289 sq mi (748 sq km)
Population: 103,000
Capital: Nuku'alofa, pop. 25,000
Currency: pa'anga
Religion: Christian
Languages: Tongan, English

COLOR KEY ● Africa ● Australia, New Zealand, and Oceania

Trinidad and Tobago

Area: 1,980 sq mi (5,128 sq km)
Population: 1,333,000
Capital: Port-of-Spain, pop. 54,000
Currency: Trinidad and Tobago dollar
Religions: Roman Catholic, Hindu, Anglican, Baptist
Languages: English, Caribbean Hindustani, French, Spanish, Chinese

Tunisia

Area: 63,170 sq mi (163,610 sq km)
Population: 10,429,000
Capital: Tunis, pop. 746,000
Currency: Tunisian dinar
Religion: Muslim
Languages: Arabic, French

Turkey

Area: 300,948 sq mi (779,452 sq km)
Population: 74,816,000
Capital: Ankara, pop. 3,715,000
Currency: new Turkish lira
Religion: Muslim (mostly Sunni)
Languages: Turkish, Kurdish, Dimli (Zaza), Azeri, Kabardian, Gagauz

Turkmenistan

Area: 188,456 sq mi (488,100 sq km)
Population: 5,110,000
Capital: Ashgabat, pop. 744,000
Currency: Turkmen manat
Religions: Muslim, Eastern Orthodox
Languages: Turkmen, Russian, Uzbek

Tuvalu

Area: 10 sq mi (26 sq km)
Population: 11,000
Capital: Funafuti, pop. 5,000
Currencies: Australian dollar; Tuvaluan dollar
Religion: Church of Tuvalu (Congregationalist)
Languages: Tuvaluan, English, Samoan, Kiribati

Uganda

Area: 93,104 sq mi (241,139 sq km)
Population: 30,700,000
Capital: Kampala, pop. 1,420,000
Currency: Ugandan shilling
Religions: Protestant, Roman Catholic, Muslim
Languages: English, Ganda, other local languages, Kiswahili, Arabic

Ukraine

Area: 233,090 sq mi (603,700 sq km)
Population: 46,030,000
Capital: Kyiv (Kiev), pop. 2,705,000
Currency: hryvnia
Religions: Ukrainian Orthodox, Orthodox, Ukrainian Greek Catholic
Languages: Ukrainian, Russian

United Arab Emirates

Area: 30,000 sq mi (77,700 sq km)
Population: 5,066,000
Capital: Abu Dhabi, pop. 604,000
Currency: Emirati dirham
Religion: Muslim
Languages: Arabic, Persian, English, Hindi, Urdu

United Kingdom

Area: 93,788 sq mi (242,910 sq km)
Population: 61,823,000
Capital: London, pop. 8,566,000
Currency: British pound
Religions: Anglican, Roman Catholic, Presbyterian, Methodist
Languages: English, Welsh, Scottish form of Gaelic

United States

Area: 3,794,083 sq mi (9,826,630 sq km)
Population: 306,805,000
Capital: Washington, DC, pop. 591,833
Currency: U.S. dollar
Religions: Protestant, Roman Catholic
Languages: English, Spanish

● Asia ● Europe ● North America ● South America

Uruguay

Area: 68,037 sq mi
(176,215 sq km)
Population: 3,364,000
Capital: Montevideo, pop. 1,514,000
Currency: Uruguayan peso
Religion: Roman Catholic
Language: Spanish

Uzbekistan

Area: 172,742 sq mi
(447,400 sq km)
Population: 27,562,000
Capital: Tashkent,
pop. 2,184,000
Currency: Uzbekistani sum
Religions: Muslim (mostly Sunni), Eastern Orthodox
Languages: Uzbek, Russian, Tajik

Vanuatu

Area: 4,707 sq mi (12,190 sq km)
Population: 239,000
Capital: Port-Vila, pop. 40,000
Currency: vatu
Religions: Presbyterian, Anglican, Roman Catholic,
other Christian, indigenous beliefs
Languages: over 100 local languages, pidgin
(known as Bislama or Bichelama)

Vatican City

Area: 0.2 sq mi (0.4 sq km)
Population: 798
Capital: Vatican City, pop. 798
Currency: euro
Religion: Roman Catholic
Languages: Italian, Latin, French

COOL CLICK

**Want to see National
Geographic photographs
from around the world? Go online
to the travel photo country gallery.**
travel.nationalgeographic.com/
travel/travel-photos

Venezuela

Area: 352,144 sq mi
(912,050 sq km)
Population: 28,368,000
Capital: Caracas, pop. 2,986,000
Currency: bolivar
Religion: Roman Catholic
Languages: Spanish, numerous indigenous dialects

Vietnam

Area: 127,844 sq mi
(331,114 sq km)
Population: 87,263,000
Capital: Hanoi, pop. 4,377,000
Currency: dong
Religions: Buddhist, Roman Catholic
Languages: Vietnamese, English, French, Chinese, Khmer

Yemen

Area: 207,286 sq mi
(536,869 sq km)
Population: 22,880,000
Capital: Sanaa, pop. 2,008,000
Currency: Yemeni rial
Religions: Muslim, including Shaf'i (Sunni)
and Zaydi (Shiite)
Language: Arabic

Zambia

Area: 290,586 sq mi
(752,614 sq km)
Population: 12,555,000
Capital: Lusaka, pop. 1,328,000
Currency: Zambian kwacha
Religions: Christian, Muslim, Hindu
Languages: English, Bemba, Kaonda, Lozi, Lunda, Luvale,
Nyanja, Tonga, about 70 other indigenous languages

Zimbabwe

Area: 150,872 sq mi
(390,757 sq km)
Population: 12,523,000
Capital: Harare, pop. 1,572,000
Currency: Zimbabwean dollar
Religions: Syncretic (part Christian, part indigenous
beliefs), Christian, indigenous beliefs
Languages: English, Shona, Sindebele, tribal dialects

COLOR KEY ● Africa ● Australia, New Zealand, and Oceania

FunStuff

ROAD TRIP

Aunt Bertha has to make five stops without making any right turns or driving on the same path twice. She must stay on the road and cannot cut through the city blocks. Find the route that will get her from home to the places on her list in order, and then home again.

ANSWER ON PAGE 339

TO DO:
1. TOLL BOOTH
2. FARMERS MARKET
3. BEATRICE'S HOUSE
4. PUMP 'N' GO
5. PARADE

THE POLITICAL
UNITED STATES

9:00 AM PACIFIC TIME

10:00 AM

MOUNTAIN TIME

Cape Flattery

Seattle
Olympia • Tacoma
WASHINGTON
• Spokane
Portland •
• Yakima
Lewiston
• Great Falls
• Minot
Grand Forks
Salem
MONTANA
NORTH DAKOTA
Eugene •
Butte • • Helena
• Bismarck
OREGON
• Billings
• Medford
• Boise
• Klamath Falls
IDAHO
SOUTH DAKOTA
Eureka •
Idaho Falls •
• Cody
• Pierre
Redding •
• Pocatello
Rapid City
Sioux Falls
WYOMING
Reno • Carson City
Great
• Ogden
Casper •
Cheyenne
NEBRASKA
Sacramento •
Lake Tahoe
Basin
Salt Lake City
Laramie
Grand Island
San Francisco • Oakland • San Jose
NEVADA
Provo •
Fort Collins
• Boulder
Denver
S. Platte
Platte
Lincoln
Salinas •
UTAH
Grand Junction
COLORADO
KANSAS
Fresno •
Mojave
Lake Powell
Colorado Springs
• Pueblo
• Dodge City
Wichita
Bakersfield •
Las Vegas
• St. George
Lake Mead
Point Conception
Desert
Grand Canyon
Colorado
Los Angeles •
Long Beach •
• Riverside
• Flagstaff
Santa Fe
Amarillo
OKLA
Oklahoma City
San Diego •
Salton Sea
Phoenix • • Mesa
ARIZONA
• Albuquerque
NEW MEXICO
• Lawton
Yuma
• Tucson
• Roswell
Wichita Falls
• Lubbock
Red
Fort Worth
Las Cruces
• Midland
• Abilene
El Paso
• Odessa
Waco
TEXAS

7:00 AM

HAWAI'I-ALEUTIAN TIME

North Slope
Brooks Range

San Antonio
Austin

Alaska Range
• Juneau
• Anchorage
ALASKA

Kaua'i
Ni'ihau
O'ahu
Moloka'i
Honolulu
Lana'i
Maui
HAWAI'I
Kaho'olawe
Hilo • Hawai'i

Corpus Christi

Laredo

Brownsville

0   400 miles
0   400 kilometers

0   150 mi
0   150 km

8:00 AM

ALASKA TIME

HAWAI'I

7:00 AM

HAWAI'I-ALEUTIAN TIME

ALEUTIAN ISLANDS

Alaska Peninsula

Like a giant quilt, the United States is made up of 50 states. Each is unique, but together they make a national fabric held together by a constitution and a federal government. State boundaries, outlined in dotted lines on the map, set apart internal political units within the country. The national capital—Washington, D.C.—is marked by a star in a double circle. The capital of each state is marked by a star in a single circle.

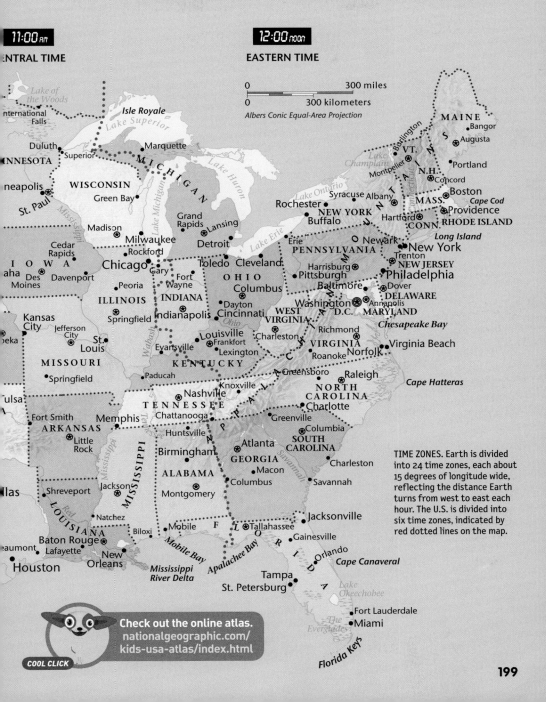

11:00 AM

CENTRAL TIME

12:00 noon

EASTERN TIME

0 — 300 miles
0 — 300 kilometers
Albers Conic Equal-Area Projection

TIME ZONES. Earth is divided into 24 time zones, each about 15 degrees of longitude wide, reflecting the distance Earth turns from west to east each hour. The U.S. is divided into six time zones, indicated by red dotted lines on the map.

Check out the online atlas.
nationalgeographic.com/
kids-usa-atlas/index.html

COOL CLICK

THE PHYSICAL UNITED STATES

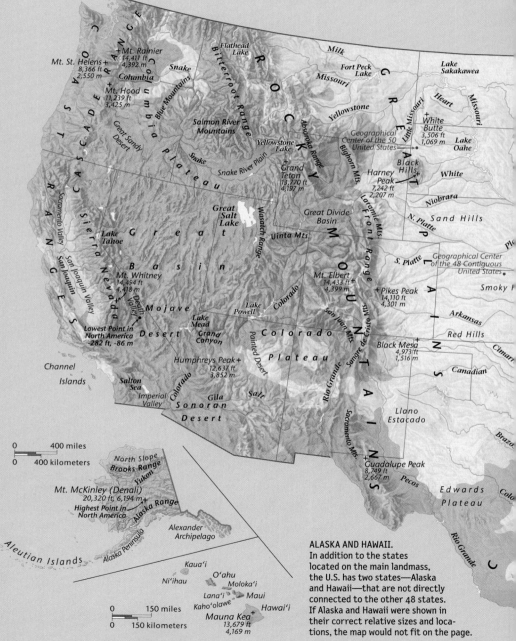

CASCADE RANGE
Mt. St. Helens+
8,366 ft
2,550 m
Mt. Rainier
14,411 ft
4,392 m
Mt. Hood
11,239 ft
3,425 m
Columbia
Snake
Great Sandy Desert
Columbia Plateau
Blue Mountains
Bitterroot Range
Flathead Lake
Salmon River Mountains
Snake
Snake River Plain
Yellowstone Lake
Absaroka Range
Grand Teton
13,770 ft
4,197 m
Milk
Missouri
Fort Peck Lake
Yellowstone
Geographical Center of the 50 United States
Bighorn Mts.
Little Missouri
Heart
White Butte
3,506 ft
1,069 m
Lake Sakakawea
Missouri
Lake Oahe
Black Hills
Harney Peak
7,242 ft
2,207 m
White
Niobrara
Sand Hills
Great Salt Lake
Wasatch Range
Uinta Mts.
Great Divide Basin
Laramie Mts.
Front Range
N. Platte
S. Platte
Geographical Center of the 48 Contiguous United States
Smoky
Lake Tahoe
Sacramento Valley
Sierra Nevada
San Joaquin Valley
Great Basin
Mt. Whitney
14,494 ft
4,418 m
Death Valley
Lowest Point in North America
−282 ft, −86 m
Mojave Desert
Lake Mead
Grand Canyon
Lake Powell
Colorado
Colorado Plateau
Painted Desert
San Juan Mts.
Sangre de Cristo Mts.
Mt. Elbert
14,433 ft
4,399 m
Pikes Peak
14,110 ft
4,301 m
Arkansas
Red Hills
Black Mesa
4,973 ft
1,516 m
Canadian
Cimarron
Humphreys Peak
12,637 ft
3,852 m
San Joaquin
Channel Islands
Salton Sea
Imperial Valley
Colorado
Gila
Salt
Sonoran Desert
Rio Grande
Sacramento Mts.
Guadalupe Peak
8,749 ft
2,667 m
Pecos
Llano Estacado
Edwards Plateau
Brazo
Rio Grande
Colo

0   400 miles
0   400 kilometers

Mt. McKinley (Denali)
20,320 ft; 6,194 m
Highest Point in North America
North Slope
Brooks Range
Yukon
Alaska Range
Alexander Archipelago
Aleutian Islands
Alaska Peninsula

Kaua'i
Ni'ihau
O'ahu
Moloka'i
Lana'i
Kaho'olawe
Maui
Hawai'i
Mauna Kea
13,679 ft
4,169 m

0   150 miles
0   150 kilometers

ALASKA AND HAWAII.
In addition to the states located on the main landmass, the U.S. has two states—Alaska and Hawaii—that are not directly connected to the other 48 states. If Alaska and Hawaii were shown in their correct relative sizes and locations, the map would not fit on the page.

Stretching from the Atlantic Ocean in the east to the Pacific Ocean in the west, the United States is the third largest country (by area) in the world. Its physical diversity ranges from mountains to fertile plains and dry deserts. Shading on the map indicates changes in elevation, while colors show different vegetation patterns.

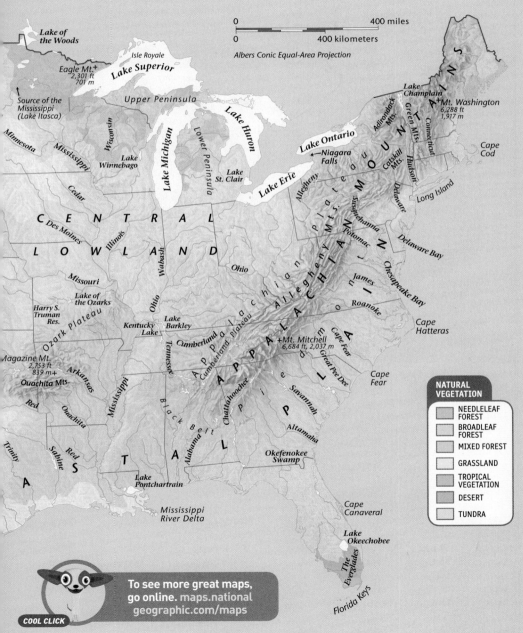

0 — 400 miles
0 — 400 kilometers

Albers Conic Equal-Area Projection

NATURAL VEGETATION

- NEEDLELEAF FOREST
- BROADLEAF FOREST
- MIXED FOREST
- GRASSLAND
- TROPICAL VEGETATION
- DESERT
- TUNDRA

COOL CLICK
To see more great maps, go online. maps.national geographic.com/maps

THE STATES

From sea to shining sea, the United States of America is a nation of diversity. In the more than 230 years since its creation, the nation has grown to become home to a wide range of peoples, industry, and cultures. The following pages present a general overview of all 50 states in the U.S.

The country is generally divided into five large regions: the Northeast, the Southeast, the Midwest, the Southwest, and the West. Though loosely defined, these zones tend to share important similarities, including climate, history, and geography. The color key below provides a guide to which states are in each region.

Flags of each state and highlights of demography and industry are also included. These details offer a brief overview of each state; there are a lot more facts about the states that can be learned online. You can check out state trees, mottos, songs, and more.

Note: U.S. population figures do not reflect the 2010 census.

Color Key by Region

Arizona

Area: 113,998 sq mi (295,256 sq km)
Population: 6,595,778
Capital: Phoenix, pop. 1,567,924
Largest city: Phoenix, pop. 1,567,924
Industry: Real estate, manufactured goods, retail, state and local government, transportation and public utilities, wholesale trade, health services, tourism
State flower/bird: Saguaro/cactus wren

Arkansas

Area: 53,179 sq mi (137,732 sq km)
Population: 2,889,450
Capital: Little Rock, pop. 189,515
Largest city: Little Rock, pop. 189,515
Industry: Services, food processing, paper products, transportation, metal products, machinery, electronics
State flower/bird: Apple blossom/mockingbird

California

Area: 163,696 sq mi (423,972 sq km)
Population: 36,961,664
Capital: Sacramento, pop. 463,794
Largest city: Los Angeles, pop. 3,833,995
Industry: Electronic components and equipment, computers and computer software, tourism, food processing, entertainment, clothing
State flower/bird: Golden poppy/California quail

Alabama

Area: 52,419 sq mi (135,765 sq km)
Population: 4,708,708
Capital: Montgomery, pop. 202,696
Largest city: Birmingham, pop. 228,798
Industry: Retail and wholesale trade, services, government, finance, insurance, real estate, transportation, construction, communication
State flower/bird: Camellia/northern flicker

There are more than 1,000 MILES (1,609 KM) OF BEACHES in California.

Alaska

Area: 663,267 sq mi (1,717,862 sq km)
Population: 698,473
Capital: Juneau, pop. 30,988
Largest city: Anchorage, pop. 279,243
Industry: Petroleum products, government, services, trade
State flower/bird: Forget-me-not/willow ptarmigan

Colorado

Area: 104,094 sq mi (269,602 sq km)
Population: 5,024,748
Capital: Denver, pop. 598,707
Largest city: Denver, pop. 598,707
Industry: Real estate, government, durable goods, communications, health and other services, nondurable goods, transportation
State flower/bird: Columbine/lark bunting

COLOR KEY ● Northeast ● Southeast

Connecticut

Area: 5,543 sq mi (14,357 sq km)
Population: 3,518,288
Capital: Hartford, pop. 124,062
Largest city: Bridgeport, pop. 136,405
Industry: Transportation equipment, metal products, machinery, electrical equipment, printing and publishing, scientific instruments, insurance
State flower/bird: Mountain laurel/robin

Delaware

Area: 2,489 sq mi (6,447 sq km)
Population: 885,122
Capital: Dover, pop. 36,107
Largest city: Wilmington, pop. 72,592
Industry: Food processing, chemicals, rubber and plastic products, scientific instruments, printing and publishing, financial services
State flower/bird: Peach blossom/blue hen chicken

Florida

Area: 65,755 sq mi (170,304 sq km)
Population: 18,537,969
Capital: Tallahassee, pop. 171,922
Largest city: Jacksonville, pop. 807,815
Industry: Tourism, health services, business services, communications, banking, electronic equipment, insurance
State flower/bird: Orange blossom/mockingbird

1. It is home to the oldest permanently occupied European settlement in the U.S., Saint Augustine.

2. Orange juice was named the state beverage in 1967.

3. Fort Lauderdale, Florida, is known as the Venice of America because it has 165 miles (266 km) of navigable waterways.

4. Florida is home to the largest subtropical wilderness in the United States—the Everglades.

5. The Florida Keys are a cluster of about 1,700 islands that begin at the southeastern tip of the Florida peninsula.

Georgia

Area: 59,425 sq mi (153,910 sq km)
Population: 9,829,211
Capital: Atlanta, pop. 537,958
Largest city: Atlanta, pop. 537,958
Industry: Textiles and clothing, transportation equipment, food processing, paper products, chemicals, electrical equipment, tourism
State flower/bird: Cherokee rose/brown thrasher

Hawaii

Area: 10,931 sq mi (28,311 sq km)
Population: 1,295,178
Capital: Honolulu, pop. 374,676
Largest city: Honolulu, pop. 374,676
Industry: Tourism, trade, finance, food processing, petroleum refining, stone, clay, glass products
State flower/bird: Hibiscus/Hawaiian goose (nene)

Idaho

Area: 83,570 sq mi (216,447 sq km)
Population: 1,545,801
Capital: Boise, pop. 205,314
Largest city: Boise, pop. 205,314
Industry: Electronics and computer equipment, tourism, food processing, forest products, mining
State flower/bird: Syringa (Lewis's mock orange)/ mountain bluebird

Illinois

Area: 57,914 sq mi (149,998 sq km)
Population: 12,910,409
Capital: Springfield, pop. 117,352
Largest city: Chicago, pop. 2,853,114
Industry: Industrial machinery, electronic equipment, food processing, chemicals, metals, printing and publishing, rubber and plastics, motor vehicles
State flower/bird: Violet/cardinal

Indiana

Area: 36,418 sq mi (94,322 sq km)
Population: 6,423,113
Capital: Indianapolis, pop. 798,382
Largest city: Indianapolis, pop. 798,382
Industry: Transportation equipment, steel, pharmaceutical and chemical products, machinery, petroleum, coal
State flower/bird: Peony/cardinal

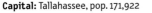

● Midwest ● Southwest ● West

COOL CLICK

Check out great state facts online. **state.me.us**
This is for Maine. For each state insert the two-letter state abbreviation (see p. 209) where "me" is now.

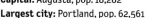

Maine

Area: 35,385 sq mi (91,646 sq km)
Population: 1,318,301
Capital: Augusta, pop. 18,282
Largest city: Portland, pop. 62,561
Industry: Health services, tourism, forest products, leather products, electrical equipment, food processing
State flower/bird: White pine cone and tassel/chickadee

Iowa

Area: 56,272 sq mi (145,743 sq km)
Population: 3,007,856
Capital: Des Moines, pop. 197,052
Largest city: Des Moines, pop. 197,052
Industry: Real estate, health services, industrial machinery, food processing, construction
State flower/bird: Wild rose/American goldfinch

Maryland

Area: 12,407 sq mi (32,133 sq km)
Population: 5,699,478
Capital: Annapolis, pop. 36,524
Largest city: Baltimore, pop. 636,919
Industry: Real estate, federal government, health services, business services, engineering services
State flower/bird: Black-eyed Susan/northern (Baltimore) oriole

Kansas

Area: 82,277 sq mi (213,097 sq km)
Population: 2,818,747
Capital: Topeka, pop. 123,446
Largest city: Wichita, pop. 366,046
Industry: Aircraft manufacturing, transportation equipment, construction, food processing, printing and publishing, health care
State flower/bird: Sunflower/western meadowlark

Massachusetts

Area: 10,555 sq mi (27,336 sq km)
Population: 6,593,587
Capital: Boston, pop. 609,023
Largest city: Boston, pop. 609,023
Industry: Electrical equipment, machinery, metal products, scientific instruments, printing and publishing, tourism
State flower/bird: Mayflower/chickadee

Kentucky

Area: 40,409 sq mi (104,659 sq km)
Population: 4,314,113
Capital: Frankfort, pop. 27,322
Largest city: Louisville, pop. 557,224
Industry: Manufacturing, services, government, finance, insurance, real estate, retail trade, transportation, wholesale trade, construction, mining
State flower/bird: Goldenrod/cardinal

Michigan

Area: 96,716 sq mi (250,495 sq km)
Population: 9,969,727
Capital: Lansing, pop. 113,968
Largest city: Detroit, pop. 912,062
Industry: Motor vehicles and parts, machinery, metal products, office furniture, tourism, chemicals
State flower/bird: Apple blossom/robin

Louisiana

Area: 51,840 sq mi (134,265 sq km)
Population: 4,492,076
Capital: Baton Rouge, pop. 223,689
Largest city: New Orleans, pop. 311,853
Industry: Chemicals, petroleum products, food processing, health services, tourism, oil and natural gas extraction, paper products
State flower/bird: Magnolia/brown pelican

Minnesota

Area: 86,939 sq mi (225,172 sq km)
Population: 5,226,214
Capital: St. Paul, pop. 279,590
Largest city: Minneapolis, pop. 382,605
Industry: estate, banking and insurance, industrial machinery, printing and publishing, food processing, scientific equipment
State flower/bird: Showy lady's slipper/common loon

COLOR KEY ● Northeast ● Southeast

Mississippi

Area: 48,430 sq mi (125,434 sq km)
Population: 2,951,996
Capital: Jackson, pop. 173,861
Largest city: Jackson, pop. 173,861
Industry: Petroleum products, health services, electronic equipment, transportation, banking, forest products, communications
State flower/bird: Magnolia/mockingbird

The **TEDDY BEAR** is the official state toy of Mississippi.

Missouri

Area: 69,704 sq mi (180,534 sq km)
Population: 5,987,580
Capital: Jefferson City, pop. 40,771
Largest city: Kansas City, pop. 451,572
Industry: Transportation equipment, food processing, chemicals, electrical equipment, metal products
State flower/bird: Hawthorn/eastern bluebird

Montana

Area: 147,042 sq mi (380,840 sq km)
Population: 974,989
Capital: Helena, pop. 29,351
Largest city: Billings, pop. 103,994
Industry: Forest products, food processing, mining, construction, tourism
State flower/bird: Bitterroot/western meadowlark

Nebraska

Area: 77,354 sq mi (200,346 sq km)
Population: 1,796,619
Capital: Lincoln, pop. 251,624
Largest city: Omaha, pop. 438,646
Industry: Food processing, machinery, electrical equipment, printing and publishing
State flower/bird: Goldenrod/western meadowlark

Nevada

Area: 110,561 sq mi (286,352 sq km)
Population: 2,643,085
Capital: Carson City, pop. 54,867
Largest city: Las Vegas, pop. 558,383
Industry: Tourism and gaming, mining, printing and publishing, food processing, electrical equipment
State flower/bird: Sagebrush/mountain bluebird

New Hampshire

Area: 9,350 sq mi (24,216 sq km)
Population: 1,324,575
Capital: Concord, pop. 42,255
Largest city: Manchester, pop. 108,586
Industry: Machinery, electronics, metal products
State flower/bird: Purple lilac/purple finch

New Jersey

Area: 8,721 sq mi (22,588 sq km)
Population: 8,707,739
Capital: Trenton, pop. 82,883
Largest city: Newark, pop. 278,980
Industry: Machinery, electronics, metal products, chemicals
State flower/bird: Violet/American goldfinch

New Mexico

Area: 121,590 sq mi (314,917 sq km)
Population: 2,009,671
Capital: Santa Fe, pop. 71,831
Largest city: Albuquerque, pop. 521,999
Industry: Electronic equipment, state and local government, real estate, business services, federal government, oil and gas extraction, health services
State flower/bird: Yucca/roadrunner

New York

Area: 54,556 sq mi (141,300 sq km)
Population: 19,541,453
Capital: Albany, pop. 93,539
Largest city: New York City, pop. 8,363,710
Industry: Printing and publishing, machinery, computer products, finance, tourism
State flower/bird: Rose/eastern bluebird

● Midwest ● Southwest ● West

North Carolina

Area: 53,819 sq mi (139,390 sq km)
Population: 9,380,884
Capital: Raleigh, pop. 392,552
Largest city: Charlotte, pop. 687,456
Industry: Real estate, health services, chemicals, tobacco products, finance, textiles
State flower/bird: Flowering dogwood/cardinal

North Dakota

Area: 70,700 sq mi (183,113 sq km)
Population: 646,844
Capital: Bismarck, pop. 60,389
Largest city: Fargo, pop. 93,531
Industry: Services, government, finance, construction, transportation, oil and gas
State flower/bird: Wild prairie rose/western meadowlark

Ohio

Area: 44,825 sq mi (116,097 sq km)
Population: 11,542,645
Capital: Columbus, pop. 754,885
Largest city: Columbus, pop. 754,885
Industry: Transportation equipment, metal products, machinery, food processing, electrical equipment
State flower/bird: Scarlet carnation/cardinal

TOMATO JUICE IS THE STATE DRINK OF OHIO.

Oklahoma

Area: 69,898 sq mi (181,036 sq km)
Population: 3,687,050
Capital: Oklahoma City, pop. 551,789
Largest city: Oklahoma City, pop. 551,789
Industry: Manufacturing, services, government, finance, insurance, real estate
State flower/bird: Mistletoe/scissor-tailed flycatcher

Oregon

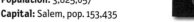

Area: 98,381 sq mi (254,806 sq km)
Population: 3,825,657
Capital: Salem, pop. 153,435
Largest city: Portland, pop. 557,706
Industry: Real estate, retail and wholesale trade, electronic equipment, health services, construction, forest products, business services
State flower/bird: Oregon grape/western meadowlark

Pennsylvania

Area: 46,055 sq mi (119,283 sq km)
Population: 12,604,767
Capital: Harrisburg, pop. 47,148
Largest city: Philadelphia, pop. 1,447,395
Industry: Machinery, printing and publishing, forest products, metal products
State flower/bird: Mountain laurel/ruffed grouse

Rhode Island

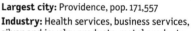

Area: 1,545 sq mi (4,002 sq km)
Population: 1,053,209
Capital: Providence, pop. 171,557
Largest city: Providence, pop. 171,557
Industry: Health services, business services, silver and jewelry products, metal products
State flower/bird: Violet/Rhode Island red

South Carolina

Area: 32,020 sq mi (82,932 sq km)
Population: 4,561,242
Capital: Columbia, pop. 127,029
Largest city: Columbia, pop. 127,029
Industry: Service industries, tourism, chemicals, textiles, machinery, forest products
State flower/bird: Yellow jessamine/Carolina wren

South Dakota

Area: 77,117 sq mi (199,732 sq km)
Population: 812,383
Capital: Pierre, pop. 13,899
Largest city: Sioux Falls, pop. 154,997
Industry: Finance, services, manufacturing, government, retail trade, transportation and utilities, wholesale trade, construction, mining
State flower/bird: Pasqueflower/ring-necked pheasant

COLOR KEY ● Northeast ● Southeast

Tennessee

Area: 42,143 sq mi (109,151 sq km)
Population: 6,296,254
Capital: Nashville, pop. 596,462
Largest city: Memphis, pop. 669,651
Industry: Service industries, chemicals, transportation equipment, processed foods, machinery
State flower/bird: Iris/mockingbird

Texas

Area: 268,581 sq mi (695,624 sq km)
Population: 24,782,302
Capital: Austin, pop. 757,688
Largest city: Houston, pop. 2,242,193
Industry: Chemicals, machinery, electronics and computers, food products, petroleum and natural gas, transportation equipment
State flower/bird: Bluebonnet/mockingbird

San Antonio, Texas, is called "The Tejano Music Capital Of The World."

Utah

Area: 84,899 sq mi (219,888 sq km)
Population: 2,784,572
Capital: Salt Lake City, pop. 181,698
Largest city: Salt Lake City, pop. 181,698
Industry: Government, manufacturing, real estate, construction, health services, business services, banking
State flower/bird: Sego lily/California gull

Vermont

Area: 9,614 sq mi (24,901 sq km)
Population: 621,760
Capital: Montpelier, pop. 7,760
Largest city: Burlington, pop. 38,897
Industry: Health services, tourism, finance, real estate, computer components, electrical parts, printing and publishing, machine tools
State flower/bird: Red clover/hermit thrush

Virginia

Area: 42,774 sq mi (110,785 sq km)
Population: 7,882,590
Capital: Richmond, pop. 202,002
Largest city: Virginia Beach, pop. 433,746
Industry: Food processing, communication and electronic equipment, transportation equipment, printing, shipbuilding, textiles
State flower/bird: Flowering dogwood/cardinal

Washington

Area: 71,300 sq mi (184,666 sq km)
Population: 6,664,195
Capital: Olympia, pop. 45,322
Largest city: Seattle, pop. 598,541
Industry: Aerospace, tourism, food processing, forest products, paper products, industrial machinery, printing and publishing, metals, computer software
State flower/bird: Coast rhododendron/Amer. goldfinch

West Virginia

Area: 24,230 sq mi (62,755 sq km)
Population: 1,819,777
Capital: Charleston, pop. 50,302
Largest city: Charleston, pop. 50,302
Industry: Tourism, coal mining, chemicals, metal manufacturing, forest products, stone, clay, oil, glass products
State flower/bird: Rhododendron/cardinal

Wisconsin

Area: 65,498 sq mi (169,639 sq km)
Population: 5,654,774
Capital: Madison, pop. 231,916
Largest city: Milwaukee, pop. 604,447
Industry: Industrial machinery, paper products, food processing, metal products, electronic equipment, transportation
State flower/bird: Wood violet/robin

Wyoming

Area: 97,814 sq mi (253,337 sq km)
Population: 544,270
Capital: Cheyenne, pop. 56,915
Largest city: Cheyenne, pop. 56,915
Industry: Oil and natural gas, mining, generation of electricity, chemicals, tourism
State flower/bird: Indian paintbrush/western meadowlark

● Midwest ● Southwest ● West

THE TERRITORIES

The United States has 14 territories—political divisions that are not states. Three of these are in the Caribbean Sea, and the other eleven are in the Pacific Ocean.

The brown tree snake probably arrived in Guam on cargo ships in the 1950s. The snake has greatly reduced the island's bird and small mammal populations and causes power outages when it climbs electrical poles.

U.S. CARIBBEAN TERRITORIES

Puerto Rico

Area: 3,508 sq mi (9,086 sq km)
Population: 3,967,288
Capital: San Juan (proper), pop. 422,665
Languages: Spanish, English

U.S. Virgin Islands

Area: 149 sq mi (386 sq km)
Population: 111,000
Capital: Charlotte Amalie, pop. 53,000
Languages: English, Spanish or Spanish Creole, French or French Creole

U.S. PACIFIC TERRITORIES

American Samoa

Area: 77 sq mi (199 sq km)
Population: 71,000
Capital: Pago Pago, pop. 58,000
Language: Samoan

Guam

Area: 217 sq mi (561 sq km)
Population: 180,000
Capital: Hagåtña (Agana), pop. 149,000
Languages: English, Chamorro, Philippine languages

Northern Mariana Islands

Area: 184 sq mi (477 sq km)
Population: 88,000
Capital: Saipan, pop. 76,000
Languages: Philippine languages, Chinese, Chamorro, English

Other U.S. Territories

Baker Island, Howland Island, Jarvis Island, Johnston Atoll, Kingman Reef, Midway Islands, Palmyra Atoll, Wake Island, Navassa Island (in the Caribbean)

THE NATION'S CAPITAL

District of Columbia

Area: 68 sq mi (177 sq km)
Population: 599,657

Abraham Lincoln, who was President during the Civil War and a strong opponent of slavery, is remembered in a monument that houses this seated statue, located at the opposite end of the National Mall from the U.S. Capitol Building.

The Smithsonian Institution, the world's largest museum, is actually made up of 19 museums. Established in 1846, the Smithsonian is sometimes referred to as the nation's attic because of its large collections.

COLOR KEY ● Territories ● Northeast

Bet you didn't know

More **TRIPLETS** are **BORN** in **NEBRASKA** than in any other state.

On average, **HAWAIIANS LIVE FIVE YEARS LONGER** than residents of Louisiana.

The town of **Liberal, Kansas**, has an **EXACT REPLICA** of Dorothy's house in **THE WIZARD OF OZ**.

WASHINGTON, D.C., was the **first planned** capital city in the world.

OREGON has the **most ghost towns** of any state in the country.

Florida and North Dakota **have had the fewest earthquakes** of any state.

Rainbow Bridge, the largest natural stone bridge in the world, **is located in Utah.**

Two-Letter Postal Abbreviations

AK	Alaska
AL	Alabama
AR	Arkansas
AS	American Samoa
AZ	Arizona
CA	California
CO	Colorado
CT	Connecticut
DC	District of Columbia
DE	Delaware
FL	Florida
GA	Georgia
GU	Guam
HI	Hawaii
IA	Iowa
ID	Idaho
IL	Illinois
IN	Indiana
KS	Kansas
KY	Kentucky
LA	Louisiana
MA	Massachusetts
MD	Maryland
ME	Maine
MI	Michigan
MN	Minnesota
MO	Missouri
MP	Northern Mariana Islands
MS	Mississippi
MT	Montana
NC	North Carolina
ND	North Dakota
NE	Nebraska
NH	New Hampshire
NJ	New Jersey
NM	New Mexico
NV	Nevada
NY	New York
OH	Ohio
OK	Oklahoma
OR	Oregon
PA	Pennsylvania
PR	Puerto Rico
RI	Rhode Island
SC	South Carolina
SD	South Dakota
TN	Tennessee
TX	Texas
UT	Utah
VA	Virginia
VI	US Virgin Islands
VT	Vermont
WA	Washington
WI	Wisconsin
WV	West Virginia
WY	Wyoming

URBAN GIANT

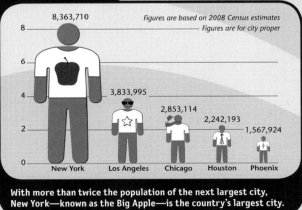

Figures are based on 2008 Census estimates
Figures are for city proper

New York: 8,363,710
Los Angeles: 3,833,995
Chicago: 2,853,114
Houston: 2,242,193
Phoenix: 1,567,924

With more than twice the population of the next largest city, New York—known as the Big Apple—is the country's largest city.

Moving Along

Migration is when people move from one locality to another, often over long distances. Immigration is when this occurs between countries. Sounds simple, right? It's actually a lot more complicated than it sounds.

Migration, and, in turn, immigration, are evolutionary forces—powerful patterns that can have a tremendous impact—on people, land, economy, history, and more. For example, imagine if you had a whole city of people who just got up and left. What would happen? The city would collapse because there would be no one to support it. That may be an extreme example of migration, but it does help to show just how influential it can be—and it's not so far from the truth! After World War II, white Americans began leaving the major cities in droves to head for the newly created suburbs. This "suburbanization" occurred because people started to believe that the cities were dangerous and that the suburbs were safer places to raise families. As a result, the demographics of American cities changed greatly. Although most migrations are elective, they are generally out of a desire to change something about the circumstances in which the people currently live. People migrate to other places for economic reasons, environmental reasons, societal reasons, and even for religious freedom. After all, that's what the Puritans were doing when they first came to the New World.

Some migrations are forced, as a result of environmental or natural disasters, or authoritarian regimes trying to drive away groups of people. This international problem, known as human displacement, can be accompanied by a great deal of violence, particularly when it is conflict-induced. This can also cause large numbers of refugees, or people who flee to a foreign country to escape danger.

Migration of all types is a hot-button issue in our ever-changing world. It generates a tremendous amount of international economic, political, and ethical debate over policies toward immigrants and refugees.

POPULATION SHIFT

Since its creation, the United States has seen a number of migration shifts. In the latter half of the 20th century, people moved from the historical, industrial, and agricultural regions of the Northeast and Midwest toward the South and West. This move was motivated by the promise of jobs, generally lower living costs, and a more relaxed way of life. States such as Nevada, Arizona, and Idaho saw more than a 25 percent change in their total populations.

Percent Change in Total Population from 1990 to 2000 (by State)

More than 25   13–25   Less than 13

NATION OF IMMIGRANTS

Mexico
3,470,000

Figures represent the total number of legal permanent residents, 2007

Philippines
570,000

India
520,000

China
510,000

Dominican Republic
440,000

Since its founding, the United States has attracted people from other lands. Today, most immigrants to the U.S. come from Latin America and Asia.

The Statue of Liberty, Liberty Island, New York-New Jersey (left), greeted immigrants arriving at Ellis Island, New York (background photo), from the 1890s to the 1930s.

United States/Mexico border fence

Learn about the American immigrant experience online. ellisisland.org

COOL CLICK

Wacky Road Trip

Check out these **5** strange-but-true roadside attractions

Enchanted Highway

REGENT, NORTH DAKOTA

Don't freak out when you spy a 40-foot (12-m) -tall pheasant standing next to a highway—there's a 45-foot (14-m) -tall farmer and a 60-foot (18-m) -long grasshopper just down the road. The Enchanted Highway is a stretch of metal sculptures displayed for 32 miles (51 km) along the road. You won't get bored on this drive.

1

2 Mac the Moose

MOOSE JAW, SASKATCHEWAN

You probably wouldn't be that surprised to see a moose in Canada, but what if it were 32-foot (10-m) -tall? Well, that's what you'll find when you head to the Moose Jaw, Saskatchewan, information center. Built in 1984 to help welcome visitors to this tourist town, Mac weighs in at a hearty 10 tons (9,072 kg).

3 Fremont Troll

SEATTLE, WASHINGTON

Even though this 18-foot (5-m) -tall troll under a bridge is—*yikes!*—clutching a real car in his left hand, a person climbing up his arm won't bother him a bit. Made of concrete over steel rods and wire, the troll took about seven weeks to build. City officials hoped that the art would prevent people from dumping trash under the bridge. Or maybe they wanted to scare away the litterbugs.

4 Giant Trumpet

SCHLADMING, AUSTRIA

This trumpet can't play music, but it sure does get a lot of attention. Located in a small mining town, the 49-foot (15-m) -long instrument is the largest trumpet in the world.

5 Muskie the Fiberglass Fish

HAYWARD, WISCONSIN

If you're wondering what life looks like from the mouth of a giant fish, this sculpture is for you. A ramp takes you into the four-and-a-half story fish and up to a lookout deck in its mouth. From there, gaze down on other giant fiberglass fish in front of the National Freshwater Fishing Hall of Fame. Don't worry—there aren't any giant hooks!

ADULT
HUMAN!

EARTH-FRIENDLY VACATIONS
How to have fun and protect the planet, too!

Going green can be a blast—especially if you do it while you're on vacation. Nothing's more fun than traveling to new places, but tourism can also hurt the environment. Cars and airplanes pollute the air. And tourists sometimes litter or damage the sites they come to see. So why be a regular tourist, when you can be an ecotourist? Earth-friendly travelers live by a golden rule: **Take only photographs, leave only footprints.** That means traveling to natural areas to observe—but not disturb—wild animals and plants. Ecotourists also explore local cultures, conserve resources such as water and fuel, and give back to the environment. Check out these cool vacations to find out how you can see the world and still be kind to the Earth.

GUIDE TO YOUR VACATION PERSONALITY

Find the symbols below that describe you. Look for them at right to pick a vacation that could be right for you.

My favorite vacations are near the water.

I love wildlife.

I'm really active.

I like learning about other cultures.

GIVE BACK TO THE EARTH

DESTINATION JAPAN

THE ADVENTURE Catch endangered Reverdin's butterflies at the base of beautiful Mount Fuji. Mark an identification number on each butterfly's wings before releasing it back into the wild.

WHY IT'S ECO-FRIENDLY The harmless markings help scientists monitor the butterfly's population.

LEARN ABOUT ANIMALS

DESTINATION SWEDEN

THE ADVENTURE Go reindeer trekking in the Arctic. For thousands of years, the Sami (SAH-me) people survived by herding reindeer in Sweden, Finland, Norway, and Russia. Live among the reindeer as Sami guides introduce you to their way of life. Sleep in a tent called a *kâta* (KAH-tah).

WHY IT'S ECO-FRIENDLY You can help the Sami save their native land from logging and other threats.

ECO-FRIENDLY LOCATIONS

DESTINATION BAHAMAS

THE ADVENTURE Strap on your snorkel and mask and slip into the Atlantic Ocean. Give a coral reef a checkup by measuring the water temperature and size of the reef. Count tropical fish species, such as parrotfish and barracuda.

WHY IT'S ECO-FRIENDLY A healthy coral reef provides a habitat for thousands of sea animals and helps protect the island from flooding during storms.

ECO-LINGO

eco-friendly Anything that's helpful, rather than harmful, to the environment.

green It's easy to be green. Just use less, and think renewable, sustainable, and eco-friendly.

SIGNS
OF THE TIMES

Do you think seeing is believing? Not always! Two of these signs are not real. Can you figure out which two are fake?

ANSWERS ON PAGE 339

1

2

HAM SANDWICH 3 ½

FINGLESHAM EASTRY R.D.C.

3

SOFT SHOULDER

4

CornDog 00 LN

6

NO TURNS 8ᴬᴹ – 7ᴾᴹ EXCEPT SUNDAY

DONT LOOK

5

READLYN

"857 friendly people AND ONE OLD GRUMP"

7

NO WAY

Galápagos Islands
VACATION

Dozens of Pacific green sea turtles slowly glide by as you snorkel along a rugged reef. Suddenly a snorkeler cuts you off. Then another. Then you realize: These aren't snorkelers. They're sea lions! That's what might happen if you visit the Galápagos Islands, a group of islands straddling the Equator west of Ecuador, in South America.

Humans aren't allowed to live on most of the Galápagos Islands, so the animals are unafraid of people. You can walk along hardened lava to see even more wildlife—fur seals, bright red crabs, blue-footed boobys (right), orcas, marine iguanas, flightless birds called cormorants, and penguins.

"The Galápagos Islands seem to break all the rules of nature," says Hannah, who was 14 years old when she visited the islands.

A trip to the Galápagos Islands may change the way you think about the world.

TOP HISTORIC
Places to Visit

1	Wachau/Melk Abbey, Austria
2	Niagara-on-the-Lake, Ontario, Canada
3	Historic Center of Ghent, Belgium
4	Nikko historic areas, Japan
5	Graz, Austria
6	Stockholm's Gamla Stan, Sweden
7	Aix-en-Provence, France
8	Potsdam historic areas, Germany
9	Dijon and Bourgogne region, France
10	Columbia, Indiana, United States

For more on these and other historic destinations, go online.
traveler.national
geographic.com

SHOPPER'S PARADISE

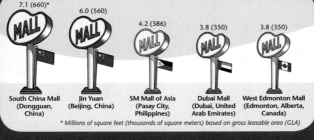

7.1 (660)* — South China Mall (Dongguan, China)
6.0 (560) — Jin Yuan (Beijing, China)
4.2 (386) — SM Mall of Asia (Pasay City, Philippines)
3.8 (350) — Dubai Mall (Dubai, United Arab Emirates)
3.8 (350) — West Edmonton Mall (Edmonton, Alberta, Canada)

* Millions of square feet (thousands of square meters) based on gross leasable area (GLA)

People love to shop, and the South China Mall in Dongguan, China, is larger than any other mall in the world.

Visiting Iceland? DON'T TIP in restaurants. It's considered an insult.

The ORIGINAL 7 of the WONDERS of the WORLD

More than 2,000 years ago, many travelers wrote about sights they had seen on their journeys. Over time, seven of those places made history as the "wonders of the ancient world." There are seven because the Greeks, who made the list, believed the number seven to be magical.

THE PYRAMIDS OF GIZA, EGYPT
BUILT: ABOUT 2600 B.C.
MASSIVE TOMBS OF EGYPTIAN PHARAOHS, THE PYRAMIDS ARE THE ONLY ANCIENT WONDERS STILL STANDING TODAY.

HANGING GARDENS OF BABYLON, IRAQ
BUILT: DATE UNKNOWN
LEGEND HAS IT THAT THIS GARDEN PARADISE WAS PLANTED ON AN ARTIFICIAL MOUNTAIN, BUT MANY EXPERTS SAY IT NEVER REALLY EXISTED.

TEMPLE OF ARTEMIS AT EPHESUS, TURKEY
BUILT: SIXTH CENTURY B.C.
THIS TOWERING TEMPLE WAS BUILT TO HONOR ARTEMIS, THE GREEK GODDESS OF THE HUNT.

STATUE OF ZEUS, GREECE
BUILT: FIFTH CENTURY B.C.
THIS 40-FOOT (12-M) STATUE DEPICTED THE KING OF THE GREEK GODS.

MAUSOLEUM AT HALICARNASSUS, TURKEY
BUILT: FOURTH CENTURY B.C.
THIS ELABORATE TOMB WAS BUILT FOR KING MAUSOLUS.

COLOSSUS OF RHODES, RHODES (AN ISLAND IN THE AEGEAN SEA)
BUILT: FOURTH CENTURY B.C.
A 110-FOOT (34-M) STATUE HONORED THE GREEK SUN GOD HELIOS.

LIGHTHOUSE OF ALEXANDRIA, EGYPT
BUILT: THIRD CENTURY B.C.
THE WORLD'S FIRST LIGHT-HOUSE, IT USED MIRRORS TO REFLECT SUNLIGHT FOR MILES OUT TO SEA.

The NEW 7 of the WONDERS of the WORLD

Why name new wonders of the world? Most of the original ancient wonders no longer exist. To be eligible for the new list, the wonders had to be man-made before the year 2000 and in preservation. They were selected through a poll of more than 100 million voters!

TAJ MAHAL, INDIA
COMPLETED: 1648
THIS LAVISH TOMB WAS BUILT AS A FINAL RESTING PLACE FOR THE BELOVED WIFE OF EMPEROR SHAH JAHAN.

PETRA, SOUTHWEST JORDAN
COMPLETED: ABOUT 200 B.C.
SOME 30,000 PEOPLE ONCE LIVED IN THIS ROCK CITY CARVED INTO CLIFF WALLS.

MACHU PICCHU, PERU
COMPLETED: ABOUT 1450
OFTEN CALLED "THE LOST CITY IN THE CLOUDS," MACHU PICCHU IS PERCHED 7,972 FEET (2,430 M) HIGH IN THE ANDES.

THE COLOSSEUM, ITALY
COMPLETED: A.D. 80
HERE, WILD ANIMALS—AND HUMANS—FOUGHT EACH OTHER TO THE DEATH BEFORE 50,000 BLOODTHIRSTY SPECTATORS.

CHRIST THE REDEEMER STATUE, BRAZIL
COMPLETED: 1931
TOWERING ATOP CORCOVADO MOUNTAIN, THIS STATUE IS TALLER THAN A 12-STORY BUILDING AND WEIGHS ABOUT 2.5 MILLION POUNDS (1.1 MILLION KG).

CHICHÉN ITZÁ, MEXICO
COMPLETED: TENTH CENTURY
ONCE THE CAPITAL CITY OF THE ANCIENT MAYA EMPIRE, CHICHÉN ITZÁ IS HOME TO THE FAMOUS PYRAMID OF KUKULCÁN.

GREAT WALL OF CHINA, CHINA
COMPLETED: 1644
THE LONGEST MAN-MADE STRUCTURE EVER BUILT, IT WINDS OVER AN ESTIMATED 4,500 MILES (7,000 KM).

10 Cool Things About the WHITE HOUSE

Only a few families know what it's like to live in the White House, but we've got inside access. Here are ten reasons why it rocks when the White House is your home.

1 The President doesn't have to wait in an airport. Whenever he flies, a **helicopter** called *Marine One,* lands right on the South Lawn of the White House to pick him up. The helicopter takes him to an air force base, where he walks right onto his plane, known as *Air Force One.*

2 Like sports? You'd love living in the White House. It has a basketball court, tennis court, swimming pool, **pool table,** putting green, and horseshoe pit.

3 If you're a guest at the White House, you might sleep in the **Lincoln Bedroom.** But Abe never slept there—it was his office. The Queens' Bedroom, next door, is named for the many queens who have stayed there.

4 There's no helping Dad paint the house at the White House. Workers use 570 gallons (2,158 L) of **paint** to cover the outside. A tower of 570 gallon-size cans is taller than the Statue of Liberty!

5 You probably won't wait for a **bathroom** at the White House. It has 35 of them, 15 of which contain bathtubs or showers.

6 Holidays at the White House are always fun for kids. On the Monday after every Easter, an Easter Egg Roll is held on the South Lawn. During Christmas, the First Family holds a special party just for kids. The White House **Christmas tree** is usually almost 20 feet (6 m) tall!

7 How'd you like to ride to school in this? The President is picked up in Cadillac One, a **special limousine** that's driven only by Secret Service agents. It's so safe that no one will even hint at what kind of security devices are installed in the car. All we can tell you is that only Secret Service agents can open and close the doors. The limo is even flown overseas when the President travels!

8
If you want a midnight snack, somewhere in the White House there's one waiting 24/7. The White House has five kitchens—a main one on the ground floor, an upstairs kitchen for the family, an underground one for the staff, one for guests, and a **pastry kitchen** just for desserts. With five chefs on duty, the food staff can prepare dinner for 140 people and snacks for more than 1,000.

9
Some claim the White House is haunted. Legend has it that President **John Adams's ghostly wife, Abigail,** hangs laundry. Other people say they've glimpsed Lincoln's ghost pacing the floor. One tale even tells of the ghost of Dolley Madison shouting at workers about to tear up her rose garden.

10
The First Family never has to go out to the movies—the White House has a **59-seat theater.** The President sees movies with family and friends, sometimes before the flicks open at the box office.

Ever wonder what's hanging on the walls of the White House? Well, it has quite the fine art collection, and it is featured throughout the building. Go online to find out more about this beautiful national collection. whitehouse.gov/history/art

COOL CLICK

WORLD'S COOLEST

CHECK OUT THIS AMAZING ROTATING BUILDING

Humans have built incredible structures, including the Great Wall of China and the pyramids of Egypt. But there's one thing that even the world's most amazing structures can't do: alter their shapes. Well, that could change.

Someday, you could live in a shape-shifting skyscraper that never stays still. The first of these buildings, which are called Dynamic Towers, will be built in Dubai, a city in the United Arab Emirates in the Middle East. It will be about two-and-a-half times taller than the Washington Monument. Each floor will be in constant motion, rotating independently and at different speeds—like an 80-story Rubik's Cube forever being twisted by invisible hands. "These buildings will never look the same," according to David Fisher, the architect behind the idea.

EVER-CHANGING

This may sound like fantasy, but in a few years the Dynamic Tower is expected to become a reality. The first 35 floors will consist of offices and a luxury hotel. Floors 36 through 70 will house numerous apartments, but each of the top ten floors in the 80-story tower will be a single apartment. While the architect will control the movement of most of the floors, anyone who owns one of the top ten apartments will be able to move them however they like. Each luxury apartment, expected to cost about $36 million, will have more space inside than five average houses in the United States put together.

IT ROTATES!

SKYSCRAPERS

GREENEST SKYSCRAPER

Wind will power the tower's motion, making it the first self-powered skyscraper in history. To generate electricity, the Dubai skyscraper will place windmill blades horizontally between each floor of the building (below). There will be 79 wind turbines. In addition, the roofs will have solar panels to capture the sun's energy. Combined, this will make enough electricity to power the entire tower—and several nearby as well.

SKYSCRAPER FACTORIES

Skyscrapers are usually built one floor at a time—but not the Dynamic Tower: It will be the world's first skyscraper to be built in a factory. Only the enormous concrete core cylinder will be built on-site, while each floor will be made at a factory. They will be shipped to the construction site ready to go: Even the furniture will be inside. All of this will make construction safer, faster, and less expensive.

SUPERSTRUCTURES

Take a look at these remarkable facts about six of the world's skyscrapers.

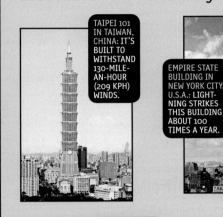

TAIPEI 101 IN TAIWAN, CHINA: IT'S BUILT TO WITHSTAND 130-MILE-AN-HOUR (209 KPH) WINDS.

EMPIRE STATE BUILDING IN NEW YORK CITY, U.S.A.: LIGHTNING STRIKES THIS BUILDING ABOUT 100 TIMES A YEAR.

WILLIS (FORMERLY SEARS) TOWER IN CHICAGO, ILLINOIS, U.S.A.: AT 1,450 FEET (442 M), IT IS THE TALLEST BUILDING IN NORTH AMERICA.

PETRONAS TOWERS IN KUALA LUMPUR, MALAYSIA: THE TOWERS HAVE 32,000 WINDOWS. IT TAKES WINDOW WASHERS A MONTH TO CLEAN EACH TOWER.

TWO INTERNATIONAL FINANCE CENTRE IN HONG KONG, CHINA: THERE ARE 62 ELEVATORS IN THE 1,362-FOOT (415-M) -TALL BUILDING.

JIN MAO TOWER IN SHANGHAI, CHINA: THIS 88-STORY BUILDING HAS AN INDOOR OBSERVATION DECK ON THE TOP FLOOR.

FINDING YOUR WAY AROUND

Every map has a story to tell, but first you have to know how to read one. Maps represent information by using a language of symbols. Knowing how to read these symbols provides access to a wide range of information. Look at the scale and compass rose or arrow to understand distance and direction (see box below).

To find out what each symbol on a map means, you must use the key. It's your secret decoder—identifying information by each symbol on the map.

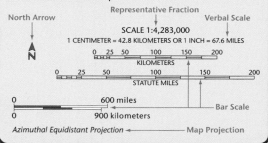

Latitude

Longitude

90°N (North Po
75°N
60°N
45°N
30°N
15°N
0°(Equator)
15°S
30°S
45°S

SYMBOLS

There are three main types of map symbols: points, lines, and areas. Points, which can be either dots or small icons, represent locations of things, such as schools, cities, or landmarks. Lines are used to show boundaries, roads, or rivers and can vary in color or thickness. Area symbols use patterns or color to show regions, such as a sandy area or a neighborhood.

POINT
A point symbol, a black dot, indicates a city, such as Omdurman.

LINE
Sudan's country boundary appears as a line symbol: a dotted line with a colored edge.

AREA
Sandy places, such as parts of the Sahara Desert, are shown by a tan, speckled area.

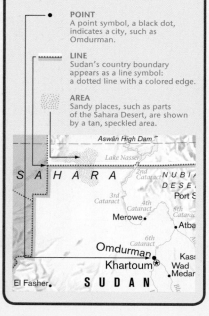

LATITUDE AND LONGITUDE LINES (above) help us determine locations on Earth. Every place on Earth has a special address called absolute location. Imaginary lines called lines of latitude run west to east, parallel to the Equator. These lines measure distance in degrees north or south from the Equator (0° latitude) to the North Pole (90°N) or to the South Pole (90°S). One degree of latitude is approximately 70 miles (113 km).

Lines of longitude run north to south, meeting at the poles. These lines measure distance in degrees east or west from 0° longitude (prime meridian) to 180° longitude. The prime meridian runs through Greenwich, England.

SCALE & DIRECTION

The scale on a map is shown as a fraction, as words, or as a line or bar. It relates distance on the map to distance in the real world. Sometimes the scale identifies the type of map projection. Maps may include an arrow or compass rose to indicate north on the map.

North Arrow

Representative Fraction

Verbal Scale

SCALE 1:4,283,000
1 CENTIMETER = 42.8 KILOMETERS OR 1 INCH = 67.6 MILES

0 25 50   100   150   200
KILOMETERS

0   25   50   100   150   200
STATUTE MILES

N

0   600 miles
0   900 kilometers

Bar Scale

Azimuthal Equidistant Projection ←   — Map Projection

WHAT'S AN ATLAS?

An atlas, or collection of maps, is usually chock-full of information, charts, and illustrations. For example, the *National Geographic World Atlas For Young Explorers* is full of photographs, statistics, quick facts, and—most of all—lots of detailed maps and charts. Plus, there is a companion website, which adds even more. The website expands upon specific subjects in the atlas and also helps you explore on your own, taking you deep into the resources of National Geographic and beyond.

Fun stuff you can do on the atlas website:
- watch animal videos
- listen to animal sounds
- listen to music from different cultures
- find country information
- download pictures and maps for your reports
- play games that allow you to explore
- send e-postcards to your friends

COOL CLICK nationalgeographic.com/kids-world-atlas

HOW TO USE THE ATLAS WEBSITE

START HERE: nationalgeographic.com/kids-world-atlas
Here are three ways to find what you are looking for from the home page: If you have the book, you can search (1) BY ATLAS PAGE NUMBER or (2) BY ICON. If you don't have the book, search (3) BY TOPIC.

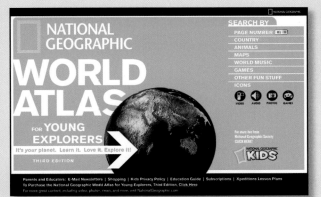

2. SEARCH BY ICON
If you want to find all the videos referenced in the atlas or all of the audio, photos, or games, click on one of the icons. A list will drop down, and you choose. Clicking on King Tut takes you to several King Tut videos.

3. SEARCH BY TOPIC
If you want to explore a specific topic, click on the entry in the topic list. You'll find vast quantities of information, photos, videos, games, and more, all arranged by subject. Say you're interested in animals. One click takes you to the animals choice page.

1. SEARCH BY ATLAS PAGE NUMBER
If you find an icon in the atlas and want to go directly to that link, use the page number pull-down menu. Just drag and click.

The statue of the 16th United States President
Abraham Lincoln in the Lincoln Memorial in Washington, D.C.

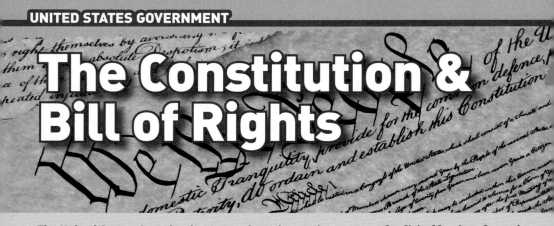

The Constitution & Bill of Rights

The United States Constitution was written in 1787 by a group of political leaders from the 13 states that made up the U.S. at the time. Thirty-nine men, including Benjamin Franklin and James Madison, signed the document to create a national government. While some feared the creation of a strong federal government, all 13 states eventually ratified, or approved, the Constitution, making it the law of the land. The Constitution has three major parts: the preamble, the articles, and the amendments.

The preamble outlines the basic purposes of the government:

We the People of the United States, in order to form a more perfect Union, establish justice, insure domestic tranquility, provide for the common defense, promote the general welfare, and secure the blessings of liberty to ourselves and our posterity, do ordain and establish this Constitution for the United States of America.

Seven articles outline the powers of Congress, the President, and the court system:

Article I outlines the legislative branch—the Senate and the House of Representatives—and its powers and responsibilities.

Article II outlines the executive branch—the presidency—and its powers and responsibilities.

Article III outlines the judicial branch—the court system—and its powers and responsibilities.

Article IV describes the individual states' rights and powers.

Article V outlines the amendment process.

Article VI establishes the Constitution as the law of the land.

Article VII gives the requirements for the Constitution to be approved.

The amendments, or additions to the Constitution, were put in later when needed. In 1791 the first ten amendments, known as the **Bill of Rights,** were added. Since then another 17 amendments have been added. This is the Bill of Rights:

1st Amendment: guarantees freedom of religion, speech, the press, and the right to assemble and petition

2nd Amendment: discusses the militia and right of people to bear arms

3rd Amendment: prohibits the military or troops from using private homes without consent

4th Amendment: protects people and their homes from search, arrest, or seizure without probable cause or a warrant

5th Amendment: grants people the right to have a trial and prevents punishment before prosecution; protects private property from being taken without compensation

6th Amendment: guarantees the right to a speedy and public trial

7th Amendment: guarantees a trial by jury in certain cases

8th Amendment: forbids "cruel and unusual punishments"

9th Amendment: states that the Constitution is not all-encompassing and does not deny people other rights, as well

10th Amendment: grants the powers not covered by the Constitution to the states and the people

HIDDEN TREASURE

THE TREASURE: DECLARATION OF INDEPENDENCE

FOUND: IN A FOUR-DOLLAR PICTURE FRAME

NOW WORTH: $8.14 MILLION

The painting was ugly and torn, but its frame seemed worth paying four dollars for. When the buyer took home his flea market find, he found a copy of the Declaration of Independence behind the painting! Convinced it must be a fake, the buyer took the document to experts at Sotheby's auction house. Not only was it real, it also had real value: it sold for $8.14 million!

The **UNITED STATES GOVERNMENT** is divided into three branches: **executive, legislative** (see p. 228), and **judicial** (see p. 228). The system of checks and balances is a way to control power and to make sure one branch can't take the reins of government. For example, most of the President's actions require the approval of Congress. Likewise, the laws passed in Congress must be signed by the President before they can take effect. This system prevents one area of government from becoming so powerful as to overly influence the business of the nation.

Executive Branch

White House

The Constitution lists the central powers of the President: to serve as Commander in Chief of the armed forces; make treaties with other nations; grant pardons; inform Congress on the state of the union; and appoint ambassadors, officials, and judges. The executive branch includes the President and the governmental departments. Originally there were three departments—State, War, and Treasury. Today there are 15 departments (see chart below).

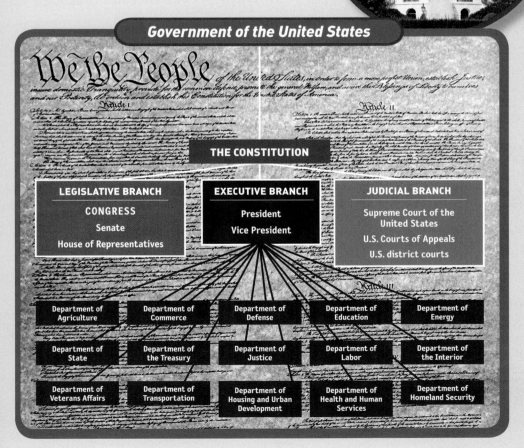

Government of the United States

We the People of the United States, in order to form a more perfect Union, establish Justice, insure domestic Tranquility, provide for the common defence, promote the general Welfare, and secure the Blessings of Liberty to ourselves and our Posterity, do ordain and establish this Constitution for the United States of America.

THE CONSTITUTION

LEGISLATIVE BRANCH

CONGRESS

Senate

House of Representatives

EXECUTIVE BRANCH

President

Vice President

JUDICIAL BRANCH

Supreme Court of the United States

U.S. Courts of Appeals

U.S. district courts

Department of Agriculture	Department of Commerce	Department of Defense	Department of Education	Department of Energy
Department of State	Department of the Treasury	Department of Justice	Department of Labor	Department of the Interior
Department of Veterans Affairs	Department of Transportation	Department of Housing and Urban Development	Department of Health and Human Services	Department of Homeland Security

Legislative Branch

This branch is made up of Congress—the Senate and the House of Representatives. The Constitution grants Congress the power to make laws. Congress is made up of elected representatives from each state. Each state has two representatives in the Senate, while the number of representatives in the House is determined by the size of the state's population. Washington, D.C., and the territories elect non-voting representatives to the House of Representatives. The Founding Fathers set up this system and the entire system of checks and balances as a compromise between states' rights.

The U.S. Capitol in Washington, D.C.

Judicial Branch

The judicial branch is composed of the federal court system—the U.S. Supreme Court, the Courts of Appeals, and the district courts. The Supreme Court is the most powerful court. Its motto is "Equal Justice Under Law." This influential court is responsible for interpreting the Constitution and applying it to the cases that it hears. The decisions of the Supreme Court are absolute—they're the final word on any legal question.

The U.S. Supreme Court building in Washington, D.C.

There are nine justices on the Supreme Court. They are appointed by the President of the United States and confirmed by the Senate.

Bet you didn't know

It's Against the Law to:

WALK A PIG along Miami Beach, in Florida.	THROW STONES in city parks in Fresno, California.
RIDE A SLED that's pulled by a car in Portland, Oregon.	THROW BANANA PEELS on the sidewalks of Mobile, Alabama.
KEEP A PET SKUNK in Virginia.	HOOT LOUDLY after 11 p.m. on weekdays in Athens, Georgia.
RIDE A BIKE with your hands off the handle-bars in Sun Prairie, Wisconsin.	RIDE A HORSE faster than ten miles an hour (16 kph) in the streets of Indianapolis, Indiana.
SPRAY SILLY STRING on Halloween in Hollywood, California.	PREDICT THE FUTURE in Yamhill, Oregon.

*NOTE: These are state and local laws and are not federally mandated.

How a Bill Becomes a Law

PROPOSAL

After an idea for a bill is formulated, the text of the bill is written. The bill must be sponsored by at least one member of the United States Congress. Most bills originate in either the Senate or the House of Representatives.

INTRODUCTION

A bill can be introduced whenever the House or Senate is in session. It is assigned a number, read on the floor, and then given to a committee for review. A copy of the bill also goes to the Library of Congress, so that it is available to the public.

CONSIDERATION

When the bill is ready, a report is created, and the bill is added to the Senate or House calendar. The bill goes to the floor for consideration, and members debate its merits and problems. Amendments may be made, and the bill can be changed again. After all amendments have been made, the chamber takes a vote.

COMMITTEE REVIEW

A committee that deals with the corresponding policy area debates the bill and may make changes (amendments). After the bill has been amended, the committee votes on the bill, at which point it can table it (stop it), send it to a subcommittee for further review, or send it back to the Senate or House floor.

VOTE

Members in attendance vote to pass or not to pass the bill. They can vote "Yea" for approval, "Nay" for disapproval, or "Present" if they choose not to take either side. If the bill receives a majority (more than 50%), it then goes to the Senate or House (wherever it did *not* originate) for a similar process.

NAY stops here   **YEA** goes on ▶

2nd CHAMBER REVIEW

The receiving chamber may vote on the bill, ignore it, or send the bill to a committee for further review. If the chamber wants to make changes in the bill's language, the bill must go for review to a committee that has members from both the Senate and the House. After agreement, the bill becomes "enrolled." Alternatively, it can be defeated in either chamber, and the bill dies.

VETO OVERRIDE

If a bill is vetoed by the President, it goes back to the chamber where it originated. Congress can drop the bill completely, or the bill can become law if objections to the veto are reviewed and debated, and a two-thirds majority overrides the veto.

PRESIDENTIAL REVIEW

When a bill passes the House and the Senate, it is sent to the President for signature. The President has three choices: ignore the bill, veto the bill, or sign it to make it law. If the President ignores the bill and Congress is in session, it will become law after ten days. If Congress is not in session, the bill dies.

Bill Becomes a Law!

The President of the United States is the chief of the executive branch, the Commander in Chief of the U.S. armed forces, and head of the federal government. Elected every four years, the President is the highest policymaker in the nation. The 22nd Amendment says that no person may be elected to the office of President more than twice. There have been 44 presidencies and 43 Presidents.

JAMES MONROE
5th President of the United States ★ 1817–1825
BORN April 28, 1758, in Westmoreland County, VA
POLITICAL PARTY Democratic-Republican
NO. OF TERMS two
VICE PRESIDENT Daniel D. Tompkins
DIED July 4, 1831, in New York, NY

GEORGE WASHINGTON
1st President of the United States ★ 1789–1797
BORN Feb. 22, 1732, in Pope's Creek, Westmoreland County, VA
POLITICAL PARTY Federalist
NO. OF TERMS two
VICE PRESIDENT John Adams
DIED Dec. 14, 1799, at Mount Vernon, VA

JOHN QUINCY ADAMS
6th President of the United States ★ 1825–1829
BORN July 11, 1767, in Braintree (now Quincy), MA
POLITICAL PARTY Democratic-Republican
NO. OF TERMS one
VICE PRESIDENT John Caldwell Calhoun
DIED Feb. 23, 1848, at the U.S. Capitol, Washington, D.C.

JOHN ADAMS
2nd President of the United States ★ 1797–1801
BORN Oct. 30, 1735, in Braintree (now Quincy), MA
POLITICAL PARTY Federalist
NO. OF TERMS one
VICE PRESIDENT Thomas Jefferson
DIED July 4, 1826, in Quincy, MA

ANDREW JACKSON
7th President of the United States ★ 1829–1837
BORN March 15, 1767, in the Waxhaw region, NC and SC
POLITICAL PARTY Democrat
NO. OF TERMS two
VICE PRESIDENTS 1st term: John Caldwell Calhoun
2nd term: Martin Van Buren
DIED June 8, 1845, in Nashville, TN

THOMAS JEFFERSON
3rd President of the United States ★ 1801–1809
BORN April 13, 1743, at Shadwell, Goochland County (now Albemarle) County, VA
POLITICAL PARTY Democratic-Republican
NO. OF TERMS two
VICE PRESIDENTS 1st term: Aaron Burr
2nd term: George Clinton
DIED July 4, 1826, at Monticello, Charlottesville, VA

MARTIN VAN BUREN
8th President of the United States ★ 1837–1841
BORN Dec. 5, 1782, in Kinderhook, NY
POLITICAL PARTY Democrat
NO. OF TERMS one
VICE PRESIDENT Richard M. Johnson
DIED July 24, 1862, in Kinderhook, NY

JAMES MADISON
4th President of the United States ★ 1809–1817
BORN March 16, 1751, at Belle Grove, Port Conway, VA
POLITICAL PARTY Democratic-Republican
NO. OF TERMS two
VICE PRESIDENTS 1st term: George Clinton
2nd term: Elbridge Gerry
DIED June 28, 1836, at Montpelier, Orange County, VA

WILLIAM HENRY HARRISON
9th President of the United States ★ 1841
BORN Feb. 9, 1773, in Charles City County, VA
POLITICAL PARTY Whig
NO. OF TERMS one (cut short by death)
VICE PRESIDENT John Tyler
DIED April 4, 1841, in the White House, Washington, D.C.

JOHN TYLER

10th President of the United States ★ *1841–1845*

BORN March 29, 1790, in Charles City County, VA
POLITICAL PARTY Whig
NO. OF TERMS one (partial)
VICE PRESIDENT none
DIED Jan. 18, 1862, in Richmond, VA

JAMES K. POLK

11th President of the United States ★ *1845–1849*

BORN Nov. 2, 1795, near Pineville, Mecklenburg County, NC
POLITICAL PARTY Democrat
NO. OF TERMS one
VICE PRESIDENT George Mifflin Dallas
DIED June 15, 1849, at Nashville, TN

ZACHARY TAYLOR

12th President of the United States ★ *1849–1850*

BORN Nov. 24, 1784, in Orange County, VA
POLITICAL PARTY Whig
NO. OF TERMS one (cut short by death)
VICE PRESIDENT Millard Fillmore
DIED July 9, 1850, in the White House, Washington, D.C.

MILLARD FILLMORE

13th President of the United States ★ *1850–1853*

BORN Jan. 7, 1800, in Cayuga County, NY
POLITICAL PARTY Whig
NO. OF TERMS one (partial)
VICE PRESIDENT none
DIED March 8, 1874, in Buffalo, NY

FRANKLIN PIERCE

14th President of the United States ★ *1853–1857*

BORN Nov. 23, 1804, in Hillsborough (now Hillsboro), NH
POLITICAL PARTY Democrat
NO. OF TERMS one
VICE PRESIDENT William Rufus De Vane King
DIED Oct. 8, 1869, in Concord, NH

JAMES BUCHANAN

15th President of the United States ★ *1857–1861*

BORN April 23, 1791, in Cove Gap, PA
POLITICAL PARTY Democrat
NO. OF TERMS one
VICE PRESIDENT John Cabell Breckinridge
DIED June 1, 1868, in Lancaster, PA

ABRAHAM LINCOLN

16th President of the United States ★ *1861–1865*

BORN Feb. 12, 1809, near Hodgenville, KY
POLITICAL PARTY Republican (formerly Whig)
NO. OF TERMS two (assassinated)
VICE PRESIDENTS 1st term: Hannibal Hamlin
2nd term: Andrew Johnson
DIED April 15, 1865, in Washington, D.C.

ANDREW JOHNSON

17th President of the United States ★ *1865–1869*

BORN Dec. 29, 1808, in Raleigh, NC
POLITICAL PARTY Democrat
NO. OF TERMS one (partial)
VICE PRESIDENT none
DIED July 31, 1875, in Carter's Station, TN

KIDS in the WHITE HOUSE

Although many presidential children are already adults or are away in college by the time their parents move into the White House, some young children have lived there.

In 1861 the Lincolns were the first to bring young children of their own to live in the White House. Among other antics, Tad Lincoln set up a White House refreshment stand and rode through a tea party on a chair pulled by his pet goats!

Sasha and Malia Obama

ULYSSES S. GRANT

18th President of the United States ★ *1869–1877*
BORN April 27, 1822,
in Point Pleasant, OH
POLITICAL PARTY Republican
NO. OF TERMS two
VICE PRESIDENTS 1st term: Schuyler Colfax;
2nd term: Henry Wilson
DIED July 23, 1885, in Mount McGregor, NY

RUTHERFORD B. HAYES

19th President of the United States ★ *1877–1881*
BORN Oct. 4, 1822,
in Delaware, OH
POLITICAL PARTY Republican
NO. OF TERMS one
VICE PRESIDENT William Almon Wheeler
DIED Jan. 17, 1893, in Fremont, OH

JAMES A. GARFIELD

20th President of the United States ★ *1881*
BORN Nov. 19, 1831, near Orange, OH
POLITICAL PARTY Republican
NO. OF TERMS one (assassinated)
VICE PRESIDENT Chester A. Arthur
DIED Sept. 19, 1881, in Elberon, NJ

CHESTER A. ARTHUR

21st President of the United States ★ *1881–1885*
BORN Oct. 5, 1829, in Fairfield, VT
POLITICAL PARTY Republican
NO. OF TERMS one (partial)
VICE PRESIDENT none
DIED Nov. 18, 1886, in New York, NY

GROVER CLEVELAND

22nd and 24th President of the United States
1885–1889 ★ *1893–1897*
BORN March 18, 1837, in Caldwell, NJ
POLITICAL PARTY Democrat
NO. OF TERMS two (nonconsecutive)
VICE PRESIDENTS 1st administration:
Thomas Andrews Hendricks
2nd administration:
Adlai Ewing Stevenson
DIED June 24, 1908, in Princeton, NJ

BENJAMIN HARRISON

23rd President of the United States ★ *1889–1893*
BORN Aug. 20, 1833,
in North Bend, OH
POLITICAL PARTY Republican
NO. OF TERMS one
VICE PRESIDENT Levi Parsons Morton
DIED March 13, 1901, in Indianapolis, IN

WILLIAM MCKINLEY

25th President of the United States ★ *1897–1901*
BORN Jan. 29, 1843, in Niles, OH
POLITICAL PARTY Republican
NO. OF TERMS two (assassinated)
VICE PRESIDENTS 1st term:
Garret Augustus Hobart
2nd term:
Theodore Roosevelt
DIED Sept. 14, 1901, in Buffalo, NY

THEODORE ROOSEVELT

26th President of the United States ★ *1901–1909*
BORN Oct. 27, 1858, in New York, NY
POLITICAL PARTY Republican
NO. OF TERMS one, plus balance of
McKinley's term
VICE PRESIDENTS 1st term: none
2nd term: Charles
Warren Fairbanks
DIED Jan. 6, 1919, in Oyster Bay, NY

WILLIAM HOWARD TAFT

27th President of the United States ★ *1909–1913*
BORN Sept. 15, 1857, in Cincinnati, OH
POLITICAL PARTY Republican
NO. OF TERMS one
VICE PRESIDENT James Schoolcraft
Sherman
DIED March 8, 1930, in Washington, D.C.

WOODROW WILSON

28th President of the United States ★ *1913–1921*
BORN Dec. 29, 1856,
in Staunton, VA
POLITICAL PARTY Democrat
NO. OF TERMS two
VICE PRESIDENT Thomas Riley Marshall
DIED Feb. 3, 1924, in Washington, D.C.

WARREN G. HARDING

29th President of the United States ★ 1921–1923

BORN Nov. 2, 1865, in Caledonia
(now Blooming Grove), OH
POLITICAL PARTY Republican
NO. OF TERMS one (died while in office)
VICE PRESIDENT Calvin Coolidge
DIED Aug. 2, 1923, in San Francisco, CA

HARRY S. TRUMAN

33rd President of the United States ★ 1945–1953

BORN May 8, 1884, in Lamar, MO
POLITICAL PARTY Democrat
NO. OF TERMS one, plus balance of
Franklin D. Roosevelt's term
VICE PRESIDENTS 1st term: none
2nd term:
Alben William Barkley
DIED Dec. 26, 1972, in Independence, MO

CALVIN COOLIDGE

30th President of the United States ★ 1923–1929

BORN July 4, 1872, in Plymouth, VT
POLITICAL PARTY Republican
NO. OF TERMS one, plus balance of
Harding's term
VICE PRESIDENTS 1st term: none
2nd term:
Charles Gates Dawes
DIED Jan. 5, 1933, in Northampton, MA

DWIGHT D. EISENHOWER

34th President of the United States ★ 1953–1961

BORN Oct. 14, 1890, in Denison, TX
POLITICAL PARTY Republican
NO. OF TERMS two
VICE PRESIDENT Richard M. Nixon
DIED March 28, 1969,
in Washington, D.C.

HERBERT HOOVER

31st President of the United States ★ 1929–1933

BORN Aug. 10, 1874,
in West Branch, IA
POLITICAL PARTY Republican
NO. OF TERMS one
VICE PRESIDENT Charles Curtis
DIED Oct. 20, 1964, in New York, NY

JOHN F. KENNEDY

35th President of the United States ★ 1961–1963

BORN May 29, 1917, in Brookline, MA
POLITICAL PARTY Democrat
NO. OF TERMS one (assassinated)
VICE PRESIDENT Lyndon B. Johnson
DIED Nov. 22, 1963,
in Dallas, TX

FRANKLIN D. ROOSEVELT

32nd President of the United States ★ 1933–1945

BORN Jan. 30, 1882, in Hyde Park, NY
POLITICAL PARTY Democrat
NO. OF TERMS four (died while in office)
VICE PRESIDENTS 1st & 2nd terms: John
Nance Garner; 3rd term:
Henry Agard Wallace; 4th
term: Harry S. Truman
DIED April 12, 1945,
in Warm Springs, GA

LYNDON B. JOHNSON

36th President of the United States ★ 1963–1969

BORN Aug. 27, 1908,
near Stonewall, TX
POLITICAL PARTY Democrat
NO. OF TERMS one, plus balance of
Kennedy's term
VICE PRESIDENTS 1st term: none
2nd term: Hubert
Horatio Humphrey
DIED Jan. 22, 1973, near San Antonio, TX

PRESIDENTIAL PETS

Barack Obama's **DOG** is named Bo; he's a boy.

George Herbert Walker Bush's dog Millie was the first presidential pet to **AUTHOR A BOOK**.

Lyndon B. Johnson and his mixed-breed dog, Yuki, **HOWLED** together for television cameras.

Woodrow Wilson's **SHEEP** grazed on the White House lawn.

When Martin Van Buren was given two **TIGER** cubs, the U.S. Congress demanded that he give them to a zoo.

Andrew Jackson left flour and bread crumbs out at night for White House **MICE** to eat.

RICHARD NIXON

37th President of the United States ★ *1969–1974*

BORN Jan. 9, 1913, in Yorba Linda, CA

POLITICAL PARTY Republican

NO. OF TERMS two (resigned)

VICE PRESIDENTS 1st term & 2nd term (partial): Spiro Theodore Agnew; 2nd term (balance): Gerald R. Ford

DIED April 22, 1994, in New York, NY

GERALD R. FORD

38th President of the United States ★ *1974–1977*

BORN July 14, 1913, in Omaha, NE

POLITICAL PARTY Republican

NO. OF TERMS one (partial)

VICE PRESIDENT Nelson Aldrich Rockefeller

DIED Dec. 26, 2006, in Rancho Mirage, CA

JIMMY CARTER

39th President of the United States ★ *1977–1981*

BORN Oct. 1, 1924, in Plains, GA

POLITICAL PARTY Democrat

NO. OF TERMS one

VICE PRESIDENT Walter Frederick (Fritz) Mondale

Bet you didn't know

Many Presidents had unusual careers before entering the White House. Harry S. Truman was a haberdasher—someone who deals in men's clothing and accessories, particularly hats. Jimmy Carter was a peanut farmer, and Ronald Reagan was a movie actor.

There have been many interesting presidential firsts. Barack Obama is our first African-American President, while John F. Kennedy was the first (and only) non-Protestant President. James Polk was the first to have his photograph taken. And Theodore Roosevelt was the first President to ride in a car while in office. His fifth cousin, Franklin D. Roosevelt, was the first to ride in an airplane.

What will be the next big presidential first? First to ride in a spaceship?

RONALD REAGAN

40th President of the United States ★ *1981–1989*

BORN Feb. 6, 1911, in Tampico, IL

POLITICAL PARTY Republican

NO. OF TERMS two

VICE PRESIDENT George H. W. Bush

DIED June 5, 2004, in Los Angeles, CA

GEORGE H. W. BUSH

41st President of the United States ★ *1989–1993*

BORN June 12, 1924, in Milton, MA

POLITICAL PARTY Republican

NO. OF TERMS one

VICE PRESIDENT James Danforth (Dan) Quayle III

BILL CLINTON

42nd President of the United States ★ *1993–2001*

BORN Aug. 19, 1946, in Hope, AR

POLITICAL PARTY Democrat

NO. OF TERMS two

VICE PRESIDENT Albert Gore, Jr.

GEORGE W. BUSH

43rd President of the United States ★ *2001–2009*

BORN July 6, 1946, in New Haven, CT

POLITICAL PARTY Republican

NO. OF TERMS two

VICE PRESIDENT Richard Bruce Cheney

BARACK OBAMA

44th President of the United States ★ *2009–present*

BORN August 4, 1961, in Honolulu, HI

POLITICAL PARTY Democrat

VICE PRESIDENT Joseph Biden

FAST FACT

SIX PRESIDENTS are portrayed on U.S. coins: Abraham Lincoln, Thomas Jefferson, Franklin D. Roosevelt, George Washington, John F. Kennedy, and Dwight D. Eisenhower.

U.S. Political Parties

Some of the Founding Fathers hoped that members of the new United States government would work together in harmony without dividing into opposing groups called parties. Yet, soon after George Washington became President, political parties began to form. Leaders partnered with others who shared their geographic background, foreign policy beliefs, or ideas for governing.

THE TWO-PARTY SYSTEM

Today, as then, the party with the largest number of elected members in the U.S. House of Representatives and the U.S. Senate holds a majority of influence over those chambers. Occasionally the same party will control both chambers of Congress and the Presidency. With that much political power, it can significantly influence the nature of government. Usually each party will control only one or two of these three areas. In that case, political parties have to compromise and cooperate with one another in order to enact new laws.

Republican elephant mascot

A LONG HISTORY

Today's leaders are primarily members of the Democratic and Republican parties. Each group can trace its origins to the 19th century.

The Democratic Party evolved from the early groups that opposed a strong federal government. Leaders such as Thomas Jefferson shaped these lawmakers into a collection of politicians known variously as the Democratic-Republicans, the National Republicans, and, eventually, the Democrats.

The modern Republican Party was formed during the 1850s to combat the spread of slavery. Its first successful presidential candidate was Abraham Lincoln. Sometimes it is referred to as the Grand Old Party (GOP).

Democratic donkey mascot

SHIFTING THE VOTE

Often the presidential ballot will include candidates from third parties, those groups that exist beyond the two major parties. Occasionally a candidate has run for office as an independent—that is, without the support of a political party. No independent or third-party candidate has ever made it to the White House. Even so, these candidates may influence an election by dividing the support of voters or by directing attention to a particular issue or cause. In recent decades, third-party and independent candidates have frequently siphoned support away from Republican and Democratic candidates in ways that helped secure a victory for the opposing major party.

SUCCESSION

If the President of the United States becomes incapacitated, dies, resigns, or is removed from office, there is an order of succession to determine who takes over as President. This order, specified by the Presidential Succession Act of 1947 and later amendments, is as follows:

1. Vice President
2. Speaker of the House of Representatives
3. President pro tempore of the Senate (highest ranking Senator)
4. Secretary of State
5. Secretary of the Treasury
6. Secretary of Defense
7. Attorney General
8. Secretary of the Interior
9. Secretary of Agriculture
10. Secretary of Commerce
11. Secretary of Labor
12. Secretary of Health and Human Services
13. Secretary of Housing and Urban Development
14. Secretary of Transportation
15. Secretary of Energy
16. Secretary of Education
17. Secretary of Veterans Affairs
18. Secretary of Homeland Security

Women of the White House

FIRST LADY	PRESIDENT	TERM	AGE AS FIRST LADY	NUMBER OF CHILDREN
Martha Dandridge Custis Washington	George Washington	1789–1797	57	none
Abigail Smith Adams	John Adams	1797–1801	52	4
Martha Wayles Skelton Jefferson* *Acting First Ladies: Dolley Madison (friend) and Martha Jefferson Randolph (daughter)	Thomas Jefferson	1801–1809	Deceased	2
Dolley Payne Todd Madison	James Madison	1809–1817	40	1
Elizabeth Kortright Monroe	James Monroe	1817–1825	48	2
Louisa Catherine Johnson Adams	John Quincy Adams	1825–1829	50	3
Rachel Donelson Jackson* *Acting First Ladies: Emily Donelson (niece) and Sarah Yorke Jackson (nephew's wife)	Andrew Jackson	1829–1837	Deceased	none
Hannah Hoes Van Buren *Acting First Lady: Angelica Singleton Van Buren (daughter–in–law)	Martin Van Buren	1837–1841	Deceased	4
Anna Tuthill Symmes Harrison	William Henry Harrison	1841	65	9
Letitia Christian Tyler* *Died while Tyler was in office.	John Tyler	1841–1845	50	8
Julia Gardiner Tyler	John Tyler	1841–1845	24	7
Sarah Childress Polk	James K. Polk	1845–1849	41	none
Margaret Mackall Smith Taylor	Zachary Taylor	1849–1850	60	4
Abigail Powers Fillmore	Millard Fillmore	1850–1853	52	2
Jane Means Appleton Pierce	Franklin Pierce	1853–1857	46	2
Harriet Lane (Niece of James Buchanan) *Two children with Henry Elliott Johnston	James Buchanan (not married)	1857–1861	26	2*
Mary Todd Lincoln	Abraham Lincoln	1861–1865	42	3
Eliza McCardle Johnson	Andrew Johnson	1865–1869	54	5
Julia Dent Grant	Ulysses S. Grant	1869–1877	43	4
Lucy Ware Webb Hayes	Rutherford B. Hayes	1877–1881	45	5
Lucretia Rudolph Garfield	James A. Garfield	1881	48	5
Ellen Lewis Herndon Arthur* *Acting First Lady: Mary Arthur McElroy (President's sister)	Chester A. Arthur	1881–1885	Deceased	2

Martha Dandridge Custis marries future President George Washington.

Michelle LaVaughn Robinson Obama, the first African-American First Lady

Former First Ladies (left to right), Lady Bird Johnson, Barbara Bush, Hillary Rodham Clinton, Betty Ford, and Nancy Reagan at the 1997 opening celebrations of the George Bush Presidential Library.

FIRST LADY	PRESIDENT	TERM	AGE AS FIRST LADY	NUMBER OF CHILDREN
Frances Folsom Cleveland* *Acting First Lady: Rose Elizabeth Cleveland (President's sister)	Grover Cleveland	1885–1889 1893–1897	21	5
Caroline Lavina Scott Harrison	Benjamin Harrison	1889–1893	56	2
Ida Saxton McKinley	William McKinley	1897–1901	49	2
Edith Kermit Carow Roosevelt	Theodore Roosevelt	1901–1909	40	5
Helen Herron Taft	William Howard Taft	1909–1913	48	3
Ellen Louise Axson Wilson* *Died while Wilson was in office. Acting First Ladies: Margaret Woodrow Wilson (daughter) and Helen Bones (President's cousin)	Woodrow Wilson	1913–1921	52	3
Edith Bolling Galt Wilson	Woodrow Wilson	1913–1921	43	none
Florence Kling Harding	Warren G. Harding	1921–1923	60	none
Grace Anna Goodhue Coolidge	Calvin Coolidge	1923–1929	44	2
Lou Henry Hoover	Herbert Hoover	1929–1933	54	2
Anna Eleanor Roosevelt	Franklin D. Roosevelt	1933–1945	48	5
Elizabeth Virginia Wallace Truman	Harry S. Truman	1945–1953	60	1
Mamie Geneva Doud Eisenhower	Dwight D. Eisenhower	1953–1961	56	1
Jacqueline Lee Bouvier Kennedy	John F. Kennedy	1961–1963	31	2
Claudia "Lady Bird" Taylor Johnson	Lyndon B. Johnson	1963–1969	50	2
Patricia Ryan Nixon	Richard Nixon	1969–1974	56	2
Elizabeth "Betty" Bloomer Ford	Gerald R. Ford	1974–1977	56	4
Rosalynn Smith Carter	Jimmy Carter	1977–1981	49	4
Nancy Davis Reagan	Ronald Reagan	1981–1989	59	2
Barbara Pierce Bush	George Bush	1989–1993	63	6
Hillary Rodham Clinton	Bill Clinton	1993–2001	45	1
Laura Welch Bush	George W. Bush	2001–2009	55	2
Michelle LaVaughn Robinson Obama	Barack Obama	2009–present	44	2

American Heroes

Pocahontas circa 1595 (Virginia, U.S.)–1617 (Gravesend, England)

About 400 years ago the young Indian princess Pocahontas became the first heroine in American history. As the story goes, she was about 12 years old when she saved the life of Captain John Smith, one of the leaders of Virginia's Jamestown Colony. This story won Pocahontas a place in history for her kindheartedness and bravery, but it may be more legend than fact. Today she is celebrated as a symbol of peace and friendship. **Did you know? The word *pocahontas* means "playful one."**

Wright Brothers
Wilbur: 1867 (Indiana, U.S.)–1912 (Ohio, U.S.)
Orville: 1871 (Ohio, U.S.)–1948 (Ohio, U.S.)

In December 1903 Wilbur and Orville Wright did what no human being had done before: They flew in a plane powered by an engine. This stunning feat ushered in the age of powered flight and made the Wright brothers the first American heroes of the 20th century. The secrets of flight had baffled great minds for centuries. Wilbur and Orville Wright focused all their intellectual and engineering skills on finding the answers. When they did, the discovery changed the world. **Did you know? Wilbur and Orville owned a cat named Old Mom when they were kids.**

Martin Luther King, Jr. 1929 (Georgia, U.S.)–1968 (Tennessee, U.S.)

Civil rights leader Martin Luther King, Jr., never backed down in his stand against racism. He dedicated his life to achieving equality and justice for all Americans of all colors. From a family of preachers, King experienced racial prejudice early in life. As an adult fighting for civil rights, his speeches, marches, and mere presence motivated people to fight for justice for all people. His March on Washington in 1963 was one of the largest activist gatherings in our nation's history. King's impact on the nation and the world is incalculable. **Did you know? King's original name was Michael, but his parents changed it to Martin after a trip to Germany in 1934.**

John Glenn 1921 (Ohio, U.S.)–

Half a century ago the United States and the nation then known as the Soviet Union (now Russia) began competing to see which country would be first to explore outer space. The Soviets captured the lead when they sent the first person into orbit around Earth. Ten months later, the United States closed the gap in the space race when American astronaut John Glenn blasted off on February 20, 1962, and circled Earth three times. Glenn became an overnight hero for his brave voyage into the unknown. **Did you know? John Glenn served as a U.S. Senator (Dem–OH) from 1974 to 1999.**

Albert Einstein 1879 (Ulm, Germany)–1955 (New Jersey, U.S.)

This German-born physicist made his first visit to the U.S. in 1921, and he later became a U.S. citizen. His mind-boggling theories dazzled the public even though very few people understood the science behind them. What everyone did know was that Einstein was the most extraordinary genius of their time—and perhaps of all time. Merely by thinking about it, he came up with a totally new explanation for time and space and the way the universe works. His revolutionary theory of relativity made him a hero. Einstein's passion for science lasted a lifetime. **Did you know? Einstein was offered the position of Israel's second president, a job he refused.**

American Wars

From before the formation of the United States to the present, there have been hundreds of military encounters, both at home and abroad. Major conflicts include the following wars:

1754–1763 French and Indian War (part of Europe's Seven Years War) A nine-year war between the British and the French for control of eastern North America.

1775–1783 Revolutionary War The 13 British colonies united to reject the rule of the British monarchy and form their own government.

1812–15 War of 1812 The U.S. declared war against Great Britain, which had imposed trade restrictions.

1846–48 Mexican-American War Mexico refused to accept the annexation of Texas by the U.S., and the two went to war over the boundary dispute.

1861–65 Civil War The Civil War was one of the most devastating wars in American history. It occurred when the northern states (the Union) went to war with the southern states, which had seceded to form the Confederate States of America. Slavery was one of the key issues in the Civil War.

1898 Spanish-American War The U.S. declared war with Spain over control of Cuba.

1914–18 World War I The U.S. entered the war after Germany sunk the British ship *Lusitania*, killing more than 120 Americans.

1941–45 World War II This massive conflict in Europe, Asia, and North Africa involved many countries that aligned with two sides: the Allies and the Axis. After the bombing of Pearl Harbor in Hawaii, the U.S. entered the war on the side of the Allies. More than 50 million people died during the war.

1950–53 Korean War During a military conflict between North and South Korea, the U.S. joined forces with the South, while China supported the North.

1950s–1975 During the **Vietnam War,** the U.S. fought on the side of South Vietnam against the communist North, which was backed by China.

1990–1991 Persian Gulf War Following the invasion of Kuwait by Iraq, the U.S. joined a coalition of nations to expel Iraq from the occupied area.

2001–present War in Afghanistan After attacks in the United States by the terrorist group Al-Qaeda, the U.S. and Britain invaded Afghanistan to find Osama Bin Laden and other Al-Qaeda members. A coalition of more than 40 countries formed the offense.

2003–present War in Iraq A coalition led by the U.S., and including Britain, Australia, and Spain, invaded Iraq over suspicions of weapons of mass destruction.

An artillery unit on Morris Island, South Carolina, during the Civil War

A World War II Army tank

CIVIL RIGHTS

In March 1965 Dr. Martin Luther King, Jr., joined marchers on a 50-mile (80-km) march to Montgomery, Alabama.

The Little Rock Nine study during the weeks when they were blocked from school.

Fighting for Your Rights:
The civil rights movement of the 1950s–1964

Although the Constitution protects the civil rights of American citizens, it has not always been able to protect all Americans from persecution or discrimination. During the first half of the 20th century, many Americans, particularly African Americans, were the subject of widespread discrimination and racism. By the mid-1950s, many people were eager to end the bonds of racism and restore freedom to all men and women.

The civil rights movement of the 1950s and 1960s sought to end the racial discrimination against African Americans, especially in the southern states. The movement wanted to restore the fundamentals of economic and social equality to those who had been oppressed. The civil rights movement benefited from powerful leaders, such as Martin Luther King, Jr., Rosa Parks, John F. Kennedy, and Malcolm X.

The Little Rock Nine

As a group of nine African-American teenagers entered an all-white high school in Little Rock, Arkansas, the world changed. In 1957 these young students became civil rights icons by challenging a racist system—and winning. For more on segregation and the Little Rock Nine, go online. nps.gov/history/nr/travel/civilrights/ar1.htm

Key Events in the Civil Rights Movement

1954 The Supreme Court case *Brown* v. *Board of Education* declares school segregation illegal.

1955 Rosa Parks refuses to give up her bus seat to a white passenger and spurs a bus boycott.

1957 The Little Rock Nine help integrate schools.

1961 Freedom Rides begin to southern states to protest segregation in transportation.

1963 Martin Luther King, Jr., leads the famous March on Washington.

1964 The Civil Rights Act, signed by President Lyndon Johnson, prohibits discrimination based on race, color, religion, sex, and national origin.

The Indian Experience

American Indians are indigenous to North and South America—they are the people who were here before Columbus and other European explorers came to these lands. They lived in nations, tribes, and bands across both continents. For decades following the arrival of Europeans in 1492, American Indians clashed with the newcomers who had ruptured the Indians' way of living.

Tribal Land

During the 19th century, both United States legislation and military action restricted the movement of American Indians, forcing them to live on reservations and attempting to dismantle tribal structures. For centuries Indians were often displaced or killed, or became assimilated. In 1924 the Indian Citizenship Act granted citizenship to all American Indians. Unfortunately this was not enough to end the social discrimination and mistreatment that many Indians have faced. Today, American Indians living in the U.S. still face many challenges.

Healing the Past

Many of the more than 560 recognized tribes in the United States live primarily on reservations. Some tribes have more than one reservation, while others have none. Many have assimilated into the general U.S. population. Together these reservations make up less than three percent of the nation's land area. The tribes have the right to form their own governments and enforce laws, similar to individual states. Many feel that this sovereignty is still not enough to right the wrongs of the past: They hope for a change in the U.S. government's relationship with American Indians.

A young Cherokee man dressed in traditional costume

Today there are about 2.3 million American Indians in the U.S. and more than a million in Canada.

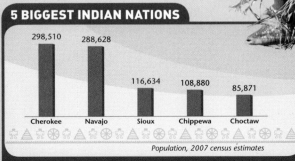

5 BIGGEST INDIAN NATIONS

Cherokee	Navajo	Sioux	Chippewa	Choctaw
298,510	288,628	116,634	108,880	85,871

Population, 2007 census estimates

One of the largest groups of American Indians living in the United States is the Cherokee nation. This nation is concentrated mainly in the Southeastern United States.

MYTHOLOGY

GREEK

EGYPTIAN

The ancient Greeks believed that many gods and goddesses ruled the universe. According to this mythology, the Olympians lived high atop Greece's Mount Olympus. Each of these 12 principal gods and goddesses had a unique personality that corresponded to particular aspects of life, such as love or death.

THE OLYMPIANS

Aphrodite was the goddess of love and beauty.

Apollo, Zeus's son, was the god of the sun, music, and healing. Artemis was his twin.

Ares, Zeus's son, was the god of war.

Artemis, Zeus's daughter and Apollo's twin, was the goddess of the hunt and childbirth.

Athena, born from the forehead of Zeus, was the goddess of wisdom and crafts.

Demeter was the goddess of fertility and nature.

Hades, Zeus's brother, was the god of the underworld and the dead.

Hephaestus, the son of Hera, was the god of fire.

Hera, the wife and older sister of Zeus, was the goddess of women and marriage.

Hermes, Zeus's son, was the messenger of the gods.

Poseidon, the brother of Zeus, was the god of the sea and earthquakes.

Zeus was the most powerful of the gods and the top Olympian. He wielded a thunderbolt and was god of the sky and thunder.

Egyptian mythology is based on a creation myth that tells of an egg that appeared on the ocean. When the egg hatched, out came Ra, the sun god. As a result, Ancient Egyptians became worshippers of the sun and the nine original deities, most of which were the children and grandchildren of Ra.

THE NINE DEITIES

Geb, son of Shu and Tefnut, was the god of the Earth.

Isis, daughter of Geb and Nut, was the goddess of fertility and motherhood.

Nephthys, daughter of Geb and Nut, was protector of the dead.

Nut, daughter of Shu and Tefnut, was the goddess of the sky.

Osiris, son of Geb and Nut, was the god of the afterlife.

Ra (Re), the sun god, is generally viewed as the creator. He represents life and health.

Seth, son of Geb and Nut, was the god of the desert and chaos.

Shu, son of Ra, was the god of air.

Tefnut, daughter of Ra, was the goddess of rain.

All cultures around the world have unique legends and traditions that have been passed down over generations. Many myths refer to gods or supernatural heroes who are responsible for occurrences in the world. For example, Norse mythology tells of the red-bearded Thor, the God of Thunder, who is responsible for creating lightning and thunderstorms. And many creation myths, especially from some of North America's native cultures, tell of an earth-diver represented as an animal that brings a piece of sand or mud up from the deep sea. From this tiny piece of earth, the entire world takes shape.

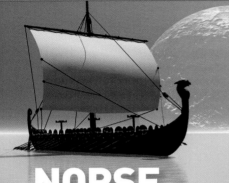

NORSE

ROMAN

Norse mythology originated in Scandinavia, in northern Europe. It was complete with gods and goddesses who lived in a heavenly place called Asgard that could be reached only by crossing a rainbow bridge.

While Norse mythology is lesser known, we use it every day. Most days of the week are named after Norse gods, including some of these major deities.

NORSE GODS

Balder was the god of light and beauty.

Freya was the goddess of love, beauty, and fertility.

Frigg, for whom Friday was named, was the queen of Asgard. She was the goddess of marriage, motherhood, and the home.

Heimdall was the watchman of the rainbow bridge and the guardian of the gods.

Hel, the daughter of Loki, was the goddess of death.

Loki, a shape shifter, was a trickster who helped the gods—and caused them problems.

Wodan, for whom Wednesday was named, was the god of war, wisdom, death, and magic.

Thor, for whom Thursday was named, was the god of thunder and lightning.

Tyr, for whom Tuesday was named, was the god of the sky and war.

Skadi was the goddess of winter and of the hunt. She is often represented as "The Snow Queen."

Much of Roman mythology was adopted from Greek mythology, but the Romans also developed a lot of original myths as well. The gods of Roman mythology lived everywhere and each had a role to play. There were thousands of Roman gods, but here are a few of the stars of Roman myths.

ANCIENT ROMAN GODS

Ceres was goddess of the harvest and motherly love.

Diana, daughter of Jupiter, was the goddess of hunting and the moon.

Juno, Jupiter's wife, was the goddess of women and fertility.

Jupiter, the patron of Rome and master of the gods, was the god of the sky.

Mars, the son of Jupiter and Juno, was the god of war.

Mercury, the son of Jupiter, was the messenger of the gods and the god of travelers.

Minerva was the goddess of wisdom, learning, and the arts and crafts.

Neptune, the brother of Jupiter, was the god of the sea.

Venus was the goddess of love and beauty.

Vesta was goddess of fire and the hearth. She was one of the most important of the Roman deities.

243

THE ROMAN EMPIRE

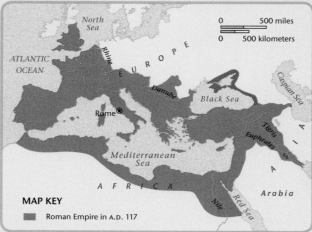

North Sea

ATLANTIC OCEAN

Rhine

E U R O P E

Danube

Black Sea

Caspian Sea

Rome

Tigris
Euphrates

A S I A

Mediterranean Sea

AFRICA

Arabia

Nile

Red Sea

0   500 miles

0   500 kilometers

MAP KEY

Roman Empire in A.D. 117

THE ANCIENT ROMANS FIRST CONQUERED the whole of Italy and then a vast empire. At its greatest extent, in A.D. 117, the Roman Empire covered some 2.3 million square miles (6 million sq. km)— that's roughly two-thirds the size of the United States—and had an estimated population of 120 million. These people were ruled by emperors, the most famous of which was Julius Caesar.

The Roman Empire had a very successful government and was a leader in war. Its people made significant advances in technology and architecture. The empire helped lay the foundations for modern Western civilization.

Daily Life in Tudor England

The history of England is broad and diverse. The Tudor period, from 1485 to 1603 (118 years), saw the reign of five powerful monarchs.

Some of these colorful monarchs were kind; others were tyrannical. From the first Tudor monarch, Henry VII, to the last queen of the period, Elizabeth I, the Tudor times were romantic and turbulent at the same time.

The Tudor period was the time of Shakespeare, frilly fashions, and exploring heroes. But it wasn't all great feasts and beautiful music. For most, living in Tudor England was hard—to say the least.

Social classes, or groups of people organized by power, were important in Tudor England, where there were four main classes. Nobility, including dukes, barons, and the royal family, made up the smallest and richest class. Just below them was the gentry, knights, and wealthy landowners who lived in mansions with tons of servants. The next class consisted of professionals, such as merchants and lawyers. The largest and lowest class included farmhands, servants, and people living in poverty.

Cities were smaller than they are now, more like big towns, and most people lived in the countryside. There were no sewers, so sewage and polluted water ran right down the streets. Rats and other pests were everywhere. The lack of sanitation led to many outbreaks of plague and smallpox, and the lack of medical knowledge meant that many people faced illness and death.

Be very happy you didn't live in Tudor England, where having a bath was a rarity!

Bet you didn't know Ancient Egyptians **BELIEVED** that **THOUGHTS** came from the **HEART**, not the brain.

SPIES who changed the world

DOSSIER 001: OPERATION MISDIRECTION | YEAR: 1944 | SPY: JUAN PUJOL GARCIA | AKA: "THE ACTOR"

It's the most powerful collection of planes, ships, armor, and troops Earth has ever seen. American, British, Canadian, and French forces are preparing for one lethal D-Day strike at the German-occupied Normandy beaches in France. Victory equals a free Europe. Defeat means, well, bad stuff.

To know where the Allies will strike, the Germans turn to their secret weapon, Juan Pujol Garcia, who is leading a network of spies against Britain. Wrong! There's no network. Garcia is really working against Germany for Britain!

As the Allies prepare to bring it on, the Germans ask Garcia where American and British soldiers will land. He tells them to move to Calais, France—15 miles (24 km) from where the Allies will actually strike.

So while most of the German army waits near Calais, the Allies battle to victory at Normandy. The defeat leads to the German surrender in 1945. When the smoke clears, Britain presents "The Actor" with a medal for heroism. And so do the Germans, never suspecting that the double agent has fooled them all along.

DOSSIER 002: OPERATION RED BLUFF | YEAR: 1962 | SPY: OLEG PENKOVSKY | AKA: "THE SPY WHO SAVED THE WORLD"

In the blue corner, hailing from the United States, President John F. Kennedy. In the red corner, his challenger from the Soviet Union (now Russia), Premier Nikita S. Khrushchev.

As the bell clangs, the two enemy superpowers begin their grudge match. *Biff! Bam! Kapow!*

At ringside is double agent Oleg Penkovsky. Khrushchev believes that the spy is on his team. In reality, he's Kennedy's go-to spy guy. And luckily for the President, Penkovsky knows Khrushchev's footwork inside and out.

Round 1: Penkovsky warns Kennedy's people of Khrushchev's punch: nuclear missile launch sites he's building in Cuba, 90 miles (145 km) off Florida's shore.

Round 2: Kennedy counters with a naval blockade of Cuba.

Round 3: Khrushchev and Kennedy are at a standoff. The U.S. and Cuba fear a nuclear attack.

Round 4: Penkovsky tells Kennedy the Soviet threat is trash talk. Kennedy agrees to remove missiles from Turkey.

Khrushchev throws in the towel. Launch site construction is halted, and the Soviets dump their missile plans in Cuba. Nuclear holocaust is averted.

Harriet Tubman: CIVIL WAR SPY

Harriet Tubman is well known for risking her life as a "conductor" on the Underground Railroad, leading escaped slaves to freedom before the United States Civil War. But did you know that the former slave also served as a spy for the Union? And that she was the first woman in American history to lead a military expedition? It's true!

Tubman decided to help the Union Army because she wanted freedom for all of the people who were forced into slavery. Tubman was five feet two inches (2 m) tall, born a slave, had a debilitating illness, and was unable to read or write. Yet, here was this tough crusader who could take charge and lead men.

SPYSPEAK

Talk like a spy with these terms.

BLACK BAG JOB: secret entry into a place to steal or copy materials

EARS ONLY: material too secret to put in writing

GHOUL: an agent who finds the names of dead people so that spies can use them as aliases

UNCLE: the headquarters of any spy service

GIRLS RULE!

Two Queens of Egypt Who Rocked the Ancient World

Girls of ancient Egypt had it a lot better than most people. By age 12 they could wear makeup. They walked their pet geese and played ball for fun. As women, they had rights that women didn't have elsewhere. They could buy and sell property, inherit stuff—even sue someone!

Still, men were usually in charge. But that didn't stop some women from defying tradition and taking over. Cleopatra and Hatshepsut were two outrageous queens who showed the ancient world what girl power was all about.

CLEOPATRA: *Political Party Girl*
(Reign: 51 B.C. to 30 B.C.)

Mark Antony was fuming. The ruler of half the Roman Empire waited impatiently for the queen of Egypt to arrive. She was late—on purpose. And when she finally glittered up the Cydnus River on a ship with silver oars, Cleopatra had the nerve to make *him* board *her* ship. How dare she?

Antony shouldn't have been surprised at the queen's bold behavior. Cleopatra had star power with the brains to match. Queen by 18, she had her hands full: bad harvests, a forced marriage to her brother, and plots to overthrow her.

Cleopatra left few words. But Egyptologists think they have found an order signed by the queen. On it, the busy ruler had scribbled, "Make it so."

HATSHEPSUT: *Built to Last*
(Reign: 1479 B.C. to 1458 B.C.)

Wearing the royal headdress, with a pharaoh's traditional fake beard on her chin, Hatshepsut was officially the "female king" of Egypt. Not bad for a girl who was forced to wed her 8-year-old half brother at 13.

Now for action! Hatshepsut waged successful warfare against fierce invaders. Organizing a five-ship expedition to faraway lands, she brought ivory, ebony, gold, and trees to Egypt. Trees? Egypt needed them to grow fragrant incense, burned by the ton in ceremonies.

Hatshepsut was an excellent ruler—so good that she kept the pharaoh-to-be on the sidelines until she died. And she lives on in spirit. In modern Egypt, Hatshepsut's wonders, from an obelisk to an incense tree, are still standing after nearly 3,500 years.

MEET THE NAT GEO EXPLORER

FREDRIK HIEBERT

Archaeologist and explorer, Hiebert has traced ancient trade routes over land and across the seas for more than 20 years.

What was your most exciting discovery?
My most memorable find is from my first dig when I was a student. I was digging an 800-year-old house of an Egyptian merchant. On the last day I pulled up an ancient reed mat from in front of the door. There, under the mat was the key to the door, left behind by the merchant for when he came back. I will never forget that connection with the last person who had been in that house hundreds of years earlier.

How would you suggest kids follow in your footsteps?
Keep exploring. If you love what you are doing, that's the best life you can have.

What is one place or thing you'd still like to explore?
I'm always eager to explore ancient cultures and places. I'm really looking forward to visiting Mongolia next.

Fearless Fliers

Charles Lindbergh

On May 20, 1927, he took off on the flight that made him world-famous. Six men had died trying to make the 3,600-mile (5,794-km) nonstop trip from New York to Paris, France, but Charles Lindbergh was going to do it. He flew alone in a small, single-engine plane. To avoid extra weight, he didn't take a radio or a parachute. The cockpit didn't have a front window, so Lindbergh used a homemade periscope to look out the side for dangers. He used charts, compasses, and the stars to guide his way. At 10,000 feet (3,048 m), it became so cold that he wore mittens and a wool-lined helmet. For two hours, he flew in total darkness. Lindbergh's flight lasted 33½ hours. Once, he even fell asleep with his eyes wide open! At 10:22 p.m. on May 21, he landed safely in Paris.

Amelia Earhart

In 1937 her plane disappeared mysteriously over the Pacific Ocean. But by then Amelia Earhart was already the world's most famous female pilot. Her dream was to follow Lindbergh's example and cross the Atlantic alone. She wanted to prove that a woman could do it. Earhart began her solo flight on May 20, 1932. For several hours she flew at 12,000 feet (3,658 m), watching the sun set and the moon come up. But a key instrument failed, and she ran into a severe storm that battered her plane. Ice formed on the wings, sending Earhart into a dangerous spin. Later, flames shot out of the engine. A fuel leak dripped gas down the back of her neck. Nearly 15 hours after starting, Earhart landed her plane in a meadow in Northern Ireland and lived to tell about it.

THE OLYMPICS

LEGEND HAS IT THAT the Olympic Games were founded in ancient times by Heracles, a son of the Greek god Zeus. Unfortunately, that can't really be proven. The first Olympic Games for which there are still written records took place in 776 B.C. There was only one event, a running race called the stade. From then on, the Olympics were played every four years until they were abolished in A.D. 393.

It wasn't until more than 1,500 years later that the Olympics were resurrected. The modern Olympic Games were held for the first time in 1896 and have continued around the world ever since.

Summer Olympic Games Sites

1896	Athens, Greece
1900	Paris, France
1904	St. Louis, Missouri, U.S.
1906	Athens, Greece
1908	London, England, U.K.
1912	Stockholm, Sweden
1920	Antwerp, Belgium
1924	Paris, France
1928	Amsterdam, Netherlands
1932	Los Angeles, California, U.S.
1936	Berlin, Germany
1948	London, England, U.K.
1952	Helsinki, Finland
1956	Melbourne, Australia
1960	Rome, Italy
1964	Tokyo, Japan
1968	Mexico City, Mexico
1972	Munich, West Germany (now Germany)
1976	Montreal, Canada
1980	Moscow, U.S.S.R. (now Russia)
1984	Los Angeles, California, U.S.
1988	Seoul, South Korea
1992	Barcelona, Spain
1996	Atlanta, Georgia, U.S.
2000	Sydney, Australia
2004	Athens, Greece
2008	Beijing, China
2012	London, England, U.K.

Winter Olympic Games Sites

1924	Chamonix, France
1928	St. Moritz, Switzerland
1932	Lake Placid, New York, U.S.
1936	Garmisch-Partenkirchen, Germany
1948	St. Moritz, Switzerland
1952	Oslo, Norway
1956	Cortina d'Ampezzo, Italy
1960	Squaw Valley, California, U.S.
1964	Innsbruck, Austria
1968	Grenoble, France
1972	Sapporo, Japan
1976	Innsbruck, Austria
1980	Lake Placid, New York, U.S.
1984	Sarajevo, Yugoslavia
1988	Calgary, Alberta, Canada
1992	Albertville, France
1994	Lillehammer, Norway
1998	Nagano, Japan
2002	Salt Lake City, Utah, U.S.
2006	Torino (Turin), Italy
2010	Vancouver, British Columbia, Canada
2014	Sochi, Russia

Note: Due to World Wars I and II, the 1916 Summer Olympics, and both the summer and winter games of 1940 and 1944 were not held.

Strange Olympic Sports of the Past & Future

There are a bunch of sports, some rather odd, that were once played in the Olympics but no longer get to make an appearance. Here are a few: **Tug-of-War • Croquet • Lacrosse • Golf • Power Boating**

The following are among a long list of sports that aren't currently played at the games, but are recognized as International Sports Federations by the Olympic Committee. So who knows, maybe one day you can win a gold medal in: **Billiards • Bridge • Chess • Lifesaving • Netball • Orienteering • Roller Sports • Waterskiing**

Who Killed the
Iceman?

Discoveries raise questions about Europe's oldest mummy

THE CRIME SCENE: In 1991 hikers found the body of a man encased in the ice of a melting glacier. Nicknamed the Iceman or Ötzi (OOTS-ee) for the Ötztal Alps where he was discovered, he was thought to have frozen to death in a snowstorm while tending sheep some 5,300 years ago. His body was mummified in the ice.

THE CRIME: Ten years later, closer study revealed that Ötzi did not die of exposure to the cold. X-rays show an arrowhead buried deep in his left shoulder. He had been shot in the back. But whodunnit? And why?

ONE DETECTIVE'S THEORY: Archaeologist Johan Reinhard, a National Geographic Society explorer-in-residence, was one of the detectives trying to solve the crime.

SUSPECTS AND MOTIVE: Reinhard believes that Ötzi may have been a victim of ritual sacrifice, killed by people to pacify mountain gods.

THE CLUES: "The place where the body was found is the kind of place where sacrifices happened in many other cultures around the world," Reinhard says. "It's a hard location to get to. I don't think a body would end up there by coincidence." And the placement of Ötzi's possessions—a bow, a backpack, and the oldest prehistoric copper ax ever found in Europe—indicates that a ceremony may have taken place there, Reinhard believes.

ANOTHER DETECTIVE'S THEORY: At the South Tyrol Museum of Archaeology, in Bolzano, Italy—where Ötzi is now kept frozen—Dr. Eduard Egarter Vigl is also working on the case. He believes that Ötzi was ambushed.

SUSPECTS AND MOTIVE: Vigl thinks Ötzi was involved in a fight—perhaps surprised while walking. He managed to escape, but later died of his wounds and exposure to the cold.

THE CLUES: A knife wound in Ötzi's hand proves that he struggled with someone before he died, Vigl says. He also points out that there is no evidence that sacrifices ever occurred in Europe during that time. And besides, most sacrifice victims aren't shot by arrows—especially in the back.

SO WHO KILLED THE ICEMAN?

Reinhard agrees that the clues are confusing. With no witnesses to tell what actually took place, there's no way to know exactly what happened. So this 5,300-year-old case may forever remain an unsolved mystery.

Reinhard believes the Iceman may have been buried by the person who killed him.

DOES BIGFOOT EXIST?

When a man admitted he pretended to be Bigfoot, many thought the question was answered. Others disagree.
NG KIDS presents both sides.

THE CASE FOR BIGFOOT:

Since the late 1800s more than 3,000 sightings of Bigfoot, also called Sasquatch, have been recorded in the United States and Canada. The reports describe a tall, hairy, apelike creature that walks on two feet and has long arms and a short neck.

The tracks, investigators say, show no claw marks like the ones a bear would leave. Their size—averaging around 16 inches (41 cm) long and 7 inches (18 cm) wide—is bigger than any human print, and the long stride would be almost impossible for a person to make.

Jeff Meldrum, an anatomy professor at Idaho State University, has collected more than 200 plaster casts of tracks. He admits some of the tracks are fakes. But the majority, he says, are

quite consistent, with flat, flexible feet; five toes; and qualities common to all primates. "Who could have made these tracks so consistently if it's all a hoax?" he says.

"Something is walking around out there." Researchers have also collected handprints, knuckle prints, knee prints—even butt prints!

The fact that no skeleton has ever been found doesn't deter investigators, either. "We're finding new fossil species all the time," Meldrum says. "It only takes one to convince people Bigfoot exists."

THE CASE AGAINST BIGFOOT:

Many Bigfoot researchers say the 1967 home movie of a tall, hairy creature proves that Bigfoot exists. But in 2002 a man who seemed to know behind-the-scenes information about the movie claimed he had posed as Bigfoot in the film.

Could Bigfoot be descended from an extinct giant ape called *Gigantopithecus?* Investigators say yes. But its fossils are found only in Asia, and there's no evidence it migrated anywhere else. "We have no fossils of this primate in North America," says anthropologist David Daegling of the University of Florida.

In fact, footprints are the only physical evidence of Bigfoot, but many scientists say they're too inconsistent to be trusted. "There are three-,

SCIENTISTS WEIGH IN

NO BIGFOOT? WHAT COULD PEOPLE BE SEEING?

Bear

Backpacker

four-, and five-toed varieties," Daegling says. And given the number of reported sightings, critics say that the creatures should be having closer encounters with humans, such as one getting hit by a car. "The biggest argument against Bigfoot is that we don't have a single body," Daegling says.

"What we have to ask about the Bigfoot evidence is, 'Is it possible that a human being could have produced this?'" Daegling says. "There is always another explanation besides a hairy monster."

Funny FILL-IN

Breaking News!

Ask someone to give you words to fill in the blanks in this story without showing it to him or her. Then read it out loud for a laugh.

REPORTER: Good evening. This is _____ reporting to you live from
famous person

_____ , where _____ claims to have spotted a mysterious
a street in your town *friend's full name, male*

creature in _____ . I have Mr. _____ here to tell us what he saw.
a park in your town *same friend's last name*

FRIEND: I was _____ right over there, when I heard a(n) _____
action verb ending in -ing *verb ending in -ing*

in the _____ . Then I heard a(n) _____ . Before I knew it, a
object in nature, plural *animal noise*

_____ appeared. It looked like it was half _____ and half _____ .
something huge *noun* *animal*

It had _____ _____ and a coat of _____ _____ . Then it
number *body part, plural* *color* *something soft, plural*

disappeared into the _____ . I have pictures here in my _____ .
object in nature, plural *high-tech gadget*

Take a look! **REPORTER:** _____ ! It looks like you placed a(n) _____
exclamation *movie character*

doll on top of a(n) _____ and hid it in the woods. **FRIEND:** You don't have
something tall

to believe me, but I know I saw the _____ ! **REPORTER:** Well, viewers,
mysterious creature

you heard it straight from the _____ 's mouth. Now back to the studio, where
animal

_____ discusses his new reality TV show.
male cartoon character

251

HISTORICAL BIOGRAPHIES THAT ROCK

A biography is the story of a person's life. It can be a brief summary or a long book. Biographers—those who write biographies—use many different sources to learn about their subjects. You can write your own biography of a famous person who you find inspiring.

How to Get Started

Choose a subject you find interesting. If you think Amelia Earhart is cool, you have a good chance of getting your reader interested, too. If you're bored by aviation, your reader will be snoring after your first paragraph.

Your subject can be almost anyone: an inventor, an author, a celebrity, a President, or a member of your family. To find someone to write about, ask yourself these simple questions:

1. Who do I want to know more about?
2. What did this person do that was special?
3. How did this person change the world?

Do Your Research

• Find out as much about your subject as possible. Read books, news articles, and encyclopedia entries. Watch video clips and movies, and search the Internet. Conduct interviews, if possible.

• Take notes, writing down important facts and interesting stories about your subject.

Writing the Biography

• Come up with a title. Include the person's name.

• Write an introduction. Consider asking a probing question about your subject.

• Include information about the person's childhood. When was this person born? Where did he or she grow up? Whom did he or she admire?

• Highlight the person's talents, accomplishments, and his or her personal attributes.

• Describe the specific events that helped to shape this person's life. Has this person ever had a problem and overcome it?

• Write a conclusion. Include your thoughts about why it is important to learn about this person.

• Once you have finished your first draft, revise and then proofread.

Here's a SAMPLE BIOGRAPHY for President Barack Obama. Of course there is so much more for you to research, uncover, and reveal!

Barack Obama—Number 44

Barack Obama is the 44th President of the United States and the first African American to hold the office.

Obama was born on August 4, 1961, in Honolulu, Hawaii. As a child he lived in Indonesia. In elementary school he once wrote an essay titled "I want to become President." Some dreams start early! Later, Obama graduated from Columbia University and earned a degree in law from Harvard Law School.

Obama was the Democratic Illinois state senator from 1997 to 2004. He gave the keynote address at the 2004 Democratic National Convention, an honor that helped him on the path to his successful presidential candidacy.

He is married to Michelle Robinson Obama and has two daughters, Malia and Sasha. Obama is a good example for them—and kids everywhere. If you work hard, your dreams can come true.

REVEAL YOUR SOURCES

A bibliography is a list of all the sources you used to get information for your essay, such as books, magazine articles, interviews, and websites. It is included at the end of your essay or report.

The bibliography should list sources in alphabetical order by author's last name. If a source doesn't have an author, then it should be alphabetized by title.

BOOK
Author (last name, first name). *Title*. City of publisher: publisher, date of publication.

Ex: Allen, Thomas B. *George Washington, Spymaster*. Washington, D.C.: National Geographic, 2004.

ENCYCLOPEDIA
Author (last name, first name) (if given). "Article title." *Name of Encyclopedia*. Edition. Volume. City of publisher: publisher, date of publication.

Ex: "Gerbil." *The Encyclopedia Britannica*. 15th ed. Vol. 5. Chicago: Encyclopedia Britannica, 2007.

MAGAZINE/NEWSPAPER ARTICLE
Author (last name, first name). "Article title." *Name of magazine*. Date: page numbers.

Ex: Kassinger, Ruth. "Gold Fever." *NATIONAL GEOGRAPHIC KIDS*. Jan–Feb 2009: pp. 8–11.

DVD/FILM
Title of film. Director's name. Year of original film's release. Format. Name of distributor, year, video/DVD/etc. produced.

Ex: *Lewis & Clark: Great Journey West*. Dir. Bruce Neibaur. 2002. Large-format film. National Geographic, 2002.

INTERVIEW
Person interviewed (last name, first name). Type of interview (personal, telephone, email, etc.). Date of interview.

Ex: Hiebert, Fredrik. Personal interview with *NATIONAL GEOGRAPHIC KIDS*. April 28, 2008.

WEBSITE
Author (last name, first name) (if given). *Title of the site*. Editor. Date and/or version number. Name of sponsoring institution. Date of access. <URL>.

Ex: *Animals*. 2006. National Geographic. January 12, 2009. <http://kids.national geographic.com/Animals>.

TIP:
If you keep track of all the sources as you use them, compiling the information to create your bibliography can be done in a snap.

COOL CLICK

Want to find out more about sources and books? The Library of Congress has a great website.
loc.gov/families

Culture Connection

Students training in the Chinese martial art Kung Fu in Henan Province, China

STRAIGHT TALK

DIFFERENT IS GOOD!

Would you hate someone just because they look different?

Unfortunately, a lot of people judge other people on the way they look, what they eat, or what they wear. But that's just not fair. It's not right to judge people. It doesn't matter where you are from, what your culture is, what religion you practice, or what you look like. We're all people, and everyone should be accepted as an individual. After all, we're all the same on the inside.

Accepting differences is like eating a burrito—without all the different meats, veggies, and cheeses, all you get is a boring tortilla. "And when I chew all the ingredients together, it's good!" says Deborah Crockett, a school psychologist in Atlanta, Georgia. Sometimes it's hard to keep an open mind about things—or people—you don't understand. So to really enjoy your next "cultural burrito," use Crockett's tips below.

COMMON GROUND. Everyone's different. But everyone also has things in common. Do you wear a baseball cap, a Jewish yarmulke, or a Muslim hijab? Yeah, they're from different cultures. But the point is, they're all head coverings.

CULTURE CLUB. Learning about other groups of people helps you understand them. Try eating foods from another culture. Or teach yourself words in another language.

BLAME GAME. Has your entire class ever had to stay in from recess because one kid couldn't keep his mouth shut? That's not fair! It's also not fair to blame an entire group of people for the actions of a few individuals.

TIME-OUT

friends?

TYPECAST. It's normal to make assumptions, we all do it. But the key is to be aware that you've done it—then try to be more open-minded the next time around.

THE CURIOUS WORLD OF TRAVEL

SHOPPING is the **NUMBER ONE** leisure activity for **international visitors** to the **UNITED STATES.**

THE SHORTEST scheduled airline flight is between two Scottish islands, Westray and Papa Westray. **Flight time: 2 MINUTES!**

The first **TRAFFIC LIGHT** was invented in 1868 by a British railroad engineer. It was a lantern with **RED AND GREEN** signals.

The 31-mile (50-km) -long **UNDERWATER TUNNEL** connecting **FRANCE** and **ENGLAND** is known as the **CHUNNEL.**

In 1987 AMERICAN AIRLINES **saved $40,000 by ELIMINATING ONE OLIVE FROM EACH SALAD** served in first class.

Around 70 percent of train trips in **GREAT BRITAIN** either start or finish in **LONDON.**

INDIGENOUS PEOPLE OF SOUTH AMERICA

Country	Percent
Bolivia	55%
Peru	45%
Ecuador	25%
Guyana	9.1%
Chile	4.6%
Paraguay	2%
Suriname	2%
Venezuela	2%
Colombia	1%
Argentina	1%
Brazil	0.4%
Uruguay	0.02%

The indigenous people of South America are concentrated in the countries of the Andes, a mountainous region in western South America.

INDIGENOUS PEOPLES are groups of people who live in a place to which they have the earliest known historical connection, such as the Inca of South America.

CELEBRATE! Holidays Around the World

1 NEW YEAR'S DAY
January 1st
Marking the beginning of a new year, celebrations for this holiday usually begin the night before. Parties, wishes for a good new year, and resolutions are among part of the usual festivities.

2 NIRVANA DAY
mid-February

Celebrated by Mahayana Buddhists, this holiday remembers the anniversary of Buddha's death. It's not a sad day, it's a day to reflect on life and celebrate.

3 PURIM
varies, usually February
This fun Jewish holiday remembers the story of how Queen Esther and Mordechai helped to save the Jews from the wicked Haman. The Megilla is read to help block out evil. Kids often dress up in costumes, while everyone eats and celebrates the day.

4 EASTER SUNDAY
varies, usually March or April
A Christian holiday that celebrates the resurrection of Jesus Christ, Easter is celebrated by giving baskets filled with gifts or candy to children.

5 PASSOVER
varies, usually March or April
A Jewish holiday that commemorates the exodus of the Jews from Egypt and their liberation from slavery. Passover is a seven-day holiday during which observers have Seders, or ritual feasts, and abstain from eating leavened bread.

6 RAMADAN AND EID AL-FITR
varies, summer
A Muslim religious holiday, Ramadan is a month long, ending in the Eid Al-Fitr celebration. Observers fast during this month, eating only after sunset, and do good deeds. Muslims pray for forgiveness and hope to purify themselves through observance.

7 ROSH HASHANAH & YOM KIPPUR
varies, usually September or October
A Jewish religious holiday marking the beginning of a new year on the Hebrew calendar, Rosh Hashanah is celebrated with prayer, ritual foods, and a day of rest. Yom Kippur, known as the "Day of Atonement," is the most solemn of all Jewish holidays. It is observed with fasting and prayer, and is marked by a feast at sundown.

8 DIWALI
varies, usually October or November
Often called the "Festival of Lights," this Hindu holiday celebrates the triumph of good over evil and the lifting of spiritual darkness.

9 HALLOWEEN
October 31st
A day for costumes, candy, scary stories, and trick-or-treating, Halloween has it's roots in a Celtic festival celebrating the end of the harvest season.

10 THANKSGIVING
4th Thursday in November
This American holiday remembers the 1621 feast of the Pilgrims and the Native Americans. Thanksgiving is celebrated with feasts shared with family and friends.

11 HANUKKAH
varies, December

Also known as the "Festival of Lights," this Jewish holiday is eight days long. It commemorates the rededication of the Temple in Jerusalem. It is observed with celebrations, the lighting of a menorah, and the exchange of gifts.

12 CHRISTMAS DAY
December 25th
A Christian holiday marking the birth of Jesus Christ, Christmas is usually celebrated by decorating trees, exchanging presents, and having festive gatherings.

ANNIVERSARIES

Annual	1 year
Biennial	2 years
Triennial	3 years
Quadrennial	4 years
Quinquennial	5 years
Sexennial	6 years
Septennial	7 years
Octennial	8 years
Novennial	9 years
Decennial	10 years
Undecennial	11 years
Duodecennial	12 years
Tredecennial	13 years
Quattuordecennial	14 years
Quindecennial	15 years
Vigintennial or vicennial	20 years
Semicentennial or quinquagenary	50 years
Semisesquicentennial	75 years
Centennial	100 years
Quasquicentennial	125 years
Sesquicentennial	150 years
Demisemiseptcentennial or quartoseptcentennial	175 years
Bicentennial	200 years
Semiquincentennial	250 years
Tercentennial or tricentennial	300 years
Semiseptcentennial	350 years
Quadricentennial or quatercentenary	400 years
Quincentennial	500 years
Sexcentennial	600 years
Septicentennial or septuacentennial	700 years
Octocentennial	800 years
Nonacentennial	900 years
Millennial	1000 years
Bimillennial	2000 years

2011 CALENDAR

JANUARY
S	M	T	W	T	F	S
						1
2	3	4	5	6	7	8
9	10	11	12	13	14	15
16	17	18	19	20	21	22
23	24	25	26	27	28	29
30	31					

FEBRUARY
S	M	T	W	T	F	S
		1	2	3	4	5
6	7	8	9	10	11	12
13	14	15	16	17	18	19
20	21	22	23	24	25	26
27	28					

MARCH
S	M	T	W	T	F	S
		1	2	3	4	5
6	7	8	9	10	11	12
13	14	15	16	17	18	19
20	21	22	23	24	25	26
27	28	29	30	31		

APRIL
S	M	T	W	T	F	S
					1	2
3	4	5	6	7	8	9
10	11	12	13	14	15	16
17	18	19	20	21	22	23
24	25	26	27	28	29	30

MAY
S	M	T	W	T	F	S
1	2	3	4	5	6	7
8	9	10	11	12	13	14
15	16	17	18	19	20	21
22	23	24	25	26	27	28
29	30	31				

JUNE
S	M	T	W	T	F	S
			1	2	3	4
5	6	7	8	9	10	11
12	13	14	15	16	17	18
19	20	21	22	23	24	25
26	27	28	29	30		

JULY
S	M	T	W	T	F	S
					1	2
3	4	5	6	7	8	9
10	11	12	13	14	15	16
17	18	19	20	21	22	23
24	25	26	27	28	29	30
31						

AUGUST
S	M	T	W	T	F	S
	1	2	3	4	5	6
7	8	9	10	11	12	13
14	15	16	17	18	19	20
21	22	23	24	25	26	27
28	29	30	31			

SEPTEMBER
S	M	T	W	T	F	S
				1	2	3
4	5	6	7	8	9	10
11	12	13	14	15	16	17
18	19	20	21	22	23	24
25	26	27	28	29	30	

OCTOBER
S	M	T	W	T	F	S
						1
2	3	4	5	6	7	8
9	10	11	12	13	14	15
16	17	18	19	20	21	22
23	24	25	26	27	28	29
30	31					

NOVEMBER
S	M	T	W	T	F	S
		1	2	3	4	5
6	7	8	9	10	11	12
13	14	15	16	17	18	19
20	21	22	23	24	25	26
27	28	29	30			

DECEMBER
S	M	T	W	T	F	S
				1	2	3
4	5	6	7	8	9	10
11	12	13	14	15	16	17
18	19	20	21	22	23	24
25	26	27	28	29	30	31

What's Your Chinese Horoscope?
Locate your birth year to find out.

In Chinese astrology the zodiac runs on a 12-year cycle, based on the lunar calendar. Each year corresponds to one of twelve animals, each representing one of twelve personality types. Read on to find out which animal year you were born in and what that might say about you.

RAT
1972, '84, '96, 2008
Say cheese! You're attractive, charming, and creative. When you get mad, you can really have sharp teeth!

RABBIT
1975, '87, '99, 2011
Your ambition and talent make you jump at opportunity. You also keep your ears open for gossip.

HORSE
1966, '78, '90, 2002
Being happy is your "mane" goal. And while you're a smart, hard worker, your teacher may ride you for talking too much.

ROOSTER
1969, '81, '93, 2005
You crow about your adventures, but inside you're really shy. You're thoughtful, capable, brave, and talented.

OX
1973, '85, '97, 2009
You're smart, patient, and as strong as an—well, you know what. Though you're a leader, you'd never brag.

DRAGON
1976, '88, 2000, '12
You're on fire! Health, energy, honesty, and bravery make you a living legend.

SHEEP
1967, '79, '91, 2003
Gentle as a lamb, you're also artistic, compassionate, and wise. You're often shy.

DOG
1970, '82, '94, 2006
Often the leader of the pack, you're loyal and honest. You can also keep a secret.

TIGER
1974, '86, '98, 2010
You may be a nice person, but no one should ever enter your room without asking—you might attack!

SNAKE
1977, '89, 2001, '13
You may not speak often, but you're very smart. You always seem to have a stash of cash.

MONKEY
1968, '80, '92, 2004
No "monkey see, monkey do" for you. You're a clever problem solver with an excellent memory.

PIG
1971, '83, '95, 2007
Even though you're courageous, honest, and kind, you never hog all the attention.

Chinese New Year

DON'T LET ANYONE TELL YOU DRAGONS ARE SCARY.
Every year they dance through the streets to celebrate Chinese New Year. Longer than 13 pickup trucks, these elaborate dragons, such as the one shown here at a parade in San Francisco, California, are controlled by at least 20 people. Tradition says the dragons help bring good luck. It's just one of many customs that ring in the Chinese New Year.

RAMADAN

30 DAYS OF FASTING? SOUNDS TOUGH, HUH?

Just ask a Muslim who celebrates the holy month of Ramadan. If you're over 12 years old and an observant Muslim, Ramadan—the ninth month of the Islamic calendar—is a time to abstain from food, drink, and other indulgences. Don't worry though, no one is starving. You're allowed to eat after sundown and before dawn.

The fasting period is meant to teach patience and spirituality. During this month, Muslims ask God for forgiveness and guidance. The end of the fasting period of Ramadan is marked by the holiday of Eid Al-Fitr, a joyous three-day holiday.

Try This! GINGERBREAD HOUSES

YOU WILL NEED

- VANILLA FROSTING
- CREAM OF TARTAR
- CARDBOARD
- GRAHAM CRACKERS (OR GINGERBREAD)
- SERRATED KNIFE (ASK FOR A PARENT'S HELP)
- ASSORTED CANDY, PRETZELS, AND COOKIES, INCLUDING SQUARE CARAMELS (NOT SHOWN)
- SHREDDED COCONUT

WHAT TO DO

MIX THE "GLUE" Frosting will hold each graham cracker building together. Combine a can of ready-made vanilla frosting with one-quarter teaspoon of cream of tartar. To apply the frosting, squeeze it out of a sealed freezer bag with a hole cut in one corner.

BUILD THE HOUSE

BASE Cut a piece of cardboard that's big enough to hold the scene.

WALLS The front and back walls are each made of a whole graham cracker turned horizontally. Ask a parent to create the two remaining sides. For each, use a serrated knife to gently saw the top of a whole graham cracker into a peak (inset, above). Run a bead of icing along the bottom edge and sides of the crackers. "Glue" them together in a rectangle on top of the cardboard. Prop up the walls while you work.

PEAKED ROOF Run icing along the tops of the walls. Place two whole graham crackers—turned horizontally—on top of the sides, using icing to hold them in place. Let the icing set overnight.

WAGON USE QUARTER CRACKERS FOR THE BOTTOM AND SIDES. USE HALF OF A QUARTER CRACKER FOR THE BACK. "GLUE" THE PIECES IN PLACE. ADD PRETZEL WHEELS AND A CARAMEL UNDER THE WAGON FOR SUPPORT.

SILO CUT OFF THE TOPS OF TWO CAKE CONES, THEN FROST THE OPEN ENDS TOGETHER. STICK ON COLORFUL LICORICE AND TOP WITH A FOIL BAKING CUP.

SNOWMAN SKEWER TWO MARSHMALLOWS ONTO A PRETZEL STICK. USE GUM-DROPS FOR THE HAT, EYES, AND NOSE; PRETZELS FOR THE ARMS; AND STRING LICORICE FOR A SCARF.

Fun Winter Gift Idea

Snow Globes

YOU WILL NEED
- small jar (a baby food jar works well)
- plastic animal or figurine that fits in the jar
- sandpaper
- instant-bonding glue (follow directions on the tube and use with adult supervision)
- nail polish remover
- baby oil
- 1/2 teaspoon white glitter

WHAT TO DO
Turn the jar's lid upside down. Use sandpaper to scuff the inside of the lid. Glue the bottom of the figurine to the center of the lid. (Nail polish remover cleans glue off skin and surfaces.) Dry for four hours. Fill the jar with baby oil. Add glitter. To seal, put glue around the rim of the jar. Close the lid tightly and dry for four hours. Turn the jar over and let it snow!

DOGHOUSE Follow the steps at left, but use quarter crackers for all sides and the roof.

BARN Use graham cracker halves for the barn's roof and sides. For the front and back, cut a peak in a whole graham cracker (inset, above left).

DECORATE "Glue" on your favorite treats to create doors, rooftops, trees, and anything else you can imagine. Let everything set overnight. Cover the cardboard base with shredded coconut to finish your snowy scene.

DOG "GLUE" TWO GUMDROPS TOGETHER TO FORM THE BODY. STICK ON PIECES OF GUMDROPS FOR THE EARS, NOSE, AND TAIL.

263

OFF THE DEEP END

UNDERWATER PUMPKIN CARVING

Trish Lee steadies the gourd as her partner takes a turn carving.

The grossest thing about carving pumpkins is pulling out the slimy guts with your bare hands, right? Well, try dodging those slimy guts as they float by your face while fish attack!

The "sport" is underwater pumpkin carving. Each Halloween, scuba divers flipper their way to the bottom of oceans, lakes, and swimming pools to participate in these wacky contests.

And talk about fun: "Where else can you see someone carving a pumpkin while they're upside down?" says Trish Lee, who participated in a contest in Monterey Bay, California.

SMASHING PUMPKINS

Armed with their carving knives and pumpkins, divers make their way to the bottom. Easy, right?

Like a 15-pound (7-kg) balloon, a pumpkin is filled with air—so it floats. Puncturing the pumpkin and filling the air pockets with water helps weigh it down, but uncooperative pumpkins tend to pop back to the surface like big orange bubbles.

Once divers get to the bottom (usually only about 20 feet (6 m) down), they can start carving. When they pull the pumpkin's top off, fish swarm to the scene to devour a free meal.

Some divers draw their pumpkin faces before carving; others sculpt free-style. Either way, it's challenging when you're under the sea.

Try This! Ways to Give Back During the Holidays

Giving back is a great thing to do year-round, but the holidays tend to bring out the charitable side in people. Try some of these ideas with your family and make a difference.

- ▶ Donate to a charitable organization.
- ▶ Invite an elderly neighbor or someone who lives alone to join your celebration. (Ask your parents first.)
- ▶ Deliver a meal to a family in need.
- ▶ Write a thoughtful note to someone special.
- ▶ Bring your host a small gift to show your appreciation, and offer to help clean up.
- ▶ Donate clothes you've outgrown.

- ▶ Donate food to a local charity or food bank.
- ▶ Volunteer at a soup kitchen.
- ▶ Send a care package to a soldier.
- ▶ Visit hospital patients.
- ▶ Foster a dog or cat.
- ▶ Adopt an endangered animal through a zoo.
- ▶ Shovel snow for a neighbor.
- ▶ Help pick up trash at a local park.

Funny FILL-IN

A Royal Vacation

Ask someone to give you words to fill in the blanks in this story without showing it to him or her. Then read out loud for a laugh.

SCREEEEECH!

This summer my family and I took a(n) _____ trip to London, England. After a(n)
                                        adjective

_____ -hour flight, we found out that the airline lost our _____. So I ended
number   plural noun

up wearing the same _____ T-shirt for the whole trip! On the way to the
                      popular singer

hotel, I was staring out the car window when I saw a(n) _____ double-decker
                                                          color

_____ coming right at us! My dad had forgotten that the British _____
noun   verb

on the _____ side of the road! He shouted, "_____!" and then
        adjective   exclamation

_____ onto the sidewalk in front of _____ Palace—the home of
past-tense verb   your neighbor's last name

_____. Luckily no one at the _____ palace seemed to notice.
famous female person   adjective

Everyone was _____ in the opposite direction. I jumped up and down
              verb ending in –ing

to see over them when my foot _____ on a piece of _____.
                               past-tense verb   food

I hit my _____ on a(n) _____, and then everything went _____.
          body part   noun   color

The next thing I knew, _____ was helping me up and inviting me
                        same famous female as above

to the _____ for dinner. She was throwing a party
        famous place

and the guest of honor was _____!
                            same singer as above

265

World Religions

Around the world, religion takes many forms. Some belief systems, such as Christianity, Islam, and Judaism, are monotheistic, meaning that followers believe in just one supreme being. Others, like Hinduism, Shintoism, and most native belief systems, are polytheistic, meaning that many of their adherents believe in multiple gods.

All of the major religions have their origins in Asia, but they have spread around the world. Christianity, with the largest number of followers, has three divisions—Roman Catholic, Eastern Orthodox, and Protestant. Islam, with about one-fifth of all believers, has two main divisions—Sunni and Shiite. Hinduism and Buddhism account for almost another one-fifth of believers. Judaism, dating back some 4,000 years, is the oldest of all the major monotheistic religions.

CHRISTIANITY

Based on the teachings of Jesus Christ, a Jew born some 2,000 years ago in the area of modern-day Israel, Christianity has spread worldwide and actively seeks converts. Followers in Switzerland (above) participate in a procession with lanterns and crosses.

BUDDHISM

Founded about 2,500 years ago in northern India by a Hindu prince, Gautama Buddha, Buddhism spread throughout East and Southeast Asia. Buddhist temples have statues, such as the Mihintale Buddha (above) in Sri Lanka.

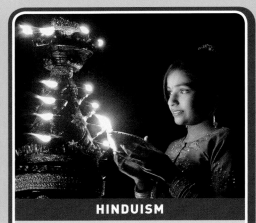

HINDUISM

Dating back more than 4,000 years, Hinduism is practiced mainly in India. Hindus follow sacred texts known as the Vedas and believe in reincarnation. During the festival of Diwali, Hindus light candles (above) to symbolize the victory of good over evil.

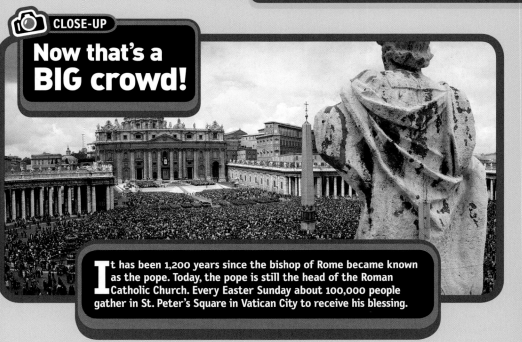

CLOSE-UP

Now that's a
BIG crowd!

It has been 1,200 years since the bishop of Rome became known as the pope. Today, the pope is still the head of the Roman Catholic Church. Every Easter Sunday about 100,000 people gather in St. Peter's Square in Vatican City to receive his blessing.

To learn more about ancient and medieval religions, go online.
historyforkids.org/learn/religion

COOL CLICK

ISLAM

Muslims believe that the Koran, Islam's sacred book, records the words of Allah (God) as revealed to the Prophet Muhammad around A.D. 610. Believers (above) circle the Kabah in the Haram Mosque in Mecca, Saudi Arabia, the spiritual center of the faith.

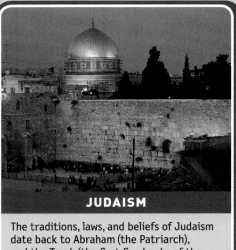

JUDAISM

The traditions, laws, and beliefs of Judaism date back to Abraham (the Patriarch), and the Torah (the first five books of the Old Testament). Followers pray before the Western Wall (above), which stands below Islam's Dome of the Rock in Jerusalem.

Languages and Literacy

Every 14 days a language dies. By 2100, more than half of the more than 7,000 languages spoken on Earth—many of them not yet recorded—may disappear, taking with them a wealth of knowledge about history, culture, and the environment.

Earth's nearly 7 billion people live in 194 independent countries and speak more than 7,000 languages. Some countries, such as Japan, have one official language. Others have many languages. India has 22 official languages. Experts believe that humans may once have spoken as many as 10,000 languages, but that number has dropped by one-third and is still declining.

Language defines a culture, through the people who speak it and what it allows speakers to say. Throughout human history, the languages of powerful groups have spread while the languages of smaller cultures have become extinct.

LITERACY is the ability to read and write in one's native language. Almost 84 percent of the people in the world (ages 15 and over) are literate.

Literacy rates vary greatly from country to country and region to region. Many factors play a role in whether people are literate; some of those factors are wealth, gender, educational availability, and locale.

There are 774 million illiterate adults (those who cannot read and write) in the world. Two-thirds of those are women, generally because women in less-developed countries often lack access to education.

COOL CLICK

To read more about preserving languages, go online.
nationalgeographic.com/mission/enduringvoices

LEADING LANGUAGES

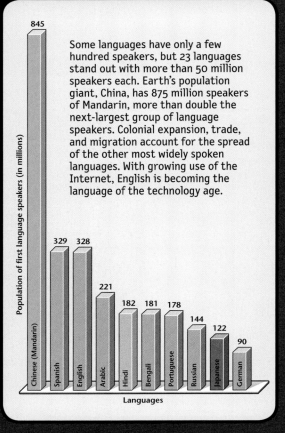

Some languages have only a few hundred speakers, but 23 languages stand out with more than 50 million speakers each. Earth's population giant, China, has 875 million speakers of Mandarin, more than double the next-largest group of language speakers. Colonial expansion, trade, and migration account for the spread of the other most widely spoken languages. With growing use of the Internet, English is becoming the language of the technology age.

Population of first language speakers (in millions)

Language	Speakers
Chinese (Mandarin)	845
Spanish	329
English	328
Arabic	221
Hindi	182
Bengali	181
Portuguese	178
Russian	144
Japanese	122
German	90

Languages

The widespread use of technology—for example, the text messaging that holds the attention of this girl using her PDA—has crossed over the language barrier. Computers, the Internet, and electronic communication devices use a universal language that knows no national borders.

MEET THE NAT GEO EXPLORER

WADE DAVIS

An ethnographer, writer, filmmaker, and photographer, Wade Davis is dedicated to the cause of protecting the world's vanishing cultures.

How did you become an explorer?
I was with my roommate in the Harvard Square cafeteria, and there was a National Geographic map in front of us. He looked at me, and I looked at him. He pointed to the Arctic, and I pointed to the Amazon. Two weeks later we were each there.

How would you suggest kids follow in your footsteps?
Just do it. It's as simple as that. But there are two lessons I like to share with kids. First, people often suggest to kids that life is linear and the only way to get through the alphabet is A to B to C. I think it's the critical crossroads that determine life's path. Cultivate your inner compass so when you come to a crossroads, you know which way to go. Second, be patient. Learn to put yourself in the way of opportunities. Do the work, and give your destiny time to find you.

What is one place or thing you'd still like to explore?
There are so many. But here's the top of my list:
- Walk Asia's Silk Road.
- Traverse the Sahara in Africa from west to east.
- Walk the network of ancient Inca highways in South America.

FINGERSPELLING

The manipulation of the fingers and hands to form the letters of a written language is called fingerspelling. These manual alphabets are used in deaf education and generally form the basis for sign languages around the world.

It is interesting to know though, that fingerspelling is not the same around the world. For example, in languages with a Latin alphabet, there are both one-handed (American Sign Language and Irish Sign Language) and two-handed (Turkish Sign Language and that of the former Yugoslavia) manual alphabets. And languages with non-Latin alphabets, such as Japanese, use handshapes to represent the written characters.

A   B   C   D

See more information on deaf culture.
pbs.org/wnet/soundandfury/culture/index.html

BRAILLE

Braille is an alphabet system used by blind people to read and write using touch. It consists of groups of dots arranged in various ways to designate certain letters, numbers, words, and punctuation to form sentences. Each character is made up of six dots within a Braille cell. The dots can be raised or not raised, creating the Braille codes. The blind can read Braille by running their fingers over the text and feeling the dot arrangements.

Braille can be adapted to languages that do not use the Latin alphabet. In this case, the codes are usually assigned to the new alphabet in relation to how it is translated into the Latin alphabet.

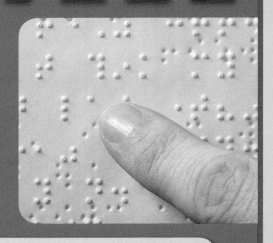

To learn more about Braille, go online. brailler.com/braille.htm

15

Ways to Say Hello

Armenian
Barev

Mandarin
Ni hao

Dutch
Goedendag

Finnish
Hei

French
Bonjour

Greek
Yia sou

Hebrew
Shalom

Hindi
Namaste

Icelandic
Halló

Italian
Ciào

Russian
Privyet

Spanish
Hola

Swahili
Jambo

Turkish
Merhaba

Welsh
Dweud

Bet you didn't know

There are more than **250,000** distinct **WORDS** in the English langage.

Hippopotomonstrosesquippedaliophobia is the **FEAR** of **LONG WORDS.**

weird (but) true

Most people spend about FIVE YEARS of their lives EATING.

A head of BROCCOLI is made up of hundreds of small FLOWER BUDS.

LEMONS can have MORE SUGAR than STRAWBERRIES.

In JAPAN it's possible to buy WATERMELONS shaped like PYRAMIDS.

The holes in SWISS CHEESE are called EYES.

SMASHING FUN!

It's OK to play with your food in Buñol, Spain. That's where the largest annual food fight is held. Every August about 120 tons (109 t) of tomatoes are tossed off of trucks to more than 38,000 people. The food fighters crush the tomatoes and then send them flying. Just don't try this in your school cafeteria!

SUSHI-SHAPED SANDWICHES

Try This!

Sushi is a Japanese food that consists of rice and fish, generally raw. Try it in a restaurant. At home you can make these sushi-shaped sandwich wraps.

Ask an adult for help when you try this recipe.

WHAT TO DO

Follow the directions below for each wrap. Just substitute the different ingredients at left.

1. Lay the wrap flat and cover it from edge to edge with the spread.
2. Cut your sandwich fillings into spears or long slices. Place the fillings in a long row, about one inch (2.54 cm) in from the edge of the wrap. Distribute all of the foods evenly.
3. If the recipe includes a topping, drizzle a small amount over the sandwich filling.
4. Roll tightly, pressing firmly as you roll. Cut wrap into 3/4-inch (2-cm) slices.
5. Decorate your plate with a side of guacamole or apples.
6. For fun, eat your sandwich "sushi" with chopsticks.

YOU WILL NEED

TASTY TEX-MEX
WRAP: SUN-DRIED TOMATO
SPREAD: SOUR CREAM
FILLING: LETTUCE, CHEDDAR CHEESE, PRE-COOKED ROASTED CHICKEN BREAST
TOPPING: SALSA

PEANUT BUTTER-BANANA SURPRISE
WRAP: WHOLE WHEAT
SPREAD: PEANUT BUTTER
FILLING: BANANA AND APPLE SLICES
TOPPING: HONEY

HAM AND CHEESE CREATION
WRAP: SPINACH
SPREAD: CREAM CHEESE
FILLING: HAM, SWISS CHEESE, PICKLES, CARROTS

DID YOU KNOW?
Sushi dates back at least to the second century A.D. It began in China as a method to preserve fish.

273

Chocolate

CHOCOLATE COMES FROM THE BEAN

of the cacao tree, and people have been delighting in it since the time of the Aztec in the 14th to 16th centuries. In fact, they often used it in a spicy drink for royal and religious celebrations. Here are some cool facts you probably never knew about the yummy stuff:

- *Theobroma cacao*, the name of the tree that produces chocolate, means "food of the gods" in Greek.

- The Aztec used cacao seeds as money.

- The Aztec sometimes fed their sacrificial victims chocolate drinks to calm them before the sacrifice.

- Chocolate bars became popular during World War I.

- In the 19th century people began adding condensed milk to cocoa to produce milk chocolate. (*Cacao* refers to the bean or tree; *cocoa* is a product derived from cacao.)

- Mexicans today use chocolate in mole, a spicy sauce made with chilies and chocolate.

Pop History

BUBBLE GUM IS MADE FROM SWEETENERS like sugar, a

variety of different flavorings, and a chewy gum base. The gum base originally was made from a product called *chicle*, which comes from *Manilkara chicle* trees. Today, the gum base is sometimes made from a latex product or a type of rubber. But these products also come from trees. Think it's weird to chew gum from a tree? People have been doing it for centuries, ever since the ancient Maya of present-day Mexico and Central America chewed chicle thousands of years ago.

Interested in learning about other food history and fun facts?

COOL CLICK

foodfunandfacts.com/foodfun.htm

WE ALL SCREAM FOR ICE CREAM

People love ice cream. Funny thing though—no one knows for sure who invented it. Get the *scoop* on the history and mystery behind this sweet treat.

Sweet Snow: A.D. 54 Roman emperor, Nero, knew how to throw a feast. For dessert, he served a one-of-a-kind treat: sweet snow. To make it, Nero's slaves ran up into the mountains and gathered snow. Then they sprinted back to the kitchen, where cooks flavored the snow with fruit, wine, or honey.

Cool Legend: 1295 Italian explorer Marco Polo returned home after 17 years in China. Among the strange things he saw was "milk dried into a kind of paste." Over time, that piece of the story grew into the legend that he brought home a recipe for ice cream. He didn't.

Rare Treat: 1660s Wealthy Europeans enjoyed a rare new treat—"water ices." Before long, creative cooks added cream to the mix. To make things really fancy, they used metal molds to form ice cream into all sorts of shapes.

Old World: 1700s At first, ice cream was mainly a treat for the rich and the royal. Before refrigeration, ice was rare and expensive. Making ice cream also took hours, so it helped to have servants who could do it.

Mighty Machine: 1843 Making ice cream took a lot of muscle—cooks had to stir the cream and shake the ice for hours. Things got much easier when the ice cream machine was invented. Turning a crank stirred the ingredients and made the ice cream freeze smoothly. With the rise of factories in the 1800s, particularly in America, ice cream became a mass-produced treat. By 1900 almost anyone could afford it.

Sundaes: 1880s The sundae is probably named for the first day of the week. One popular tale is that many places banned selling sodas on Sunday. In response, a crafty merchant put just ice cream and syrup into a dish—a total hit.

First Cone? 1904 Countless visitors attended the World's Fair in St. Louis, Missouri. Many marveled at their first sight of an ice-cream cone. But just who invented it? Generally the glory goes to Ernest Hamwi, a Syrian immigrant who was selling thin, waffle-shaped cakes. Next to him was an ice-cream stand. When the ice-cream seller ran out of dishes, Hamwi quickly shaped his cakes into cones that could hold ice cream.

Far-out Flavors: Some things about ice cream haven't changed. Back in the 1790s a New York cookbook included recipes for parmesan, ginger, and brown bread ice cream. Today, people can try rose, ketchup, or potato chip. Ice cream is as flavorful as ever!

275

World Economies

The way a country manages its resources (money, land, transportation, natural resources, etc.) to produce, distribute, and consume goods (cars, food, etc.) and services (transportation, etc.) is called its economy.

It can be divided into three parts, or sectors—agriculture, industry, and services. The economies of the United States, Western Europe, and Japan are dominated by the service sector. These economies enjoy a high GDP (gross domestic product) per capita—the value of goods and services produced each year, averaged per person in each country.

In contrast, some economies in Africa and Asia still depend mostly on agriculture, where farmers produce only enough crops to support their own families. These countries have a low standard of living. Other economies, such as those of oil-producing countries of the Middle East, have a very high GDP per capita, but wealth is very unevenly divided among the population.

No country produces everything its people need or want. Therefore, trade is also a critical part of the world economy.

The economies of the world impact each other and global trends, such as recessions, can also develop.

HIGHEST GDP PER CAPITA

1.	Liechtenstein	$118,000
2.	Qatar	$111,000
3.	Luxembourg	$81.200
4.	Norway	$59,500
5.	Kuwait	$57,500
6.	Singapore	$51,600
7.	Brunei	$51,300
8.	United States	$47,500
9.	Ireland	$45,500
10.	United Arab Emirates	$44,600

LOWEST GDP PER CAPITA

1.	Zimbabwe	$200
2.	Democratic Republic of the Congo	$300
3.	Burundi	$300
4.	Liberia	$500
5.	Somalia	$600
6.	Guinea-Bissau	$600
7.	Eritrea	$700
8.	Niger	$700
9.	Central African Republic	$700
10.	Malawi	$800

* Data from 2007–2008

MIDEAST OIL RESERVES

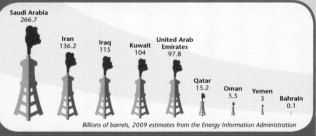

Billions of barrels, 2009 estimates from the Energy Information Administration

Saudi Arabia leads the region and the world in oil reserves and production, but four other countries in the Middle East also rank near the top.

AUTO GIANTS

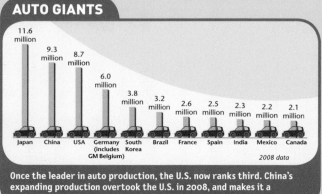

2008 data

Once the leader in auto production, the U.S. now ranks third. China's expanding production overtook the U.S. in 2008, and makes it a contender for the top place in the future.

FISHING AND AQUACULTURE

The world's yearly catch of ocean fish is more than four times what it was in 1950. The most heavily harvested areas are in the North Atlantic and western Pacific Oceans. Overfishing is becoming a serious problem. At least seven of the most-fished species are considered to be at their limit.

Aquaculture—raising fish and seaweed in controlled ponds—accounts for some 40 percent of the fish people eat. This practice began some 4,000 years ago in China, where it continues today. Fish are among the most widely traded food products, with 75 percent of the total catch sold on the international market each year.

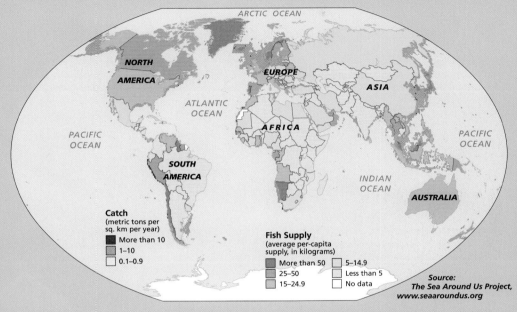

Catch
(metric tons per sq. km per year)
- More than 10
- 1–10
- 0.1–0.9

Fish Supply
(average per-capita supply, in kilograms)
- More than 50
- 25–50
- 15–24.9
- 5–14.9
- Less than 5
- No data

Source:
The Sea Around Us Project,
www.seaaroundus.org

STAPLE GRAINS

CORN

A staple in prehistoric Mexico and Peru, corn (or maize) is native to the New World and was plentiful in the Americas. But before Columbus arrived in 1492, no one in Europe had even tasted corn.

WHEAT

Among the oldest grains, wheat was important in ancient Mediterranean civilizations. Today, it is the most widely cultivated grain. Wheat grows best in temperate climates.

RICE

Originating in Asia many millennia ago, rice is the staple grain for about half the world's people. It is a labor-intensive plant that grows primarily in paddies (flooded fields) and thrives in the hot, humid tropics.

Currency Around

Canada—Canadian Dollar (CAD)
The slang term "buck" originated in Canada.

Iran—Iranian Rial (IRR)
A map of Iran appears on the 50,000 rial note.

Colombia—Colombian Peso (COP)
The official symbol of the peso is $.

Israel—Shekel (ILS)
The plural of shekel is shekalim.

Egypt—Egyptian Pound (EGP)
The Qaitbay Mosque appears on the one-pound note.

Japan—Japanese Yen (JPY)
The yen is based on ancient Chinese coins called yuar

European Union—Euro
The euro is the official currency of the European Union.

New Zealand—New Zealand Dollar (NZD)
The five-dollar note has a drawing of a penguin.

the World

Nigeria—Naira (NGN)
Naira use red, blue, green, purple, and mauve colors.

Russia—Russian Federation Rouble (RUB)
100 kopeck coins equal one ruble.

South Korea—South Korean Won (KRW)
The 10,000 won note is the highest in circulation.

United Kingdom—British Pound (GBP)
The pound is divided into 100 coins called new pence.

HIDDEN TREASURE

THE TREASURE: A BOX OF SILVER COINS

FOUND: IN AN ATTIC

NOW WORTH: $2,000

This was real buried treasure—but it was buried under insulation in an attic. While working on his home's wiring, Matt Rogers discovered a box tucked beneath the insulation. Inside was $2,000 worth of silver dollars and quarters, along with notes from a father to his family. Instead of keeping the cash, he returned the box to the original family. "If the roles had been reversed, I would have wanted my family heirlooms back," Rogers says. "It was the right thing to do."

In 2007, the
ROYAL CANADIAN MINT
made the world's largest coin, a 220-pound (100-kg)
GOLD COIN WORTH A MILLION DOLLARS.

MORE THAN 10,000,000 MILLIONAIRES ARE ALIVE TODAY.

WRITE A COUNTRY REPORT

You're a **student**, but you're also a citizen of the world. Writing a report on a foreign nation or your own country is a great way to better understand and appreciate how people in other parts of the world live. Pick the country of your ancestors, one that's been in the news, or one that you'd like to visit someday.

Passport to Success

A country report follows the format of an expository essay (see p. 300 for "How to Write a Perfect Essay") because you're "exposing" information about the country you choose.

Simple Steps

1. RESEARCH Gathering information is the most important step in writing a good country report. Look to Internet sources, encyclopedias, books, magazine and newspaper articles, and other sources to find important and interesting details about your subject.

2. ORGANIZE YOUR NOTES Put the information you gathered into a rough outline. For example, sort everything you found about the country's system of government, climate, etc.

3. WRITE IT UP Follow the basic structure of good writing: introduction, body, and conclusion. Remember that each paragraph should have a topic sentence that is supported by facts and details. Incorporate the information from your notes, but make sure it's in your own words. And make your writing flow with good transitions and descriptive language.

4. JAZZ IT UP Include maps, diagrams, photos, and other visual aides.

5. PROOFREAD AND REVISE Correct any mistakes, and polish your language. Do your best!

6. CITE YOUR SOURCES Be sure to keep a record of your sources (see p. 253 for "Reveal Your Sources").

TIP: Choose a country that's in the news. For example, think about the ongoing war efforts around the world, such as in Iraq or Afghanistan. These places would make ideal topics for your next country report.

Key Information

You may be assigned to write a report on a specific aspect of a country, such as its political system, or your report may be more general. In writing a broad survey, be sure to touch on the following areas:

GEOGRAPHY—the country's location, size, capital, major cities, topography, and other physical details

NATURE—the country's various climates, ecosystems (rain forest, desert, etc.), and unique wildlife

HISTORY—major events, wars, and other moments that affected the country and its people

GOVERNMENT—the country's political system (democracy, dictatorship, etc.) and the role of the individual citizen in the country's governance

ECONOMY / INDUSTRY—the country's economic system (capitalism, socialism, etc.), major industries and exports, and the country's place in the world economy

PEOPLE AND CULTURE—the country's major religions, spoken languages, unique foods, holidays, rituals, and traditions

GO BEYOND THE BASICS.

✔ Explain the history of the country's flag and the meaning of its colors and symbols. crwflags. com/fotw/flags

✔ Play the country's national anthem. Download the anthem, words, and sheet music. nationalanthems.info

✔ Figure out how much your country's currency and a U.S. dollar are worth. xe.com/ucc

✔ Check the local weather. Go to the website below and click on "World" at the top of the page, then search for the country or city. weather.com

✔ Figure out the time difference between the country you're studying and where you live. worldtimeserver.com

COOL CLICKS

✔ Still want more information? Go to National Geographic's One-Stop Research site for maps, photos, art, games, and other information to make your report stand out. nationalgeographic. com/onestop

Write With Power

Using good transitions makes any kind of writing read more smoothly. It gives organization and helps the reader to understand and improve connections between thoughts. Here are a few examples of good transitions you might want to use:

Addition
also, again, as well as, besides, coupled with, furthermore, in addition, likewise, moreover, similarly

Generalizing
as a rule, as usual, for the most part, generally, generally speaking, ordinarily, usually

Emphasis
above all, chiefly, with attention to, especially, particularly, singularly

Similarity
comparatively, coupled with, correspondingly, identically, likewise, similar, moreover, together with

Restatement
in essence, in other words, namely, that is, that is to say, in short, in brief, to put it differently

Contrast and Comparison
by the same token, conversely, instead, likewise, on one hand, on the other hand, on the contrary, rather, similarly, yet, but, however, still, nevertheless, in contrast

Awesome Adventure

Two ice climbers scale Columbia Icefield in Alberta, Canada. Located in the Canadian Rockies, the icefield is one of the largest accumulations of ice and snow below the Arctic Circle.

DARE TO E⟩

Do you have what it takes to be a great explorer? Read the stories of thr

SUE, THE *T. REX*, AND HER DISCOVERER, PALEONTOLOGIST SUE HENDRICKSON WITH HER DOG

THE PALEONTOLOGIST

Sue Hendrickson, on discovering the most complete skeleton of a *Tyrannosaurus rex* (named Sue, after the explorer) ever recorded:

"My team had spent two weeks in South Dakota searching a large area, but there was one area I still wanted to check out. On our last day, everyone went into town, but I explored the area we'd missed. My dog and I wandered through the dense fog for miles. Then, about eight feet (2 m) up a cliff, I saw six *T. rex* bones sticking out. It was like hitting the lottery 50 million times! Sue had been there all along, calling, wanting me to find her."

Want to be a paleontologist?

STUDY: Natural sciences such as biology and art to train the eye

WATCH: *Jurassic Park*

READ: *Bones Rock! Everything You Need to Know to Be a Paleontologist*, by Peter Larson and Kristin Donman

DO: Modelmaking to practice applying glue, handling small brushes, etc.

ADVICE: "Never give up, and be afraid of nothing."

THE MOUNTAIN CLIMBER

Samantha Larson, the youngest person to climb the highest mountains on each continent, on reaching the top of Mount Everest, the world's highest peak:

"During the last stretch before Everest's summit, I began to doubt I would make it. It seemed to take forever. When I finally reached the top, I was exhausted. I used any extra energy I had to hold back tears of awe and disbelief. I was standing on top of the world! A guide asked me if it was worth the view, but it was such a blur that I didn't know the answer. Whenever I think of my time up there, I realize that it definitely was."

Want to climb mountains?

STUDY: Geography, geology, biology

WATCH: *Kilimanjaro: To the Roof of Africa*

READ: *Within Reach: My Everest Story*, by Mark Pfetzer and Jack Galvin

DO: Anything outdoorsy: hiking, camping, skiing

ADVICE: "Push your limits to discover what you're able to do."

XPLORE

mous adventurers, and see how you can get started on the same path.

ROBERT BALLARD

THE *TITANIC* UNDER
THE ATLANTIC OCEAN

THE OCEANOGRAPHER

Robert Ballard, on discovering the lost wreckage of the R.M.S. *Titanic*, the cruise ship that hit an iceberg and sank in 1912:

"My team had been watching the ocean floor with an underwater camera for days—and all we'd seen was mud. Late one evening, our camera suddenly passed over a ship's boiler. There was a picture of the *Titanic*'s boiler hanging on our cabin wall. We all looked up at the picture. Then we looked back at the screen—and at that moment, we knew. It was as if Neptune, the Roman god of the sea, knew we'd been searching for almost two months and finally pulled back the curtain to show us it was right under our noses all along. The *Titanic* wasn't gone. It was out there. And we'd found it." (To learn more about Robert Ballard, see p. 325.)

LARSON SCALES A PORTABLE LADDER ON HER WAY UP TO EVEREST'S SUMMIT.

Want to be an oceanographer?

STUDY: Physical sciences such as geology

WATCH: *20,000 Leagues Under the Sea*

READ: *Exploring the Titanic*, by Robert D. Ballard

DO: Any kind of team sport because oceanography is a team effort

ADVICE: "You may fail, and you may get knocked down, but you have to get back up."

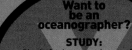

SAMANTHA LARSON

285

CHINA CONNECTION

DUDE: Marco Polo

EXPEDITION: One of the first Europeans to explore China

WHEN: Starting in 1271

Marco Polo's father and uncle ask him to travel with them from Italy to China—on horseback! The adventurous 17-year-old says yes! On his journey, Marco claims to hear "spirit voices" in the desert. But it's worth it when he reaches the huge, glittering palace of Kublai Khan, China's ruler. There he marvels at paper money, tattoos, and rhinoceroses. Marco turns his travels into a book, which later inspires another Italian with adventurous ambitions: Christopher Columbus.

WHAT'S IN IT FOR YOU: The discovery of America

These stories make *Lost* look like episodes of the *Teletubbies*. Braving everything from raging seas to blazing deserts, these five awesome adventurers explored Earth's uncharted, unforgiving unknown. If you think *that's* extreme, along the way one of them wrestled a lion. Another chowed down on rats. And a third wore an American flag— as underwear. Explore on—if you dare!

WELCOME TO THE SUNSHINE STATE

DUDE: Ponce de León

EXPEDITION: Discovered Florida, now a U.S. state

WHEN: 1513

Wealth. Fame. The chance to be young again. That, according to legend, is what awaits the first person who dips his toes into the Fountain of Youth. But the problem is no one knows where the fabled fountain is located. Spanish explorer Ponce de León sails the Caribbean to Grand Turk Island. No fountain there. San Salvador Island, too, is fountain-free. Although Ponce never finds the fountain, he scores wealth and fame by being the first European to set foot in a land he calls Pascua Florida (Flowery Easter), or Florida to you and me.

WHAT'S IN IT FOR YOU: The discovery of the future home of Disney World

AFRICA

COOL DUDES WHO CHANGED THE WORLD

INTO AFRICA

DUDE: David Livingstone

EXPEDITION: First European to explore Central Africa extensively

WHEN: 1841 to 1873

For Scottish doctor-missionary David Livingstone, trudging through the deserts, rain forests, and mountains of unexplored Africa (and taking lots of notes) is a dream come true. He wrestles a lion and nearly loses an arm. He sees one of the world's largest waterfalls and names it Victoria, for England's queen. He searches for the source of the Nile River and drops from sight. Five years later newspaper reporter Henry Stanley tracks down Livingstone outside a grass hut and utters the famous line, "Dr. Livingstone, I presume?"

WHAT'S IN IT FOR YOU: The knowledge that you really *should* keep distance between yourself and a lion

IT'S LONELY AT THE TOP. COLD, TOO.

DUDE: Robert Peary

EXPEDITION: Led the expedition that was first to reach the geographic North Pole

WHEN: 1909

Robert Peary, his trusted partner Matthew Henson—a talented African-American explorer— and four other men are heading north. *Way* north. They scale 50-foot (15-m) cliffs of ice and endure subzero temperatures and dark fog. When they finally reach the North Pole, Peary unfurls an American flag sewn by his wife—which he's worn as a warm undergarment—and rightfully feels he's on top of the world.

WHAT'S IN IT FOR YOU: The knowledge that when exploring new territory, you should always pack a flag—it could come in handy!

AROUND THE WORLD IN ... THREE YEARS

DUDE: Ferdinand Magellan

EXPEDITION: Led the first expedition to sail around the world

WHEN: Starting in 1519

Back then people thought the world was round, but no one had actually *proven* it by sailing all the way around the world—until Magellan. Terrible storms nearly sink his ships. Food runs so low that they eat rats. Three years later just one of five ships returns home. But it carries the first men to sail around the world.

WHAT'S IN IT FOR YOU: The knowledge that you won't ever fall off the edge of Earth

+ NORTH POLE

GOING TO
EXTREMES

Researchers hunt for life that seems out of this world.

D iving into a maze of underwater caves is all in a day's work for extremophile-hunting scientists and researchers. Extremophiles are microscopic life-forms that live in extreme environments that are too dry, too hot, too cold, too dark, or too toxic for the likes of us.

Microbiologist Hazel Barton eyes a small fish as she explores an underwater cave.

Scientists know that human beings are nature's wimps. We need a cushy environment to survive—lots of water, abundant sunshine, oxygen, and moderate temperatures. Most places on Earth—and in the rest of the solar system—just aren't like that.

SEARCHING THE DEEP

Finding extremophiles can be dangerous because of the remote places in which they live and grow. But some daring scientists are willing to take the risks because the rewards could be great.

The next important antibiotic could come from one of these organisms. Some have already helped scientists make new tests to identify people who are more likely to get certain diseases.

Heat-loving extremophiles were probably among the earliest forms of life on Earth. Scientists are even working with samples from caves to support the idea that microbes once lived under the surface of planets like Mars.

With so much to gain, scientists will keep chipping rock from cliffs, scraping scum from hot springs, and sampling the walls of deep ice caves to find extremophiles. Scientists are really going to extremes in the search for life.

288

Bet you
didn't
know

There is
CELL
PHONE
RECEPTION
at the
SUMMIT
of Mount
Everest.

Rising to an elevation of almost 11,000 feet (3,353 m), Fitzroy Massif in southern Argentina's Patagonia region presents major challenges to adventurous climbers who must contend with strong winds and bitter cold.

DINOSAUR FOOTPRINTS

TRACKS TELL PREHISTORIC SECRETS

Footprints impressed on the Earth millions of years ago are changing the field of dinosaur paleontology.

"There is much to be learned from a corpse, even one that has been dead for millions of years," says Rich McCrea, a curator at the Peace Region Paleontology Research Centre in British Columbia, Canada. He is a member of a small but growing field of scientists who have dedicated themselves to the study of fossilized dinosaur tracks. "Tracks, even those millions of years old, represent the activity of animals that were living," he said.

LEARNING FROM TRACKS

Tracks are one of the closest ways a human can get to understanding dinosaurs as breathing, functioning animals. They show where and how dinosaurs walked, their posture, and gait. They show which dinosaurs roamed solo and which traveled in groups.

Coal mining sites have revealed thousands of footprints of dinosaurs. For example, McCrea spends much of his time studying tracks near the mining town of Grande Cache, Alberta, Canada. "There are only a couple of sites where there is a real diversity of tracks," says McCrea. In the few places with multiple tracks, he found traces of small, medium, and large meat-eating, two-footed theropod dinosaurs, and also those of birds.

TRACK HUNTING

When scientists hunt for dinosaur tracks, they look for areas where ancient layers of sedimentary rock are exposed, such as cliffs, sea coasts, quarries, open-pit mines, and along the banks of rivers and streams.

Usually, tracks are not found in the same location as bones. This is mostly because the conditions that are ideal for preserving tracks are not very good for the fossilization of bone.

"It doesn't mean the bones weren't there, but after 70 million years the bones would dissolve whereas the tracks wouldn't," says Anthony Martin, an ichnologist (one who studies tracks). "We can look forward to the discovery of tracks of more groups of extinct animals."

Paleontologist Paul Sereno

MEET THE NAT GEO EXPLORERS

DERECK AND BEVERLY JOUBERT

Award-winning filmmakers from Botswana, the Jouberts have been filming, researching, and exploring Africa for more than 25 years.

How did you become explorers?
We were both born to be explorers! You know how sometimes when you just know—we knew. School was just like going to the gym—a way to get mentally and physically fit to go exploring.

What was your closest call in the field?
We have been hit by elephants; bitten by snakes, scorpions, and mosquitoes; knocked down by buffalo; crashed two planes; and generally had a hard life—every day is potentially a close call.

What is one place or thing you'd still like to explore?
Exploration is as much of the mind as it is of a place. There are still things to be done, things to be discovered, and greater understanding to bring to humankind.

TREASURES OF THE TOMB

Discovering King Tut's INCREDIBLE RICHES

It's pitch-black. His hands trembling, British archaeologist Howard Carter makes a small hole in the tomb's second door. He inserts a candle. Next to him, British millionaire Lord Carnarvon blurts out, "Can you see anything?" After a moment of stunned silence, Carter replies, "Yes, wonderful things."

What Carter sees looks like the inside of a giant treasure chest. Gold gleams everywhere! There are glittering statues, a throne, and fabulous golden beds with posts shaped like the heads of wild animals. Precious items are heaped all over the room.

It's 1922. It has taken years of digging in the Valley of the Kings—a graveyard for ancient Egypt's richest kings—and $500,000 (in today's money) of Lord Carnarvon's cash, but Carter hit the jackpot. He discovered the tomb of Tutankhamun (Tut, for short), who became pharaoh at age nine and died ten years later around 1323 B.C.

HIDDEN TREASURES
Carter, Lord Carnarvon, and two others enter the cluttered first room, which they call the antechamber. Under a bed with posts in the shape of hippopotamus heads, Lord Carnarvon finds the entrance to another room. Soon known as the annex, this tiny chamber holds more than 2,000 everyday objects. They include boomerangs, shields, a box containing eye makeup, and 116 baskets of food. When Carter clears the annex out later, his workers need to be suspended by ropes to keep from stepping on things.

Curse of the Pharaohs

Many people believe in the curse of the pharaohs. They think that the souls of the ancient Egyptian dead will haunt those who uncover their bodies and disturb their rest. These ancient ghosts often get blamed when things go wrong, including accidents, illnesses, and even deaths.

Does Egyptologist and National Geographic Explorer-in-Residence Zahi Hawass believe in the curse? Nope. "Even if it does exist, I do not fear it, although many strange things have happened to me during my years excavating, or digging, at sites around Egypt," says Hawass.

Buckle showing King Tut and his queen

Collar on Tut's mummy

Ceremonial instruments of royal authority

Fan

Mummy's gold sandals

Hippo's head bedpost

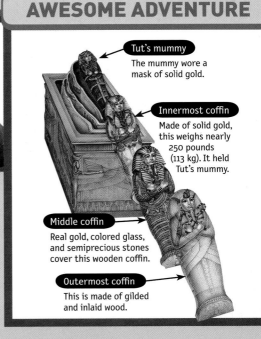

Tut's mummy
The mummy wore a mask of solid gold.

Innermost coffin
Made of solid gold, this weighs nearly 250 pounds (113 kg). It held Tut's mummy.

Middle coffin
Real gold, colored glass, and semiprecious stones cover this wooden coffin.

Outermost coffin
This is made of gilded and inlaid wood.

The disorder in the annex indicates ancient grave robbers had looted the tomb. They left behind footprints and gold rings wrapped in cloth. Luckily, they'd been caught and the tomb resealed. That was more than 3,000 years ago.

ANCIENT GUARD

The explorers are fascinated by two tall statues in the antechamber showing Tut dressed in gold. The figures seem to be guarding another room. Sweltering in the heat, the group crawls through a hole created by the ancient robbers.

Before them stands a huge wooden box, or shrine, that glitters with a layer of gold. This room must be Tut's burial chamber! At the very center of the shrine is a carved sarcophagus, or coffin. Inside it are three nested coffins, each one more richly decorated than the one before. Inside the last, made of solid gold, lies the mummy of Tutankhamun. A 22-pound (10-kg) gold mask (far left) covers its head and shoulders. A collar made from 171 separate gold pieces rests on the mummy's chest, and gold sandals are on its feet.

On one side of the burial chamber is an open doorway revealing the fourth room of the tomb— the treasury. Towering over the other objects is a gold-covered shrine guarded by goddesses. It holds Tut's liver, lungs, stomach, and intestines. Each vital organ is preserved, wrapped in linen, and placed in its very own small coffin.

Today, millions of people visit Cairo's Egyptian Museum each year to see Tut's treasures. The ancient Egyptians believed that "to speak the name of the dead is to make them live again." If that is true, Tutankhamun certainly lives on.

MUMMIES EVERYWHERE!

A city of the dead sat undisturbed for centuries. Then, in 1996 a donkey passing through the Egyptian oasis town of Bahariya stumbled into a hole. As the donkey's owner worked to free its hoof, he saw a flash of gold in the sand. The donkey had punched a hole in the roof of a long-buried tomb. Archaeologists found mummies—more than have ever been found in one place before. The mummies of Bahariya were entombed during Egypt's Greco-Roman period, which lasted from 332 B.C. until the fourth century A.D.

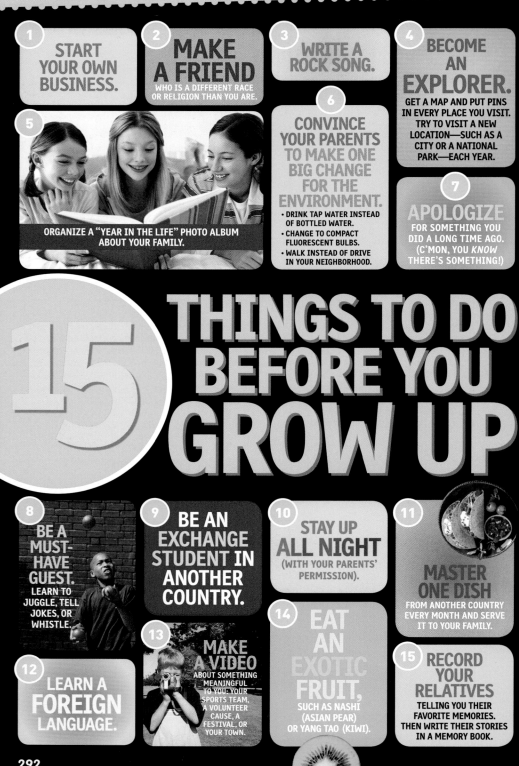

1 START YOUR OWN BUSINESS.

2 MAKE A FRIEND WHO IS A DIFFERENT RACE OR RELIGION THAN YOU ARE.

3 WRITE A ROCK SONG.

4 BECOME AN EXPLORER. GET A MAP AND PUT PINS IN EVERY PLACE YOU VISIT. TRY TO VISIT A NEW LOCATION—SUCH AS A CITY OR A NATIONAL PARK—EACH YEAR.

5 ORGANIZE A "YEAR IN THE LIFE" PHOTO ALBUM ABOUT YOUR FAMILY.

6 CONVINCE YOUR PARENTS TO MAKE ONE BIG CHANGE FOR THE ENVIRONMENT.
- DRINK TAP WATER INSTEAD OF BOTTLED WATER.
- CHANGE TO COMPACT FLUORESCENT BULBS.
- WALK INSTEAD OF DRIVE IN YOUR NEIGHBORHOOD.

7 APOLOGIZE FOR SOMETHING YOU DID A LONG TIME AGO. (C'MON, YOU KNOW THERE'S SOMETHING!)

15 THINGS TO DO BEFORE YOU GROW UP

8 BE A MUST-HAVE GUEST. LEARN TO JUGGLE, TELL JOKES, OR WHISTLE.

9 BE AN EXCHANGE STUDENT IN ANOTHER COUNTRY.

10 STAY UP ALL NIGHT (WITH YOUR PARENTS' PERMISSION).

11 MASTER ONE DISH FROM ANOTHER COUNTRY EVERY MONTH AND SERVE IT TO YOUR FAMILY.

12 LEARN A FOREIGN LANGUAGE.

13 MAKE A VIDEO ABOUT SOMETHING MEANINGFUL TO YOU: YOUR SPORTS TEAM, A VOLUNTEER CAUSE, A FESTIVAL, OR YOUR TOWN.

14 EAT AN EXOTIC FRUIT, SUCH AS NASHI (ASIAN PEAR) OR YANG TAO (KIWI).

15 RECORD YOUR RELATIVES TELLING YOU THEIR FAVORITE MEMORIES. THEN WRITE THEIR STORIES IN A MEMORY BOOK.

CLIFF Hanger

A FIRST-PERSON ACCOUNT OF A TOWERING CONQUEST

Yosemite Valley, California, U.S.A.

It's 1 a.m. I'm 2,500 feet (762 m) above the ground, sleeping on a portable cot I've attached to the near-vertical face of the rocky valley wall, when—*BOOM*—my cot suddenly collapses, plunging me through darkness.

Suddenly my waist belt—tied to a bolt in the rock where my cot used to be—snatches me under the armpits and stops my fall. Dangling in midair, I realize how lucky I am that I didn't fall headfirst and slam into the rock. With frustration, I grunt it back up my rope to my gear and close my eyes.

That was at Yosemite National Park, in California. I was climbing 3,000 feet (914 m) up a valley wall known as El Capitan for the fourth time. But even a fall from one of America's tallest and sheerest rock faces didn't stop me—I kept going, hand over hand, toe over toe, until I reached the top. You just can't admit failure in rock climbing.

To climb El Cap alone is kind of like climbing it twice. See, as I climb up the rock face, I pound tools into cracks in the rock to support my hands and feet. When I run out, I tie my rope to one of them. Then I rappel down to pull out my tools.

After I retrieve my 110 pounds (50 kg) of gear, I use my ascenders to slide back up the rope. Up, down, up, about every 160 feet (49 m). The first time I made it to the top by myself was when I was 15. That made me one of the youngest solo climbers to scale El Capitan's slick granite face.

Climbing El Cap is like putting together a big puzzle: figuring out which way to go, which crack to cram your toe in. I do everything while dangling from the rock— eat food, try to nap, even use a plastic "poop" tube. When I finally scramble to El Cap's summit, I always have this big smile on my face. Sure, El Capitan is tough, but I love it. Every time I get on, it teaches me who's boss.

Adventurer Scott Thelan hangs from ropes as he scales the mountain.

To the Top

Want to climb a mountain? First get in shape with these tips:

Keep your heart strong by biking, swimming, or running.

Build up your endurance: Always take the stairs.

Strong arms are essential. Strengthen them by carrying groceries in from the car.

Mental conditioning counts, so pay attention to the weather, wind, and geography around you.

KidsDidIt!

Inches from the HUGE OPEN JAWS of a great white shark,

Members of a NATIONAL GEOGRAPHIC KIDS expedition team

Wiley Dotzenroth's eyes bug out of their sockets. *"Woo-hoo!* Awesome!" he yells as he surfaces. He's standing safely in a protective steel shark cage lowered over the side of the boat.

Wiley, of Wayzata, Minnesota, was one of 15 explorers on a NATIONAL GEOGRAPHIC KIDS Expedition team who traveled to the country of South Africa. The 10- to 14-year-olds were winners of the annual NG KIDS photo and essay competition—the Hands-On Explorer Challenge (HOEC).

In just the first few hours of the expedition, the team saw great white sharks, Cape fur seals, and southern right whales. They also were granted special permission to go ashore on Dyer Island, a protected nesting ground for African penguins where injured birds are cared for and released back to the wild when they are well.

The NG KIDS team traveled to Bush Lodge at Sabi Sabi Private Game Reserve, where mischievous vervet monkeys greeted them. Every morning and evening the team explored the reserve. They spotted many wild animals, including South Africa's "big five": elephants, rhinos, African buffalo, lions, and leopards.

Before the expedition began team members raised more than $10,000. They used that money to buy a computer and Internet access for the Sam Nzima Primary School, in the village of Lilydale. Most exciting for the team: The knowledge that they can email new friends made during their visit to the school.

Caged team members got this view of a great white shark.

AFRICA

SOUTH AFRICA

Burchell's zebras live in small herds.

For more about the NG KIDS Hands-On Explorer Challenge, go online. kids.nationalgeographic.com

COOL CLICK

WILL MY TOY CAR SURVIVE A
CROC ATTACK?

My name is Brady Barr, and part of my job as a scientist is catching crocodiles. Crocs are big, fast, good at hiding, and always alert. They're not easy to catch, but I need to get hold of them to attach tracking tags and to gather data.

I talked with some creative kids who gave me a few great ideas to help me catch crocs. So on my next trip to Africa, I set off with my scientific equipment and toys (the kids' suggestion).

I'm helping wildlife biologists put tracking tags on a threatened population of Nile crocodiles. From our boat we spot a cluster of crocs. I set a remote-control car on the beach and steer it toward the basking crocs. I speed the car right up to one—chomp! The croc's teeth just miss the car, and it's not giving up! It chases the car and I work the joystick as if my life depends on it.

My little car is no match for a Nile crocodile—the croc's jaws close over my toy—and, temporarily, over my plans. The size and quick movements of the toy car must trigger a crocodile's predatory instinct. Conclusion: Use a faster car and improve my driving skills!

The kids' second idea: to disguise myself as a croc. I get into the water wearing a big rubber croc mask. My goal: Get close enough to wrestle a croc into our boat. When one giant male approaches, I raise the snout of my mask, which in "croc talk" lets him know I'm not looking for trouble. But he's angry—he arches his back and slaps the water with his chin. He thinks I'm a rival! At first I stand my ground, but as he comes closer, it gets too dangerous. I get out of the water . . . fast! Conclusion: The disguise works.

Idea number three—I steer a remote-control boat, fitted with a small rubber croc head and a snare, toward the real crocs. Success! They act as if the boat's one of them and ignore it. Then, just as the boat's in position to snare one, the batteries die! Conclusion: The boat works, but next time I've got to remember more batteries!

A field test involves a lot of trial and error. What I learned this time will mean success the next time. Meanwhile, I reached my goal to be the first person to catch all 23 species of crocodilians!

18 EXTREME FEARS

PHOBIA	A FEAR OF
Aeronausiphobia	Airsickness
Euphobia	Hearing good news
Oneirophobia	Dreams
Panophobia	Everything
Osmophobia	Body odors
Amaxophobia	Riding in a car
Consecotaleophobia	Chopsticks
Chorophobia	Dancing
Philemaphobia	Kissing
Ombrophobia	Rain
Optophobia	Opening one's eyes
Potamophobia	Running water
Zoophobia	Animals
Dentophobia	Dentists
Geliophobia	Laughter
Carnophobia	Meat
Scoleciphobia	Worms
Scriptophobia	Writing in public

HOW TO SURVIVE ...

ADRIFT AT SEA

1 GO UNDERCOVER
Slap on some sunscreen, a baseball cap, your best sunglasses, and a jacket. That will help you avoid sunburn, sunstroke, and dehydration—which could *so* ruin your day.

2 MADE IN THE SHADES
No sunglasses? No problem! Cut two narrow eye slits in your socks, and tie them around your head with string. Now you've got a smelly pair of shades!

3 OFF THE HOOK
Getting hungry? Fashion a fishing line from a rope, string, or scrap of cloth. Make a hook with the pop-top from a soda can. Soon you'll have sushi!

4 HERE'S FISH IN YOUR EYE
The ocean may look like one huge salt-flavored Big Gulp. But too much seawater can cause vomiting and hallucinations. Instead, catch rainwater. Or you can suck liquid out of a fish eye. Slurp!

5 CATCH SOME RAYS
Use a mirror to reflect sunlight and signal your search team. Then fix your hair. You'll want to be ready for your close-up when you're rescued!

QUICKSAND

BEWARE! QUICKSAND

1 NO MORE "SOUP-ERSTITIONS"
Quicksand isn't some bottomless pit waiting to suck you in. It's a soupy mixture of sand and water found near riverbanks, shorelines, and marshes. It's rarely more than a few feet (meters) deep, though it can be deeper.

2 GO WITH THE FLOAT
Not that you'd want to, but quicksand is actually easier to float on than water. So lean back, place your arms straight out from your sides, and let the sopping sand support your weight.

3 YOU FLAIL, YOU FAIL
Don't kick or struggle. That creates a vacuum, which only pulls you down. Ignore the gritty goop squishing into your underpants and remain calm.

4 LEG LIFTS
Conquer the quicksand with a slow stand. As you're lying back with your arms out, carefully inch one leg, then the other, to the surface.

5 ROLL OVER!
When both legs are afloat, pretend you're performing a dog trick. Keeping your face out of the muck, gently roll over the quicksand until you're on solid ground.

A Near FATAL Attraction

Using Snake Venom To Save Lives

Snake venom is dangerous, complex, medically promising— and the ultimate adrenaline rush. What's not to love?

"It was the last night of a very long week," says herpetologist and molecular biologist Bryan Grieg Fry, describing the bite he suffered from one of the deadliest snakes on Earth. "Of course it's always the last night. They never get you when you're fresh, and it was a new species, one that we hadn't caught before."

THE SNAKE WHISPERER

Fry is the director of the Australian Venom Research Unit at the University of Melbourne. In groundbreaking research on the toxins that squirt out of snake fangs, he has painted a startling new picture of the complexity of venom, and he has derived potential new drugs by studying its scary effects on human physiology, occasionally by experiencing those effects firsthand.

LOVE AT FIRST BITE

In the case of this deadly bite, he and his wife, Alexia, had flown to Weipa, Australia, to collect venom samples from a variety of sea snake (left) species, including Hardwick's sea snakes, elegant sea snakes, and rare Stokes sea snakes. Because the whole operation involved a lot of exposure to awfully dangerous animals—sea snakes are among the world's most poisonous reptiles, and their venom can cause horrible pain and a quick and ugly death—Fry had taken his standard precautions. He had contacted the head of the local emergency ward, explained what he'd be up to, and packed big syringes full of adrenaline and strong antihistamines. Then he got on with having a good time.

AMAZING SNAKES

Sea snakes have astonishing aquatic adaptations, such as valved nostrils to seal in air and lungs that can hold a breath for hours, but they do have to surface to breathe once in a while. When they do, a spotlight will catch a ripple of coils in its glare and Alexia and Fry will snatch them up.

Snake venoms are remarkable, Fry points out, for the sheer number of horrible effects that they can cause simultaneously. The venom of the seven-foot (2-m) -long Australian inland taipan (above, left and right), for example, carries more than 50 toxins, including some that abruptly lower blood pressure or destroy nerves.

It is precisely this complexity, however, that has led to Fry's most interesting discoveries. For decades it was assumed that snake venom had evolved separately in a range of snake species, based on the fact that many venomous snakes had close nonvenomous relatives. But modern research has allowed Fry to show that snake venom had a single point of biological origin, in the earliest of snakes, and that even the apparently nonvenomous snakes have active venom glands—they just lack a means for delivering it. Fry's research has raised the number of known venomous snakes from around 200 to 2,000-plus.

TIPS FROM A PRO
How to Take Great Photos

As far as the eye can see there are photographs waiting to be captured or to be created. Life swirls around us without stopping, but as a photographer, you can put a frame around moments in time. A lot more goes into taking a good photograph than just pushing a button, though.

Learn how to use a camera, but most of all, learn how to think like a photographer. Here are some valuable tips from expert photographer Neil Johnson to help you get started on your way.

LIGHT

- When lighting a subject, it is important to consider not only the direction of the light (front, side, back), but also the color of the background.
- Light does not always have to fall on the front of your subject.
- On-camera flash is most useful for subjects that are 10 to 15 feet (3 to 4 m) away.

COMPOSITION

- Making your subject the focus of attention does not mean that you have to put it in the middle of the frame. Placing the subject slightly off center can help lead the viewer into the picture.

SUBJECTS

- When taking pictures of animals, getting down to their eye level and moving in close will improve your photographs.
- When taking pictures of people, try to get them to forget about the camera and just go about doing what they enjoy.

QUICK TIPS!

- **Don't rush your pictures.**
- **Take your time and experiment.**
- ***Snap. Snap. Snap.* Take as many pictures as you can.**
- **Study them. Ask yourself why some work and others don't.**
- **Learn from your mistakes, but most important, keep shooting.**

PHOTO TERMS

Composition: the arrangement of everything in your picture—the subject, foreground, background, and surrounding elements

Exposure: the amount of light coming into the camera and the length of time it strikes the film or digital medium

Lens: one or more pieces of glass or plastic designed to collect and focus light on a piece of film or digital medium

Shutter: the device in a camera that opens to allow light to strike the film or digital medium

Tripod: a three-legged stand for supporting a camera

CAUGHT ON CAMERA

WHAT IS IT?
a gray whale, up close and personal

PLACE
off the coast of Mexico

I'm Annie Griffiths Belt, and as a National Geographic photographer, I am lucky enough to go to some pretty wild places. A big part of the fun is how I get there. I have ridden elephants and camels, and traveled in helicopters, fishing boats, and hot-air balloons.

One of the most exciting adventures I ever had was in Mexico, when I went to photograph gray whales. I was floating in a rubber raft and watching for whales. Suddenly, I felt a bump. The rubber raft actually began lifting out of the water!

A friendly whale had decided to play with us. She gently lifted our raft up out of the water, and slowly lowered us down again. She circled around us with her baby calf, so close that we could touch her nose and stroke her calf.

For more, read Annie's book, *A Camera, Two Kids and a Camel: My Journey in Photographs.*

Raging Danger!

On New Britain Island, part of Papua New Guinea, a white-water river vanishes into a limestone cave. Following the torrent underground, a team discovers breathtaking waterfalls and theater-size chambers. The island is home to a massive sinkhole, also called a doline. The team of 12 cavers from Britain, France, and the United States traveled to New Britain Island to descend into Ora, one of the island's largest sinkholes, and probe the cave at the bottom.

"In Ora you remain wet almost all the time," says explorer Herb Laeger. Following the riverbank underground, the team was forced to cross several times when the bank vanished. Complicated and dangerous, the crossings required one team member to swim the river and fix a line for the others.

During their two-month expedition, the team explored some 8 miles (13 km) of river caves, discovering waterfalls, lakes, and spectacular mineral formations. Exploring the damp, dark world by headlamp, expedition leader David Gill says that most of the time "you're watching where you're putting your feet."

Near the end of the expedition, the team spotted a previously unknown doline from the air, a river visible deep within it. "You cannot really get much better than this," says expedition leader David Gill. "It's an incredibly exotic, beautiful, untouched area."

HOW TO WRITE A PERFECT ESSAY

Need to write an essay? Does the assignment feel as big as climbing Mount Everest? Fear not, brave adventurer. You're up to the challenge! The following step-by-step tips will help you with this monumental task.

1 **BRAINSTORM.** Sometimes the subject matter of your essay is assigned to you, sometimes it's not. Either way, you have to decide what you want to say. Start by brainstorming some ideas, writing down any thoughts you have about the subject. Then read over everything you've come up with and consider which idea you think is the strongest. Ask yourself what you want to write about the most. Keep in mind the goal of your essay. (The four main types of essays are described on the next page.) Can you achieve the goal of the assignment with this topic? If so, you're good to go.

2 **WRITE A TOPIC SENTENCE.** This is the main idea of your essay, a statement of your thoughts on the subject. Again, consider the goal of your essay. Think of the topic sentence as an introduction that tells your reader what the rest of your essay will be about.

3 **OUTLINE YOUR IDEAS.** Once you have a good topic sentence, then you need to support that main idea with more detailed information, facts, thoughts, and examples. These supporting points answer one question about your topic sentence—"Why?" This is where research and perhaps more brainstorming come in. Then organize these points in the way you think makes the most sense, probably in order of importance. Now you have an outline for your essay.

4 **ON YOUR MARK, GET SET, WRITE!** Follow your outline, using each of your supporting points as the topic sentence of its own paragraph. Use descriptive words to get your ideas across to the reader. Go into detail, using specific information to tell your story or make your point. Stay on track, making sure that everything you include is somehow related to the main idea of your essay. Use transitions (see p. 281) to make your writing flow.

5 **WRAP IT UP.** Finish your essay with a conclusion that summarizes your entire essay and restates your main idea.

6 **PROOFREAD AND REVISE.** Check for errors in spelling, capitalization, punctuation, and grammar. Look for ways to make your writing clear, understandable, and interesting. Use descriptive verbs, adjectives, or adverbs when possible. It also helps to have someone else read your work to point out things you might have missed. Then make the necessary corrections and changes in a second draft. Repeat this revision process once more to make your final draft as good as you can.

Types of Essays

NARRATIVE ESSAY

Purpose: A narrative essay tells a story about an event.

Example: "Caught on Camera" (p. 299)

Helpful Hints:
- Pick a topic that really interests you. Your excitement will come through in your writing.
- Tell your story with a clear beginning, middle, and end.
- Add fun or exciting details to highlight dramatic or unexpected moments.
- Use descriptive words to help give your reader a sense of what it was like to be there.

EXPOSITORY ESSAY

Purpose: An expository essay gives facts and information about a person, place, thing, or idea. Book reports, research papers, and biographies are types of expository writing.

Example: "Going to Extremes: Researchers Hunt for Life That Seems Out of This World" (p. 288)

Helpful Hints:
- Dig deep in your research to find interesting details.
- State your topic right away.
- Use transitional phrases to make your essay flow smoothly.

DESCRIPTIVE ESSAY

Purpose: A descriptive essay describes a person, place, or thing using sensory details to give the reader a better idea of what the subject is really like.

Example: "Discovering King Tut's Incredible Riches" (p. 290)

Helpful Hints:
- Describe how the subject looks, sounds, tastes, smells, and feels.
- Use interesting comparisons.
- Be specific; find just the right adjectives and adverbs.

PERSUASIVE ESSAY

Purpose: A persuasive essay tries to convince the reader of your point of view using facts, statistics, details, and logic to make an argument.

Example: "Does Bigfoot Exist?" (p. 250)

Helpful Hints:
- State your opinion in the topic sentence.
- Use evidence to support your point of view.
- Consider the opposing views.
- Present a strong conclusion.

DON'T BE A COPYCAT

Plagiarism is presenting an idea or piece of writing as your own original work when it was actually created by someone else. It's a serious offense and will get you into trouble. Obvious examples of plagiarism include buying an essay from the Internet and handing it in as your own, or copying from a friend. Plagiarism can also occur by not citing your sources, so be careful.

In writing, you must give credit whenever you use information taken from another source. This is called citing your sources. Follow these basic guidelines to avoid plagiarism:

- **Take good notes** when researching. Keep a list of all research material you use, including details (title, author, page numbers, websites, etc.) about where you got specific pieces of information.

- **Use your own words.** Copying sentence structure but changing a few words is still plagiarism. Don't use more than three words in a row taken directly from another source.

- **Plagiarism** is not restricted to textbooks—don't copy material from the Internet, either.

- **Place quotation marks** around any phrase or sentence you take directly from another source, and cite it.

- **Double-check** your final text with your notes. Be sure that you've given credit where credit is due.

Beware! Plagiarism can result in suspension or expulsion from school.

The caldera of Pu'u O'o overflows with lava
in Hawaii Volcanoes National Park, Hawaii, U.S.A.

Wonders of Nature

World Climate

Weather is the condition of the atmosphere—temperature, precipitation, humidity, wind—at a given place at a given time. Climate, however, is the average weather for a particular place over a long period of time. Different places on Earth have different climates, but climate is not a random occurrence. There is a pattern that is controlled by factors such as latitude, elevation, prevailing winds, the temperature of ocean currents, and location on land relative to water. Climate is generally constant, but many scientists believe that human activity is causing a change in the patterns of climate.

CLIMATE FACTS

Data collected by satellites suggests that the Sahara, Earth's largest hot desert, had a wet climate that supported vast forests some 12,000 years ago. Extremely dry conditions did not begin until about 5,000 years ago.

According to climatologists, Earth had what is called the Little Ice Age, which lasted from the 17th century to the late 18th century. During that time, temperatures were cold enough to cause glaciers to advance.

Ice cores taken from Antarctica and Greenland have enabled scientists to gain detailed information about the history of Earth's climate and its atmosphere—especially the presence of greenhouse gases—dating back thousands of years.

According to the National Oceanic and Atmospheric Administration (NOAA), the 2009 annual temperature tied with 2006 as the fifth warmest year on record for Earth. All of the top ten hottest years have occurred since 1998.

GLOBAL CLIMATE ZONES

ARCTIC OCEAN
ATLANTIC OCEAN
PACIFIC OCEAN
PACIFIC OCEAN
INDIAN OCEAN

Climate

Tropical   Dry   Temperate   Cold   Polar

Climatologists, people who study climate, have created different systems for classifying climates. An often-used system is called the Köppen system, which classifies climate zones according to precipitation, temperature, and vegetation. It has five major categories—Tropical, Dry, Temperate, Cold, and Polar—with a sixth category for locations where high elevations override other factors. Climate zones can shift over time, but the changes are likely accelerated by human activity.

Go online for more fun weather information.
kids.nationalgeographic.com/
Games/PuzzlesQuizzes/Weather-word-search

COOL CLICK

Bet you didn't know

WEATHER REPORT

There are some **16 MILLION THUNDERSTORMS** on Earth **EVERY YEAR.**

TORNADOES usually **SPIN** in the opposite directions **ABOVE** and **BELOW** the **EQUATOR.**

DIRTY snow **MELTS FASTER** than **CLEAN** snow.

A **CLOUD** can **WEIGH MORE** than a **BILLION POUNDS.**

A **RAINBOW** looks **DIFFERENT** to every **PERSON** who sees it.

Temperature Tips

There are two types of temperature scales in the world, **Fahrenheit** (used in the U.S.) and **Celsius** (used in most countries of the world). Although they both measure temperature, the numbers are different. For example, **water freezes at 32°F or 0°C.**

To convert from Fahrenheit to Celsius, subtract 32, then multiply by 5, and divide by 9.

To convert from Celsius to Fahrenheit, multiply by 9, divide by 5, and then add 32.

Example: If water boils at 100°C, and we want to know what temperature that is in Fahrenheit, we'd use the second formula: 100°C x 9 = 900 900 ÷ 5 = 180 180 + 32 = 212°F

CLIMATE CHANGE

Earth's climate history has been a story of ups and downs, with warm periods followed by periods of bitter cold. The early part of the 20th century was marked by colder than average temperatures (see graph below), followed by a period of gradual and then steady increase. Scientists are concerned that the current warming trend is more than a natural cycle. Evidence indicates that human activity is adding to the warming. One sign of change is melting glaciers in Greenland and Antarctica. If glaciers continue to melt, areas of Florida (shown above in red) and other coastal land will be underwater.

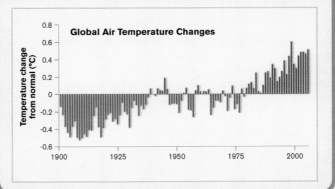

305

Lightning!

A bolt of lightning is about 54,000°F (30,000°C); more than five times hotter than the Sun.

Clouds suddenly appeared on the horizon, the sky turned dark, and it started to rain as Sabrina was hiking through the Grand Canyon with her parents.

As lightning flashed around them, Sabrina and her parents ran for cover. "When it stopped raining, we thought it was safe," says Sabrina. They started to hike back to their car along the trail. Then *zap!* A lightning bolt struck nearby. It happened so fast that the family didn't know what it hit. A jolt of electricity shot through their bodies. "It felt like a strong tingling over my whole body," says Sabrina. "It really hurt."

Sabrina and her family were lucky. The lightning didn't zap them directly, and they recovered within minutes. Some people aren't so lucky. Lightning kills about 100 people in the United States each year. It injures hundreds more.

Lightning is a giant electric spark similar to the small spark you get when you walk across a carpet and touch a metal doorknob—but much stronger. One flash can contain a billion volts of electricity—enough to light a 100-watt incandescent bulb for three months. Lightning crackles through the air at a temperature five times hotter than the surface of the sun. The intense heat makes the surrounding air expand rapidly, creating a sound we know as thunder. Getting hit by lightning is rare, but everyone must be careful.

"For the first few years after I was struck, I was so scared every time there was a storm," says Sabrina. "Now I'm not scared. But I'm always cautious."

LIGHTNING SAFETY TIPS

INSIDE

Stay inside for 30 minutes after the last lightning or thunder.

Don't take baths or showers or wash dishes.

Avoid the use of landline phones (cell phones are OK), computers, TVs, and other electrical equipment.

OUTSIDE

Get into an enclosed structure or vehicle and shut the windows.

Stay away from bodies of water.

Avoid tall objects such as trees.

If you're in the open, crouch down (but do not lie flat) in the lowest place you can find.

8 cool facts that are too hot to touch!

1 **NINE OUT OF TEN** lightning strike victims **SURVIVE.**

2 **A BASEBALL** will travel **FARTHER** in HOT weather than in COLD weather.

3 **RAIN** contains vitamin **B12.**

4 **HOT COFFEE** is the name of a town in **Mississippi.**

5 The **SUN** has enough ENERGY TO BURN for **100 billion more years.**

6 A light wind is called a **ZEPHYR.**

7 **A camel** doesn't sweat until its body temperature reaches **106°F (41°C).**

8 The **hottest** stars are **BLUE.**

307

Natural Disasters

Every world region has its share of natural disasters—the menacing mix just varies from place to place. The Ring of Fire—grinding tectonic plate boundaries that follow the coasts of the Pacific Ocean—shakes with volcanic eruptions and earthquakes. Coastal lives and livelihoods here and along other oceans can be swept away by tsunamis. The U.S. heartland endures blizzards in winter and dangerous tornadoes that can strike in spring, summer, or fall. Tropical cyclones batter many coastal areas with ripping winds, torrents of rain, and huge storm surges along their deadly paths.

KINDS OF DISASTERS

EARTHQUAKE
A shaking of Earth's crust caused by a volcanic eruption or by the release of energy along a fault in the crust

TORNADO
A violently rotating column of air that touches Earth's surface during intense thunderstorm activity

HURRICANE
A large weather system, fueled by warm water, that can become a rotating storm packing winds of at least 74 miles an hour (119 kph). The storms are called hurricanes in the Atlantic Ocean and eastern Pacific, cyclones in the Indian Ocean, and typhoons in the western Pacific.

TSUNAMI
Huge ocean waves caused by an undersea earthquake or by a volcanic eruption

VOLCANIC ERUPTION
The upward movement and usually forceful release of molten material and gases from Earth's interior onto the surface

Christmas 2011 is the seven-year anniversary of a tsunami—a series of massive waves—that hit coastlines around the Indian Ocean. In minutes, buildings were destroyed and people lost their families. Rina Kamal, then five years old, was one of them. She was found on the shore; her mother and sisters had been swept away.

This tsunami began with a powerful undersea earthquake. Waves began to roll across the ocean in a series. They traveled behind each other very fast—at about the speed of a jet plane.

Closer to shore, the waves slowed. The ones at the back got closer to the waves in the front. One after another they crashed ashore. Some were as tall as a four-story building. The devastating tsunami killed more than 225,000 people.

All over the world people rushed to help the tsunami's survivors. Some sent blankets, school supplies, and canned goods. Others found unique ways to raise funds. Kids helped, too; in Benson, North Carolina, first-grade students collected pennies—158,451 of them!

Meanwhile, Rina's father never stopped looking for his wife and daughters. A month after the tsunami, he found Rina's name on a list of survivors. Volunteers brought him to where Rina was living. At last father and daughter were reunited and could begin to rebuild their lives together.

Scale of Hurricane Intensity

CATEGORY	ONE	TWO	THREE	FOUR	FIVE
DAMAGE	Minimal	Moderate	Extensive	Extreme	Catastrophic
WINDS	74–95 mph (119–153 kph)	96–110 mph (154–177 kph)	111–130 mph (178–209 kph)	131–155 mph (210–249 kph)	Over 155 mph (249+ kph)
(DAMAGE refers to wind and water damage combined.)					

Avalanche!

A million tons (907, 184 t) of snow rumble eight miles (13 km) downhill, kicking up a cloud of snow dust visible a hundred miles (161 km) away.

This is not a scene from a disaster movie—this describes reality one day in April 1981. The mountain was Mount Sanford in Alaska, and the event was one of history's bigger avalanches. Amazingly, no one was hurt, and luckily, avalanches this big are rare.

An avalanche is a moving mass of snow that may contain ice, soil, rocks, and uprooted trees. The height of a mountain, the steepness of its slope, and the type of snow lying on it all help determine the likelihood of an avalanche. Avalanches begin when an unstable mass of snow breaks away from a mountainside and moves downhill. The growing river of snow picks up speed as it rushes down the mountain. Avalanches have been known to reach speeds of 155 miles an hour (249 kph)—about the same as the record for downhill skiing.

This winter in the western United States alone, thousands upon thousands of avalanches will tumble down mountainsides. In the United States and Canada crashing walls of white will bowl over about 300 people. Most will be skiers, snowboarders, or snowmobilers who set out to have fun. Many will be buried by snow. Most will survive; some will not. Follow the safety tips below to help stay safe when you play in the mountains.

France has had the greatest number of avalanche fatalities.

Safety Tips

SAFETY FIRST
Before heading out, check for avalanche warnings.

EQUIPMENT
When hiking, carry safety equipment, including a long probe, a small shovel, and an emergency avalanche rescue beacon that signals your location.

NEVER GO IT ALONE
Don't hike in the mountain wilderness without a companion. Keep plenty of distance between party members, so if there is an avalanche not everyone is swept away.

CAUGHT
If caught in the path of an avalanche, try to get to the side of it. If you can't, grab a tree as an anchor. If swept into an avalanche, "swim" with the slide to stay as close to the surface as you can.

Tornado

"One time a tornado we were filming was coming right at us," says filmmaker Sean Casey. "As it moved closer, the wind picked up, and we felt as if the wind were pulling us into the tornado." Casey wants to film the perfect tornado. So when he sees one, he plants himself nearby with his cameras. That's not the safest thing to do. "The trick is knowing when to get out of there," says Casey.

With swirling winds that can top 300 miles an hour (483 kph), twisters can rip up trees, turn houses into piles of twisted wood, and toss cars around like toys. They're nature's most violent storms.

People like Casey chase tornadoes to make large-format films. But to find the storms, Casey tags along with a group of meteorologists, or weather scientists, who chase storms to find out why tornadoes form in some thunderstorms but not in others. The data that these meteorologists collect could make it easier to predict tornadoes.

Casey's team of filmmakers and scientists have had close calls. "We were following a storm one day and the wind pushed our 13-ton (11.8-t) radar truck backward," remembers Casey.

The chase has its exciting moments. But it can also be long and tedious. Seeing a tornado up close is exciting. But what's even more important is that storm chasers gain insight about twisters that could one day save lives.

Earthquake

The people of Northridge, California, will never forget the morning the ground started to shake, rattle, and roll. It was 4:30 a.m. when a huge block of rock 11 miles (18 km) under the city suddenly jolted upward several inches. As the ground above it bounced and buckled, thousands of buildings cracked and crumbled. Bridges snapped like toothpicks, and cracks opened in the ground. Gas lines broke, starting fires. The 1994 earthquake lasted only 30 seconds but caused 57 deaths, 9,000 injuries, and left thousands of people homeless.

Earthquakes are common; thousands occur each day. But unlike the Northridge quake, most are too weak to feel. Even some strong quakes are harmless because they happen in isolated, unpopulated areas. "Earthquakes don't kill people, falling buildings do," says Lucy Jones, a seismologist, or scientist who studies earthquakes. "You can't stop an earthquake," says Jones, who works for the U.S. Geological Survey in California. "The best thing you can do is prepare."

SURVIVE! A quake in Japan caused this damage. If you're in an earthquake, follow these tips. Outside, find an open space away from heavy structures and utility poles. Inside, avoid windows. Get under a sturdy table and stay there, or move into a hallway and press yourself against an inside wall.

Volcanic Eruption

So you're climbing your favorite mountain, just minding your own business, when *ba-da-bing, ba-da-boom!* It explodes! But don't blow your top. Just stay cool and follow these **VOLCANO SURVIVAL TIPS.**

SHAKE YOUR BOOTIES
Volcanic eruptions are often preceded by earth tremors. So if you feel the mountain start to mambo, make like Scooby-Doo and—*zoinks!*—get outta there!

CARRY A DISGUISE
Volcanoes may not erupt for hundreds of years, but you might want to bring a breathing mask and goggles just in case. They'll protect your eyes and lungs from harmful ash and noxious gases. (Plus they make a really cool Halloween costume!)

DON'T WADE AROUND
Ooey-gooey lava can reach temperatures of 2200°F (1204°C). That'll turn your toenails into toast! So don't go with the (lava) flow. Hotfoot it to safety before your shoes scorch!

ROCKS 'N' ROLL
Question: How do red-hot rocks flying toward you feel? Answer: Don't find out! Run up the closest nonexploding, 100-foot (30-m) hill, the "safety zone" outside the spew range.

HANG 10, DUDE
A volcanic blast can trigger a huge tidal wave, so even after you're off the volcano, you still could be all washed up. If you see a towering wall of water crashing your way, hightail it to high ground.

Signs That "It's Gonna Blow!"

1 In and around a volcano, the frequency and intensity of earthquakes increase.

2 The ground at the eruption site deforms or bulges.

3 The amount of gas released by the volcano increases.

A volcano's "fireworks" begin deep underground.

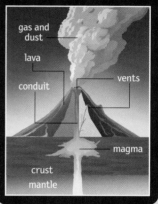

gas and dust
lava
conduit
vents
magma
crust
mantle

weird but true

A VOLCANO IN ITALY HAS BEEN ACTIVE FOR 2,000 YEARS.

Biomes

A biome, often called a major life zone, is one of the natural world's major communities where plants and animals adapt to their specific surroundings. Biomes are classified depending on the predominant vegetation, climate, and geography of a region. They can be divided into six major types: forest, freshwater, marine, desert, grassland, and tundra. Each biome consists of many ecosystems.

Biomes are extremely important. Balanced ecological relationships between biomes help to maintain the environment and life on Earth as we know it. For example, an increase in one species of plant, such as an invasive one, can cause a ripple effect throughout the whole biome and possibly the whole Earth.

Since biomes can be fragile in this way, it is important to protect them from negative human activity, such as deforestation, pollution, and other exploitation. We must work to conserve these biomes and the unique organisms that live within them.

FOREST

The forest biomes have been evolving for about 420 million years. Today, forests occupy about one-third of Earth's land area. There are three major types of forests: tropical, temperate, and boreal (taiga). Forests are home to a diversity of plants, some of which may hold medicinal qualities for humans, as well as thousands of unseen and undiscovered species. Forests can also absorb carbon dioxide, a greenhouse gas, and help mitigate its negative effects.

FRESHWATER

Freshwater biomes are home to one of our greatest natural resources—water. As the basis for all life, water is needed for drinking, crop irrigation, and general support of animal life. Most water on Earth is salty, but freshwater ecosystems include lakes, ponds, rivers, and streams. They are home to countless animal and plant species. Throughout the world, people use food, medicine, oil, and other resources from this biome, making it extremely important to life on Earth.

MARINE

The marine biome covers almost three-fourths of Earth's surface, making it the largest habitat on our planet. The five oceans, coral reefs, and estuaries make up the majority of the marine biome. Coral reefs are considered to be the most biodiverse of any of the biome habitats. The marine biome is home to more than one million plant and animal species. Many of the animals in the marine biome are the largest animals on Earth, such as the blue whale.

DESERT

Covering about one-fifth of Earth's surface, deserts are places where precipitation is less than 10 inches (25 cm) per year. Although most deserts are hot, there are other kinds, as well. The four major kinds of deserts in the world include: hot, semi-arid, coastal, and cold. Far from being barren wastelands, deserts are biologically rich habitats with a vast array of animals and plants that have adapted to the harsh conditions there.

GRASSLAND

Biomes called grassland are characterized by having grasses instead of large shrubs or trees. Grasslands generally have precipitation for only about half to three-fourths of the year. If it was more, they would become forests. Widespread around the world, grasslands can be divided into two types: tropical (savannas) and temperate. Grasslands are home to some of the largest land animals on Earth, such as elephants, hippopotamus, and lions.

TUNDRA

The coldest of all biomes, tundras are characterized by an extremely cold climate, simple vegetation, little precipitation, poor nutrients, and short growing seasons. There are two types of tundra: arctic and alpine. A very fragile environment, tundras are home to few kinds of vegetation. Surprisingly though, there are quite a few species that can survive the tundra's extremes, such as wolves, caribou, and even mosquitoes.

Countries Around the World
Where Crystals and Gems Are Mined

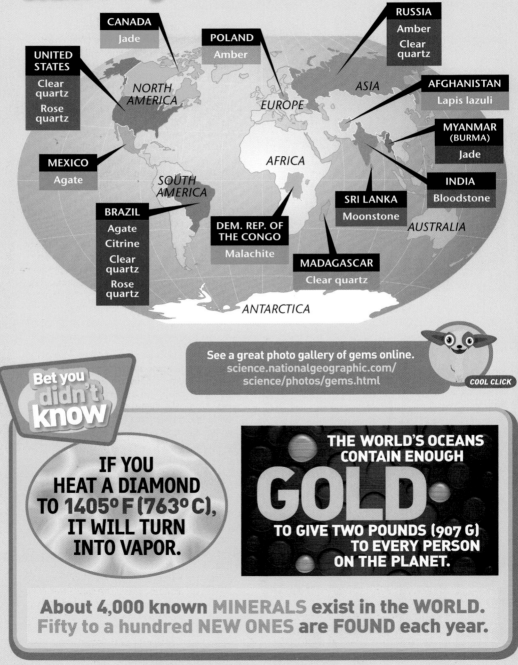

CANADA
Jade

POLAND
Amber

RUSSIA
Amber
Clear quartz

UNITED STATES
Clear quartz
Rose quartz

NORTH AMERICA

ASIA

EUROPE

AFGHANISTAN
Lapis lazuli

MYANMAR (BURMA)
Jade

MEXICO
Agate

AFRICA

SOUTH AMERICA

INDIA
Bloodstone

SRI LANKA
Moonstone

AUSTRALIA

BRAZIL
Agate
Citrine
Clear quartz
Rose quartz

DEM. REP. OF THE CONGO
Malachite

MADAGASCAR
Clear quartz

ANTARCTICA

See a great photo gallery of gems online.
science.nationalgeographic.com/
science/photos/gems.html

COOL CLICK

Bet you didn't know

IF YOU HEAT A DIAMOND TO 1405° F (763° C), IT WILL TURN INTO VAPOR.

THE WORLD'S OCEANS CONTAIN ENOUGH

GOLD

TO GIVE TWO POUNDS (907 G) TO EVERY PERSON ON THE PLANET.

About 4,000 known MINERALS exist in the WORLD.
Fifty to a hundred NEW ONES are FOUND each year.

BIRTHSTONES

GARNET LOYALTY

January Garnets were once thought to hold medicinal value and protect against poisons, wounds, and bad dreams. They come in red, black, green, or are colorless.

AMETHYST SINCERITY

February Amethysts were believed to help people stay awake and think clearly. They are found in geodes (rock formations) and range in color from light mauve to deep purple.

AQUAMARINE COURAGE
March This gem was thought to heal illnesses of the stomach, liver, jaws, and throat. They range from deep blue to blue-green. The most valued and rare are the deep blue gems.

DIAMOND ENDURING LOVE
April People associate these gems with romance, mystery, power, greed, and magic. The hardest natural substance on Earth, diamonds are a form of carbon.

EMERALD PURE LOVE
May Emeralds were thought to prevent epilepsy, stop bleeding, cure fevers and diarrhea, and keep the wearer from panicking. These gems are light to deep green.

PEARL INNOCENCE

June Pearls were thought to possess magical powers, as a result there used to be laws about who could own and wear them (powerful, rich people). No two pearls are exactly alike.

RUBY CONTENTMENT

July A ruby supposedly brought good health, cured bleeding, guarded against wickedness, and foretold misfortune. Rubies are a red form of the mineral corundum.

PERIDOT HAPPINESS
August People felt that peridots could ward off anxiety, help one speak better, and improve relationships. Peridot is the only gem ever found in meteorites.

SAPPHIRE CLEAR THINKING

September Once a source of protection for travelers, sapphires brought peace and wisdom. Some are pale; others are brilliant blue. They also come in orange, green, yellow, and pink.

OPAL HOPE
October An opal was believed to bring beauty, success, and happiness, as well as to ward off heart and kidney failure and prevent fainting. Opals form over a long, long time.

TOPAZ FAITHFULNESS
November Legends proclaimed that a topaz made one clear-sighted, increased strength, and warned of poison. Topazes come in a range of colors: gold, pink, green, or colorless.

TURQUOISE SUCCESS

December Some believed turquoise was a love charm. If a man gave a woman turquoise jewelry, he was pledging his love for her. It forms where mineral-rich water seeps into rocky gaps.

HOW DOES Your Garden GROW?

More than 300,000 organisms strong, the plant kingdom is growing wild! Plants are found all over the world—on top of mountains, in the sea, in frigid temperatures—everywhere. Without plants, life on Earth would not be able to survive. Plants provide food and oxygen for animals and humans.

There are three characteristics that make plants distinct:

1 Most have chlorophyll (a green pigment that makes photosynthesis work and turns sunlight into glucose), while some are parasitic.

2 They cannot change their location on their own.

3 Their cell walls are made from cellulose.

Photosynthesis

light

oxygen

carbon dioxide

water

Plants are lucky—they don't have to hunt or shop for food. Most use the sun to produce their own food. In a process called photosynthesis, the plant's chloroplast (the part of the plant where the chemical chlorophyll is located) captures the sun's energy and combines it with carbon dioxide from the air and nutrient-rich water from the ground to produce glucose, a sugar. Plants use the glucose to help them grow. As a waste product, plants emit oxygen, which humans need to breathe. When we breathe, we exhale carbon dioxide, which the plants then use for more photosynthesis—it's all a big, finely tuned system. So the next time you pass a lonely houseplant, give it thanks for helping you live.

Try This!

Recycled Shoe Flower Pots

Instead of throwing away the shoes you've outgrown, use them as pots for plants. It's a great gift to give to the eco-conscious people in your life.

YOU WILL NEED

- Seedlings
- Old shoes (sneakers or closed-toed shoes work best)
- Potting soil
- Drill

HERE'S HOW

Ask an adult to drill two small holes into the soles of the old shoes for drainage. Fill up the shoe with potting soil. Place seedlings into soil. Top off with more soil. Water your plant.

NOTE: Make sure you consider light conditions when selecting plants.

Green Invaders

They're taking over! No, not invaders from space. Plants! Sometimes these "green invaders" can overtake native plants in a region. For example, in the United States, there are so many invasive plant species, they're crowding out the plants that have lived there for centuries.

And that's a problem, says Dr. Doug Tallamy, an entomologist at the University of Delaware in the U.S.A. He explains that almost all plant-eating insects are specialized. That means they eat only certain plants. Orange-and-black monarch caterpillars, for example, can only dine on one plant: milkweed. If people cut down milkweed and replace it with something else, the caterpillars would starve. And the trouble goes across the food web.

Fewer of the right plants mean fewer bugs, and fewer bugs mean fewer birds. And that's bad for Earth, because we need a variety of living things to keep the planet healthy. The good news is, gardeners are working hard to protect native plants and get rid of invaders.

WORLD WATER

Earth's most precious resource

More than two-thirds of Earth is covered by water, but fresh water, which is needed by plants and animals—including humans—makes up less than 3 percent of all the water on Earth. Much of this fresh water is trapped deep underground or frozen in ice sheets and glaciers. Of the small amount of water that is fresh, less than one percent is available for human use.

Unfortunately, human activity often puts great stress on vital watersheds. For example, in Brazil plans are being made to build large dams on the Amazon River. This will alter the natural flow of water in this giant watershed and help provide water and electricity. In the United States, heavy use of chemical fertilizers and pesticides has created toxic runoff that threatens the health of the Mississippi River watershed.

Access to clean fresh water is critical for human health. But in many places, safe water is scarce due to population pressure and pollution.

Water Facts

Rivers that have been dammed to generate electricity are the source of almost 20 percent of the renewable energy used.

If all the glaciers and ice sheets on Earth's surface melted, they would raise the level of Earth's oceans by about 230 feet (70 m). It is estimated that during the last ice age, when glaciers covered about one-third of the land, the sea level was 400 feet (122 m) lower than it is today.

Desalination is the process of removing salt from ocean water so that it can be used for irrigation and for people and livestock to drink. Most of the world's desalination plants are in the arid countries of the Arabian Peninsula.

Water consists of three atoms, two hydrogen and one oxygen, that are bonded together by electrical charges.

If all the world's water were placed in a gallon jug, the fresh water available for humans to use would equal only about one tablespoon.

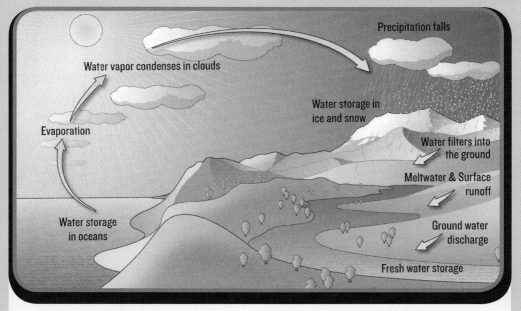

Precipitation falls

Water vapor condenses in clouds

Water storage in ice and snow

Evaporation

Water filters into the ground

Meltwater & Surface runoff

Water storage in oceans

Ground water discharge

Fresh water storage

WATER CYCLE

The amount of water on Earth is more or less constant—only the form changes. As the sun warms Earth's surface, liquid water is changed to water vapor in a process called **evaporation.** Plants lose water from the surface of leaves in a process called **transpiration.** As water vapor rises into the air, it cools and changes form again. This time it becomes clouds in a process called **condensation.** Water droplets fall from the clouds as **precipitation,** which then travels as groundwater or runoff back to the lakes, rivers, and oceans, where the cycle (shown above) starts all over again.

Bet you didn't know

Although a person can LIVE WITHOUT FOOD for more than A MONTH, a person can only LIVE WITHOUT WATER for approximately ONE WEEK.

As a result of wind, a waterfall in Hawaii sometimes GOES UP instead of DOWN.

AN EAR OF CORN IS MADE UP OF 70 PERCENT WATER.

WAYS YOU CAN PRESERVE FRESH WATER SUPPLIES

Don't clean sidewalks with a hose. Use a broom instead.

Turn off the tap while brushing your teeth. Letting the faucet run wastes a gallon (3.8 L) of water each time. If you brush your teeth twice a day, that's 730 gallons (2,763 L) of water a year!

Keeping the lawn green can be tough on the environment. Fertilizers wash into neighborhood storm drains, creating unhealthy algae growth in rivers and streams.

Every living thing depends on water.

Water Isn't Everywhere

Lake Itasca, Minnesota
Fresh water is always a fresh subject for photographer Jim Richardson, who has been taking pictures for NATIONAL GEOGRAPHIC since 1984. Many of his photographs, including the one here, deal with fresh water. "The world's supply of fresh water is dwindling," he says.

"In some places, entire suburbs are being built where the supply of fresh water will run out in a matter of years." Cleanliness is just as important as supply, according to Richardson. "But good water isn't always crystal clear," he says. "Healthy fresh water can also be muddy and full of nutrients for the animals that depend on it."

Bet you didn't know

WATER is the **ONLY** substance on Earth to be found naturally in three forms— **SOLID, GAS,** and **LIQUID.**

COOL CLICKS

Check out some of these websites to learn more about water.

National Integrated Drought Information System
drought.gov

Water Conservation Tips
monolake.org/waterconservation

Healthy Water Crossword Puzzle
epa.gov/waterscience/learn/files/crossword.pdf

We're Parched!

We live in a thirsty world, and water is our drink of necessity. Our world would not survive without water—plants would not grow, and animals would not live.

Drought is when there is a prolonged period of lack of rainfall. If the amount of rain lessens too much, particularly if it's combined with unpredictable wind patterns and high temperatures, we can end up in a severe drought. When droughts persist, water often has to be rationed, or given out in limited amounts. Crops and animals won't get the water that they need to survive, which can lead to food shortages. Droughts can also cause dust storms and fires.

Since drought is related to weather, it may seem like there is nothing we can do to help prevent it, but that is wrong. As humans, the activities we engage in, like burning fossil fuels, contribute to the process of global warming, which is gradually changing the climate of our planet. To help prevent devastating droughts and slow global warming, we need to burn less fossil fuel, conserve water, change farming methods, and treat our planet with care. Because if the water runs out, we will, too.

Drought Drives Them Out

A lost world lies hidden in the rain forests that lie from southern Mexico to South America. Hundreds of cities and towns stand among the trees. Once they were home to millions of people known as the Maya.

The Maya have lived in the jungles of the Americas for 3,000 years. They built an incredible civilization. It was at its peak for about 750 years. The peak ended about 1,000 years ago.

Today the Maya cities are empty. Trees and vines embrace the old buildings. Many once proud temples and palaces are now ruins.

Tikal, located in present-day Guatemala, was one of the greatest Maya cities. Thirteen hundred years ago there were some 55,000 people and roughly 3,000 major buildings.

Yet, one day, its people were all gone. Why? Archaeologists think Tikal suffered a drought that made it hard to grow corn, beans, squash, and other foods. Warfare may also have weakened Tikal.

That's not all. Drought and war probably shook the people's faith in their king. The Maya thought of their rulers as gods. When the king couldn't bring rain or victory, though, people may have stopped listening to him. Their community fell apart. They left behind a great city and a great mystery.

ruins of a temple in Palenque, an ancient Maya city in southern Mexico

THE OC

PACIFIC OCEAN

STATS

Surface area
65,436,200 sq mi (169,479,000 sq km)

Percent of Earth's water area
47

Greatest depth
Challenger Deep
(in the Mariana Trench)
-35,827 ft (-10,920 m)

Surface temperatures
Summer high: 90°F (32°C)
Winter low: 28°F (-2°C)

Tides
Highest: 30 ft (9 m)
near Korean peninsula
Lowest: 1 ft (0.3 m)
near Midway Islands

GEO WHIZ

The Pacific Ocean has tens of thousands of islands, more than any other ocean.

The ocean's name comes from the Latin *Mare Pacificum,* meaning "peaceful sea," but earthquakes and volcanic activity along its coasts generate powerful waves called tsunamis, which cause death and destruction when they slam ashore.

The Pacific is home to the largest number of coral reefs, including Earth's longest: Australia's 1,429-mile (2,300-km) -long Great Barrier Reef.

The Hawaiian monk seal, the most endangered marine mammal in U.S. waters, lives on only a few islands in the remote northwestern end of the Hawaiian archipelago.

ATLANTIC OCEAN

STATS

Surface area
35,338,500 sq mi (91,526,400 sq km)

Percent of Earth's water area
25

Greatest depth
Puerto Rico Trench
-28,232 ft (-8,605 m)

Surface temperatures
Summer high: 90°F (32°C)
Winter low: 28°F (-2°C)

Tides
Highest: 52 ft (16 m)
Bay of Fundy, Canada
Lowest: 1.5 ft (0.5 m)
Gulf of Mexico and Mediterranean Sea

GEO WHIZ

In 2005 the Atlantic Ocean produced a record-setting 15 hurricanes. For the first time in a single season, four hurricanes—Emily, Katrina, Rita, and Wilma—reached category 5 level, with sustained winds of at least 155 miles per hour (249 kph).

The Atlantic Ocean is about half the size of the Pacific, but it's growing. Spreading along the Mid-Atlantic Ridge—an undersea mountain range—allows molten rock from Earth's interior to escape and form new ocean floor.

Of all of the world's oceans, the Atlantic is the youngest. It is thought to have been created during the Jurassic Period.

The amount of water that flows into the Atlantic Ocean from the Amazon River in South America is equal to 20 percent of Earth's available fresh water.

EANS

INDIAN OCEAN

STATS

Surface area
28,839,800 sq mi (74,694,800 sq km)

Percent of Earth's water area
21

Greatest depth
Java Trench
-23,376 ft (-7,125 m)

Surface temperatures
Summer high: 93°F (34°C)
Winter low: 28°F (-2°C)

Tides
Highest: 36 ft (11 m)
Lowest: 2 ft (0.6 m)
Both along Australia's west coast

GEO WHIZ

Each day tankers carrying 17 million barrels of crude oil from the Persian Gulf enter the waters of the Indian Ocean, transporting their cargo for distribution around the world.

Some of the world's largest breeding grounds for humpback whales are in the Indian Ocean, the Arabian Sea, and off the east coast of Africa.

The Bay of Bengal, off the coast of India, is sometimes called Cyclone Alley because of the large number of tropical storms that occur each year between May and November.

Sailors from what is now Indonesia used seasonal winds called monsoons to reach Africa's east coast. They arrived on the continent long before Europeans did.

Ancient Sanskrit literature refers to the Indian Ocean as *Ratnakara*, which means "the creator of jewels." Sanskrit is one of the 22 official languages of India.

ARCTIC OCEAN

STATS

Surface area
5,390,000 sq mi (13,960,100 sq km)

Percent of Earth's water area
4

Greatest depth
Molloy Deep
-18,599 ft (-5,669 m)

Surface temperatures
Summer high: 41°F (5°C)
Winter low: 28°F (-2°C)

Tides
Less than 1 ft (0.3 m)
variation throughout the ocean

GEO WHIZ

Satellite monitoring of Arctic sea ice, which began in the late 1970s, shows that the extent of the sea ice is shrinking by approximately 11 percent every 10 years. Scientists continue to research and think this is caused by global warming.

The geographic North Pole lies roughly in the middle of the Arctic Ocean under 13,000 feet (3,962 m) of water.

Many of the features on the Arctic Ocean floor are named for early Arctic explorers and bordering landmasses.

There are at least 12 volcanoes on the floor of the Arctic Ocean.

The Atlantic, Indian, and Pacific Oceans merge into ice waters around Antarctica. Some define this as an ocean—calling it the Antarctic Ocean, Austral Ocean, or Southern Ocean—but there is no agreement on the name and the extent of a fifth ocean.

To see the major oceans and bays in relation to landmasses, look at the map on pages 154 and 155.

How Deep It Is!

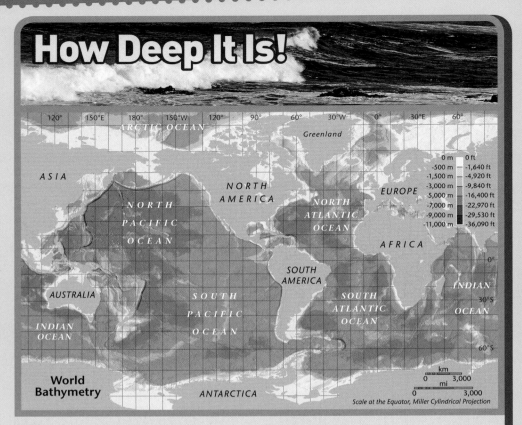

ARCTIC OCEAN

Greenland

ASIA

NORTH
AMERICA

EUROPE

0 m	0 ft
-500 m	-1,640 ft
-1,500 m	-4,920 ft
-3,000 m	-9,840 ft
-5,000 m	-16,400 ft
-7,000 m	-22,970 ft
-9,000 m	-29,530 ft
-11,000 m	-36,090 ft

NORTH
PACIFIC
OCEAN

NORTH
ATLANTIC
OCEAN

AFRICA

SOUTH
AMERICA

INDIAN

AUSTRALIA

SOUTH
PACIFIC
OCEAN

SOUTH
ATLANTIC
OCEAN

OCEAN

INDIAN
OCEAN

**World
Bathymetry**

ANTARCTICA

Scale at the Equator, Miller Cylindrical Projection

Explorers can't just march across the floor of the Pacific Ocean, which in places descends to more than 35,000 feet (10,668 m) below the surface of the water. Luckily, the science of world bathymetry maps and measures the depths of the oceans. It is quite challenging, as the ocean floor is as varied as the surface of the continents. The map above shows that more than 70 percent of Earth's surface is underwater, mainly covered by the oceans, which are really interconnected bodies of water that together form one global ocean.

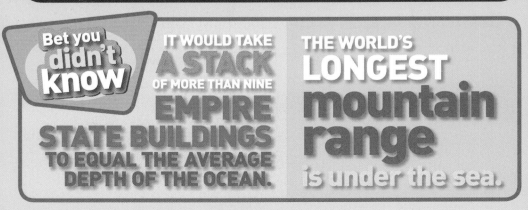

Bet you didn't know

IT WOULD TAKE A STACK OF MORE THAN NINE EMPIRE STATE BUILDINGS TO EQUAL THE AVERAGE DEPTH OF THE OCEAN.

THE WORLD'S LONGEST mountain range is under the sea.

MEET THE NAT GEO EXPLORER

ROBERT BALLARD

Among the most accomplished of the world's deep-sea explorers, Robert Ballard is best known for his historic discovery of the sunken R.M.S. *Titanic*. During his long career he has conducted more than 120 deep-sea expeditions, and he is a trailblazer in the use of deep-diving submarines.

How did you become an explorer?
I became an explorer the moment I could walk.

What was your closest call in the field?
I have had several: a fire in a bathyscaphe (a kind of submersible) in the rift valley of the Mid-Atlantic Ridge at 9,000 feet (2,743 m), crashing into the side of a volcano in the Cayman Trough in 20,000 feet (6,096 m) of water, and almost getting entangled in the cables of a World War II Australian heavy cruiser in Iron Bottom Sound in the Solomon Islands.

How would you suggest kids follow in your footsteps?
Follow your own dreams wherever they take you—your passion to do something, to become someone, is the driving energy you will need to overcome setbacks in your life.

What is one place or thing you'd still like to explore?
I want to go where no one has ever gone on planet Earth—a quest that will keep me busy for the rest of my life. (To read about the discovery of the *Titanic*, see p.285)

UNDERWATER LANDSCAPES

The landscape of the ocean floor is varied and constantly changing. A continental edge that slopes gently beneath the water is called a continental shelf. Mountain ranges, called mid-ocean ridges, rise where ocean plates are spreading. Other plates plunge into trenches more than 6 miles (10 km) deep. Magma rises through vents called hot spots, pushes through ocean plates, and creates seamounts and volcanoes.

Continents on the Move

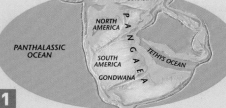

1 **PANGAEA** About 240 million years ago, Earth's landmasses were joined together in one super-continent that extended from pole to pole.

2 **BREAKUP** By 94 million years ago, Pangaea had broken apart into landmasses that would become today's continents. Dinosaurs roamed Earth during a period of warmer climates.

3 **EXTINCTION** About 65 million years ago, an asteroid smashed into Earth, creating the Gulf of Mexico. This impact may have resulted in the extinction of half the world's species, including the dinosaurs. This was one of several major mass extinctions.

4 **ICE AGE** By 18,000 years ago, the continents had drifted close to their present positions, but most far northern and far southern lands were buried beneath huge glaciers.

A LOOK WITHIN

The distance from Earth's surface to its center is 3,963 miles (6,378 km). There are four layers: a thin, rigid crust; the rocky mantle; the outer core, which is a layer of molten iron; and finally the inner core, which is solid iron.

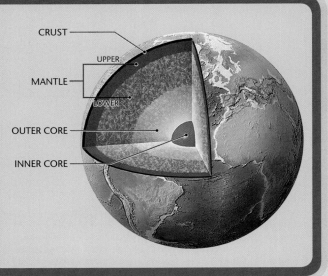

CRUST

UPPER

MANTLE

LOWER

OUTER CORE

INNER CORE

TIME ZONES

Long ago, when people lived in relative isolation, they measured time by the position of the sun overhead. That meant that noon in one place was not the same as noon in a place 100 miles (160 km) to the west. Later, with the development of long-distance railroads, people needed to coordinate time. In 1884 a system of 24 standard time zones was adopted. Each time zone reflects the fact that Earth rotates west to east 15 degrees each hour. Time is counted from the prime meridian, which runs through Greenwich, England.

Earth Shapers

Earth's features are constantly undergoing change—being built up, destroyed, or just rearranged. Plates are in constant, very slow motion. Some plates collide, others pull apart, and still others slowly grind past each other. As the plates move, mountains are uplifted, volcanoes erupt, and new land is created.

▲ **VOLCANOES** form when molten rock, called magma, rises to Earth's surface. Some volcanoes occur as one plate pushes beneath another plate. Other volcanoes result when a plate passes over a column of magma, called a hot spot, rising from the mantle.

◀ **FAULTING** happens when two plates grind past each other, creating large cracks along the edges of the plates.

▶ **COLLISION** of two continental plates causes plate edges to break and fold, creating mountains, Earth's highest landforms.

◀ **SPREADING** results when oceanic plates move apart. The ocean floor cracks, magma rises, and new crust is created. The Mid-Atlantic Ridge spreads about an inch—a few centimeters—a year, pushing Europe and North America farther apart.

◀ **SUBDUCTION** occurs when an oceanic plate dives under a continental plate. This often results in volcanoes and earthquakes, as well as mountain building.

SPEAK NATURALLY
Oral Reports Made Easy

Does the thought of public speaking start your stomach churning like a tornado? Would you rather get caught in an avalanche than give a speech?

Giving an oral report does not have to be a natural disaster. The basic format is very similar to a written essay. There are two main elements that make up a good oral report—the writing and the presentation. As you write your oral report, remember that your audience will be hearing the information as opposed to reading it. Follow the guidelines below, and there will be clear skies ahead.

TIP: Remember to dress nicely on the day you give your report. Your appearance is a form of nonverbal communication and makes an impact on your audience.

Writing Your Material

Follow the steps in the "How to Write A Perfect Essay" section on p. 300, but prepare your report to be spoken rather than written.

Try to keep your sentences short and simple. Long, complex sentences are harder to follow. Limit yourself to just a few key points. You don't want to overwhelm your audience with too much information. To be most effective, hit your key points in the introduction, elaborate on them in the body, and then repeat them once again in your conclusion.

An oral report has three basic parts:

- **Introduction**—This is your chance to engage your audience and really capture their interest in the subject you are presenting. Use a funny personal experience, a dramatic story, or start with an intriguing question.

- **Body**—This is the longest part of your report. Here you elaborate on the facts and ideas you want to convey. Give information that supports your main idea and expand on it with specific examples or details. In other words, structure your oral report in the same way you would a written essay so that your thoughts are presented in a clear and organized manner.

- **Conclusion**—This is the time to summarize the information and emphasize your most important points to the audience one last time.

Preparing Your Delivery

1 Practice makes perfect.
Practice! Practice! Practice! Confidence, enthusiasm, and energy are key to delivering an effective oral report, and they can best be achieved through rehearsal. Ask family and friends to be your practice audience, and ask them for feedback when you're done. Were they able to follow your ideas? Did you seem knowledgeable and confident? Did you speak too slow or too fast, too soft or too loud? The more times you practice giving your report, the more you'll master the material. Then you won't have to rely so heavily on your notes or papers and can give your report in a relaxed and confident manner

2 Present with everything you've got.
Be as creative as you can. Incorporate videos, sound clips, slide presentations, charts, diagrams, and photos. Visual aids help stimulate your audience's senses and keep them intrigued and engaged. They can also help to reinforce your key points. And remember that when you're giving an oral report, you're a performer. Take charge of the spotlight and be as animated and entertaining as you can. Have fun with it.

COOL CLICK

Need a good subject? Go online. kidsblogs.national geographic.com/kidsnews

3 Keep your nerves under control.

Everyone gets a little nervous when speaking in front of a group. That's normal. But the better prepared you are—including good research, well-organized material, and plenty of rehearsal—the more confident you'll be. Preparation is the key. And if you make a mistake or stumble over your words, just regroup and keep going. Nobody's perfect, and nobody expects you to be.

PRESENTATION CHECKLIST

✓ Get a good night's sleep before your presentation.

✓ Have a healthy meal or nutritious snack beforehand.

✓ When you think you're fully prepared, practice it one more time.

✓ Maintain eye contact with your audience throughout your report.

✓ Take a deep breath, relax, and have fun with it.

FUN TIP
If you're fighting nerves, try to picture your listeners in their underwear.

CONNECTING WORDS

Effective use of connecting words will make your oral report go smoothly. Connecting words help the listener understand as you transition from one idea to the next.

Here are some words you can use to make your oral report flow:

also	next
anyway	nonetheless
consequently	now that
finally	otherwise
furthermore	since
however	still
incidentally	then
instead	therefore
likewise	thus
meanwhile	until
moreover	whether
nevertheless	while

Future World

ELECTRIC IMAGE

It's the future! Blast off to Paris in minutes aboard your rocketplane. Or, you can hit the space station before lunch!

8 Future Possibilities

It's 2035. You have a job, spouse, kids ... and guess what? It's a totally techno world full of amazing possibilities. Step into your future life and check out 8 cool things you might see there.

1 The kitchen is your personal shopper. All food packaging contains a **Radio Frequency Identification (RFID)** tag, a tiny electronic version of a bar code. Your kitchen reads RFIDs, so it knows whether the milk is about to go sour and when you ate the last cookie. It automatically adds them to your grocery list and even e-shops to have your favorite foods delivered.

2 Change your outfit without undressing! Interactive **smart clothes**, made of smart materials and RFIDs, change color, texture, pattern, and even smell. Tired of stripes? Turn your pants plaid. Have your shirt change patterns to match the beat of the music you're listening to. Going hiking? Wear a jacket that repels insects. Clothes can stretch, shrink, translate languages, play music, pay bills, find your keys, give you a massage, and even read your email aloud.

3 **Robots** make your life easier, often taking over tasks you find boring. They come in various forms and sizes. Robotics expert Reid Simmons envisions tiny dust-eating bugs that will work together to keep things clean. Other robots will slurp up spills, mow the lawn, or feed the dog. Will robots do your kid's homework? Maybe, but the teacher's grouchy robot may not accept it!

4 Need a little advice on what to wear? The **mirror** in your bathroom can help you. It will select a shirt in your closet that'll match the pants you've chosen and suggest the best clothes for the weather. A display in the mirror lets you read your e-mail, watch TV, or check your schedule as you finish getting ready.

CLOTHING WITH RFID

SUPER SA

RECIPE

HOLOCONSO

SMART MIRROR

SPILL
ALERT!

5 Play **video games** that blend reality with virtual reality for amazing action and adventure. When you are wearing the game glasses, three-dimensional characters become part of your world. The blending of the digital world and the real world is so flawless that you actually see a pterodactyl swooping toward you on the climbing wall, a monster creeping up the bridge in town, or aliens zooming alongside the car!

6 A wall in your living room, the side of a bus, a cereal box—nearly any surface doubles as a **video display** to give you information about a product. You see some sort of video display all around you—in your home and around town. When you're picking out a DVD, its cover shows a 30-second clip, making your choice much easier. Hungry after fighting a virtual reality battle? Check the video on food packaging for appealing snack suggestions.

BEDROOM OF STARS

7 Your **home** responds to you, predicting your every need. Just like everything else, your house uses invisible embedded electronics to come alive when you walk in. It automatically turns on the lights, tints your windows, plays your favorite music, tells you who's at the door, and starts dinner. Tell every wall in the house to beam you a reminder to take out the trash (unless your robot does that for you!). Even your ceilings are cool. Like to sleep under the stars? Program the ceiling, walls, and floor in your bedroom to recreate a night sky.

C ACTIVATED
F ACTIVATED
S ACTIVATED
enabled
n to reset

kids
on the move!

8 Thanks to **holographic technology,** you can have a face-to-face discussion with a virtual Einstein to help you solve a tough math problem. Or maybe you'd like to swim with a great white shark without becoming lunch. Museums in the future will be accessible from your home and will bring music, history, science, and other subjects alive (almost!).

3-D MAGAZINE

SPACE HOTEL

The space taxi is waiting. Mars-bound astronauts climb into the little craft, buckle up, and lift off from Earth. Soon they see their next stop: a huge spaceship soaring past in the dark. Their pilot pulls alongside, carefully bringing the taxi's speed to 13,000 miles an hour (21,000 kph) to match the speed of the big crafts. With a few more delicate maneuvers, the pilot docks the taxi, and the astronauts enter their new home away from home: the moving Mars hotel. Traveling to Mars on a regular spacecraft has some serious problems: The journey would require a huge amount of expensive fuel, and being weightless for a long time can badly weaken human bones and muscles. But "space hotels," also called cyclers, would ride the solar system's gravitational forces in a never-ending loop between Mars and Earth. They wouldn't require much fuel, and each one would spin to create a kind of artificial gravity for the travelers inside. Cycler hotels could be the healthiest, cheapest, and most comfortable way to visit our planetary neighbor—if they ever actually happen!

Solar Sailing

One day travelers in the solar system may see a glorious sight: a craft pulled through space by a huge, delicate, mirrorlike sail. The force pushing the sail forward would be nothing more than light from the sun.

The idea behind solar sailing is pretty simple. Light is made of extremely tiny particles called photons. When photons bounce off objects, they push on those objects just a little bit. On Earth we don't notice this because other forces, such as friction in the air, are so much stronger. But in space, where there is no air to get in the way, the gentle pressure of photons from the sun is enough to move a lightweight object.

Sunlight bouncing off a solar sail would move it—and the spacecraft attached to it—very slowly at first. Over time, the solar sailer would pick up speed, moving faster and faster. By the time the sailer passed the outer planets, it could be traveling at 200,000 miles per hour (324,000 kph), ten times as fast as today's space shuttle.

Although it's not luxurious, this imagined space hotel has comfortable little cabins, exercise machines, and games to play.

ROBOT REVOLUTION

CUTTING-EDGE TECHNOLOGY IS COMING YOUR WAY.

WALKING ON WATER

Designing a robot to walk on land is challenging enough, but scientists have actually designed a robot that can walk on water! Called the Water Runner, the robot was created using secrets scientists learned from a lizard. To escape predators, the basilisk lizard sprints across the surface of water without sinking. Scientists hope the next generation of Water Runners will be able to walk on both land and water. Someday a robot might walk to your cooler, grab a cold drink, and then run across the pool to hand it to you as you float on a raft. Be sure it doesn't forget your sunscreen.

THE AMAZING ASIMO

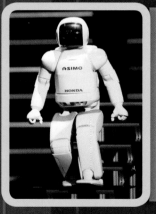

This robot once looked like a giant toaster with legs and now looks like a kid in a white space suit. It's Asimo—considered by many to be the most advanced human-shaped robot in the world. Honda has worked on Asimo for more than 20 years and hopes one day it will fight fires, clean up toxic waste, do chores, and help the sick. Right now, Asimo can walk, climb stairs, recognize faces, and even run very slowly. But don't get too excited. While you're able to go for days without food and can recharge (eat) on the run, Asimo's battery can drain in less than an hour. It also cost about a million dollars to make! Looks like you'll be doing your own chores for a little while longer.

SHAPE SHIFTING

Scientists have designed robots in hundreds of shapes, with each shape having certain advantages. But why choose just one? Imagine a swarm of microscopic robots, called nanobots, connected together that can rearrange themselves into the shape of a screwdriver, antenna, or just about anything else. Scientists designing nanobots think that someday virus-eating nanobots (example, right) may help you get rid of a cold!

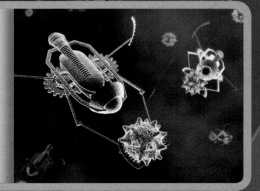

GAME ANSWERS

Wild Guess
(from inside front cover):

1. An adult *T. rex* stood as tall as 20 feet (6 m); adult giraffes are up to 19 feet (5.8 m) tall.
2. Thunder can be heard up to 12 miles (19 km) away; a lion's roar can be heard 5 miles (8 km) away.
3. The Leaning Tower of Pisa weighs 32 million pounds (14 million kg); the space shuttle weighs 4 million pounds (2 million kg).
4. Riding the 8,133-foot (2,479-m) -long Steel Dragon roller coaster in Japan took 3 minutes, 40 seconds; microwave popcorn cooks for an average of two to three minutes.
5. California is 163,696 square miles (423,972 sq km); Italy is 116,345 square miles (301,333 sq km).

City Gone Wild!
(from page 37):

Penguin Party
(from page 59):

1. B   2. D   3. F   4. G   5. C   6. A
7. I   8. J   9. H   10. E

What in the World?
(from page 103):

Top row: **toucan, lantern bug, leopard**
Middle row: **snail, red-eyed tree frog, ring-tailed lemur**
Bottom row: **emerald tree boa, monkey, millipede**

Road Trip
(from page 197):

Signs of the Times
(from page 215):
Signs **#1** and **#6** are fake.

ABBREVIATIONS:

AA: Animals Animals
AP: Associated Press
AWS: Archivo White Star
BAL: The Bridgeman Art Library
CB: Corbis
DA: David Aguilar
GI: Getty Images
IS: iStockphoto.com
JI: Jupiter Images
MP: Minden Pictures
MW: Martin Walz
NGS: NationalGeographicStock.com
PR: Photo Researchers, Inc.
SS: Shutterstock
WHHA: White House Historical Association
ZSD: Zoological Society of San Diego

All Maps
By NGS unless otherwise noted

All Illustrations & Charts
By Stuart Armstrong unless otherwise noted

Zipper Artwork
By Nathan Jurevicius

Front Cover
(jaguar), Steve Winter/NGS; (penguin), John Eastcott & Yva Momatiuk; (volcano), Julien Grondin/SS; (camel), Frederic Pacorel/Workbook Stock/GI

Back Cover
(giraffe), EML/SS; (earth), Alex Staroseltsev/SS; (ice cream), Donald Erickson/IS; (river), Maria Stenzel/NGS; (diamond), IS; (turtle), Eric Isselée/SS; (Taj Mahal), Holger Mette/SS; (zebras), SS; (polar bear), SS

Spine
(camel), Frederic Pacorel/Workbook Stock/GI; (volcano) Julien Grondin/SS; (penguin), John Eastcott & Yva Momatiuk

Inside Front Cover
(giraffe), Roy Toft/NGS; (*T. rex*), CB; (lion), Kristian Sekulic/SS; (lightning), Jhaz Photography/SS; (popcorn), GWImages/S; (roller coaster), GI; (space shuttle), NASA; (tower of Pisa), CB;

Front Matter (2–7)
2–3, Konrad Wothe/MP; 5 (A), SS; 5 (B), Peter Kneffel/Newscom; 5 (C), Michele Westmorland/CB; 5 (D), Piotr Naskrecki/MP; 6 (A), Robert Clark/NGS; 6 (B), Frans Lanting/CB; 6 (C), Rudy Sulgan/CB; 6 (D), Justin Guariglia/CB; 7 (UP), Jim Brandenburg/MP; 7 (CTR), Frans Lanting/CB; 7 (LO), David Mattingly

Your World 2011 (8–17)
8–9, Peter Kneffel/Newscom; 10 (UP), NASA; 10 (LO), Mattias Breiter/MP; 11, Flip Nicklin/MP/NGS; 11 (INSET), John Calambokidis/Cascadia Research; 12 (UP), Phil Borges; 12 (LO), Tom Till/Photographer's Choice/GI; 13 (BOTH), Achmad Ibrahim/AP; 14 (UP), Oregon Zoo/Michael Durham; 14 (LO), NASA; 15 (LO), courtesy of the Monterey Bay Aquarium Research Institute; 15 (UP), Vincent Castello; 16 (A), New Line Cinema/ZUMA Press; 16 (B), NASA; 16 (C), IS; 16 (D), IS; 16 (E), Audrey Snider-Bell/SS; 16 (F), Edd Westmacott/SS; 16 (G), Darth Emma; 17 (LO LE), DreamWorks

Entertainment/ZUMA Press; 17 (LO CTR), Heyday Films/ZUMA Press; 17 (LO RT), AP; 17 (UP), Imaginechina/AP

Amazing Animals (18–91)
18–19, Michele Westmorland/CB; 20 (RT), EML/SS; 20 (LE), Eric Isselée/SS; 21 (UP LE), Johan Swanepoel/SS; 21 (LO RT), Dennis Sabo/SS; 21 (UP RT), Michele Westmorland/Photodisc/GI; 21 (LO LE), mashe/SS; 21 (LO), Eric Isselée/SS; 22 (UP), John Mayor/Rex USA; 22 (LO), Henner Frankenfeld; 23 (UP), Karine Aigner/NGS Staff; 23 (LO), Karine Aigner/NGS Staff; 24, Michael K. Nichols/NGS; 25 (ALL), Tom Richmond; 26 (UP LE), Stuart Westmoreland/CB; 26 (UP CTR), Galen Rowell/CB; 26 (UP RT), Erwin & Peggy Bauer; 26 (LO), Sebastian Knight/SS; 27, David Lohman; 28, Tim Davis/CB; 29, Joel Sartore/NGS; 30 (UP), Johnny Johnson/AA; 30 (LO), Nick Norman/NGS; 31, Keren Su/Digital Vision/GI; 31 (LO), MW; 32, Keren Su/CB; 33, Joel Sartore/NGS; 34 (UP), Henk Bentlage/SS; 34 (LO), WEDA/EPA/Sipa; 35, Randy Olson/NGS; 36, Anne Keiser/NGS; 37, James Yamasaki; 38 (UP), George Grall/NGS; 38 (LO), Chris Collins; 39 (UP LE), Michael Gadomski/AA; 39 (UP RT), Joe McDonald/Photoshot; 39 (A), Dr. Paul A. Zahl/PR; 39 (B), Martjan Lammertink; 39 (C), Michael Fogden/Photoshot; 39 (D), G. Carleton Ray/PR; 40, Howard Noel/SS; 41, gallimaufry/SS; 42 (LE), Milton Heiberg; 42 (RT), Bill Bachman; 43 (UP), uri press gmbh/safaripark-Udo Richter; 43 (LO), Sergei Karpukhin/Reuters; 44 (LO), Renee Lynn/CB; 44 (CTR LE), Randy Green/Taxi/GI; 44 (CTR RT), Lynn M. Stone/naturepl.com; 44 (UP), Peter Blackwell/naturepl.com; 45 (B), Art Wolfe; 45 (A), Dr. Gertrud Neumann-Denzau/naturepl.com; 45 (C), Henk Bentlage/SS; 45 (D), Anup Shah/naturepl.com; 45 (E), Lynda Richardson/CB; 45 (F), Jonathan & ange Scott/JI; 45 (G), Fritz Polking/Frank Lane Picture Agency/CB; 45 (H), Joel Sartore/NGS; 45 (I), Philip Perry/Frank Lane Picture Agency/CB; 46, Ipatov/SS; 47, Jeff Hunter/Photographer's Choice/GI; 48, Chris Johns/NGS; 50, Eric Isselée/IS; 51 (LO), Rodney Griffiths; 51 (UP), Erwin & Peggy Bauer; 52–53, Doug Perrine/Nature Picture Library; 52 (UP), SeaPics.com; 52 (CTR), WWF/Philippines/Mavic Matillano; 52 (LO), Brandon Cole; 53 (LE), Hiroya Minakuchi/MP; 53 (A), Doug Perrine/Nature Picture Library; 53 (B), Guy Crittenden/Photographer's Choice RR/GI; 53 (C), Doug Perrine/Nature Picture Library; 53 (D), SeaPics.com; 54 (UP), © 2005 Norbert Wu/www.norbertwu.com; 54 (LO), Sissie Brimgberg & Cotton Coulson/NGS; 55 (UP), Tyson Mangelsdorf; 56, Mike Parry/MP/NGS; 57, Design Pics Inc/Alamy; 58 (UP), Mark Thiessen/NGS; 58 (LO), Paul Souders/Photodisc/GI; 59 (A), Fred Bavendam/MP; 59 (B), Rinie Van Meurs/Foto Natura/MP; 59 (C), Tui De Roy/MP; 59 (D), Tony Heald/Nature Picture Library; 59 (E), Peter Steyn/Ardea; 59 (F), DLILLC/CB; 59 (G), David Tipling/Photolibrary; 59 (H), Digital Vision/GI; 59 (I), Tim Davis/CB; 59 (J), Kevin Schafer; 60, SecondShot/SS; 61 (UP), Fritz Polking; Frank Lane Picture Agency/CB; 61 (LO), Michael Kern and the Gardens of Eden/All Rights Reserved; 62 (A, C, D, E, F), Ken Bohn/ZSD; 62 (B), FeatureChina/BH Ruan/Newscom; 63 (UP), Keith Levit/SS; 63 (LO), W. Perry Conway; 64 (UP), Bob Cranston/Seapics.com; 64–65, Nana Grosse-Woodley; 65, Richard Austin/Secret

World Wildlife Rescue; 66 (UP), David Haring/Duke University Primate Center; 66 (LO LE), Siede Preis/Photodisc/GI; 66 (LO RT), Hans Neleman/The Image Bank/GI; 66 (INSET), MW; 66 (INSET), MW; 67, Cyril Ruoso/JH Editorial/MP; 68 (LE), Karel Brož/SS; 68 (RT), Melinda Fawver/SS; 69, Stephen Dalton/MP; 70, Romanchuck Dimitry/SS; 71 (UP), Robert Lubeck/AA-Earth Scenes; 71 (CTR), Michael and Patricia Fogden/MP; 71 (LO), Stephen Dalton/MP; 72, Michael Pettigrew/IS; 73 (UP), Stefan Klein/IS; 73 (LO), Liesl Morin; 74 (UP LE), P+S Images/age footstock; 74 (UP RT), Denise Kappa/SS; 74 (CTR RT), Richard Kolar/AA; 74 (LO LE), Norma Thruman; 74 (LO RT), Demark/SS; 75 (UP), Mary Evans Picture Library/Alamy; 75 (UP), Hemera Technologies/JI; 75 (CTR), Image 100/JI; 75 (LO), Mark Thiessen, NGP; 76 (UP), Chris Butler/PR; 76 (CTR), Publiphoto/PR; 76 (LO), Pixeldust Studios/NGS; 77 (UP), Chris Butler/PR; 77 (C), Chris Butler/PR; 77 (D), Publiphoto/PR; 77 (E), courtesy of Project Exploration; 77 (A), Publiphoto/PR; 78 (LE), Martha Cooper/NGS; 78–79, Pixeldust Studios/NGS; 79 (BOTH), Ira Block/NGS; 80 (LE), Paul B. Moore/SS; 80 (RT), Andreas Meyer/SS; 81 (UP), Franco Tempesta; 82, Franco Tempesta; 83, Franco Tempesta; 84, Franco Tempesta; 85 (UP), Franco Tempesta; 85 (A), Franco Tempesta; 86 (UP), Raul Martin; 86 (LO), SS; 87 (UP), Andrea Danti/SS; 87 (LO), Atlantic Digital/Dorling Kindersley RF/GI; 88, 89, © 2007 NGHT, Inc.; 90, Walter Meayers Edwards/NGS; 91, Gelpi/SS

Going Green (92–115)
92–93, Piotr Naskrecki/MP/NGS; 95, Index Stock Imagery/Photolibrary; 96 (INSET), UncleGenePhoto/SS; 96, Burcu Arat Sup/IS; 97 (UP), image 100/CB; 98 (LO), Michael & Patricia Fogden/CB; 98 (UP), Olga Kolos/SS; 98 (LO), Mosista Pambudi/SS; 99, Don Wilkie/IS; 100, Nik Niklz/SS; 101 (LO), NGS; 101 (UP), Paul Marcus/SS; 102, Comstock Images/Jupiterimages; 103, Jim Tuten/AA; 103, David Lazenby/AA; 103, Tim Laman/NGS; 103, Peter Weimann/AA; 103, Digital Vision/GI; 103, John Downer/GI; 103, McDonald Wildlife Photography/AA; 103, Manoj Shah/AA; 103, Patricia Fogden/CB; 105 (LE), Walter Rawlings/Robert Harding World Imagery/CB; 105 (UP RT), Sarah Leen/NGS; 105 (LO LE), Richard Nowitz/NGS; 105 (LO RT), Marc Moritsch/NGS; 106, Goodshoot/JupiterImages; 107 (UP), Jim Parkin/SS; 107 (LO), James Weishaar; 109, Mondolithic Studios; 110, Lynn Seeden/IS; 111, Arco Images GmbH/Alamy; 111 (LO), BlueMoon Stock/SuperStock; 111 (UP), Catherine D. Hughes/NGS Staff; 112 (UP LE), Jim Craigmyle/CB; 112 (UP RT), Richard Heinzen/SuperStock; 112 (CTR), Evan Sklar/JI; 112 (LO LE), Big Cheese Photo/SuperStock; 112 (LO RT), Lori Adamski/JI; 113 (UP), Tom Stewart/CB; 113 (CTR), Purestock/SuperStock; 113 (LO LE), Brand X Pictures/JI; 113 (LO RT), Mitsuaki Iwago/MP; 114, SS

Super Science (116–149)
116–117, Robert Clark/NGS; 118 (A), Sebastian Kaulitzki/SS; 118 (B), SS; 118 (C), IS; (D), Arie v.d. Wolde/SS 118 (E), sgame/SS; 118; 118 (F), Hydromet/SS; 118 (G), Benjamin Jesso/IS; 119–121, DA; 122 (BOTH), NASA; 123, DA; 124–125, DA; 126, DA; 127 (UP), Neo Edmund/SS; 127 (CTR), Michael Taylor/SS; 128 (LO), NASA; 128, British Library, London, UK/BAL; 128–129, Giovanni Benintende/SS; 129 (LO), Maisei

Raman/SS; 130 (UP), Courtesy of Franziska Faoro; 130 (CTR), Courtesy of Franziska Faoro; 130 (LO), Imaging by Curventa; 131 (UP), Courtesy of Jonathan Black, Raytheon Company; 131 (LO), Social Retailing/Icon Nicholson/Yun Rhee; 132, Zafer Kizilkaya; 133, Michele Romero; 134 (A, B), Robert Clark/NGS; 134 (C), op-Pics TBK/Alamy; 134 (D), Tibor Bognar/Alamy; 135, Courtesy of Lockheed Martin; 135 (RT), Johnee Bee; 136, SS; 136 (UP), Ian Hooton/SPL/Alamy; 137, Joachim Angeltun/Photodisc/GI; 138 (UP), Sebastian Kaulitzki/SS; 138 (LO), Suzanne Tucker/SS; 139, Robert Llewellyn/CB; 140 (UP), Dennis Cooper/zefa/CB; 140 (LO), Linda Nye; 142, Robert J. Demarest; 143, Blake Thornton; 144, USDA; 145, Mark Thiessen, NGP; 146 (CTR), Mark Thiessen, NGP; 146 (LE), Burke/Triolo/Brand X Pictures/Jupiterimages; 146 (RT), Akiko Ida/GI; 147, Michael Flippo/IS; 148, IS; 149 (LO), IS; 149 (UP), Rob Marmion/SS

Geography Rocks (150–223)

150–151, Frans Lanting/CB; 157 (A), Maria Stenzel/NGS; 157 (B), Bill Hatcher/NGS; 157 (C), Carsten Peter/NGS; 157 (D), Carsten Peter/NGS; 157 (E), Gordon Wiltsie/NGS; 157 (F), James P. Blair/NGS; 157 (G), Thomas J. Abercrombie/NGS; 157 (H), Bill Curtsinger/NGS; 158 (LO LE), Eric Isselée/SS; 158–159, MW; 159 (UP LE), Katja Kreder/JI; 159 (UP RT), Yoshio Tomii/SuperStock; 159 (LO LE), Comstock/CB; 159 (LO RT), Radius Images/JI; 160, George F. Mobley/NGS; 161, Yva Momatiuk & John Eastcott/MP/NGS; 162–163, Tui De Roy/MP; 164, Robin MacDougall/Photographer's Choice/GI; 165 (UP), Mike Hollman/IS; 165 (LO), IS; 166 (UP), Penny Tweedie/CB; 166 (LC), Panoramic Images/GI; 167, Dean Turner/IS; 168 (UP), Harald Sund/Photographer's Choice/GI; 168 (LO), Jorma Jaemsen/zefa/CB; 169, Brian Lawrence/Photographer's Choice/GI; 170 (LO), Elena Ioachim/IS; 171 (INSET), Suzann Julien/IS; 171, Graça Victoria/SS; 172, Rex USA; 173 (LO), Jarno Gonzalez Zarraonandia/SS; 173 (UP), Juan Silva/Iconica/GI; 181, Vladimir Korostyshevskiy/SS; 187, David Edwards; 188, Robb Kendrick/Aurora Photos; 191, David Evans; 197, Joe Rocco; 202, Lowe Llaguno/SS; 206, Silke Heyer/IS; 208 (UP), GI; 208 (LO LE), PhotoDisc; 208 (LO RT), PhotoDisc; 210–211, SS; 211 (LE), Glenn Taylor/IS; 211 (RT), James Steidl/SS; 212–213, Layne Kennedy/CB; 212 (UP), Matt Boulton; 213 (UP), David Barnes/Danita Delimont.com; 213 (CTR), Zoltan Szabo; 213 (LO), RoadsideAmerica.com; 214, Photos.com; 215 (A), Matthias Clamer/Stone/GI; 215 (B), Rick Strange/Index Stock Imagery/Photolibrary; 215 (C), CB; 215 (D), Layne Kennedy/CB; 215 (E), Annie Griffiths Belt; 215 (G), Doug Plummer/Photonica/GI; 215 (F), Roger Wood/CB; 216 (UP), Jeremy Woodhous/Photodisc Green/GI; 217 (A), David Sutherland/The Image Bank/GI; 217 (B, C, D, F), Ferdinand Knab/BAL/GI; 217 (E), Wilhelm van Ehrenberg/BAL/GI; 217 (G), De Agostini Picture Library/GI; 217 (H, I), Holger Mette/SS; 217 (J, N), Jarno Gonzalez Zarraonandia/SS; 217 (K), David Iliff/SS; 217 (L), Ostill/SS; 217 (M), Hannamariah/SS; 218–219, Clayton Hanmer; 220, Dynamic Architecture TM/David Fisher Architect/All Rights Reserved 2008 © International Patent Pending; 220 (INSET), Dynamic Architecture TM/David Fisher Architect/All Rights Reserved 2008 © International Patent Pending; 221 (A), Digital Vision/Alamy; 221 (B),

Sandra Baker/Alamy; 221 (C), Jon Arnold Images LTD/Alamy; 221 (D), International Photobank/Alamy; 221 (E), Daniel Hewlett/Alamy; 221 (F), Digital Vision/Alamy; 221 (G), Dynamic Architecture TM/David Fisher Architect/All Rights Reserved 2008 © International Patent Pending; 221 (H), Dynamic Architecture TM/David Fisher Architect/All Rights Reserved 2008 © International Patent Pending; 222, NGS; 223 (BOTH), NGS

History Happens (224–253)

224–225, Rudy Sulgan/CB; 224 (F), WHHA; 226 (UP), Scott Rothstein/SS; 226 (LO), Courtesy of Declaration of Independence Road Inc; 227 (UP), Cristina Ciochina/SS; 227 (LO), Stephen Coburn/SS; 228 (LE), Gary Blakeley/SS; 228 (RT), S.Borisov/SS; 230 (ALL), WHHA; 231 (ALL), WHHA; 231 (kids), Charles Dharapak/AP; 232 (ALL), WHHA; 233 (ALL), WHHA; 234 (A, B, C, D, E), WHHA; 234 (G, H), The White House; 235 (BOTH), Cory Thoman/SS; 236 (LE), The Granger Collection, NY; 236 (RT), Ron Edmonds/AP; 237, JohnMottern/AFP/GI; 238 (A), AP; 238 (B), Bettmann/CB; 238 (C), GI; 238 (D), MPI/Hulton Archives/GI; 238 (E), Johnson Space Center/NASA; 239 (UP), Ivan Cholakov Gostock-dot-net/SS; 239, Library of Congress; 240 (UP), Associated Press; 240 (LO), Bettmann/CB; 241, Aga/SS; 242 (UP LE), images.com; 242 (UP RT), Jose Ignacio Soto/SS; 242 (LO), Photosani/SS; 243 (LE), Cory Ford/Dreamstime.com; 243 (RT), IS; 245, Chip Wass; 246, Kimberly Schamber/www.schamber.com; 247 (UP), NGS; 247 (CTR), Bettmann/CB; 247 (LO), Bettmann/CB; 248, Bob Thomas/Popperfoto/GI; 249, South Tyrol Museum of Archaeology; 250 (A), Erik and Martin Dahinden; 250 (B), Erik and Martin Dahinden; 250 (C), Paul A. Souders/CB; 250 (D), Dale C. Spartas/CB; 251, Marty Baumann; 252, Pablo Martinez Monsivais/AP; 253 (LO), Bluehill/SS

Culture Connection (254–281)

254–255, Justin Guariglia/CB; 256 (UP), Annie Griffiths Belt; 256 (LO), Graham Smith/Art-Masters; 258 (A), Madlen/SS; 258 (B), Smith & Smith/SS; 258 (C, D, E), Comstock; 260, Scott Matthews; 261 (UP), Phil Schemeister; 261 (LO), Ed Kashi/NGS; 262 (UP), Rebecca Hale, NGP; 262–263, Mark Thiessen, NGP; 263 (UP), Rebecca Hale, NGP; 263 (CTR), Rebecca Hale, NGP; 264, Bradley-Ireland Productions; 265, Marty Baumann; 266 (UP), Randy Olson/NGS; 266 (LO LE), Martin Gray/NGS; 266 (LO RT), Amit Dave/Reuters/CB; 267 (LO LE), Reza/NGS; 267 (LO RT), Richard Nowitz/NGS; 267 (UP), Winfield Parks/NGS; 269 (UP), Doug Schneider/IS; 269 (LO), NGS; 270 (LO), Mary Terriberry/SS; 270 (UP), Andrew Howe/IS; 272 (F), Edyta Pawłowska/IS; 272 (D), Toru Yamanaka/AFP/GI; 272 (C), Dean Turner/IS; 272 (B), IS; 272 (A), Jason Reekie/IS; 272 (E), IS; 273 (LO), Patricia Brabant/Cole Group/GI; 273 (UP), Reuters/CB; 273 (CTR), Mark Thiessen, NGP; 274 (UP LE), J. Helgason/SS; 274 (LO), IS; 274 (CTR), Maram/SS; 275 (LO), Donald Erickson/IS; 275 (UP), Adrian Weinbrecht/GI; 277 (LE), Stephen St. John/NGS; 277 (CTR), Joel Sartore/NGS; 277 (RT), Michael Nichols/NGS; 278 (A), Taylor Kennedy/NGS; 278 (B), SS; 278 (C), Charles & Josette Lenars/CB; 278 (D), SS; 278 (E), Matt Trommer/SS; 278 (F), Pavel Bernshtam/SS; 278 (G), Gregor Schuster/CB; 278 (H), SS; 279 (A), SS;

279 (B), Alexey Gostev/SS; 279 (C), Wolfgang Kaehler/CB; 279 (D), Josh Westrich/CB; 279 (UP RT), William Cooley/Novato Advance; 280 (LO), Joanne van Hoof/SS; 280 (UP), Route66/SS; 280 (CTR), Joel Blit/SS

Awesome Adventure (282–301)

282–283, Jim Brandenburg/MP; 284 (LE), Field Museum of Natural History; 284–285, Wim Smets; 285–29 (CTR), David Mclain/SS; 285 (RT), Joseph B. Macinnis/SS; 285 (LO), David Larson; 286 (UP), Tom Richmond; 286 (UP), Tom Richmond; 286 (CTR), Tom Richmond; 286 (LO), Tom Richmond; 286 (A), MW; 286 (B), MW; 286 (C), MW; 287 (UP), Tom Richmond; 287 (LO), Tom Richmond; 287 (A), MW; 287 (B), MW; 288 (A), Radius Images/JI; 288 (B), John Birdsall/age fotostock; 288 (C), Philip Kaake/Photonica/GI; 288 (D), JI; 288 (E), JI; 289, Aurora Photos; 289 (UP), MW; 290 (LE), www.macfreefilms.com; 290 (RT), Jimmy Chin/NGS; 291 (UP), George Steinmetz/NGS; 291 (LO), NGS; 292 (UP), Araldo De Luca/AWS; 292 (ALL), Araldo De Luca/AWS; 293 (UP LE), Araldo De Luca/AWS; 293 (UP CTR), Araldo De Luca/AWS; 293 (UP RT), Elisabetta Ferrero/White Star; 293 (LO), Patti Fasen/Extraordinair Art; 294 (CTR), Stephen Frink/Digital Vision/GI; 294 (LO), SS; 294 (UP), Annie Griffiths Belt; 294 (LO LE), MW; 295 (UP), Martin Harvey, www.wildimagesonline.co.za; 296 (UP), Eric Gevaert/SS; 296 (LO), Barbara Kinney; 297 (UP), Nicole Duplaix/NGS; 297 (CTR), Stephen Frink/CB; 297 (LO), Jason Edwards/NGS; 298 (LE), Losevsky Pavel/SS; 298 (CTR), Trutta/SS; 298 (RT), Rebecca Roth; 299 (UP), Annie Griffiths Belt; 299 (LO), Stephen Alvarez/NGS; 300, Killroy Productions/SS

Wonders of Nature (302–329)

302–303, Frans Lanting/CB; 305 (LE), Artem Efimov/SS; 305 (CTR), Weiss and Overpeck, The University of Arizona; 305 (RT), Weiss and Overpeck, The University of Arizona; 306, Digital Vision/GI; 308, Eric Skitzi/AP; 309, Galen Rowell/CB; 310 (LE), Kimimasa Mayama/Reuters/CB; 310 (UP), Richard Olsenius/NGS; 311, Stuart Armstrong; 312 (UP), IS; 312 (LO), Brad Wynnyk/SS; 313 (A), Rich Carey/SS; 313 (B), Richard Walters/IS; 313 (C), IS; 313 (LO), Michio Hoshino/MP/NGS; 315, JewelryStock/Alamy; 315 (LO LE), SS; 315 (RT), Rago Arts/SS; 315 (LO), Nguyen Thai/SS; 316, David Nicholls/Science Photo Library/PR; 317, Lyssa White; 318, Jarvis Grey/SS; 319, Stuart Armstrong; 320, Jim Richardson; 321, James L. Stanfield/NGS; 321 (LO), SS; 322–323, Jason Edwards/NGS; 324–293, Chris Anderson/SS; 325 (UP), NGS; 325 (LO), NGS; 326, NGS; 327 (UP), NGS; 327 (A), Shusei Nagaoka/NGS; 327 (B, C, D, E), Susan Sandford/NGS; 329, SS

Future World (330–337)

330–331, David Mattingly; 332–335, Mondolithic Studios; 336, DA; 337 (UP), Michael P. Murphy; 337 (CTR), Robyn Beck/AFP/GI; 337 (LO), Hybrid Medical Animation/PR; 337, Age Fotostock/Superstock

Published by the
National Geographic Society

John M. Fahey, Jr.
President and Chief Executive Officer

Gilbert M. Grosvenor
Chairman of the Board

Tim T. Kelly
President, Global Media Group

John Q. Griffin
Executive Vice President; President, Publishing

Nina D. Hoffman
*Executive Vice President,
President, Book Publishing Group*

Melina Gerosa Bellows
Executive Vice President, Children's Publishing

Prepared by the Book Division

Nancy Laties Feresten, *Vice President,
Editor in Chief, Children's Books*
Jonathan Halling, *Design Director,
Children's Publishing*
Jennifer Emmett, *Executive Editor,
Reference and Solo, Children's Books*
Carl Mehler, *Director of Maps*
R. Gary Colbert, *Production Director*
Jennifer Thornton, *Managing Editor*

Staff for this Book

Robin Terry, *Project Editor*
Susan Kehnemui Donnelly, *Editor*
James Hiscott, Jr., *Art Director*
Ruthie Thompson, *Designer*
Lori Epstein, Rebecca Roth, *Illustrations Editors*
Michelle Harris, *Researcher*
Michael McNey, *Map Production*
Stuart Armstrong, *Graphics Illustrator*
Kate Olesin, *Editorial Assistant*
Grace Hill, *Associate Managing Editor*
Lewis R. Bassford, *Production Manager*
Susan Borke, *Legal and Business Affairs*

Manufacturing and Quality Management

Christopher A. Liedel, *Chief Financial Officer*
Phillip L. Schlosser, *Vice President*
Chris Brown, *Technical Director*
Rachel Faulise, *Manager*
Nicole Elliott, *Manager*

In Partnership with
NATIONAL GEOGRAPHIC KIDS Magazine

Julie Vosburgh Agnone, *Executive Editor*
Rachel Buchholz, *Managing Editor*
Catherine D. Hughes, *Science Editor*
Jill E. Yaworski, *Assistant Editor*
Photo: Jay Sumner, *Photo Director;*
Karine Aigner, *Senior Editor;* Kelley Miller, *Editor*

Art: Eva Absher, *Art Director;*
Nicole M. Lazarus, *Associate Art Director;*
Julide Obuz Dengel, *Designer*
Erin Taylor Monroney, Eleanor Shannahan, Sharon
Thompson, *Writer-Researchers*
Administration: Margaret J. Krauss, *Editorial
Assistant;* Tammi Colleary, *Business Specialist*
Production: David V. Showers, *Director*

The National Geographic Society is one of the
world's largest nonprofit scientific and educational
organizations. Founded in 1888 to "increase and
diffuse geographic knowledge," the Society works
to inspire people to care about the planet. National
Geographic reflects the world through its magazines,
television programs, films, music and radio, books,
DVDs, maps, exhibitions, live events, school publishing programs, interactive media and merchandise.
National Geographic magazine, the Society's official
journal, published in English and 32 local-language
editions, is read by more than 35 million people each
month. The National Geographic Channel reaches 310
million households in 34 languages in 165 countries.
National Geographic Digital Media receives more
than 13 million visitors a month. National Geographic
has funded more than 9,200 scientific research,
conservation and exploration projects and supports
an education program promoting geography literacy.
For more information, visit nationalgeographic.com.

For more information, please call
1-800-NGS LINE (647-5463) or write
to the following address:
NATIONAL GEOGRAPHIC SOCIETY
1145 17th Street NW
Washington, D.C. 20036-4688 U.S.A.

Visit us online at nationalgeographic.com/books
For librarians and teachers: ngchildrensbooks.org

More for kids from National Geographic:
kids.nationalgeographic.com

For information about special discounts for bulk
purchases, please contact National Geographic Books
Special Sales: ngspecsales@ngs.org

For rights or permissions inquiries, please contact
National Geographic Books Subsidiary Rights:
ngbookrights@ngs.org

Printed in the United States of America
10/CML-CK/2